Implementing Splunk

Second Edition

A comprehensive guide to help you transform Big Data into valuable business insights with Splunk 6.2

Vincent Bumgarner

James D. Miller

[PACKT] PUBLISHING

enterprise
professional expertise distilled

BIRMINGHAM - MUMBAI

Implementing Splunk
Second Edition

First published: January 2013

Second edition: July 2015

Production reference: 1220715

Published by Packt Publishing Ltd.
Livery Place
35 Livery Street
Birmingham B3 2PB, UK.

ISBN 978-1-78439-160-7

www.packtpub.com

Credits

Authors
Vincent Bumgarner
James D. Miller

Reviewers
Gabriel D'Antona
Travis Marlette
Brian Warehime
Alan Williams

Commissioning Editor
Dipika Gaonkar

Acquisition Editor
Tushar Gupta

Content Development Editor
Arwa Manasawala

Technical Editor
Siddhesh Patil

Copy Editors
Sarang Chari
Sonia Mathur

Project Coordinator
Shweta Birwatkar

Proofreader
Safis Editing

Indexer
Monica Mehta

Graphics
Disha Haria

Production Coordinator
Conidon Miranda

Cover Work
Conidon Miranda

About the Authors

Vincent Bumgarner has been designing software for over 20 years, working with many languages on nearly as many platforms. He started using Splunk in 2007 and has enjoyed watching the product evolve over the years.

While working for Splunk, he has helped many companies train dozens of users to drive, extend, and administer this extremely flexible product. At least one person in every company he has worked with has asked for a book, and he hopes that this book will help fill their shelves.

James D. Miller is an IBM-certified, accomplished senior engagement leader and application / system architect / developer / integrator with over 35 years of extensive application and system design and development experience. He has held positions such as National FPM practice leader, certified solutions expert, technical leader, technical instructor, and best practice evangelist. His experience includes business intelligence, predictive analytics, web architecture and design, business process analysis, GUI design and testing, data and database modeling and systems analysis, design, and development of applications, systems and models based on cloud, client/server, web and mainframe.

His responsibilities have included all aspects of solution design and development, including business process analysis and reengineering, requirement documentation, estimating and planning/management of projects, architectural evaluation and optimization, test preparation, and the management of resources. Other experience includes the development of ETL infrastructures—such as data transfer automation between mainframe (DB2, Lawson, Great Plains, and so on) systems and the client/server model-based SQL server—web-based applications, and the integration of enterprise applications and data sources.

In addition, he has acted as an Internet application development manager and was responsible for the design, development, QA, and delivery of multiple websites, including online trading applications, warehouse process control and scheduling systems, and administrative and control applications. Mr. Miller was also responsible for the design, development, and administration of a web-based financial reporting system for a $450-million organization, reporting directly to the CFO and his executive team.

In various other leadership roles, such as project and team leader, lead developer, and applications development director, Mr. Miller has managed and directed multiple resources using a variety of technologies and platforms.

James has authored *IBM Cognos TM1 Developer's Certification Guide* and *Mastering Splunk*, both by *Packt Publishing* and a number of whitepapers on best practices, such as *Establishing a Center of Excellence*. He continues to post blogs on a number of relevant topics based on personal experiences and industry best practices.

James also holds the following current technical certifications:

- IBM Certified Developer Cognos TM1
- IBM Certified Analyst Cognos TM1
- IBM Certified Administrator Cognos TM1
- IBM Cognos 10 BI Administrator C2020-622
- IBM Cognos TM1 Master 385 Certification
- IBM OpenPages Developer Fundamentals C2020-001-ENU
- IBM Certified Advanced Solution Expert Cognos TM1

His technology specialties include IBM Cognos BI and TM1, SPSS, Splunk, dynaSight/ArcPlan, ASP, DHTML, XML, IIS, MS Visual Basic and VBA, Visual Studio, PERL, WebSuite, MS SQL Server, Oracle, SQL Server on Sybase, miscellaneous OLAP tools, and so on.

As always, I'd like to thank my wife and soulmate, Nanette L. Miller, who is always on my mind.

About the Reviewers

Gabriel D'Antona has been working in the information technology industry since 1998, mainly in the media/telecommunications business. He has been a Splunk advocate since 2012, introducing the system for the first time to his current employer. He is also an open source and technology enthusiast, actively working on projects such as Multiple Arcade Machine Emulator (MAME)—a multi-system emulator—and researching the HTML5/Javascript technologies privately.

Travis Marlette has been championing Splunk in the organizations he has worked with over the past 6 years. He has architected and implemented multiple Splunk deployments, leveraging both clustered and distributed deployments in medium- to enterprise-class institutions, primarily for the cutting-edge financial services industry. His experience ranges from the newest of technologies, such as Hadoop and AWS, to more legacy infrastructure, such as mainframe technologies, and the integration of Splunk into both old and modern data center environments.

Having recently focused on operational efficiency and intelligence, Travis has also leveraged Splunk for:

- Business intelligence
- Executive-level overview
- Marketing analysis using big data
- ROI tracking
- High availability and disaster recovery for Splunk
- Splunk for Security (the replacement for SIEM)

He has also worked on beta testing many of the new functionalities of Splunk during their product releases and assisted in troubleshooting the Splunk platform as a whole.

He has worked for companies such as Lehman Brothers, Barclays, and Bank of New York and is currently working with another Fortune 100 company to implement its goal for Splunk and operational excellence. The scope of the yearlong project consists of consolidating toolsets to create a single pane of glass for the enterprise tier 1 and tier 2 support staff to maximize work efficiencies and reduce MTTR by at least 20 percent over the next year while allowing full access to remote application administration and remote monitoring to all customers to share intelligence and increase knowledge sharing between silos. This is being done even as they reduce operational expenditure by replacing legacy toolsets.

He truly enjoys what he does, bringing to light many of the underlying opportunities organizations have to streamline efficiency and gain real value from some of the most cryptic or antiquated machine information. Giving this intelligence to the right eyes in an organization is part of his passion.

> *How do you find a problem that you don't know exists? Splunk it.*
>
> *–Travis Marlette*

> *I get the most abstract, and innocuous problems to ever arise in an organization as a Big Data and forensic expert. Splunk saves me the time to ensure my quality of life.*
>
> *-Travis Marlette*

Brian Warehime is an analyst by trade and has come to use Splunk in his day-to-day operations as a crucial tool for analysis and research. He came to use and administer Splunk a few years ago and has enjoyed using it ever since as it has helped him in many different components of his job.

Brian is currently working at Aplura LLC, which is a small consulting firm specializing in Splunk Professional Services. While at Aplura, he started working with a large marketing company and originally helped deploy its Splunk infrastructure and set up various inputs; however, he currently works on the security team and uses Splunk every day to investigate incidents and analyze threats.

www.PacktPub.com

Support files, eBooks, discount offers, and more

For support files and downloads related to your book, please visit www.PacktPub.com.

Did you know that Packt offers eBook versions of every book published, with PDF and ePub files available? You can upgrade to the eBook version at www.PacktPub.com and as a print book customer, you are entitled to a discount on the eBook copy. Get in touch with us at service@packtpub.com for more details.

At www.PacktPub.com, you can also read a collection of free technical articles, sign up for a range of free newsletters and receive exclusive discounts and offers on Packt books and eBooks.

https://www2.packtpub.com/books/subscription/packtlib

Do you need instant solutions to your IT questions? PacktLib is Packt's online digital book library. Here, you can search, access, and read Packt's entire library of books.

Why subscribe?

- Fully searchable across every book published by Packt
- Copy and paste, print, and bookmark content
- On demand and accessible via a web browser

Free access for Packt account holders

If you have an account with Packt at www.PacktPub.com, you can use this to access PacktLib today and view 9 entirely free books. Simply use your login credentials for immediate access.

Instant updates on new Packt books

Get notified! Find out when new books are published by following @PacktEnterprise on Twitter or the *Packt Enterprise* Facebook page.

Table of Contents

Preface

Splunk is a powerful tool to collect, store, alert, report, and study machine data. This machine data usually comes from server logs, but it could also be collected from other sources. Splunk is, by far, the most flexible and scalable solution available to tackle the huge problem of making machine data useful.

The goal of the original version of this book was to serve as an organized and curated guide to Splunk 4.3. This version endeavors to preserve that objective, while focusing on the latest version (at the time of writing) of Splunk—6.2.0. In fact, care has been taken to call out the differences between the versions. In addition, new content has been added, covering search acceleration methods, backfilling, data replication, and Hunk.

As the documentation and community resources available to Splunk are vast, finding important pieces of knowledge can be daunting at times. My goal is to present what is needed for the effective implementation of Splunk in as concise and useful a manner as possible.

What this book covers

Chapter 1, The Splunk Interface, walks you through the elements of the user interface.

Chapter 2, Understanding Search, covers the basics of the searches, paying particular attention to writing efficient queries.

Chapter 3, Tables, Charts, and Fields, shows you how you can use fields for reporting and then covers the process of building your own fields.

Chapter 4, Data Models and Pivots, explains and defines Splunk data models and pivots, along with the pivot editor, pivot elements and filters, Sparklines, and more.

Chapter 5, Simple XML Dashboards, first uses the Splunk web interface to build our first dashboards. The chapter then examines how you can build forms and more efficient dashboards.

Chapter 6, Advanced Search Examples, walks you through examples of using Splunk's powerful search language in interesting ways.

Chapter 7, Extending Search, exposes a number of features in Splunk to help you to categorize events and act upon search results in powerful ways.

Chapter 8, Working with Apps, covers the concepts of an app, helps you in installing a couple of popular apps, and then helps you in building your own app.

Chapter 9, Building Advanced Dashboards, explains the concepts of advanced XML dashboards and covers practical ways to transition from simple XML to advanced XML dashboards.

Chapter 10, Summary Indexes and CSV Files, introduces the concept of summary indexes and shows you how they can be used to improve performance. It also discusses how CSV files can be used in interesting ways.

Chapter 11, Configuring Splunk, explains the structure and meaning of common configurations in Splunk. The chapter also explains the process of merging configurations in great detail.

Chapter 12, Advanced Deployments, covers common questions about multi-machine Splunk deployments, including data inputs, syslog, configuration management, and scaling up.

Chapter 13, Extending Splunk, demonstrates ways in which code can be used to extend Splunk for data input, external querying, rendering, custom commands, and custom actions.

What you need for this book

To work through the examples in this book, you will need an installation of Splunk, preferably a nonproduction instance. If you are already working with Splunk, then the concepts introduced by the examples should be applicable to your own data.

Splunk can be downloaded for free from `http://www.splunk.com/download`, for most popular platforms.

The sample code was developed on a UNIX system, so you will probably have better luck using an installation of Splunk that is running on a UNIX operating system. Knowledge of Python is necessary to follow certain examples in the later chapters.

Who this book is for

This book should be useful to new users, seasoned users, dashboard designers, and system administrators alike. This book does not try to act as a replacement for the official Splunk documentation but should serve as a shortcut for many concepts.

For some sections, a good understanding of regular expressions would be helpful.

For some sections, the ability to read Python would be helpful.

Conventions

In this book, you will find a number of text styles that distinguish between different kinds of information. Here are some examples of these styles and an explanation of their meaning.

Code words in text, database table names, folder names, filenames, file extensions, pathnames, dummy URLs, user input, and Twitter handles are shown as follows: " The address will look like `http://mysplunkserver:8000` or `http://mysplunkserver.mycompany.com:8000`"

A block of code is set as follows:

```
sourcetype="impl_splunk_gen" (mary AND error) NOT debug NOT worthless
NOT logoutclass
```

Any command-line input or output is written as follows:

```
$SPLUNK_HOME/bin/splunk reload deploy-server
```

New terms and **important words** are shown in bold. Words that you see on the screen, for example, in menus or dialog boxes, appear in the text like this: " Clicking on **Settings**, on the top bar, takes you to the **Settings** page."

 Warnings or important notes appear in a box like this.

 Tips and tricks appear like this.

Reader feedback

Feedback from our readers is always welcome. Let us know what you think about this book—what you liked or disliked. Reader feedback is important for us as it helps us develop titles that you will really get the most out of.

To send us general feedback, simply e-mail feedback@packtpub.com, and mention the book's title in the subject of your message.

If there is a topic that you have expertise in and you are interested in either writing or contributing to a book, see our author guide at www.packtpub.com/authors.

Customer support

Now that you are the proud owner of a Packt book, we have a number of things to help you to get the most from your purchase.

Downloading the example code

You can download the example code files from your account at http://www.packtpub.com for all the Packt Publishing books you have purchased. If you purchased this book elsewhere, you can visit http://www.packtpub.com/support and register to have the files e-mailed directly to you.

Errata

Although we have taken every care to ensure the accuracy of our content, mistakes do happen. If you find a mistake in one of our books—maybe a mistake in the text or the code—we would be grateful if you could report this to us. By doing so, you can save other readers from frustration and help us improve subsequent versions of this book. If you find any errata, please report them by visiting http://www.packtpub.com/submit-errata, selecting your book, clicking on the **Errata Submission Form** link, and entering the details of your errata. Once your errata are verified, your submission will be accepted and the errata will be uploaded to our website or added to any list of existing errata under the Errata section of that title.

To view the previously submitted errata, go to https://www.packtpub.com/books/content/support and enter the name of the book in the search field. The required information will appear under the **Errata** section.

Piracy

Piracy of copyrighted material on the Internet is an ongoing problem across all media. At Packt, we take the protection of our copyright and licenses very seriously. If you come across any illegal copies of our works in any form on the Internet, please provide us with the location address or website name immediately so that we can pursue a remedy.

Please contact us at copyright@packtpub.com with a link to the suspected pirated material.

We appreciate your help in protecting our authors and our ability to bring you valuable content.

Questions

If you have a problem with any aspect of this book, you can contact us at questions@packtpub.com, and we will do our best to address the problem.

1
The Splunk Interface

This chapter will walk you through the most common elements in the Splunk interface, and will touch upon concepts that will be covered in greater detail, in later chapters. You may want to dive right into the search section, but an overview of the user interface elements might save you some frustration later. We will cover the following topics in this chapter:

- Logging in and app selection
- A detailed explanation of the search interface widgets
- A quick overview of the admin interface

Logging into Splunk

The Splunk GUI interface (Splunk is also accessible through its command-line interface [CLI] and REST API) is web-based, which means that no client needs to be installed. Newer browsers with fast JavaScript engines, such as Chrome, Firefox, and Safari, work better with the interface. As of Splunk Version 6.2.0, no browser extensions are required. Splunk Versions 4.2 and earlier require Flash to render graphs. Flash can still be used by older browsers, or for older apps that reference Flash explicitly. The default port for a Splunk installation is 8000.

The address will look like: http://mysplunkserver:8000 or http://
mysplunkserver.mycompany.com:8000.

The Splunk interface

If you have installed Splunk on your local machine, the address can be some variant
of http://localhost:8000, http://127.0.0.1:8000, http://machinename:8000,
or http://machinename.local:8000.

Once you determine the address, the first page you will see is the login screen. The
default username is *admin* with the password *changeme*. The first time you log in,
you will be prompted to change the password for the admin user. It is a good idea to
change this password to prevent unwanted changes to your deployment.

By default, accounts are configured and stored within Splunk. Authentication can
be configured to use another system, for instance **Lightweight Directory Access
Protocol (LDAP)**. By default, Splunk authenticates locally. If LDAP is set up, the
order is as follows: LDAP / Local.

The home app

After logging in, the default app is the **Launcher** app (some may refer to this as **Home**). This app is a launching pad for apps and tutorials.

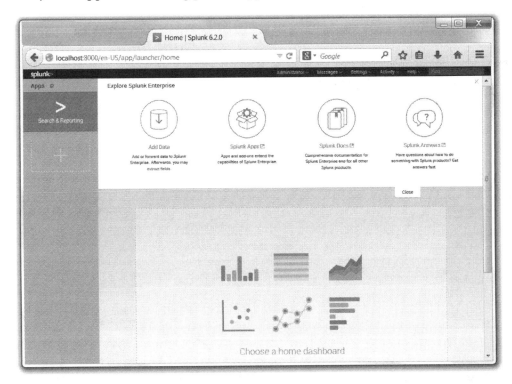

In earlier versions of Splunk, the **Welcome** tab provided two important shortcuts, **Add data** and the **Launch search** app. In version 6.2.0, the **Home** app is divided into distinct areas, or panes, that provide easy access to **Explore Splunk Enterprise** (**Add Data, Splunk Apps, Splunk Docs,** and **Splunk Answers**) as well as **Apps** (the App management page) **Search & Reporting** (the link to the **Search** app), and an area where you can set your default dashboard (choose a home dashboard). We'll cover apps & dashboards in later chapters of this book.

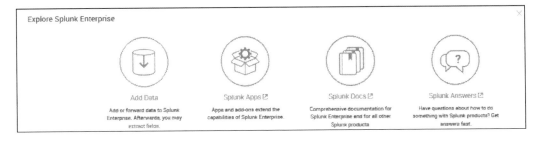

The **Explore Splunk Enterprise** pane shows links to:

- **Add data**: This links **Add Data** to the Splunk page. This interface is a great start for getting local data flowing into Splunk (making it available to Splunk users). The **Preview data** interface takes an enormous amount of complexity out of configuring dates and line breaking. We won't go through those interfaces here, but we will go through the configuration files that these wizards produce in *Chapter 11, Configuring Splunk*.

- **Splunk Apps**: This allows you to find and install more apps from the Splunk Apps Marketplace (`http://apps.splunk.com`). This marketplace is a useful resource where Splunk users and employees post Splunk apps, mostly free but some premium ones as well.

- **Splunk Answers**: This is one of your links to the wide amount of Splunk documentation available, specifically `http://answers.splunk.com`, where you can engage with the Splunk community on Splunkbase (`https://splunkbase.splunk.com/`) and learn how to get the most out of your Splunk deployment.

The **Apps** section shows the apps that have GUI elements on your instance of Splunk. App is an overloaded term in Splunk. An app doesn't necessarily have a GUI at all; it is simply a collection of configurations wrapped into a directory structure that means something to Splunk. We will discuss apps in a more detailed manner in *Chapter 8, Working with Apps*.

Search & Reporting is the link to the Splunk Search & Reporting app.

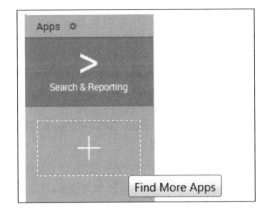

Beneath the **Search & Reporting** link, Splunk provides an outline which, when you hover over it, displays a **Find More Apps** balloon tip. Clicking on the link opens the same **Browse more apps** page as the **Splunk Apps** link mentioned earlier.

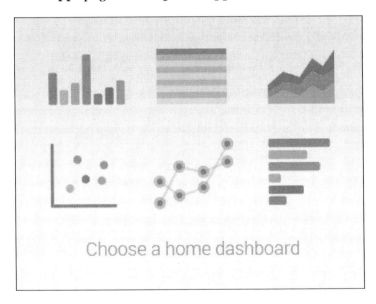

Choose a home dashboard provides an intuitive way to select an existing (simple XML) dashboard and set it as part of your Splunk **Welcome** or **Home** page. This sets you at a familiar starting point each time you enter Splunk. The following image displays the **Choose Default Dashboard** dialog:

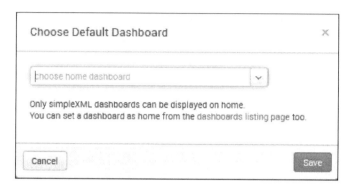

Once you select an existing dashboard from the dropdown list, it will be part of your welcome screen every time you log into Splunk – until you change it. There are no dashboards installed by default after installing Splunk, except the **Search & Reporting** app. Once you have created additional dashboards, they can be selected as the default.

The top bar

The bar across the top of the window contains information about where you are, as well as quick links to preferences, other apps, and administration.

The current app is specified in the upper-left corner. The following image shows the upper-left Splunk bar when using the **Search & Reporting** app:

Clicking on the text takes you to the default page for that app. In most apps, the text next to the logo is simply changed, but the whole block can be customized with logos and alternate text by modifying the app's CSS. We will cover this in *Chapter 8, Working with Apps*.

The upper-right corner of the window, as seen in the previous image, contains action links that are almost always available:

- The name of the user who is currently logged in appears first. In this case, the user is **Administrator**. Clicking on the username allows you to select **Edit Account** (which will take you to the **Your account** page) or to **Logout** (of Splunk). Logout ends the session and forces the user to login again. The following screenshot shows what the **Your account** page looks like:

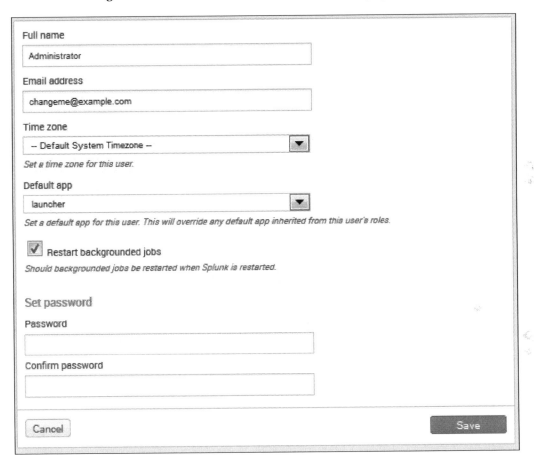

This form presents the global preferences that a user is allowed to change. Other settings that affect users are configured through permissions on objects and settings on roles. (Note: preferences can also be configured using the CLI or by modifying specific Splunk configuration files).

- **Full name** and **Email address** are stored for the administrator's convenience.

- **Time zone** can be changed for the logged-in user. This is a new feature in Splunk 4.3.

> Setting the time zone only affects the time zone used to display the data. It is very important that the date is parsed properly when events are indexed. We will discuss this in detail in *Chapter 2, Understanding Search*.

- **Default app** controls the starting page after login. Most users will want to change this to search.

- **Restart backgrounded jobs** controls whether unfinished queries should run again if Splunk is restarted.

- **Set password** allows you to change your password. This is only relevant if Splunk is configured to use internal authentication. For instance, if the system is configured to use Windows Active Directory via LDAP (a very common configuration), users must change their password in Windows.

- **Messages** allows you to view any system-level error messages you may have pending. When there is a new message for you to review, a notification displays as a count next to the Messages menu. You can click the **X** to remove a message.

Downloading the example code

You can download the example code files from your account at http://www.packtpub.com for all the Packt Publishing books you have purchased. If you purchased this book elsewhere, you can visit http://www.packtpub.com/support and register to have the files e-mailed directly to you.

- The **Settings** link presents the user with the configuration pages for all Splunk **Knowledge** objects, **Distributed Environment** settings, **System** and **Licensing, Data,** and **Users and Authentication** settings. If you do not see some of these options, you do not have the permissions to view or edit them.

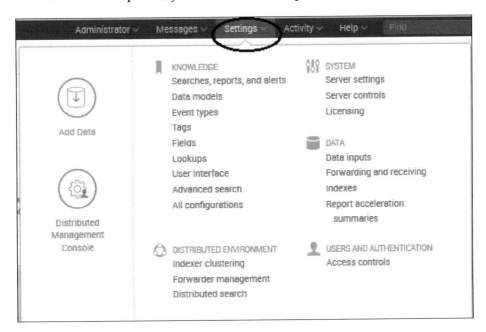

- The **Activity** menu lists shortcuts to Splunk **Jobs, Triggered Alerts,** and **System Activity** views. You can click **Jobs** (to open the search jobs manager window, where you can view and manage currently running searches), click **Triggered Alerts** (to view scheduled alerts that are triggered) or click **System Activity** (to see dashboards about user activity and the status of the system).

- **Help** lists links to video **Tutorials**, **Splunk Answers**, the Splunk **Contact Support** portal, and online **Documentation**.

- **Find** can be used to search for objects within your Splunk Enterprise instance. For example, if you type in error, it returns the saved objects that contain the term *error*. These saved objects include **Reports**, **Dashboards**, **Alerts**, and so on. You can also search for error in the **Search & Reporting** app by clicking **Open error** in search.

The search & reporting app

The **Search & Reporting** app (or just the search app) is where most actions in Splunk start. This app is a dashboard where you will begin your searching.

The data generator

If you want to follow the examples that appear in the next few chapters, install the *ImplementingSplunkDataGenerator* demo app by following these steps:

1. Download ImplementingSplunkDataGenerator.tar.gz from the code bundle available on the site http://www.packtpub.com/support.
2. Choose **Manage apps...** from the **Apps** menu.
3. Click on the button labeled **Install app from file**.
4. Click on **Choose File**, select the file, and then click on **Upload**.

This data generator app will produce about 16 megabytes of output per day. The app can be disabled so that it stops producing data by using **Manage apps...**, under the **App** menu.

The summary view

Within the **Search & Reporting** app, the user is presented with the **Summary** view, which contains information about the data which that user searches for by default. This is an important distinction—in a mature Splunk installation, not all users will always search all data by default. But at first, if this is your first trip into **Search & Reporting**, you'll see the following:

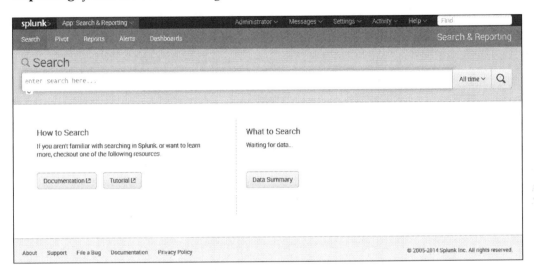

From the screen depicted in the previous screenshot, you can access the Splunk documentation related to **What to Search** and **How to Search**. Once you have at least some data indexed (a topic we'll discuss later in the *The settings section*), Splunk will provide some statistics on the available data under **What to Search** (remember that this reflects only the indexes that this particular user searches by default; there are other events that are indexed by Splunk, including events that Splunk indexes about itself. We will discuss indexes in *Chapter 9, Building Advanced Dashboards*). This is seen in the following image:

In previous versions of Splunk, panels such as the **All indexed data** panel provided statistics for a user's indexed data. Other panels gave a breakdown of data using three important pieces of metadata—**Source**, **Sourcetype**, and **Hosts**. In the current version—6.2.0—you access this information by clicking on the button labeled **Data Summary**, which presents the following to the user:

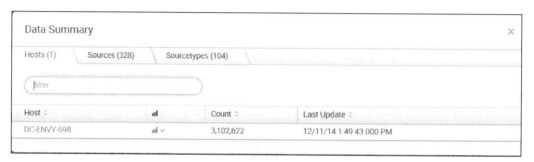

This dialog splits the information into three tabs—**Hosts**, **Sources** and **Sourcetypes**.

- A host is a captured hostname for an event. In the majority of cases, the host field is set to the name of the machine where the data originated. There are cases where this is not known, so the host can also be configured arbitrarily.

- A source in Splunk is a unique path or name. In a large installation, there may be thousands of machines submitting data, but all data on the same path across these machines counts as one source. When the data source is not a file, the value of the source can be arbitrary, for instance, the name of a script or network port.

- A source type is an arbitrary categorization of events. There may be many sources across many hosts, in the same source type. For instance, given the sources /var/log/access.2012-03-01.log and /var/log/access.2012-03-02.log on the hosts fred and wilma, you could reference all these logs with source type access or any other name that you like.

Let's move on now and discuss each of the Splunk widgets (just below the app name). The first widget is the navigation bar.

As a general rule, within Splunk, items with downward triangles are menus. Items without a downward triangle are links.

We will cover customizing the navigation bar in *Chapter 8, Working with Apps.*

Next we find the **Search** bar. This is where the magic starts. We'll go into great detail shortly.

Search

Okay, we've finally made it to search. This is where the real power of Splunk lies.

For our first search, we will search for the word (not case specific); error. Click in the search bar, type the word error, and then either press *Enter* or click on the magnifying glass to the right of the bar.

Upon initiating the search, we are taken to the search results page.

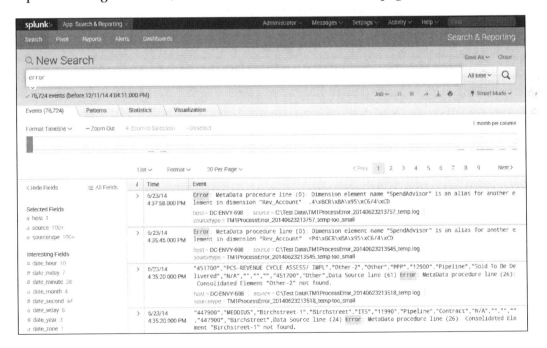

Note that the search we just executed was across **All time** (by default); to change the search time, you can utilize the Splunk time picker.

Refer to the *Using the time picker* section for details on changing the time frame of your search.

Actions

Let's inspect the elements on this page. Below the **Search** bar, we have the event count, action icons, and menus.

Starting from the left, we have the following:

- The **number of events** matched by the base search. Technically, this may not be the number of results pulled from disk, depending on your search. Also, if your query uses commands, this number may not match what is shown in the event listing.

- **Job**: This opens the **Search job inspector** window, which provides very detailed information about the query that was run.

- **Pause**: This causes the current search to stop locating events but keeps the job open. This is useful if you want to inspect the current results to determine whether you want to continue a long running search.

- **Stop**: This stops the execution of the current search but keeps the results generated so far. This is useful when you have found enough and want to inspect or share the results found so far.

- **Share**: This shares the search job. This option extends the job's lifetime to seven days and sets the read permissions to everyone.

- **Export**: This exports the results. Select this option to output to CSV, raw events, XML, or **JavaScript Object Notation (JSON)** and specify the number of results to export.

- **Print**: This formats the page for printing and instructs the browser to print.

- **Smart Mode**: This controls the search experience. You can set it to speed up searches by cutting down on the event data it returns and, additionally, by reducing the number of fields that Splunk will extract by default from the data (*Fast mode*). You can, otherwise, set it to return as much event information as possible (*Verbose mode*). In Smart mode (the default setting) it toggles search behavior based on the type of search you're running.

Timeline

Now we'll skip to the timeline below the action icons.

Along with providing a quick overview of the event distribution over a period of time, the timeline is also a very useful tool for selecting sections of time. Placing the pointer over the timeline displays a pop-up for the number of events in that slice of time. Clicking on the timeline selects the events for a particular slice of time.

Clicking and dragging selects a range of time.

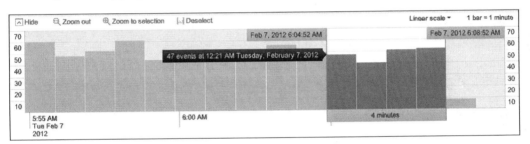

Once you have selected a period of time, clicking on **Zoom to selection** changes the time frame and reruns the search for that specific slice of time. Repeating this process is an effective way to drill down to specific events.

Deselect shows all events for the time range selected in the time picker.

Zoom out changes the window of time to a larger period around the events in the current time frame

The field picker

To the left of the search results, we find the field picker. This is a great tool for discovering patterns and filtering search results.

< Hide Fields   ☰ All Fields

Selected Fields
a host 1
a source 100+
a sourcetype 100+

Interesting Fields
date_hour 10
date_mday 7
date_minute 38
a date_month 4
date_second 44
a date_wday 5
date_year 3
a date_zone 1
a index 1
linecount 2
a punct 100+
a splunk_server 1
timeendpos 4
timestartpos 4

1 more field
⊕ Extract New Fields

Fields

The field list contains two lists:

- **Selected Fields**, which have their values displayed under the search event in the search results
- **Interesting Fields**, which are other fields that Splunk has picked out for you

Above the field list are two links: **Hide Fields** and **All Fields**.

- **Hide Fields**: Hides the field list area from view.
- **All Fields**: Takes you to the **Selected Fields** window.

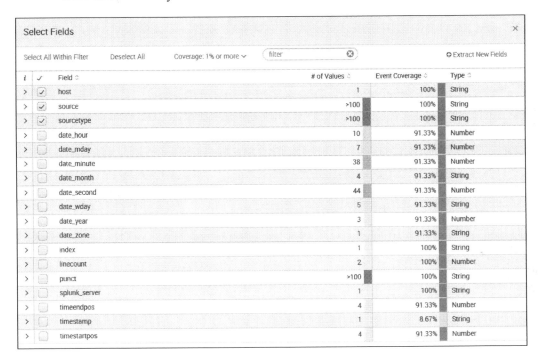

Search results

We are almost through with all the widgets on the page. We still have a number of items to cover in the search results section though, just to be thorough.

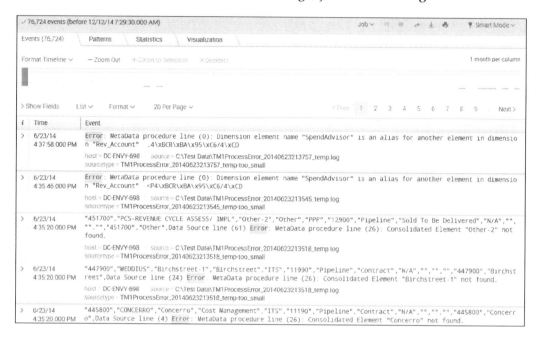

As you can see in the previous screenshot, at the top of this section, we have the number of events displayed. When viewing all results in their raw form, this number will match the number above the timeline. This value can be changed either by making a selection on the timeline or by using other search commands.

Next, we have the action icons (described earlier) that affect these particular results.

Under the action icons, we have four results tabs:

- **Events** list, which will show the raw events. This is the default view when running a simple search, as we have done so far.

- **Patterns** streamlines the event pattern detection. It displays a list of the most common patterns among the set of events returned by your search. Each of these patterns represents the number of events that share a similar structure.

- **Statistics** populates when you run a search with transforming commands such as stats, top, chart, and so on. The previous keyword search for *error* does not display any results in this tab because it does not have any transforming commands.

- **Visualization** transforms searches and also populates the **Visualization** tab. The results area of the **Visualization** tab includes a chart and the statistics table used to generate the chart. Not all searches are eligible for visualization – a concept which will be covered later in *Chapter 3, Tables, Charts, and Fields*.

Under the tabs described just now, is the timeline which we will cover in more detail later in this chapter in the section *Using the time picker*.

Options

Beneath the timeline, (starting at the left) is a row of option links that include:

- **Show Fields**: shows the **Selected Fields** screen
- **List**: allows you to select an output option (**Raw**, **List**, or **Table**) for displaying the search results
- **Format**: provides the ability to set **Result display options**, such as **Show row numbers**, **Wrap results**, the **Max lines** (to display) and **Drilldown** as *on* or *off*.
- **NN Per Page**: is where you can indicate the number of results to show per page (**10, 20,** or **50**).

To the right are options that you can use to choose a page of results, and to change the number of events per page.

 In prior versions of Splunk, these options were available from the **Results display options** popup dialog.

The events viewer

Finally, we make it to the actual events. Let's examine a single event.

```
>  1  6/23/14        Error: MetaData procedure line (0): Dimension element name "SpendAdvisor" is an alias for another element in
       4:37:58.000 PM  dimension "Rev_Account"   .4\xBCR\xBA\x95\xC6/4\xCD

                       host = DC-ENVY-698    source = C:\Test Data\TM1ProcessError_20140623213757_temp.log
                       sourcetype = TM1ProcessError_20140623213757_temp-too_small
```

Starting at the left, we have:

- **Event Details**: Clicking here (indicated by the *right facing arrow*) opens the selected event, providing specific information about the event by type, field, and value, and allows you the ability to perform specific actions on a particular event field. In addition, Splunk version 6.2.0 offers a button labeled **Event Actions** to access workflow actions, a few of which are always available.

- **Build Eventtype**: Event types are a way to name events that match a certain query. We will dive into event types in *Chapter 7, Extending Search*.

- **Extract Fields**: This launches an interface for creating custom field extractions. We will cover field extraction in *Chapter 3, Tables, Charts, and Fields*.

- **Show Source**: This pops up a window with a simulated view of the original source.

- **The event number**: Raw search results are always returned in the order *most recent first*.

- Next to appear are any workflow actions that have been configured. Workflow actions let you create new searches or links to other sites, using data from an event. We will discuss workflow actions in *Chapter 7, Extending Search*.

- Next comes the parsed date from this event, displayed in the time zone selected by the user. This is an important and often confusing distinction. In most installations, everything is in one time zone—the servers, the user, and the events. When one of these three things is not in the same time zone as the others, things can get confusing. We will discuss time in great detail in *Chapter 2, Understanding Search*.

- Next, we see the raw event itself. This is what Splunk saw as an event. With no help, Splunk can do a good job finding the date and breaking lines appropriately, but as we will see later, with a little help, event parsing can be more reliable and more efficient.

- Below the event are the fields that were selected in the field picker. Clicking on the value adds the field value to the search.

Using the time picker

Now that we've looked through all the widgets, let's use them to modify our search. First we will change our time. The default setting of **All time** is fine when there are few events, but when Splunk has been gathering events over a period time (perhaps for weeks or months), this is less than optimal. Let's change our search time to one hour.

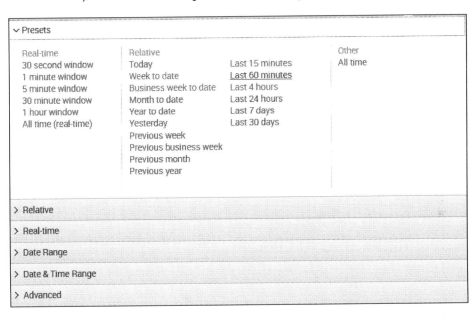

The search will run again, and now we see results for the last hour only. Let's try a custom time. **Date Range** is an option.

If you know specifically when an event happened, you can drill down to whatever time range you want here. We will examine the other options in *Chapter 2, Understanding Search*.

The time zone used in **Custom Time Range** is the time zone selected in the user's preferences, which is, by default, the time zone of the Splunk server.

Using the field picker

The field picker is very useful for investigating and navigating data. Clicking on any field in the field picker pops open a panel with a wealth of information about that field in the results of your search.

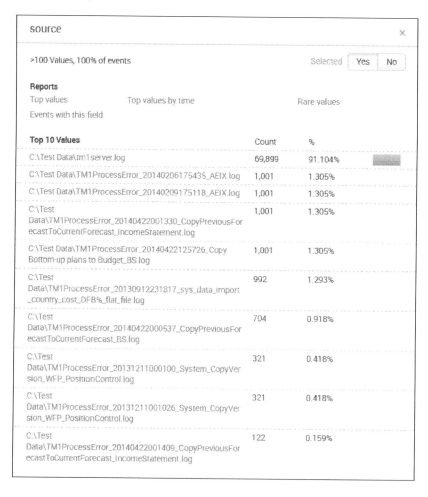

Looking through the information, we observe the following:

- Number (of) Values, **Appears in X% of results** tells you how many events contain a value for this field.

- **Selected** indicates if the field is a selected field.

- **Top values** and **Top values by time** (allows referring to the **Top 10 Values** returned in the search) present graphs about the data in this search. This is a great way to dive into reporting and graphing. We will use this as a launching point later in *Chapter 3, Tables, Charts, and Fields*.

- **Rare Values** displays the least common values of a field.

- Show only **Events with this field** will modify the query to show only those events that have this field defined.

- The links are actually a quick representation of the top values overall. Clicking on a link adds that value to the query. Let's click on `c:\\Test Data\\tm1server.log`.

```
error source="C:\\Test Data\\tm1server.log"
```

This will rerun the search, now looking for errors that affect only the source value `c:\\Test Data\\tm1server.log`.

The settings section

The **Settings** section, in a nutshell, is an interface for managing configuration files. The number of files and options in these configuration files is truly daunting, so the web interface concentrates on the most commonly used options across the different configuration types.

Splunk is controlled exclusively by plain text configuration files. Feel free to take a look at the configuration files that are being modified as you make changes in the admin interface. You will find them by hitting the following commands:

```
$SPLUNK_HOME/etc/system/local/
```

```
$SPLUNK_HOME/etc/apps/
```

You may notice configuration files with the same name at different locations. We will cover in detail; the different configuration files, their purposes, and how these configurations merge together in *Chapter 11, Configuring Splunk*. Don't start modifying the configurations directly until you understand what they do and how they merge.

Clicking on **Settings**, on the top bar, takes you to the **Settings** page.

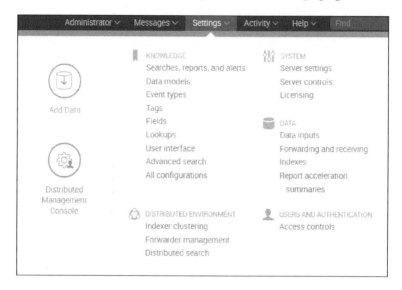

The options are organized into logical groupings, as follows:

*   **Knowledge**: Each of the links under Knowledge allows you to control one of the many object types that are used at search time. The following screenshot shows an example of one object type, workflow actions: **Searches, reports, and alerts**:

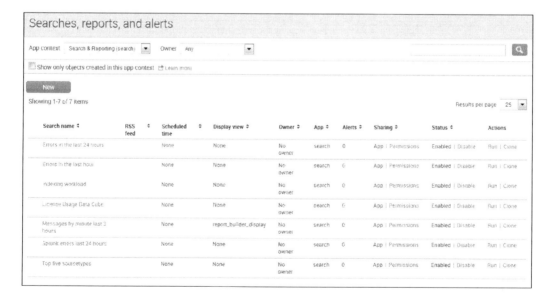

- **System**: The options under this section control system-wide settings.
    - ◦ **System settings** covers network settings, the default location to store indexes, outbound e-mail server settings, and how much data Splunk logs about itself
    - ◦ **Server controls** contains a single page that lets you restart Splunk from the web interface
    - ◦ **Licensing** lets you add license files or configure Splunk as a slave to a Splunk license server

- **Data**: This section is where you manage data flow.
    - ◦ **Data Inputs**: Splunk can receive data by reading files (either in batch mode or in real time), listening to network ports, or running scripts.
    - ◦ **Forwarding and receiving**: Splunk instances don't typically stand alone. Most installations consist of at least one Splunk indexer and many Splunk forwarders. Using this interface, you can configure each side of this relationship and more complicated setups (we will discuss this in more detail in *Chapter 12, Advanced Deployments*).
    - ◦ **Indexes**: An Index is essentially a datastore. Under the covers, it is simply a set of directories, created and managed by Splunk. For small installations, a single index is usually acceptable. For larger installations, using multiple indexes allows flexibility in security, retention, and performance tuning, as well as better use of hardware. We will discuss this further in *Chapter 11, Configuring Splunk*.
    - ◦ **Report acceleration summaries**: Accesses automatically-created summaries to speed up completion times for certain kinds of reports.

- **Distributed Environment**: The three options here relate to distributed deployments (we will cover these options in detail in *Chapter 12, Advanced Deployments*):
    - ◦ **Indexer clustering**: Access to enabling and configuring Splunk **Indexer clustering**, which we will discuss later in *Chapter 10, Summary Indexes and CSV Files*.
    - ◦ **Forwarder management**: Access to the forwarder management UI distributes deployment apps to Splunk clients.
    - ◦ **Distributed search**: Any Splunk instance running searches can utilize itself and other Splunk instances to retrieve results. This interface allows you to configure access to other Splunk instances.

- **Users and authentication**: This section provides authentication controls and an account link.

  ◦ **Access controls**: This section is for controlling how Splunk authenticates users and what users are allowed to see and do. We will discuss this further in *Chapter 11, Configuring Splunk*.

  ◦ In addition to the links, the **Settings** page also presents a panel on the left side of the page. This panel includes two icons **Add Data** and **Distributed Management Console**.

  ◦ **Add Data** links to the **Add Data** page. This page presents you with three options for getting data into your Splunk Enterprise instance: **Upload, Monitor**, and **Forward**.

  ◦ **Distributed Management Console**, where you can view detailed performance information about your Splunk Enterprise deployment.

Summary

As you have seen in this chapter, the Splunk GUI provides a rich interface for working with search results. We have really only scratched the surface and will cover more elements as we use them in later chapters.

In the next chapter, we will dive into the nuts and bolts of how search works, so that you can make efficient searches to populate the cool reports that we will make in *Chapter 3, Tables, Charts, and Fields*, and beyond.

2
Understanding Search

To successfully use Splunk, it is vital that you write effective searches. Using the index efficiently will make your initial discoveries faster, and the reports you create will run faster for you and for others. In this chapter, we will cover the following topics:

- How to write effective searches
- How to search using fields
- Understanding time
- Saving and sharing searches

Using search terms effectively

The key to creating an effective search is to take advantage of the index. The Splunk index is effectively a huge word index, sliced by time. The single most important factor for the performance of your searches is how many events are pulled from the disk. The following few key points should be committed to memory:

- **Search terms are case insensitive**: Searches for error, Error, ERROR, and ErRoR are all the same thing.
- **Search terms are additive**: Given the search item, *mary error*, only events that contain both words will be found. There are Boolean and grouping operators to change this behavior; we will discuss in this chapter under *Boolean and grouping operators*.
- **Only the time frame specified is queried**: This may seem obvious, but it's very different from a database, which would always have a single index across all events in a table. Since each index is sliced into new buckets over time, only the buckets that contain events for the time frame in question need to be queried.
- **Search terms are words, including parts of words**: A search for *foo* will also match *foobar*.

With just these concepts, you can write fairly effective searches. Let's dig a little deeper, though:

- **A word is anything surrounded by whitespace or punctuation**: For instance, given the log line `2012-02-07T01:03:31.104-0600 INFO AuthClass Hello world. [user=Bobby, ip=1.2.3.3]`, the "words" indexed are `2012,02, 07T01, 03, 31, 104, 0600, INFO, AuthClass, Hello, world, user, Bobby, ip, 1, 2, 3,` and `3`. This may seem strange, and possibly a bit wasteful, but this is what Splunk's index is really, really good at—dealing with huge numbers of words across a huge number of events.

- **Splunk is not grep with an interface**: One of the most common questions is whether Splunk uses regular expressions for your searches. Technically, the answer is no. Splunk does use regex internally to extract fields, including the auto generated fields, but most of what you would do with regular expressions is available in other ways. Using the index as it is designed is the best way to build fast searches. Regular expressions can then be used to further filter results or extract fields.

- **Numbers are not numbers until after they have been parsed at search time**: This means that searching for `foo>5` will not use the index, as the value of `foo` is not known until it has been parsed out of the event at search time. There are different ways to deal with this behavior, depending on the question you're trying to answer.

- **Field names are case sensitive**: When searching for `host=myhost`, host must be lowercase. Likewise, any extracted or configured fields have case sensitive field names, but the values are case insensitive.
    - `Host=myhost` will not work
    - `host=myhost` will work
    - `host=MyHost` will work

- **Fields do not have to be defined before indexing data**: An indexed field is a field that is added to the metadata of an event at index time. There are legitimate reasons to define indexed fields, but in the vast majority of cases it is unnecessary and is actually wasteful. We will discuss this in *Chapter 3, Tables, Charts, and Fields*.

 It should be noted that some of the queries used throughout this book may yield different results or in some cases return no events since these searches were based on random data indexed by Splunk in our test environment.

Boolean and grouping operators

There are a few operators that you can use to refine your searches (note that these operators must be in uppercase to not be considered search terms):

- **AND** is implied between terms. For instance, `error mary` (two words separated by a space) is the same as `error AND mary`.

- **OR** allows you to specify multiple values. For instance, `error OR mary` means find any event that contains either word.

- **NOT** applies to the next term or group. For example, `error NOT mary` would find events that contain `error` but do not contain `mary`.

- **The quote marks ("")** identify a phrase. For example, `"Out of this world"` will find this exact sequence of words. `Out of this world` would find any event that contains all of these words, but not necessarily in that order.

- **Parentheses (( ))** is used for grouping terms. Parentheses can help avoid confusion in logic. For instance, these two statements are equivalent:

  - `bob error OR warn NOT debug`
  - `(bob AND (error OR warn)) AND NOT debug`

- **The equal sign (=)** is reserved for specifying fields. Searching for an equal sign can be accomplished by wrapping it in quotes. You can also escape characters to search for them. `\=` is the same as `"="`.

- **Brackets ([ ])** are used to perform a subsearch. We will discuss this in *Chapter 6, Advanced Search Examples*.

You can use these operators in fairly complicated ways if you want to be very specific, or even to find multiple sets of events in a single query. The following are a few examples:

- `error mary NOT jacky`

- `error NOT (mary warn) NOT (jacky error)`

- `index=myapplicationindex ( sourcetype=sourcetype1 AND ( (bob NOT error) OR (mary AND warn) ) ) OR ( sourcetype=sourcetype2 (jacky info) )`

This can also be written with some whitespace for clarity:

```
index=myapplicationindex
(
sourcetype=security
AND
(
```

```
(bob NOT error)
OR
(mary AND warn)
)
)
OR
(
sourcetype=application
(jacky info)
)
```

Clicking to modify your search

Though you can probably figure it out by just clicking around, it is worth discussing the behavior of the GUI when moving your mouse around and clicking.

- Clicking on any word or field value will give you the option to **Add to search** or **Exclude from search** (the existing search) or (create a) **New search**:

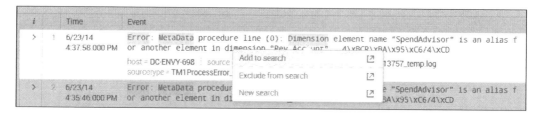

- Clicking on a word or a field value that is already in the query will give you the option to *remove it* (from the existing query) or, as above, (create a) *new* (search):

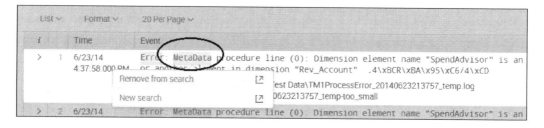

Event segmentation

In previous versions of Splunk, event segmentation was configurable through a setting in the **Options** dialog. In version 6.2, the options dialog is not present – although segmentation (discussed later in this chapter under *field widgets* section) is still an important concept, it is not accessible through the web interface/options dialog in this version.

Field widgets

Clicking on values in the **Select Fields** dialog (the *field picker*), or in the field value widgets underneath an event, will again give us an option to append (add to) or exclude (remove from) our search or, as before, to start a new search.

For instance, if source="C:\Test Data\TM1ProcessError_20140623213757_temp. log" appears under your event, clicking on that value and selecting **Add to search** will append source="C:\\Test Data\\TM1ProcessError_20140623213757_temp. log" to your search:

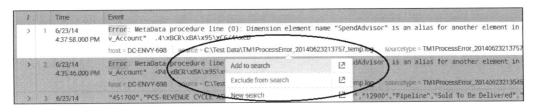

To use the field picker, you can click on the link **All Fields** (see the following image):

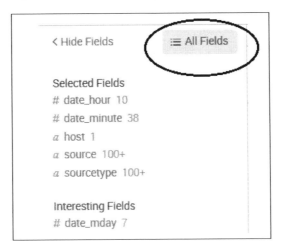

Expand the results window by clicking on > in the far-left column. Clicking on a result will append that item to the current search:

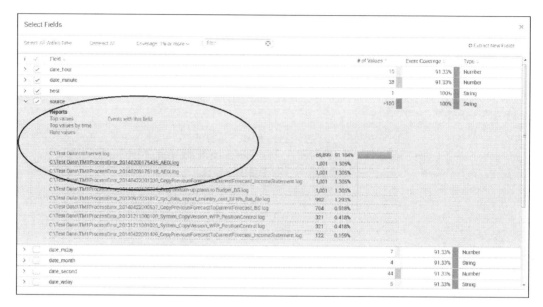

If a field value looks like `key=value` in the text of an event, you will want to use one of the field widgets instead of clicking on the raw text of the event. Depending on your event segmentation setting, clicking on the word will either add the value or `key=value`. The former will not take advantage of the field definition; instead, it will simply search for the word. The latter will work for events that contain the exact quoted text, but not for other events that actually contain the same field value extracted in a different way.

Time

Clicking on the time next to an event will open the **_time** dialog (shown in the following image) allowing you to change the search to select **Events Before** or **After** a particular time period, and will also have the following choices:

- **Before this time**
- **After this time**
- **At this time**

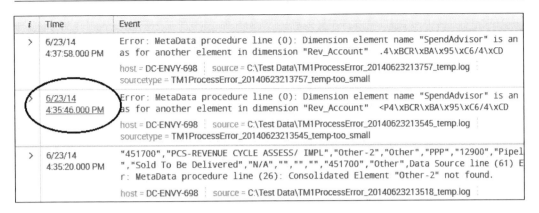

In addition, you can select **Nearby Events** within *plus, minus,* or *plus or minus*, a number of seconds (the default), *milliseconds, minutes, hours, days,* or *weeks*:

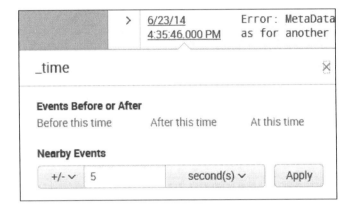

One search trick is to click on the time of an event, select **At this time, and** then use the **Zoom out** (above the timeline) until the appropriate time frame is reached.

Using fields to search

When we explored the GUI in *Chapter 1, The Splunk Interface*, you probably noticed fields everywhere. Fields appear in the field picker on the left and under every event. Where fields actually come from is transparent to the user, who simply searches for `key=value`. We will discuss adding new fields in *Chapter 3, Tables, Charts, and Fields*, and in *Chapter 11, Configuring Splunk*.

Using the field picker

The field picker gives us easy access to the fields (currently defined) for the results of our query. Splunk will extract some fields from event data without your help, such as **host**, **source**, and **sourcetype** values, timestamps, and others. Additional fields to be extracted can be defined by you. Clicking on any field presents us with the details about that field in our current search results:

As we go through the following items in this widget, we see a wealth of information right away:

- *N Value, X% of events* is a good indication of whether we are getting the results we think we're getting. If every event in your results should contain this field, and this is not 100 percent, either your search can be made more specific or a field definition needs to be modified. In addition, N Value indicates the number of unique values that this field contains.

- **Selected — Yes** or **No** indicates whether the field is selected (is part of the search query results) or not (simply listed as interesting additional fields found by Splunk within the data).

- **Reports — Top Values**, **Top Values by time**, **Rare values**, and **Events with this field**
  - ° **Top values** (overall) shows a table of the most common values for this field for the time frame searched.
  - ° **Top values by time** shows a graph of the most common values occurring in the time frame searched.
  - ° **Rare values** shows a table of the most unique values for this field for the time frame searched.

- (Show only) **Events with this field** adds `fieldname="*"` to your existing search to make sure that you only get the events that have this field. If the events you are searching for always contain the name of the field, in this case network, your query will be more efficient if you also add the field name to the query. In this case, the query would look like this: `sourcetype="impl_splunk_gen" network="*" network`.

- **Values** shows a very useful snapshot of the top ten most common values, **Count** is the number found for each of these values and % is the percentage that the value is found in this field in the results of the search.

Using wildcards efficiently

Though the index is based on words, it is possible to use wildcards when needed, albeit a little carefully. Take a look at some interesting facts about wildcards:

- Only trailing wildcards are efficient: Stated simply, `bob*` will find events containing Bobby efficiently, but `*by` or `*ob*` will not. The latter cases will scan all events in the time frame specified.

- Wildcards are tested last: Wildcards are tested after all other terms. Given the search: `authclass *ob* hello world`, all other terms besides `*ob*` will be searched first. The more you can limit the results using full words and fields, the better your search will perform.

Supplementing wildcards in fields

Given the following events, a search for world would return both events:

```
2012-02-07T01:04:31.102-0600 INFO AuthClass Hello world. [user=Bobby,
ip=1.2.3.3]
2012-02-07T01:23:34.204-0600 INFO BarClass Goodbye. [user=Bobby,
ip=1.2.3.3, message="Out of this world"]
```

What if you only wanted the second event, but all you know is that the event contains world somewhere in the field message? The query `message="*world*"` would work but is very inefficient because Splunk must scan every event looking for `*world`, and then determine whether world is in the field message.

You can take advantage of the behavior mentioned earlier — wildcards are tested last. Rewriting the query as world `message="*world*"` gives Splunk a chance to find all the records with world, and then inspect those events for the more specific wildcard condition.

All about time

Time is an important and confusing topic in Splunk. If you want to skip this section, absorb one concept—time must be parsed properly on the way into the index as it cannot be changed later without indexing the raw data again.

How Splunk parses time

If given the date `11-03-04`, how would you interpret this date? Your answer probably depends on where you live. In the United States, you would probably read this as November 3, 2004. In Europe, you would probably read this as March 11, 2004. It would also be reasonable to read this as March 4, 2011.

Luckily, most dates are not this ambiguous, and Splunk makes a good effort to find and extract them, but it is absolutely worth the trouble to give Splunk a little help by configuring the time format. We'll discuss the relevant configurations in *Chapter 11, Configuring Splunk*.

How Splunk stores time

Once the date is parsed, the date stored in Splunk is always stored as GMT epoch. Epoch time is the number of seconds since January 1, 1970. By storing all events using a single time zone, there is never a problem lining up events that happen in different time zones. This, of course, only works properly if the time zone of the event can be determined when it is indexed. This numeric value is stored in the field `_time`.

How Splunk displays time

The text of the original event, and the date it contains, is never modified. It is always displayed as it was received. The date displayed to the left of the event is determined by the time zone of the Splunk instance or the user's preference, as specified in **Your account**.

i	Time	Event
>	6/23/14 4:35:20.000 PM	"451700","PCS-REVENUE CYCLE ,"Sold To Be Delivered","N/ MetaData procedure line (2

How time zones are determined and why it matters

Since all events are stored according to their GMT time, the time zone of an event only matters at parse time, but it is vital to get it right. Once the event is written into the index, it cannot be changed without reindexing the raw data.

The time zone can come from a number of places, in the following order of precedence:

- The time zone specified in the log. For instance, the date `2012-02-07T01:03:23.575-0600`, `-0600` indicates that the zone is 6 hours behind GMT. Likewise, `Tue 02 Feb, 01:03:23 CST 2012` represents the same date.

- The configuration associated with a source, host, or sourcetype, in that order. This is specified in `props.conf`. This can actually be used to override the time zone listed in the log itself, if needed. We will discuss this in *Chapter 11, Configuring Splunk*.

- The time zone of the Splunk instance forwarding the events. The time zone is relayed along with the events, just in case it is not specified elsewhere. This is usually an acceptable default. The exception is when different logs are written with different time zones on the same host, without the time zone in the logs. In that case, it needs to be specified in `props.conf`.

- The time zone of the Splunk instance parsing the events. This is sometimes acceptable and can be used in interesting ways in distributed environments.

- The important takeaway, again, is that the time zone needs to be known at the time of parsing and indexing the event.

Different ways to search against time

Now that we have our time indexed properly, how do we search against time?
The **Date & Time Range** picker provides a neat set of options for dealing with
search times:

This picker widget is organized by:

- **Presets**
- **Relative**
- **Real-time**
- **Data Range**
- **Date & Time Range** and
- **Advanced**

Let's take a look at understanding each of these.

Presets

Presets are time ranges that are pre-defined for you in Splunk Enterprise. You should be aware, though, that if you are searching potentially large amounts of data, results will return faster if you run the search over a smaller time period (rather than **All time**).

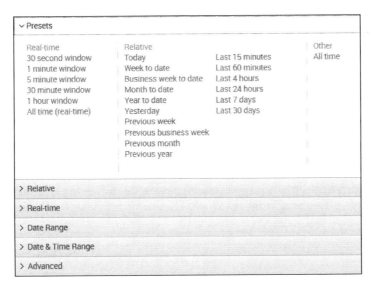

Relative

If the **Relative** presets are not what you need, you can use the custom **Relative** time range options to specify a time range for your search that is relative to now. You can select from the list of time range units, **Seconds Ago**, **Minutes Ago**, and so on:

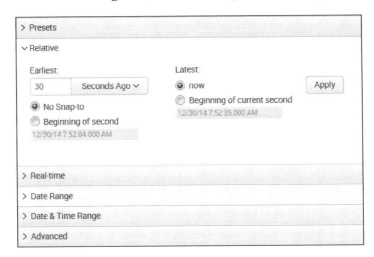

Splunk also provides the ability to use **Beginning of second** (the default) or a **No Snap-to** time unit to indicate the nearest or latest time to which your time amount rounds up to. If you don't specify a *snap to* time unit, Splunk snaps automatically to the second. Unlike the **Presets**, to actually apply your (**Relative**) selections to the search, you need to click the **Apply** button.

Real-time

The custom **Real-time** option gives you the ability to set the start time for your real-time time range window. Keep in mind that the search time ranges for historical searches are set at the time at which the search runs. With real-time searches, the time ranges are constantly updating and the results accumulate from the beginning of your search.

You can also specify a time range that represents a sliding window of data, for example, the last 30 seconds.

When you specify a sliding window, Splunk takes that amount of time to accumulate data. For example, if your sliding window is 5 minutes, you will not start to see data until after the first 5 minutes have passed.

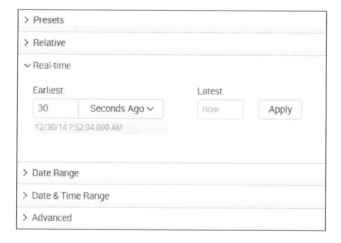

Windowed real-time versus all-time real-time searches

When designing your searches, it's important to keep in mind that there is a difference between Splunk real-time searches that take place within a set window (like **30** seconds or 1 minute) and real-time searches that are set to **All time**.

In windowed real-time searches, the events in the search can disappear as they fall outside of the window, and events that are newer than the time the search job was created can appear in the window when they occur.

In all-time real-time searches, the window spans all of your events, so events do not disappear once they appear in the window. But events that are newer than the time the search job was created, can appear in the window as they occur.

In comparison, in historical searches, events never disappear from within the set range of time that you are searching and the latest event is always earlier than the job creation time (with the exception of searches that include events that have future-dated timestamps).

Date range

You can use the custom **Date Range** option to add calendar dates to your search. You can choose among options to return events: **Between** a beginning and end date, **Before** a date, and **Since** a date (for these fields, you can either type the date into the text box, or select the date from a calendar).

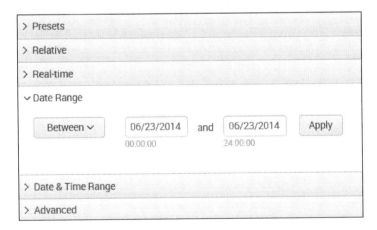

Date and time range

Use the custom **Date & Time Range** option to specify calendar dates and times for the beginning and ending of your search. Again, you can type the date into the text box or select the date from a calendar.

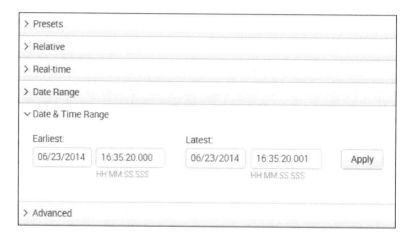

Advanced

Use the **Advanced** option to specify the earliest and latest search times. You can write the times in Unix (epoch) time or relative time notation. The epoch time value that you enter is converted to local time. This timestamp is displayed under the text field so that you can verify your entry.

Specifying time in-line in your search

You can also directly use relative and exact times in your searches. For instance, given the search item `bob error`, you can specify the time frame you want to use directly in the search, using the fields earliest and latest.

- To search for errors affecting `bob` in the last 60 minutes, use `earliest=-60m bob error`

- To search for errors affecting `bob` in the last 3 hours, snap to the beginning of the hour using `earliest=-3h@h bob error`

- To search for errors affecting `bob` yesterday, use `earliest=-1d@d latest=-0d@d bob error`

- To search for errors affecting `bob` since Monday midnight, use `earliest=-0@w1 bob error`

You cannot use different time ranges in the same query; for instance, in a Boolean search, (`earliest=-1d@d latest=-0d@d bob error`) OR (`earliest=-2d@d latest=-1d@d mary error`) will not work. The *append* command provides a way of accomplishing this.

_indextime versus _time

It is important to note that events are generally not received at the same time as stated in the event. In most installations, the discrepancy is usually of a few seconds, but if logs arrive in batches, the latency can be much larger. The time at which an event is actually written in the Splunk index is kept in the internal field `_indextime`.

The time that is parsed out of the event is stored in `_time`.

You will probably never search against `_indextime`, but you should understand that the time you are searching against is the time parsed from the event, not the time at which the event was indexed.

Making searches faster

We have talked about using the index to make searches faster. When starting a new investigation, the following few steps will help you get results faster:

1. Set the time to the minimum time that you believe will be required to locate relevant events. For a chatty log, this may be as little as a minute. If you don't know when the events occurred, you might search a larger time frame and then zoom in by clicking on the timeline while the search is running.

2. Specify the index if you have multiple indexes. It's good to get into the habit of starting your queries with the index name. For example, `index=myapplicationindex error bob`.

3. Specify other fields that are relevant. The most common fields to specify are *sourcetype* and *host*. For example, `index=myapplicationindex sourcetype="impl_splunk_gen" error bob`. If you find yourself specifying the field source on a regular basis, you could probably benefit from defining more source types. Avoid using the `sourcetype` field to capture other information, for instance datacenter or environment. You would be better off using a lookup against host or creating another indexed field for those cases.

4. Add more words from the relevant messages as and when you find them. This can be done simply by clicking on words or field values in events, or field values in the field picker. For example, `index=myapplicationindex sourcetype="impl_splunk_gen" error bob authclass OR fooclass`.

5. Expand your time range once you have found the events that you need, and then refine the search further.

6. Disable **Field discovery** in earlier versions of Splunk - there was a toggle at the top of the field picker. In version 6.2, the feature is a bit different. You can simply open the field picker and use the **Select All Within Filter** or **Deselect All** checkbox to remove any unneeded fields from the list that Splunk will extract. This can greatly improve speed, particularly if your query retrieves a lot of events. Extracting all the fields from events simply takes a lot of computing time, and disabling this option prevents Splunk from doing all that work when not needed. Take a look at the following screenshot:

If the query you are running is taking a long time to run, and you will be running this query on a regular basis—perhaps for an alert or a dashboard—using a summary index may be appropriate. We will discuss this in *Chapter 10, Summary Indexes and CSV Files*.

Sharing results with others

It is often convenient to share a specific set of results with another user. You could always export the results to a CSV file and share it, but this is cumbersome. In earlier versions of Splunk, a URL could be saved and shared; in version 6.2, things are a bit different (although you still can save your search as a bookmarked URL).

The URL

To share your search as a bookmarked URL, you can click on the share icon to view the **Share Job** dialog:

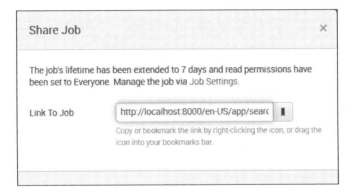

From here, you can simply right-click on the share icon and bookmark your search for later use:

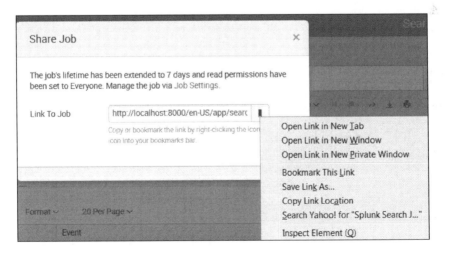

You can also share your search and search results in a variety of other ways, starting by clicking on the **Save As** link:

This lists your options for saving the search and search results. Your choices are the following:

- **Report**
- **Dashboard Panel**
- **Alert**
- **Event Type**

Save as report

To save your search as a report, click on the **Report** link. This opens the **Save As Report** dialog:

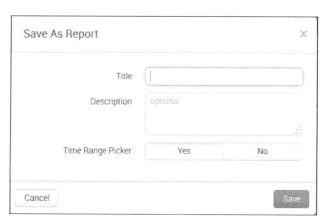

From here, you need to do the following:

1. Enter a **Title** (or name) for your report.
2. Enter an optional **Description** to remind users what your report does.
3. Indicate if you'd like to include the Splunk **Time Range Picker** as a part of your report.

Once you click **Save**, Splunk prompts you to either review **Additional Settings** for your newly created report (**Permissions, Schedule, Acceleration,** and **Embed**), **Add** (the report) **to Dashboard** (we will talk more about dashboards in *Chapter 5, Simple XML Dashboards*), **View** the report, or **Continue Editing** the search:

In my example, I named my report **My Error Report**, added a description (**a simple example of a save as report**), and included the **Time Range Picker**. The following screenshot displays the saved report after clicking **View**:

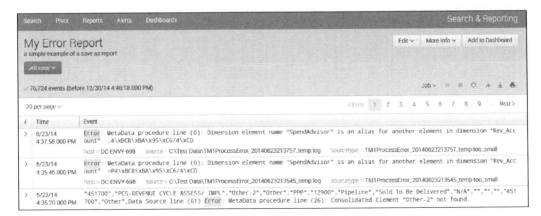

The additional settings that can be made to the report are given as follows:

- **Permissions**: Allows you to set how the saved report is displayed: by owner, by app, or for all apps. In addition, you can make the report read only or writeable (can be edited).

- **Schedule**: Allows you to schedule the report (for Splunk to run/refresh it based upon your schedule). For example, an interval like every week, on Monday at 6 AM, and for a particular time range.

- **Acceleration**: Not all saved reports qualify for acceleration and not all users (not even admins) have the ability to accelerate reports. Generally speaking, Splunk Enterprise will build a report acceleration summary for the report if it determines that the report would benefit from summarization (acceleration). More on this topic later in *Chapter 2, Understanding Search*.

- **Embed**: Report embedding lets you bring the results of your reports to large numbers of report stakeholders. With report embedding, you can embed scheduled reports in external (non-Splunk) websites, dashboards, and portals. Embedded reports can display results in the form of event views, tables, charts, maps, single values, or any other visualization type. They use the same formatting as the originating report. When you embed a saved report, you do this by copying a Splunk generated URL into an HTML-based web page.

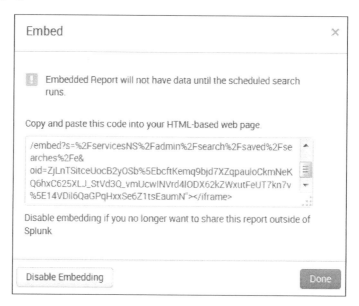

Save as dashboard panel

We'll be discussing dashboards in *Chapter 5*, *Simple XML Dashboards* but, for now, you should know that you can save your search as a new dashboard or as a new panel in an existing one. Permissions can also be set:

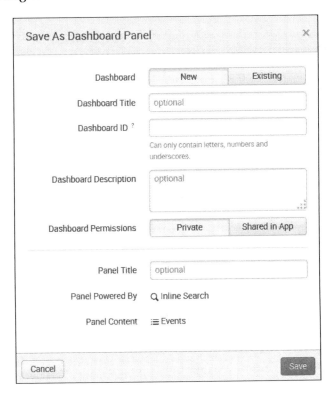

Save as alert

An alert is an action that a saved search triggers based on specified results of the search. When creating an alert, you specify a condition that triggers the alert (basically, a saved search with trigger conditions). When you select **Save as Alert**, the following dialog is provided to configure search as an alert:

Save as event type

Event types are a categorization system to help you make sense of your user-defined data fields. It simplifies searches by letting you categorize events. Event types let you classify events that have common characteristics. When your search results come back, they're checked against known event types. An event type is applied to an event at search time if that event matches the event type definition.

The simplest way to create a new event type is through Splunk Web. After you run a search that would make a good event type, click Save As and select Event Type. This opens the Save as Event Type dialog, where you can provide the event type name and optionally apply tags to it:

Search job settings

Once you run a search, you can access and manage information about the search job (an individual instance of a running or completed search, pivot, or report, along with its related output) without leaving the **Search** page. This is done by clicking **Job** and choosing from the available options:

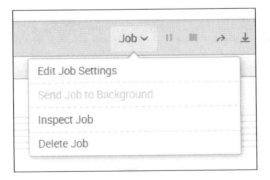

You can also perform the following tasks:

- **Edit Job Settings**: Select this to open the **Job Settings** dialog, where you can change the job's read permissions, extend the job's lifespan, and get a URL for the job which you can use to share the job with others. You can also put a link to the job in your browser's bookmark bar.

- **Send Job to Background**: Select this if the search job is slow to complete and you would like to run the job in the background while you work on other Splunk Enterprise activities (including running a new search job).

- **Inspect Job**: Opens a separate window and displays information and metrics for the search job via the **Search Job Inspector**.

- **Delete Job**: Use this to delete a job that is currently running, is paused, or which has finalized. After you have deleted the job, you can still save the search as a report.

Saving searches for reuse

As an example, let's build a search query, save it (as a report), and then make an alert out of it. First, let's find errors that affect mary, one of our most important users. This can simply be the query mary error. Looking at some sample log messages that match this query, we see that some of these events probably don't matter (the dates have been removed to shorten the lines).

```
ERROR LogoutClass error, ERROR, Error! [user=mary, ip=3.2.4.5]
WARN AuthClass error, ERROR, Error! [user=mary, ip=1.2.3.3]
ERROR BarCLass Hello world. [user=mary, ip=4.3.2.1]
WARN LogoutClass error, ERROR, Error! [user=mary, ip=1.2.3.4]
DEBUG FooClass error, ERROR, Error! [user=mary, ip=3.2.4.5]
ERROR AuthClass Nothing happened. This is worthless. Don't log this.
[user=mary, ip=1.2.3.3]
```

We can probably skip the DEBUG messages; the LogoutClass messages look harmless, and the last message actually says that it's worthless. mary error NOT debug NOT worthless NOT logoutclass limits the results to:

```
WARN AuthClass error, ERROR, Error! [user=mary, ip=1.2.3.3]
ERROR BarCLass Hello world. [user=mary, ip=4.3.2.1]
```

For good measure, let's add the sourcetype field and some parentheses.

```
sourcetype="impl_splunk_gen" (mary AND error) NOT debug NOT worthless
NOT logoutclass
```

Another way of writing the same thing is as follows:

```
sourcetype="impl_splunk_gen" mary error NOT (debug OR worthless OR
logoutclass)
```

So that we don't have to type our query every time, let's go ahead and save it as a report for quick retrieval.

First, choose **Save As...**, and then, **Report**.

The **Save As Report** window appears.

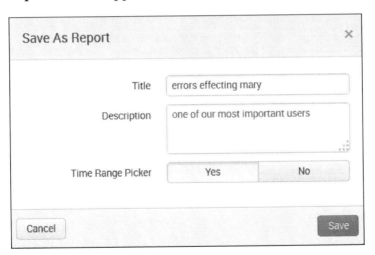

Enter a value for **Title**, in our case, errors affecting `mary`. Optionally, we can add a short description of the search. The time range is filled in based on what was selected in the time picker, and we decide to include the **Time Range Picker** in the saved report. Click **Save**.

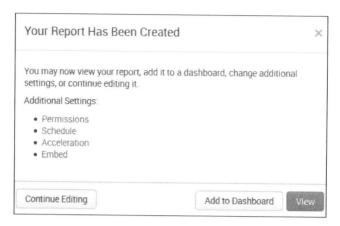

Once we see the preceding window (**Your Report Has Been Created**), we click on **Permissions** and see the **Edit Permissions** window:

For **Display For**, let's click on **App** (rather than the default **Owner**, as shown in the preceding screenshot):

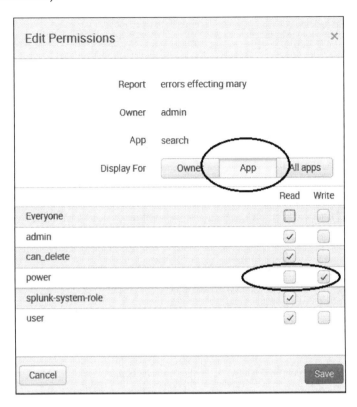

Next, we'll check **Read** for all user roles except for **power**, since we know that certain users in our Splunk environment are members of this group (including our friend `mary`). Finally, we can click **Save**.

The search report is then available under **Reports**:

Selecting search/report from the menu runs the search using the latest data available.

Creating alerts from searches

Let's continue with our example. We want to take our original search query, schedule it, and then set a triggered response.

Any saved search can also be run on a schedule. One use for scheduled searches is firing alerts. Let's get started with our example. Go to the **Reports** page (shown in the previous screenshot) and click on **Open in Search** for our report (`errors affecting mary`). This opens our saved report not as a report but as a search query (it also runs the search). From there, we can click on `Save As` and choose `Alert`:

Using the **Save As Alert** window (shown in the next screenshot), we can fill in the appropriate details for our alert:

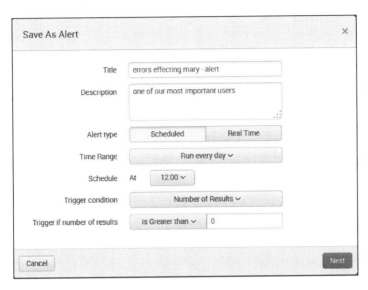

- **Title**: I kept the original search title (`errors affecting mary`) but added the word `alert`
- **Description**: I kept this the same, but in reality, we'd want to add more of a description
- **Alert Type**: I selected **Scheduled**, since I want this alert search to be run every day
- **Time Range**: I selected the preset **Run every day**
- **Schedule At**: I selected the preset **12:00**
- **Trigger condition**: I selected the preset **Number of Results** since I'd like to trigger an event if my search finds any errors generated by our favorite user, `mary`
- **Trigger if number of results**: I selected the preset **Is Greater than** and filled in zero (this means that I am interested in any errors that are found by my search)

After filling in the above, I can click on **Next**; we can see that we have more information to provide:

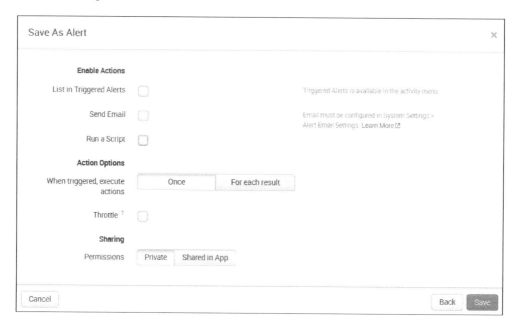

This time, the window is divided into the following areas: **Enable Actions**, **Action Options,** and **Sharing**.

Enable actions

- **List in Triggered Alerts**: You can check this if you want to display your triggered alert in the Splunk Alert Manager which lists details of triggered alerts for 24 hours or a specified duration

- **Send Email**: You can configure your alert to send an e-mail to specified users when the alert gets triggered

- **Run a Script**: You can have Splunk run a script when your alert gets triggered

Action options

- **When triggered, execute actions**: **Once** or **For each result**. For example, should the alert trigger for each error that `mary` receives or once for all errors within a time range?

- **Throttle?**: You can use throttling (usually based upon time and/or event count) to reduce the frequency at which an alert triggers since an alert can trigger frequently based on similar results that the search returns or the schedule to run the alert.

Sharing

Permissions—**Private** or **Shared in App**. Should this alert be shared with other users?

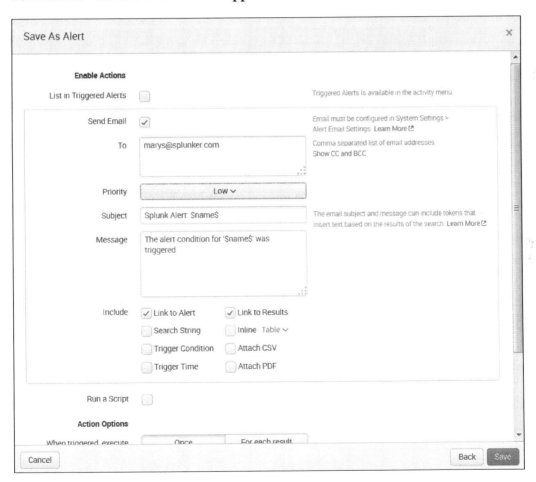

For our example, I've elected to trigger an e-mail to `mary` (`marys@slunker.com`) with a link to both the alert and the alert results within the e-mail so that she can review her errors. In addition (as shown in the next screenshot), I have decided to send an e-mail **Once** (for all events/errors within the time range, not for each one) and leave the alert **Private**.

After hitting **Save**, our alert is ready to go:

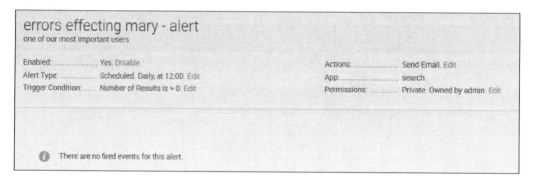

Summary

In this chapter, we covered searching in Splunk and doing a few useful things with those search results. There are lots of little tricks that we will touch upon as we go forward.

In the next chapter, we will start using fields for more than searches; we'll build tables and graphs, and then, we'll learn how to make our own fields.

3
Tables, Charts, and Fields

Up to this point, we have learned how to search for and retrieve raw events, but you will most likely want to create tables and charts to expose useful patterns. Thankfully, the reporting commands in Splunk make short work of most reporting tasks. We will step through a few common-use cases in this chapter. Later in the chapter, we will learn how to create custom fields for even more custom reports.

Specifically, in this chapter we will cover the following topics:

- The pipe symbol
- Using top to show common field values
- Using stats to aggregate values
- Using chart to turn data
- Using timechart to show values over time
- Working with fields
- Acceleration

About the pipe symbol

Before we dive into the actual commands, it is important to understand what the pipe symbol (|) is used for in Splunk. In a command line, the pipe symbol is used to represent the sending of data from one process to another. For example, in a Unix-style operating system, you might say:

```
grep foo access.log | grep bar
```

The first command finds, in the file access.log, lines that contain foo. Its output is taken and piped to the input of the next grep command, which finds lines that contain bar. The final output goes wherever it was destined, usually to the terminal window.

The pipe symbol is different in Splunk in a few important ways:

- Unlike the command line, events are not simply text, but rather each is a set of key/value pairs. You can think of each event as a database row, a Python dictionary, a JavaScript object, a Java map, or a Perl associative array. Some fields are hidden from the user but are available for use. Many of these hidden fields are prefixed with an underscore; for instance _raw, which contains the original event text, and _time, which contains the parsed time in UTC epoch form. Unlike a database, events do not adhere to a schema, and fields are created dynamically.

- Commands can do anything to the events that they are handed. Usually, a command does one of the following:
  - Modifies or creates fields—for example, eval, rex
  - Filters events—for example, head, where
  - Replaces events with a report—for example, top, stats
  - Sorts the results of a search—using sort

- Some commands can act as generators, which produce what you might call synthetic events, such as |metadata and |inputcsv.

We will get to know the pipe symbol very well through examples.

Using top to show common field values

A very common question that may often arise is, "What values are most common?" When looking for errors, you are probably interested in figuring out what piece of code has the most errors. The top command provides a very simple way to answer this question.

Let's step through a few examples.

First, run a search for errors:

```
sourcetype="tm1*" error
```

The preceding example searches for the word error in all sourcetypes starting with the character string "tm1*" (with the asterisk being the wildcard character).

In my data, we find events containing the word `error`, a sample of which is listed in the following screenshot:

i	Event
>	`Error: MetaData procedure line (0): Dimension element name "SpendAdvisor" is an alias for another element in dimen` `ount"` `.4\xBCR\xBA\x95\xC6/4\xCD`
>	`Error: MetaData procedure line (0): Dimension element name "SpendAdvisor" is an alias for another element in dimen` `ount"` `<P4\xBCR\xBA\x95\xC6/4\xCD`
>	`"451700","PCS-REVENUE CYCLE ASSESS/ IMPL","Other-2","Other","PPP","12900","Pipeline","Sold To Be Delivered","N/A",` `700","Other",Data Source line (61) Error: MetaData procedure line (26): Consolidated Element "Other-2" not found.`
>	`"447900","MEDDIUS","Birchstreet-1","Birchstreet","ITS","11990","Pipeline","Contract","N/A","","","","447900","Birc` `Source line (24) Error: MetaData procedure line (26): Consolidated Element "Birchstreet-1" not found.`
>	`"445800","CONCERRO","Concerro","Cost Management","ITS","11190","Pipeline","Contract","N/A","","","","445800","Conc` `urce line (4) Error: MetaData procedure line (26): Consolidated Element "Concerro" not found.`
>	`"446700","SPEND ADVISOR","SpendAdvisor","Cost Management","ITS","11190","Pipeline","Contract","N/A","","","","4467` `isor",Data Source line (3) Error: MetaData procedure line (26): Consolidated Element "SpendAdvisor" not found.`
>	`Error: MetaData procedure line (0): Dimension element name "SpendAdvisor" is an alias for another element in dimen` `ount"` `%4\xBCR\xBA\x95\xC6/4\xCD`

Since I happen to know that the data I am searching is made up of application log files generated throughout the year, it might be interesting to see the month that had the most errors logged. To do that, we can simply add | `top date_month` to our search, like so:

```
sourcetype="tm1*" error | top date_month
```

The results are transformed by `top` into a table like the following one:

date_month ⌄	count ⌄	percent ⌄
october	69899	99.757382
december	165	0.235482
june	5	0.007136

From these results, we see that **october** is logging significantly more errors than any other month. We should probably take a closer look at the activity that occurred during that month.

Next, perhaps we would like to determine if there is a particular day of the week when these errors are happening. Adding another field name to the end of the command instructs `top` to slice the data again. For example, let's add `date_wday` to the end of our previous query, like so:

```
sourcetype="tm1*" error | top date_month date_wday
```

The results might look like the following screenshot:

date_month	date_wday	count	percent
october	wednesday	69889	99.743110
december	wednesday	98	0.139862
december	tuesday	67	0.095620
october	tuesday	9	0.012844
june	friday	3	0.004281
october	thursday	1	0.001427
june	thursday	1	0.001427
june	monday	1	0.001427

In these results, we see that **wednesday** is logging the most errors from the month of **october**. If we simply wanted to see the distribution of errors by **date_wday**, you could specify only the user field, like so:

```
sourcetype=tm1* error | top date_wday
```

Controlling the output of top

The default behavior for `top` is to show the 10 largest counts. The possible row count is the product of all fields specified, in this case `date_month` and `date_wday`. Using our data in this example, there are 8 possible combinations. If you would like to see less than 10 rows (or in our example, less than 8), add the argument limit, like so:

```
sourcetype=tm1* error | top limit=4 date_month date_wday
```

Arguments change the behavior of a command; they take the form of `name=value`. Many commands require the arguments to immediately follow the command name, so it's a good idea to always follow this structure.

Each command has different arguments, as appropriate. As you type in the search bar, a help drop-down box will appear for the last command in your search, as shown in the following screenshot:

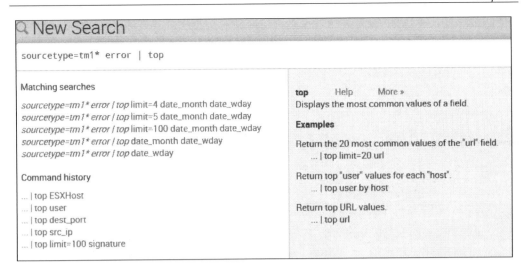

The **Help** option takes you to the documentation for that command at http://www. splunk.com and **More >>** provides concise documentation inline.

Let's use a few arguments to make a shorter list but also roll all other results into another line:

```
sourcetype=tm1* error
| top
limit=4
useother=true
otherstr="everything else
date_month date_wday
```

This produces results like those shown in the following screenshot:

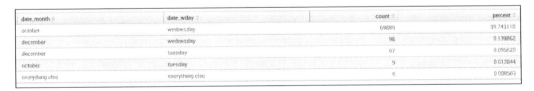

The last line represents everything that didn't fit into the top four. The (top) option, useother, enables this last row, while option otherstr controls the value printed instead of the default value other.

The reader may review the Splunk documentation for additional information on the `top` command and options at `http://docs.splunk.com/Documentation/Splunk/6.2.3/SearchReference/Top`

For the opposite of `top`, see the `rare` command.

Using stats to aggregate values

While `top` is very convenient, `stats` is extremely versatile. The basic structure of a `stats` statement is:

```
stats functions by fields
```

Many of the functions available in `stats` mimic similar functions in SQL or Excel, but there are many functions unique to Splunk. The simplest `stats` function is `count`. Given the following query, the results will contain exactly one row, with a value for the field count:

```
sourcetype=tm1* error | stats count
```

Using the `by` clause, `stats` will produce a row per unique value for each field listed, which is similar to the behavior of `top`. Run the following query:

```
sourcetype=tm1* error | stats count by date_month date_wday
```

It will produce a table like that shown in the following screenshot:

date_month ⌄	date_wday ⌄	count ⌄
december	tuesday	67
december	wednesday	98
june	friday	3
june	monday	1
june	thursday	1
october	thursday	1
october	tuesday	9
october	wednesday	69889

There are a few things to notice about these results:

- The results are sorted against the values of the *by* fields, in this case **date_month** followed by **date_wday**. Unlike `top`, the largest value will not necessarily be at the top of the list. You can sort in the GUI simply by clicking on the field names at the `top` of the table, or by using the `sort` command.
- There is no limit to the number of rows produced. The number of rows will equal all possible combinations of field values.
- The function results are displayed last. In the next example, we will add a few more functions, and this will become more obvious.

Using `stats`, you can add as many by fields or functions as you want into a single statement. Let's run this query:

```
sourcetype=tml* error | stats count avg(linecount) max(linecount)
as "Slowest Time" by date_month date_wday
```

The results look like those in the following screenshot:

date_month	date_wday	count	avg(linecount)	Slowest Time
april	tuesday	3	1.000000	1
december	friday	16	257.000000	257
december	monday	13	257.000000	257
december	saturday	15	239.933333	257
december	sunday	10	257.000000	257
december	thursday	20	257.000000	257
december	tuesday	69	8.420290	257
december	wednesday	116	38.603448	257
february	friday	5	257.000000	257
february	monday	12	257.000000	257
february	saturday	10	257.000000	257

Let's step through every part of this query, just to be clear:

- `sourcetype=tml* error` is the query itself
- `| stats` starts the `stats` command
- `count` will return the number of events
- `avg(linecount)` produces an average value of the `linecount` field
- `max(linecount) as Slowest Time` finds the maximum value of the `linecount` field and places the value in a field called `Slowest Time`

The quotes are necessary because the field name contains a space.

- `by` indicates that we are done listing functions and want to list the fields to slice the data by. If the data does not need to be sliced, `by` and the fields following it can be omitted.

- `date_month` and `date_wday` are our fields for slicing the data. All functions are actually run against each set of data produced per each possible combination of `date_month` and `date_user`.

If an event is missing a field that is referenced in a `stats` command, you may not see the results you are expecting. For instance, when computing an average, you may wish for events missing a field to count as zeros in the average. Also, for events that do not contain a field listed in the `by` fields, the event will simply be ignored.

To deal with both of these cases, you can use the `fillnull` command to make sure that the fields you want exist. We will cover this in *Chapter 6, Advanced Search Examples*.

Let's look at another example, using a time-based function and a little trick. Let's say we wanted to know the most recent time at which a particular user saw an error each day.

We can use the following query:

```
sourcetype=tm1* Error TheUser="Admin" | stats count
first(date_wday) max(_time) as _time by source
```

This query produces the following table:

source	count	first(date_wday)	_time
C:\Test Data\tm1s20131210184347.log	8	tuesday	2013-12-10 18.43.41
C:\Test Data\tm1s20131211140307.log	7	wednesday	2013-12-11 13.44.02

Let's step through this example:

- `sourcetype=tm1* Error TheUser="Admin"` is the query that will find all errors logged by the user `"Admin"`.

- `| stats` is our command.

- `count` shows how many times this user saw an error each day.

- `first(date_wday)` gives us the weekday that was most recently logged for this user. This will be the most recent event, since results are returned in the order of the most recent first.

- `max(_time) as _time` returns the time at which the user most recently saw an error that day. This takes advantage of three aspects of time in Splunk:

  - `_time` is always present in raw events. As discussed in *Chapter 2, Understanding Search*, the value is the number of seconds since January 1, 1970, UTC.

  - `_time` is stored as a number and can be treated as such.

  - If there is a field called `_time` in the results, Splunk will always display the value as the first column of a table in the time zone selected by the user.

- `by source` is our field to split the results against and in this example it is by data `source` or the error log file that the error(s) were found in.

We have only seen a few functions in `stats`. There are dozens of functions and some advanced syntax that we will touch upon in later chapters. The simplest way to find the full listing is to search with your favorite search engine for the Splunk `stats` functions.

Using chart to turn data

The `chart` command is useful for turning data across two dimensions. It is useful for both tables and charts. Let's start with one of our examples from `stats`:

```
sourcetype="tm1*" error | chart count over date_month by date_wday
```

The resulting table looks like this:

date_month	friday	monday	thursday	tuesday	wednesday
december	0	0	0	67	98
june	3	1	1	0	0
october	0	0	1	9	69889

If you look back at the results from `stats`, the data is presented as one row per combination. Instead of a row per combination, `chart` generates the intersection of the two fields. You can specify multiple functions, but you may only specify one field each for `over` and `by`.

Switching the fields (by rearranging our search statement a bit) turns the data the other way.

date_wday ⌄	december ⌄	june ⌄	october ⌄
friday	0	3	0
monday	0	1	0
thursday	0	1	1
tuesday	67	0	9
wednesday	98	0	69889

By simply clicking on the **Visualization** tab (to the right of the **Statistics** tab), we can see these results in a chart:

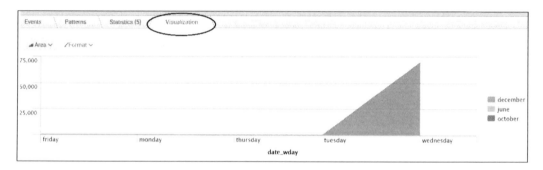

This is an **Area** chart, with particular format options set. Within the chart area, you can click on **Area** to change the chart type (**Line, Area, Column, Bar,** and so on) or **Format** to change the format options (**Stack, Null Values, Multi-series Mode,** and **Drilldown**).

Chart types are pretty self-explanatory, so let's go ahead and take a look at the (chart) **Format** options. These options are grouped as:

- **General**: Under general, you have the option to set the **Stack Model** (which indicates how Splunk will display your chart columns for different series (alongside each other or as a single column), determine how to handle **Null Values** (you can leave gaps for null data points, connect to zero data points, or just connect to the next positive data point), set the **Multi-series mode** (**Yes** or **No**), and turn **Drilldown** (active or inactive) on or off.

- **X-Axis**: Is mostly visual, you can set a custom title, allow truncation of label captions, and set the rotation of the text for your chart labels.

- **Y-Axis**: Here you can set not just a custom title, but also the scale (linear or log), the interval, and the min and max values.

- **Chart Overlay**: Here you can set the following options:
  - ◦ **Overlay**: Select a field to show as an overlay.
  - ◦ **View as Axis**: Select **On** to map the overlay to a second Y-axis.
  - ◦ **Title**: Specify a title for the overlay.
  - ◦ **Scale**: Select **Inherit**, **Linear**, or **Log**. **Inherit** uses the scale for the base chart. **Log** provides a logarithmic scale, useful for minimizing the display of large peak values.
  - ◦ **Interval**: Enter the units between tick marks in the axis.
  - ◦ **Min Value**: The minimum value to display. Values less than the **Min Value** do not appear on the chart.
  - ◦ **Max Value**: The maximum value to display. Values greater than the **Max Value** do not appear on the chart.

- **Legend**: Finally, under **Legend**, you can set **Position** (where to place the legend (or to not include the legend) in the visualization.) and **Truncation** (set how to represent names that are too long to display). Keep in mind that, depending on your search results and the visualization options that you select, you may or may not get a useable result. Some experimentation with the various options is recommended.

Using timechart to show values over time

Timechart lets us show numerical values over time. It is similar to the `chart` command, except that time is always plotted on the *x* axis. Here are a couple of things to note:

- The events must have a `_time` field. If you are simply sending the results of a search to the timechart, this will always be true. If you are using interim commands, you will need to be mindful of this requirement.
- Time is always bucketed, meaning that there is no way to draw a point per event.

Let's see how many errors have been occurring:

```
sourcetype="tm1*" error | timechart count
```

The default chart will look something like this:

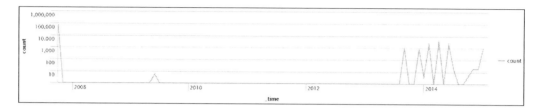

Now let's see how many errors have occurred per weekday over the same time period.

We simply need to add by user to the query:

```
sourcetype="tm1*" error | timechart count by date_wday
```

This produces the following chart:

As we stated earlier, the *x* axis is always time. The *y* axis can be:

- One or more functions
- A single function with a by clause
- Multiple functions with a by clause (a new feature in Splunk 4.3). An example of a timechart with multiple functions might be as follows:

```
sourcetype="tm1*" error | timechart count as "Error Count"
count(sourcetype) as "Source Count"
```

This would produce a graph like this:

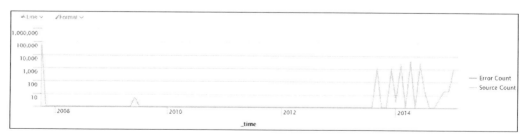

Timechart options

Timechart has many arguments and formatting options. We'll touch upon a few examples of formatting, but they are too numerous to cover in detail. We will use other chart types in later chapters. Let's throw a few options in (to a simple search) and see what they do.

```
sourcetype="*" GET | timechart bins=100 limit=3 useother=false
usenull=false count as "Error count" by user
```

Let's step through each of these arguments:

- `sourcetype="*" GET` is our search query
- `bins` defines how many bins to slice time into. The number of bins will probably not be exactly 100 as the time will be sliced into logical units. In our example, this comes to 10 minutes per bin. To be more exact, you can use span (for example, `span=1h`) for hourly slices, but note that if your span value creates too many time slices, the chart will be truncated.
- `limit` changes the number of series returned. The series with the largest values are returned, much like in `top`. In this case, the most common values of a user will be returned.
- `useother` instructs timechart whether to group all series beyond the limit into an other bucket. The default value is `true`.
- `usenull` instructs timechart whether to bucket, into the group NULL, events that do not have a value for the fields in the by clause. The default value is `true`.

This combination of arguments produces a graph similar to this:

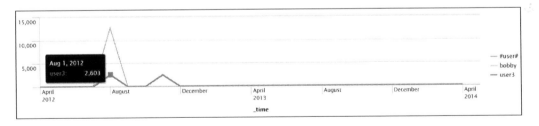

As mentioned earlier in the section *Using chart to turn data*, Splunk offers us a variety of **Formatting options** for our visualizations. Clicking on the drop-down selector on the **Visualization** tab in the following graph gives us quite a few options to work with.

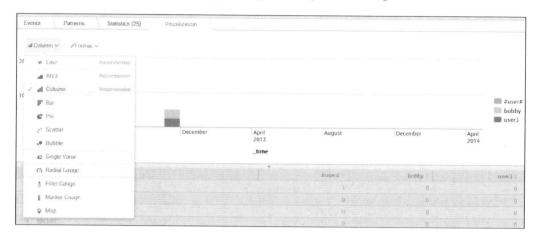

The preceding graph shows a common chart style, the stacked column. This graph is useful for showing how many events of a certain kind occurred, but with colors to give us an idea of the distribution. Some great examples of all of the available chart styles are available at `http://www.splunk.com/`, and we will touch upon more styles in later chapters.

Working with fields

All the fields that we have used so far were either indexed fields (such as `host`, `sourcetype`, and `_time`) or fields that were automatically extracted from `key=value` pairs. Unfortunately, most logs don't follow this format, especially for the first few values in each event. New fields can be created either inline, by using commands, or through configuration.

A regular expression primer

Most of the ways to create new fields in Splunk involve regular expressions (sometimes referred to as REGEX). As mentioned in the Splunk documentation:

> "*Regex is a powerful part of the Splunk search interface, and understanding it is an essential component of Splunk search best practices*".

There are many books and sites dedicated to regular expressions, so we will only touch upon the subject here. The following examples are really provided for completeness; the Splunk web interface may suffice for most users.

Given the `log` snippet `ip=1.2.3.4`, let's pull out the `subnet` (`1.2.3`) into a new field called subnet. The simplest pattern would be the following literal string:

```
ip=(?P<subnet>1.2.3).4
```

This is not terribly useful as it will only find the subnet of that one IP address. Let's try a slightly more complicated example:

```
ip=(?P<subnet>\d+\.\d+\.\d+)\.\d+
```

Let's step through this pattern:

- `ip=` simply looks for the raw string `ip=`.
- `(` starts a *capture buffer*. Everything until the closing parenthesis is part of this capture buffer.
- `?P<subnet>` immediately inside the parenthesis, says *create a field called subnet from the results of this capture buffer*.
- `\d` matches any single digit, from 0 to 9.
- `+` says *one or more of the item immediately before*.
- `\.` matches a literal period. A period without the backslash matches any character.
- `\d+\.\d+` matches the next two parts of the IP address.
- `)` ends our capture buffer.
- `\.\d+` matches the last part of the IP address. Since it is outside the capture buffer, it will be discarded.

Now let's step through an overly complicated pattern to illustrate a few more concepts:

```
ip=(?P<subnet>\d+.\d*\.[01234-9]+)\.\d+
```

Let's step through this pattern:

- `ip=` simply looks for the raw string `ip=`.
- `(?P<subnet>` starts our capture buffer and defines our field name.
- `\d` means digit. This is one of the many backslash character combinations that represent some sets of characters.
- `+` says *one or more of what came before*, in this case `\d`.
- `.` matches a single character. This will match the period after the first set of digits, though it would match any single character.
- `\d*` means zero or more digits.

- `\.` matches a literal period. The backslash negates the special meaning of any special punctuation character. Not all punctuation marks have a special meaning, but so many do that there is no harm adding a backslash before a punctuation mark that you want to literally match.

- `[` starts a character set. Anything inside the brackets will match a single character in the character set.

- `01234-9` means the characters 0, 1, 2, 3, and the range 4-9.

- `]` closes the character set.

- `+` says *one or more of what came before*, in this case the character set.

- `)` ends our capture buffer.

- `\.\d+` is the final part of the IP address that we are throwing away. It is not actually necessary to include this, but it ensures that we only match if there were, in fact, four sets of numbers.

There are a number of different ways to accomplish the task at hand. Here are a few examples that will work:

- `ip=(?P<subnet>\d+\.\d+\.\d+)\.\d+`

- `ip=(?P<subnet>(\d+\.){2}\d+)\.\d+`

- `ip=(?P<subnet>[\d\.]+)\.\d`

- `ip=(?P<subnet>.*?\..*?\..*?)\.`

- `ip=(?P<subnet>\S+)\.`

For more information about regular expressions, consult the man pages for **Perl Compatible Regular Expressions (PCRE)**, which can be found online at `http://www.pcre.org/pcre.txt`, or one of the many regular expression books or websites dedicated to the subject. We will build more expressions as we work through different configurations and searches, but it's definitely worthwhile to have a reference handy.

Commands that create fields

In Splunk, fields are extracted from the event data; to fully leverage the power of Splunk, you have the ability to create additional fields or to have Splunk extract additional fields that you define. This allows you to capture and track information that is important to your needs, but which is not automatically discovered and extracted by Splunk.

There are a number of commands that create new fields, but the most commonly used are `eval` and `rex`.

eval

The `eval` command allows you to use functions to build new fields, much as you would build a formula column in Excel, for example:

```
sourcetype="impl_splunk_gen" | eval
req_time_seconds=date_second/1000 | stats avg(req_time_seconds)
```

This creates a new field called `req_time_seconds` on every event that has a value for `date_second`. Commands after this statement see the field as if it were part of the original event. The `stats` command then creates a table of the average value of our newly created field.

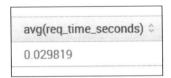

There are a huge number of functions available for use with `eval`. The simplest way to find the full listing is to search Google for *Splunk eval functions*. I would suggest bookmarking this page as you will find yourself referring to it often.

rex

The `rex` command lets you use regular expressions to create fields. It can work against any existing field but, by default, will use the field `_raw`. Let's try one of the patterns that we wrote in our short regular expression primer:

```
sourcetype="impl_splunk_gen" | rex
"ip=(?P<subnet>\d+\.\d+\.\d+)\.\d+" | chart values(subnet) by
date_minute
```

This would create a table like this:

	date_minute ⇕	values(subnet) ⇕
20 Per Page ⌄ Format ⌄ Preview ⌄		
	0	118.192.35
		123.125.67
		173.174.50
		208.115.113
		209.85.238
		220.181.51
		27.159.200
		27.159.213
		31.3.244
		46.17.97
		65.60.148
	1	173.174.50
		188.230.91
		208.115.111
		209.85.238

With the addition of the field argument, we can work against the ip field that is already being created automatically from the `name=value` pair in the event.

```
sourcetype="impl_splunk_gen" | rex field=ip "(?P<subnet>.*)\."|
chart values(subnet) by date_minute
```

This will create exactly the same result as the previous example.

Extracting loglevel

In some of our examples, we searched for the raw word *error*. You may have noticed that many of the events weren't actually errors, but simply contained the word error somewhere in the message. For example, given the following events, we probably only care about the second event:

```
2012-03-21T18:59:55.472-0500 INFO This is not an error
2012-03-21T18:59:42.907-0500 ERROR Something bad happened
```

Using an extracted field, we can easily create fields in our data without re-indexing, that allows you to search for values that occur at a specific location in your events.

Using the extract fields interface

There are several ways to define a field. Let's start by using the **Extract Fields** interface. To access this interface, choose **Extract Fields** from the workflow actions menu next to any event:

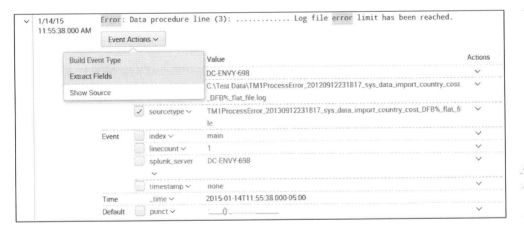

This menu launches the **Extract Fields** view:

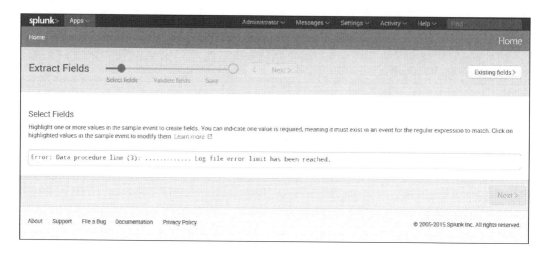

In Splunk version 6.2, we have access to a wizard which helps us provide the information required for Splunk to attempt to build a regular expression that matches.

Although you may choose multiple fields, in this case, we specify **Error**:

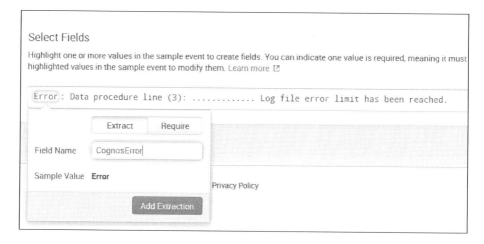

In the popup, you can provide a custom **Field Name** (I chose `CognosError`) and then click the button labeled **Add Extraction**.

Under **Preview,** you can see two tabs – **Events** and our new field **CongosError**:

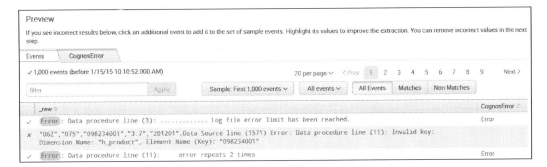

Under **Events**, we get a preview of what data was matched in context, and under **CongosError** we can see our new field.

Finally, under **Show Regular Pattern**, we see the regular expression that Splunk generated, which is as follows:

```
^(?P<CognosError>\w+)
```

You can step through the pattern and, if you are so inclined, make edits to it.

Clicking on the button labeled **Edit the Regular Expression** (shown in the preceding screenshot) presents a dialog to let you modify the pattern manually:

Once you make any edits to the pattern, **Preview** will be enabled and will launch a new search with the pattern loaded into a very useful query that shows the most common values extracted.

Tables, Charts, and Fields

Save prompts you for a name for your new field. Assuming that you modified the originally generated pattern string, you can enter a new name (rather than `CongosError`), and then select the desired permissions for accessing this new field:

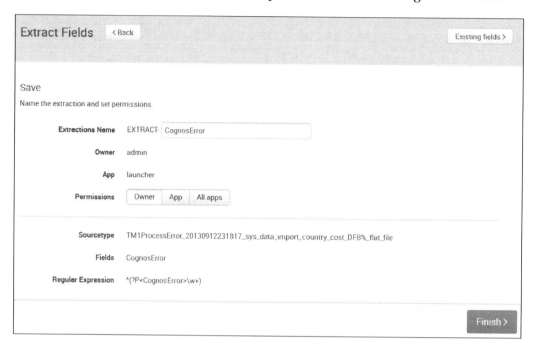

Now that we've defined our field, we can use it in a number of ways, as follows:

- We can search for the value using the fieldname; for instance, `loglevel=CognosError`

- When searching for values by fieldname, the fieldname is case sensitive, but the value is not case sensitive. In this case `loglevel=CognosError` would work just fine, but `LogLevel=cognoserror` would not.

- We can report on the field, whether we searched for it or not. For instance: `sourcetype="impl_splunk_gen" user=mary | top loglevel`

- We can search for only events that contain our field: `sourcetype="impl_splunk_gen" user=mary loglevel="*"`

Using rex to prototype a field

When defining fields, it is often convenient to build the pattern directly in the query and then copy the pattern into the configuration. You might have noticed that the test in the **Extract Fields** workflow used `rex`.

Let's turn the subnet pattern which we built within the section *A regular expression primer* into a field. First, we build the query with the `rex` statement:

```
sourcetype="impl_splunk_gen" ip="*"
| rex "ip=(?P<subnet>\d\.\d\.\d+)\.\d+"
| table ip subnet
```

Since we know there will be an `ip` field in the events which we care about, we can use `ip="*"` to limit the results only to events that have a value for that field.

The `table` command takes a list of fields and displays a table, one row per event:

ip ⌃	subnet ⌃
64.134.155.137	
64.134.155.137	
64.134.155.137	
64.134.155.137	
64.134.155.137	
64.134.155.137	
64.134.155.137	
64.134.155.137	
64.134.155.137	
64.134.155.137	
64.134.155.137	

As we can see, the `rex` statement doesn't always work. Looking at the pattern again, you may notice that the first two instances of \d are now missing their trailing +. Without the plus sign, only addresses with a single digit in both their first and second sections will match. After adding the missing plus signs to our pattern, all rows will have a subnet.

```
sourcetype="impl_splunk_gen" ip="*"
| rex "ip=(?P<subnet>\d+\.\d+\.\d+)\.\d+"
| table ip subnet
```

ip ⬍	subnet ⬍
64.134.155.137	64.134.155
64.134.155.137	64.134.155
64.134.155.137	64.134.155
64.134.155.137	64.134.155
64.134.155.137	64.134.155
64.134.155.137	64.134.155
64.134.155.137	64.134.155
64.134.155.137	64.134.155
64.134.155.137	64.134.155
64.134.155.137	64.134.155
64.134.155.137	64.134.155
173.174.50.156	173.174.50

We can now take the pattern from the `rex` statement and use it to build a configuration.

Using the admin interface to build a field

Taking our pattern from the previous example, we can build the configuration to wire up this extract.

First, click on **Settings** in the upper menu bar. From there, select `Fields`. The `Fields` section contains everything, funnily enough, about fields.

Here you can view, edit, and set permissions on field extractions, define event workflow actions, field aliases, and even rename sourcetypes.

For now, we're interested in **Field extractions**.

> **Field extractions**
>
> View and edit all field extractions. Add new field extractions and update permissions.

After clicking on **Add new** to the right of **Field extractions**, or on the **New** button after clicking on **Field extractions**, we are presented with the interface for creating a new field.

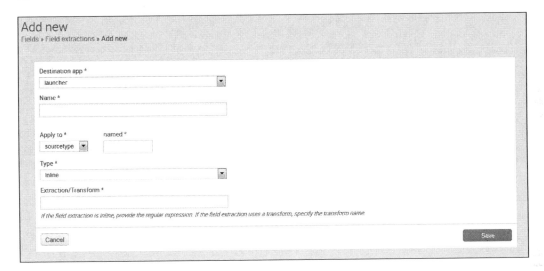

Now, we step through the fields:

- **Destination app** lets us choose the app where this extraction will live and where it will take effect, by default. We will discuss the scope of configurations in *Chapter 11, Configuring Splunk*.
- **Name** is simply a display name for the extraction. Make it as descriptive as you like.
- **Apply to** lets you choose what to bind this extraction to. Your choices are **sourcetype**, **source**, and **host**. The usual choice is **sourcetype**.
- **named** is the name of the item we are binding our extraction to.

- **Type** lets you choose **Inline**, which means specifying the regular expression here, or **Uses transform**, which means we will specify a named transform that exists already in the configuration.

- **Extraction/Transform** is where we place either our pattern, if we chose a **Type** option of **Inline**, or the name of a **Transform** object.

Once you click on **Save**, you will return to the listing of extractions. By default, your extraction will be private to you and will only function in the application it was created in. If you have the rights to do so, you can share the extraction with other users and change the scope of where it runs. Click on **Permissions** in the listing to see the permissions page, which most objects in Splunk use.

Object should appear in		
● Keep private ○ This app only (search) ○ All apps		

Permissions

Roles	Read	Write
Everyone	○	○
admin	○	○
can_delete	○	○
power	○	○
user	○	○

The top section controls the context in which this extraction will run. Think about when the field would be useful, and limit the extractions accordingly. An excessive number of extractions can affect performance, so it is a good idea to limit the extracts to a specific app when appropriate. We will talk more about creating apps in *Chapter 8, Working with Apps*.

The second section controls what roles can read or write this configuration. The usual selections are the **Read** option for the **Everyone** parameter and the **Write** option for the admin parameter. As you build objects going forward, you will become very familiar with this dialog. Permissions and security, in general, can be complex and affect where an app will eventually be visible—the reader is advised to take the time to review whether the permissions set for apps are actually what is expected.

Indexed fields versus extracted fields

When an event is written to an index, the raw text of the event is captured along with a set of indexed fields. The default indexed fields include `host`, `sourcetype`, `source`, and `_time`. There are distinct advantages and a few serious disadvantages to using indexed fields.

First, let's look at the advantages of an indexed field (we will actually discuss configuring indexed fields in *Chapter 11, Configuring Splunk*):

- As an indexed field is stored in the index with the event itself, it is only calculated at index time and, in fact, can only be calculated once at index time.
- It can make finding specific instances of common terms efficient. See *Indexed field case 1 – rare instances of a common term* in the following section, as an example.
- You can create new words to search against those which simply don't exist in the raw text or are embedded inside a word. See from *Indexed field cases 2 – splitting words* to *Indexed field cases 4 – slow requests* in the following sections.
- You can efficiently search for words in other indexed fields. See the *Indexed field case 3 – application from source* section.

Now for the disadvantages of an indexed field:

- It is not retroactive. This is different from extracted fields where all events, past and present, will gain the newly defined field if the pattern matches. This is the biggest disadvantage of indexed fields and has a few implications, as follows:
    - Only newly indexed events will gain a newly defined indexed field. If the pattern is wrong in certain cases, there is no practical way to apply the field to already indexed events.
    - Likewise, if the log format changes, the indexed field may not be generated (or generated incorrectly).
- It adds to the size of your index on disk.
- It counts against your license.
- Any changes will require a restart to be applied and disrupt data flow temporarily.
- In most cases, the value of the field is already an indexed word, in which case creating an indexed field will likely have no benefit, except in the rare cases where that value is very common.

With the disadvantages out of the way, let's look at a few cases where an indexed field would improve search performance and then at one case where it would probably make no difference.

Indexed field case 1 – rare instances of a common term

Let's say your log captures process exit codes. If `1` represents a failure, you probably want to be able to search for this efficiently. Consider a log that looks something like this:

```
4/1/12 6:35:50.000 PM process=important_process.sh, exitcode=1
```

It would be easy to search for this log entry using `exitcode=1`. The problem is that when working with extracted fields, the search is effectively reduced to this:

```
1 | search exitcode="1"
```

Since the date contains `1`, this search would find every event for the entire day and then filter the events to the few that we are looking for. In contrast, if `exitcode` were defined as an indexed field, the query would immediately find the events, only retrieving the appropriate events from the disk. Please note that binding an indexed field to any time (stamp) is risky. This wreaks havoc on data integrity and is not considered best practice.

Indexed field case 2 – splitting words

In some log formats, multiple pieces of information may be encoded into a single word without whitespace or punctuation to separate the useful pieces of information. For instance, consider a log message such as this:

```
4/2/12 6:35:50.000 PM kernel: abc5s2: 0xc014 (UNDEFINED).
```

Let's pretend that `5s2` (a made-up string of characters for an example) is an important piece of information that we need to be able to search for efficiently. The query `*5s2` would find the events but would be a very inefficient search (in essence, a full table scan). By defining an indexed field, you can very efficiently search for this instance of the string `5s2`, because essentially, we create a new word in the metadata of this event.

Defining an indexed field only makes sense if you know the format of the logs before indexing, if you believe the field will actually make the query more efficient (see previous section), and if you will be searching for the field value. If you will only be reporting on the values of this field, an extracted field will be sufficient, except in the most extreme performance cases.

Indexed field case 3 – application from source

A common requirement is to be able to search for events from a particular web application. Often, the only easy way to determine the application that created the logs is by inspecting the path to the logs, which Splunk stores in the indexed field source. For example, given the following path, the application name is `app_one`:

```
/opt/instance19/apps/app_one/logs/important.log
```

You could search for this instance using `source="*/app_one/*"`, but this effectively initiates a full table scan. You could define an extracted field and then search for `app="app_one"`, but unfortunately, this approach will be no more efficient because the word we're looking for is not contained in the field `_raw`. If we define this field as an indexed field, `app="app_one"` will be an efficient search.

Once again, if you only need this field for reporting, the extracted field is just fine.

Indexed field case 4 – slow requests

Consider a web access log with a trailing request time in microseconds:

```
[31/Jan/2012:18:18:07 +0000] "GET / HTTP/1.1" 200 7918 ""
"Mozilla/5.0..." 11/11033255
```

Let's say we want to find all requests that took longer than 10 seconds. We can easily extract the value into a field, perhaps `request_ms`. We could then run the search `request_ms>10000000`. This query will work, but it requires scanning every event in the given time frame. Whether the field is extracted or indexed, we would face the same problem as Splunk has to convert the field value to a number before it can test the value.

What if we could define a field and instead search for `slow_request=1`? To do this, we can take advantage of the fact that, when defining an indexed field, the value can be a static value. Having Splunk search for a static value – rather than examining the value of every event and then trying to match it – would improve the efficiency of the search. This could be accomplished with a transform, like so:

```
REGEX = .*/(\d{7,})$
FORMAT = slow_request::1
```

We will cover transforms, and the configurations involved, in *Chapter 11, Configuring Splunk*.

Once again, this is only worth the trouble if you need to efficiently search for these events and not simply report on the value of `request_ms`.

Indexed field case 5 – unneeded work

Once you learn to make indexed fields, it may be tempting to convert all your important fields into indexed fields. In most cases, it is essentially a wasted effort and ends up using extra disk space, wasting license, and adding no performance boost.

For example, consider this log message:

```
4/2/12 6:35:50.000 PM [vincentbumgarner] [893783] sudo bash
```

Assuming that the layout of this message is as follows, it might be tempting to put both userid and pid into indexed fields:

```
date [userid] [pid] action
```

Since the values are uncommon, and are unlikely to occur in unrelated locations, defining these fields as indexed fields is most likely wasteful. It is much simpler to define these fields as extracted fields and shield ourselves from the disadvantages of indexed fields.

Summary

This has been a very dense chapter, but we have really just scratched the surface of a number of important topics. In future chapters, we will use these commands and techniques in more and more interesting ways. The possibilities can be a bit dizzying, so we will step through a multitude of examples to illustrate as many scenarios as possible.

In the next chapter, we will cover data models and pivots; covering a definition of each, the pivot editor, pivot elements and filters, and sparklines.

4
Data Models and Pivots

In this chapter, we will introduce the following:

- Data Models
- Pivots (along with pivot elements and filters)
- Sparklines

So let's get started.

In Splunk, data models and pivots should be discussed together because data models drive (Splunk) pivots. So let's start by defining data models.

What is a data model?

The Splunk product documentation (2015) defines a data model as:

> *a hierarchically structured, search-time mapping of semantic knowledge about one or more datasets (that encode the domain knowledge necessary to generate specialized searches of those datasets) so that Splunk can use these specialized searches to generate reports and charts for pivot users.*

Data models enable you to create Splunk reports and dashboards without having to develop Splunk searches (required to create those reports and dashboards), and can play a big part in Splunk app development. You can create your own data models, but before you do, you should review the data models that your organization may have already developed. Typically, data models are designed by those that understand the specifics around the format, the semantics of certain data, and the manner in which users may expect to work with that data. In building a typical data model, knowledge managers use knowledge object types (such as lookups, transactions, search-time field extractions, and calculated fields).

Another way to perhaps understand data models, if you are familiar with relational databases, is to think of a Splunk data model as a sort of database schema. Using the **Splunk pivot editor**, they let you generate statistical tables, charts, and visualizations based on column and row configurations that you select.

What does a data model search?

Splunk data models are really a group or set of specific information (referred to as objects) pulled together to create specific Splunk search strings, each used to generate a search that returns a particular dataset. That dataset, returned by the object you select, is governed by particular object constraints and attributes.

Data model objects

As I mentioned, data models are constructed of a series of objects and these objects will be one of four types – Event, Search, Transaction, or Child. They are arranged hierarchically with child objects inheriting from the parent objects that they are associated with.

- *Event objects* are the most common data model object, broadly representing a type of event. Event objects are typically defined by a constraint (which we will discuss next).

- *Transaction objects* enable you to create data models that represent transactions (groups of related events that span time) using fields that have already been added to the model via an event or search object, which means that you can't create data models that are composed only of transaction objects and their child objects. Before you create a transaction object, you must already have some event or search object trees in your model.

- *Search objects* use an arbitrary Splunk search that includes transforming commands to define the dataset that they represent.

- The most top-level objects in a data model are referred to as *root objects,* and each can be a parent object to many child objects. Splunk calls the relationship of a parent and child object an *object tree.* The data that this object tree represents is first selected by the root and then refined by each of its child objects.

Object constraining

All data model objects are defined by sets of constraints that will filter out information that is not pertinent to the object. A constraint may be a simple Splunk search (with no pipes or additional commands), a more complex search, or even a transaction. Constraints are inherited by child objects. Constraint inheritance ensures that each child object represents a subset of the data represented by its parent objects. So, for example, a data model may have a root object which defines a particular indexed source (sourcetype=speciallogs_*), while a child object of that root might narrow down that search to only the errors that appear in that datasource (error*). You might use this data model if you know that you only want to report on *errors* within the events that belong to the speciallogs sourcetype.

Attributes

Data model objects also include attributes, which are simply fields (exposed for use in reporting) associated with the dataset that the object represents. There are five types of object attributes: Auto-extracted (fields that Splunk derives at search time), eval expressions (field derived from an eval expression that you enter in the attribute definition), lookups (lookups add fields from external data sources such as CSV files and scripts), Regular Expressions (a field that is extracted from the object event data using a regular expression) and Geo IP (of lookup that adds geographical attributes, such as latitude, longitude, country, and city to events in the object dataset).

Attributes fall into one of three categories: *inherited attributes* (from the object's parent), *extracted attributes* (that you add to an object), or *calculated* (attributes that are the result of a calculation or a lookup).

When you define data model attributes, you can define (for each object in the data model) whether it is *visible* or *hidden*. Attributes are visible by default. This is particularly important if each object in your data model has many attributes but only a few are essential for your user's needs. Determining what attributes to include in a Splunk data model, and which attributes to expose, is a critical part of the overall design of the model. Typically, it's often helpful if each object exposes only the data that is relevant to that object, making it easier to understand and use for your average Splunk user.

In addition to attribute visibility, it is also possible to make any attribute either, required or optional. Indicating that an attribute is required means that every event represented by the object must have that attribute. When you define an attribute as optional, it means that the object may have events that do not have that attribute at all.

Creating a data model

So now that we have a general idea of what a Splunk data model is, let's go ahead and create one. Before we can get started, we need to verify that our user ID is set up with the proper access required to create a data model. By default, only users with the admin or a power role can create data models. For other users, the ability to create a data model depends on whether their roles have write access to an app.

To begin (once you have verified that you do have the access to create a data model), you can click on **Settings** and then **Data models** (under **KNOWLEDGE**):

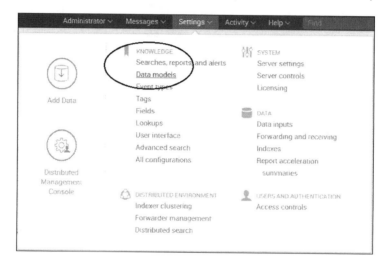

This takes you to the **Data Models** (management) page (shown in the next screenshot). This is where a list of data models is displayed. From here, you can manage the permissions, acceleration, cloning, and removal of existing data models. You can also use this page to upload a data model or create new data models, using the **Upload Data Model** and **New Data Model** buttons in the upper-right corner, respectively.

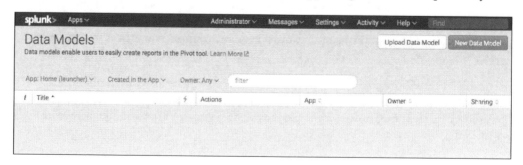

Since this is a new data model, you can click on the button labeled **New Data Model**. This will open the **New Data Model** dialog box (shown in the following image). We can fill in the required information in this dialog box:

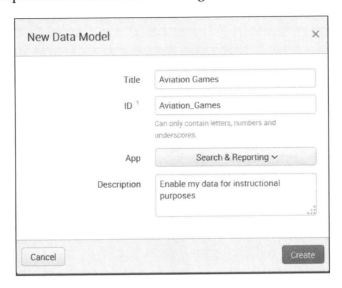

Filling in the new data model dialog

You have four fields to fill in order to describe your new Splunk data model: **Title, ID, App,** and **Description**:

- **Title**: here you must enter a **Title** for your data model. This field accepts any character, as well as spaces. The value you enter here is what will appear on the data model listing page.

- **ID**: this is an optional field. It gets prepopulated with what you entered for your data model title (with any spaces replaced with underscores. Take a minute to make sure you have a good one, since once you enter the data model **ID**, you can't change it.

- **App**: Here you select (from a drop-down list) the Splunk app that your data model will serve.

- **Description**: the description is also an optional field, but I recommend adding something descriptive to later identify your data model.

Once you have filled in these fields, you can click the button labeled **Create**. This opens the data model (in our example, **Aviation Games**) in the Splunk **Edit Objects** page (shown in the following screenshot).

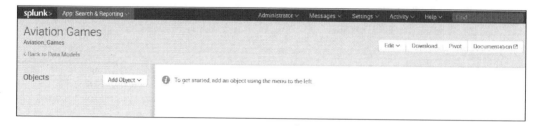

The next step in defining a data model is to add the first object. As we have already stated, data models are typically composed of object hierarchies built on root event objects. Each root event object represents a set of data that is defined by a constraint, which is a simple search that filters out events that are not relevant to the object.

Getting back to our example, let's create an object for our data model to track purchase requests on our **Aviation Games** website.

To define our first event-based object, click **Add Object** (as shown in the following screenshot):

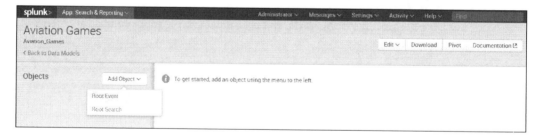

Our data model's first object can either be a **Root Event,** or **Root Search**. We're going to add a **Root Event**, so select **Root Event**. This will take you to the **Add Event Object** editor:

Our example event will expose events that contain the phrase `error` which represents processing errors that have occurred within our data source. So for the **Object Name,** we will enter `Processing Errors`.

The **Object ID** will automatically populate when you type in the **Object Name** (you can edit it if you want to change it). For our object's constraint, we'll enter `sourcetype=tm1* error`. This constraint defines the events that will be reported on (all events that contain the phrase `error` that are indexed in the data sources starting with `tm1`). After providing **Constraints** for the event-based object, you can click **Preview** to test whether the constraints you've supplied return the kind of events that you want.

The following screenshot depicts the preview of the constraints given in this example:

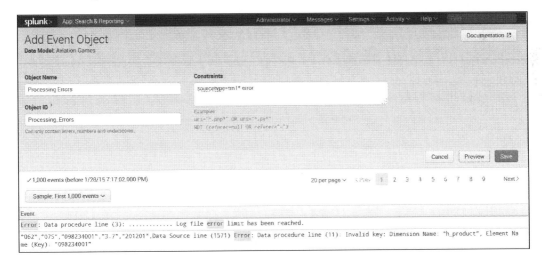

After reviewing the output, Click **Save**. The list of attributes for our root object are displayed: **host**, **source**, **sourcetype**, and **_time**. If you want to add child objects to client and server errors, you need to edit the attributes list to include additional attributes:

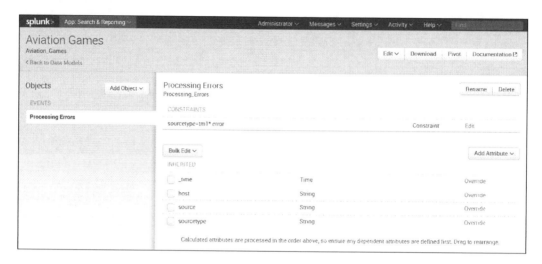

Editing attributes

Let's add an auto-extracted attribute, as mentioned earlier in this chapter, to our data model. Remember, auto-extracted attributes are derived by Splunk at search time. To start, click **Add Attribute**:

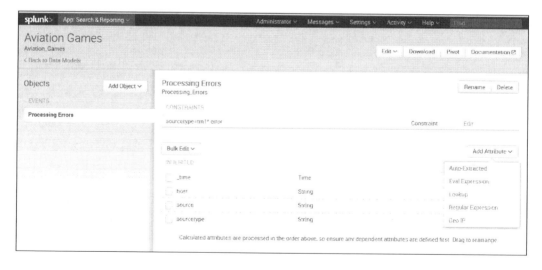

Next, select **Auto-Extracted**. The **Add Auto-Extracted Field** window opens:

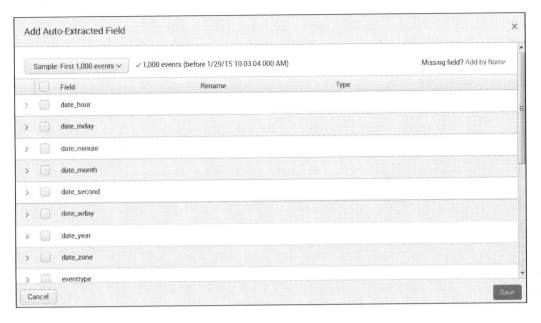

You can scroll through the list of automatically extracted fields and check the fields that you want to include. Since my data model example deals with errors that occurred, I've selected **date_mday**, **date_month,** and **date_year**.

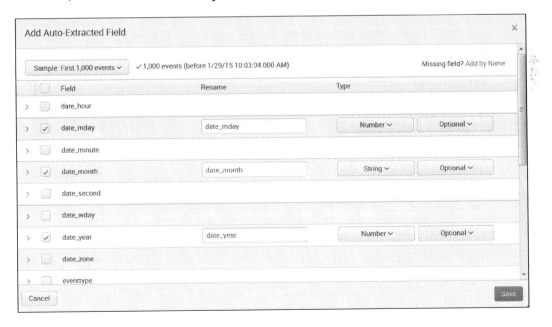

Notice that to the right of the field list, you have the opportunity to rename and type set each of the fields that you selected. **Rename** is self-explanatory, but for type, Splunk allows you to select *String*, *Number*, *Boolean*, or *IPV$* and indicate if the attribute is *Required*, *Optional*, *Hidden*, or *Hidden & Required*. Optional means that the attribute doesn't have to appear in every event represented by the object. The attribute may appear in some of the object events and not others.

Once you have reviewed your selected field types, Click **Save**.

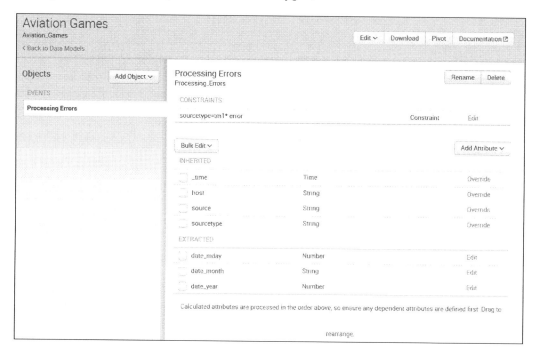

Lookup attributes

Lets discuss lookup attributes now. Splunk can use the existing lookup definitions to match the values of an attribute that you select to values of a field in the specified lookup table. It then returns the corresponding field/value combinations and applies them to your object as (lookup) attributes.

Once again, if you click **Add Attribute** and select **Lookup**, Splunk opens the **Add Attributes with a Lookup** page (shown in the following screenshot) where you can select from your currently defined lookup definitions. For this example, we select **dnslookup**:

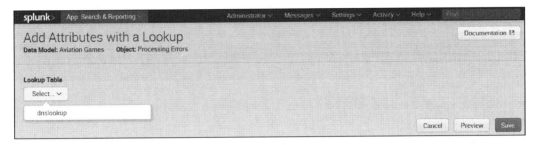

The **dnslookup** converts clienthost to clientip. We can configure a lookup attribute using this lookup to add that result to the processing errors objects.

Under **Input**, select **host** for the **Field in Lookup** and **Attribute**. **Field in Lookup** is the field to be used in the lookup table. **Attribute** is the name of the field used in the event data. In our simple example, Splunk will match the field **clienthost** with the field **host**.

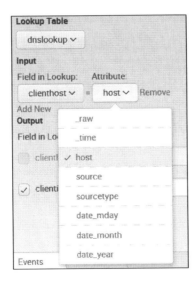

Under **Output**, I have selected **host** as the output field to be matched with the lookup. You can provide a **Display Name** for the selected field. This display name is the name used for the field in your events. I simply typed `AviationLookupName` for my display name (see the following screenshot):

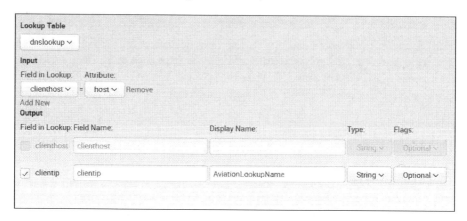

Again, Splunk allows you to click **Preview** to review the fields that you want to add. You can use the tabs to view the **Events** in a table, or view the values of each of the fields that you selected in **Output**. For example, the following screenshot shows the values of **AviationLookupName**:

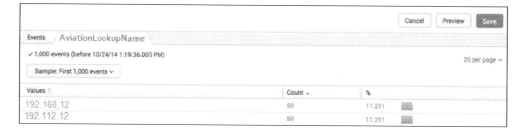

Finally, we can click **Save**.

Children

We have just added a root (or parent) object to our data model. The next step is to add some children. Although a child object inherits all the constraints and attributes from its parent, when you create a child, you will give it additional constraints with the intention of further filtering the dataset that the object represents.

To add a child object to our data model, click **Add Object** and select **Child**:

Splunk then opens the editor window, **Add Child Object** (shown in the following screenshot):

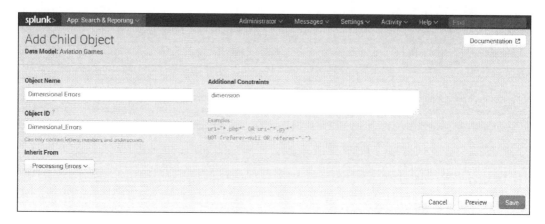

On this page, follow these steps:

- Enter the **Object Name**: `Dimensional Errors`
- Leave the **Object ID**: `Dimensional_Errors`
- Under **Inherit From**, select **Processing Errors**. This means that this child object will inherit all the attributes from the parent object, **Processing Errors**
- Add the **Additional Constraints**: `dimension`, which means that the data models search for the events in this object; when expanded, it will look something like this: `sourcetype=tm1* error dimension`
- Finally, Click **Save** to save your changes

Following the above outlined steps, you can add additional objects, each continuing to filter the results until you have the results that you need.

At this point, the next step in implementing a Splunk data model is to use it. So let's continue and determine how.

What is a pivot?

As we stated earlier in this chapter, data models drive (Splunk) pivots. So what is a pivot? A pivot is created by using the Splunk Pivot Editor and can be a simple (or complex) table, chart, or dashboard. You use the pivot editor to map fields of data that you have defined in a data model to a specific data visualization without having to deal with the Splunk Enterprise Search Processing Language.

The Splunk pivot is a simple *drag and drop* interface that uses your (predefined) data models and data model objects. These data models (designed by the knowledge managers in your organization using the method that we outlined in the previous sections) are used by the pivot tool to define and subdivide, and to set attributes for the event data that you are interested in.

You can create a Splunk pivot table by following these steps:

1. Go to the Splunk **Home** page and click **Pivot** for the app workspace that you want to use (I chose **Search & Reporting**):

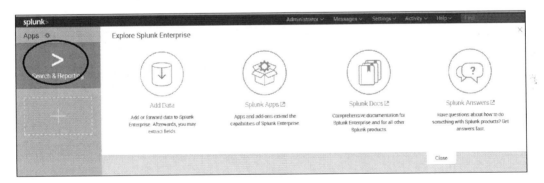

2. Then click on **Pivot**:

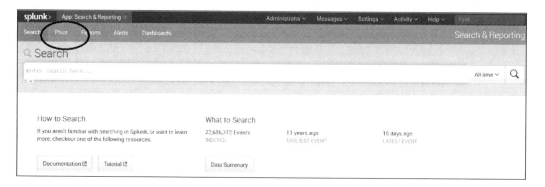

3. Next, from the **Select a Data Model** page, you can indicate a specific data model (identifying which dataset to work with):

4. Once you select a data model, you can select from the list of objects (which can be an event, transaction, search, or child type of object, and represent a specific view or slice of a Splunk search result) within that data model (or click **Edit Objects** to edit or add to the objects within the data model) to work with:

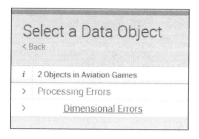

5. After you select a specific object, Splunk will take you to the pivot editor where you can create your pivot:

The pivot editor

Splunk will start the pivot editor in what is referred to as the *pivot table mode*.

In the pivot table mode, the editor displays only one row that represents the object's total result count over all time, based upon the type of object you've selected:

- **Event type**: the total number of events (selected by the object)
- **Transaction type**: the total number of transactions (identified by the object)
- **Search type**: the total number of table rows (returned by the base search in the object)

Pivot tables are defined by you, using Splunk pivot elements, which are of four basic pivot element categories: *filters*, *split rows*, *split columns*, and *column values*.

Only two pivot elements will be defined when you start, a filter element (always set to **All time**) and a column values element (always set to the **Count_of**, which is based upon the object type of your selected object).

Using the editor, you can add, define, and remove multiple pivot elements from each pivot element category to define your pivot table:

- **Filters**: To reduce the result count for the object
- **Split rows**: To split out the pivot results by rows
- **Split columns**: To break up field values by columns
- **Column values**: To show aggregate results like counts, sums, and averages

Working with pivot elements

Within the pivot editor, all pivot element categories can be managed in the same way:

- Click the **+** icon to open up the element dialog, where you choose an attribute, and then define how the element uses that attribute
- Click the pencil icon on the element to open the element dialog and edit how a pivot element is defined
- Drag and drop elements within its pivot element category to reorder them
- Drag and drop the elements between pivot element categories to transfer the element to the desired pivot category (there are some restrictions on what can and cannot be transferred by drag and drop)
- Click the pencil icon on the element to open the element dialog and click **Remove** to remove the element (or you can click on the element and shake it up and down until it turns red, then drop it—my favorite method)

The management of the pivot elements is done using the pivot element dialog. The element dialog is broken up into two steps: choose (or change) the element, and configure the element (configuration). Let's look at each category:

Filtering your pivots

Splunk Pivots can be filtered using filter elements.

Splunk supports three kinds of filter elements for use with pivots. It's important to understand each and they are explained as follows:

- **Time**: (always present) and cannot be removed. Time defines the time range for which your pivot will return results
- **Match**: enables the ability to set up matching for strings, numbers, timestamps, Booleans, and IPv4 addresses (although currently only as *AND* not *OR* matches)

- **Limit**: enables you to restrict the number of results returned by your pivot

 Configuration options for the match and the limit filter element depend on the type of attribute that you've chosen for the element.

Split (row or column)

The Splunk configuration options that are available for split (row and column) depend upon the type of attribute you choose for them.

 Some split configuration options are specific to either row or column elements while others are available to either element type.

Those configuration options, regardless of attribute type, are:

- Both split row and split column:
  - **Max rows and max columns**: This is the maximum number of rows or columns that can appear in the results table
  - **Totals**: Indicates whether to include a row or column that represents the total of all the others in an attribute called *ALL*

- Only split row elements:
  - **Label**: is used to override the attribute name with a different text or character string
  - **Sort**: Used to reorder the split rows

- Only split column:
  - **Group Others**: Indicates whether to group any results excluded by the *max columns limit* into a separate *OTHER* column

Configuration options dependent upon attribute type are:

- String attributes:
  - There are no configuration options specific to string attributes that are common to both split row and split column elements

- Numeric attributes:
  - **Create ranges**: Indicates whether you want your numeric values represented as ranges (*Yes*) or listed separately (*No*)

- Boolean attributes:
  - You can provide alternate labels for true and false values
- Timestamp attributes:
  - **Period**: Use this to bucket your timestamp results by *Year, Month, Day, Hour, Minute,* or *Second*

Column values

You will find a column value element providing the total results returned by a selected object over all time. You have the option to keep this element, change its label, or remove it. In addition, you can add new column value elements such as:

- List distinct values
- First/last value
- Count/distinct count
- Sum
- Average
- Max/min
- Standard deviation
- List distinct values
- Duration
- Earliest/latest

Pivot table formatting

You can format the results of your pivot in many ways. You can set the number of results displayed per page (10, 20, or 50) by using the pagination dropdown.

If you use **Format dropdown,** you can even control table wrapping, the display of row numbers, and determine drilldown and data overlay behavior. Pivot table drilldown is set to *cell mode* by default and works similar to the Splunk table drilldown.

A quick example

Once you have selected a data model (in our case **Aviation Games**), from the **Select an object** page, we can choose **Processing Errors**, which will land us on the **New Pivot** (Pivot Editor):

To build a simple pivot, we can take the following quick steps:

1. Add/verify the filters.

   Remember, **All time** is the default; this will include all results found over all time. You can click on the pencil and amend this filter to be based upon any of Splunk's **Presets** or a specific **Date Range**:

   For this example, we'll just leave the default selection.

2. Configure the **Split Rows**

   Directly under **Filters** is **Split Rows**. For **Split Rows**, I've selected **date_month**:

   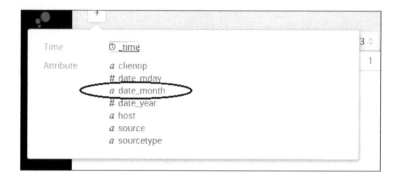

3. After making the selection, you are able to provide additional settings for the selected row:

   I've provided a new name (**Label**) for the row (my_Month) and left the defaults for **Sort**, **Max Rows** (to display), and **Totals**.

4. Configure the **Split Columns**

Moving to the upper-right side of the **Pivot** page, we have **Split Columns**. For **Split Columns**, I've selected **date_mday**:

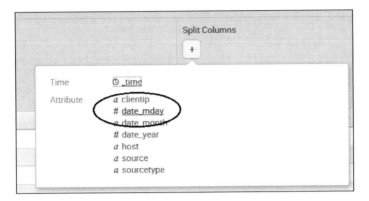

Once you select **date_mday**, you are given the opportunity to set some additional values:

We'll leave the defaults again and click on the button labeled **Add To Table**.

5. Configure the **Column Values**

   Finally, for the **Column Values**, (by clicking on the pencil) you can see that
   Splunk defaulted to providing a **count** (of Processing Errors) found in the
   indexed data (shown in the following screenshot). You can click the button
   labelled **Update**:

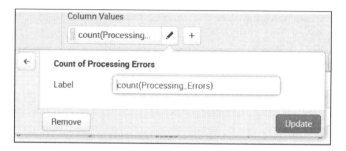

6. View the results of our sample Pivot in the following screenshot:

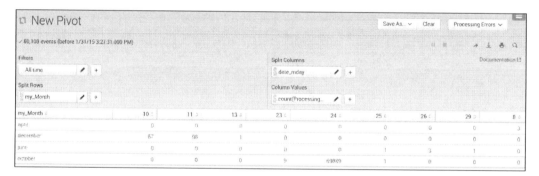

From here, you have the option to **Clear the Pivot** (and start over), or click
on **Save As** and save the pivot as a Splunk report or as a dashboard panel for
later use.

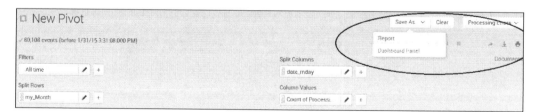

Sparklines

Growing in popularity as a data visualization option, Sparklines are inline charts that represent the general shape of a variation (typically over time) in some measurement (such as miles per gallon or home value), in a simple and highly condensed way. Splunk provides the ability for you to add Sparklines to stats and chart searches, improving their usefulness and overall information density.

A simple Splunk search example like

```
sourcetype=csv "0001" "USD" | chart AVG(Jan) by PERIOD
```

creates the following results table:

As you can see, the preceding example of a search, generates a table that shows average amounts by the field **PERIOD**—just two columns.

If you add the keyword *sparkline* to the search pipeline, you can have Splunk include Sparklines with the results.

 You always use the Sparklines feature in conjunction with chart and stats because it is a function (of those two search commands) and not a command by itself.

```
sourcetype=csv "0001" "USD" | chart sparkline AVG(Jan) by PERIOD
```

If we run the preceding Splunk search, it generates a table similar to the preceding one, except that now, for each row, you have a sparkline chart:

Here is an additional example—using Sparklines—to view the variations of an amount (the rounded value of **Jan**) by **COMPANY**:

```
sourcetype=csv "0001" "USD" | eval RJan= round(Jan) | chart
sparkline Sum(RJan) by COMPANY
```

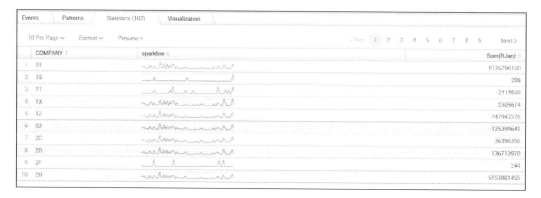

Now you can more easily see patterns in the data that may have been unseen before.

 The Splunk sparkline displays information in relation to the events represented in that sparkline but not in relation to other Sparklines.

Summary

In this chapter, we introduced and provided a definition for Splunk's Data Models, Pivots (along with pivot elements and filters) as well as Sparklines. By going through the given, simple examples, the reader has hopefully grasped the power of these features.

In the next chapter, we will cover simple XML dashboards including their purpose, using wizards to build, schedule the generation of, and edit (XML) directly, and the building of forms.

5
Simple XML Dashboards

Dashboards are a way for you to capture, group, and automate tables and charts into useful and informative views.

In this chapter, we will quickly cover the wizards provided in Splunk 6.2 and then dig into the underlying XML. With XML, you can easily build interactive forms, further customize panels, and use the same query for multiple panels, among other things (XML—an industry standard meta language—is a powerful tool. It is suggested that the reader have some knowledge of its fundamentals. A variety of sources are currently available outside of this book). We will also cover how and when to schedule the generation of dashboards to reduce both the wait time for users and the load on the server. This chapter is laid out under the following topics:

- The purpose of dashboards
- Using wizards to build dashboards
- Scheduling the generation of dashboards
- Editing the XML directly
- UI Examples app
- Building forms

The purpose of dashboards

Any search, table, or chart that you create can be saved and made to appear in the menus for other users to see. With that power, why would you bother creating a dashboard?

Here are a few reasons:

- A dashboard can contain multiple panels, each running a different query.
- Every dashboard has a unique URL, which is easy to share.
- Dashboards are more customizable than an individual query.
- The search bar is removed, making it less intimidating to many users.
- Forms allow you to present the user with a custom search interface that only requires specific values.
- Dashboards look great. Many organizations place dashboards on projectors and monitors for at-a-glance information about their environment.
- Dashboards can be scheduled for PDF delivery by e-mail. This feature is not the most robust, but with some consideration, it can be used effectively. With all of this said, if a saved search is working the way it is, there is no strong reason to turn it into a dashboard.

Using wizards to build dashboards

Since the goal of this chapter is understanding Splunk dashboards (and not the fundamentals of searching), we'll utilize several new simple search strings as well as some of the queries from previous chapters to illustrate certain points. So, let's start by making an operational dashboard for showing **Forecast Events** within our indexed data. The following is a simple search string to begin our exercise:

```
sourcetype="*" Forecast | timechart count as "Forecast Events" by
date_month
```

In addition to our search string, I've selected **Previous Year** from the Splunk presets (see the preceding image).

This will produce a graph like this one:

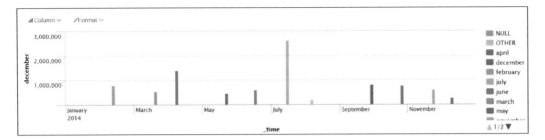

To add this to a dashboard, we can perform the following steps:

1. Click on **Save As** and then choose **Dashboard Panel**.

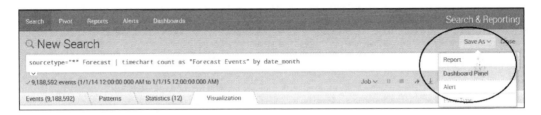

2. This opens a dialog that guides you through saving the query as a dashboard:

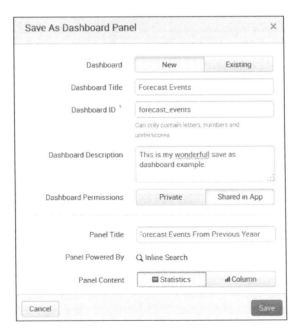

3. Enter the following details and click on the **Save** button:

  ○ **Dashboard—New/Existing**: This allows you to indicate if your search is to be saved as part of an existing dashboard or as a new one. In our example, I've selected **New**.

  ○ **Dashboard Title**: Simply provide a title for your dashboard to display.

  ○ **Dashboard ID**: This is the Splunk dashboard ID, which defaults to whatever you have entered for your title, with special characters (like spaces) replaced.

  ○ **Dashboard Description**: This is where you can provide a short note as to what your dashboard does.

  ○ **Dashboard Permissions**: Select whether your dashboard will be private (not accessible to other users) or shared within an App.

  ○ **Panel Title**: This is a sort of sub title which means that it will be the title/caption displayed for the dashboard panel (where your search runs).

  ○ **Panel Powered By**: This is set by Splunk. Our example is powered by an inline search string.

  ○ **Panel Content**: This is where you indicate a format for the search results.

4. You should now receive the following:

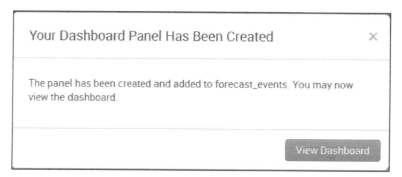

Your new dashboard is ready to use. It is that simple.

As you create more dashboards, you will end up creating a lot of searches. A naming convention will help you keep track of which search belongs to which dashboard. Here is one possible approach:

```
Dashboard - [dashboard name] - [search name and panel type].
```

When the number of dashboards and searches becomes large, apps can be used to group dashboards and searches together, providing yet another way to organize and share assets.

After saving our dashboard, it will now be available under the **Dashboards** menu (see the following screenshot):

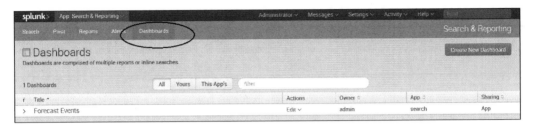

On the **Dashboards** page, if you click on our dashboard name (**Forecast Events**), Splunk displays our single panel dashboard:

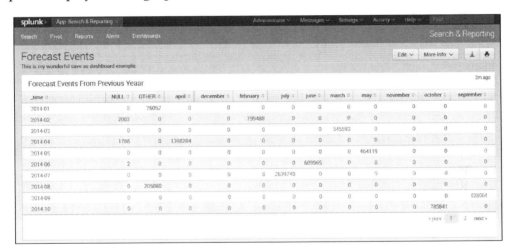

Adding another panel

Perhaps we would like to add a second panel to our dashboard. To do that, we can open the dashboard and click on **Edit**:

There are many options under **Edit**, but let's select **Edit Panels**:

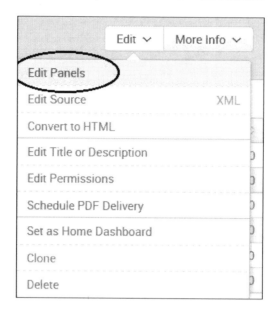

Splunk now gives us the following selections (where we will—for now—select **Add Panel**):

The following options are displayed:

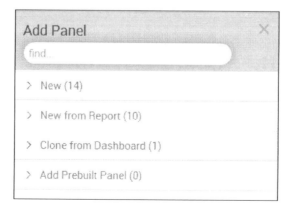

Here we have the ability to add a new panel to our dashboard from a variety of sources:

- **New**: creates one from scratch
- **New from Report**: creates a panel from an existing report
- **Clone from Dashboard**: creates a panel from an existing dashboard
- **Add Prebuilt Panel**: like what it says, adds a "prebuilt panel" to our dashboard

So for our example, let's select **New**:

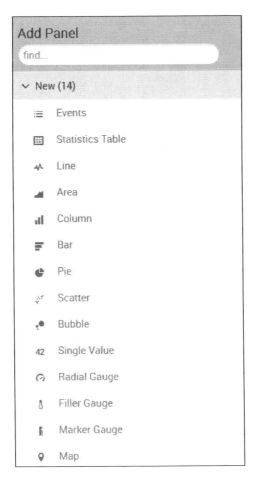

Again, various options are displayed. For illustrative purposes, let's select **Pie** and fill in the **New Pie** options (shown in the following screenshot). I simply plugged in the original time preset (**Previous year**), added a **Content Title,** and provided the same search string. The idea here is to present the same information as our initial dashboard panel but in a different format:

Next, click on the button labeled **Add to Dashboard**:

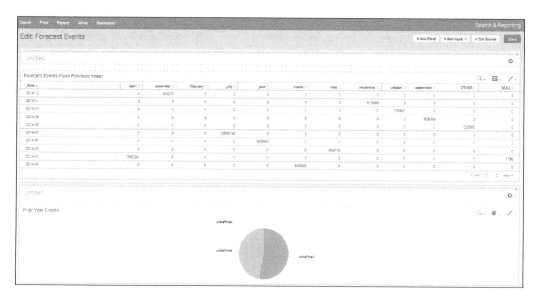

The preceding screenshot is what our new, two-panel dashboard looks like. To be sure, the pie chart isn't very interesting, so let's make a change. You'll notice three icons in the upper-right corner of the lower panel. If you click on the middle one (which looks like a tiny pie chart), you'll see that you have the option of changing the visualization type, and that Splunk has looked at your data and made some recommendations:

You can try out the different choices — I selected **Area**:

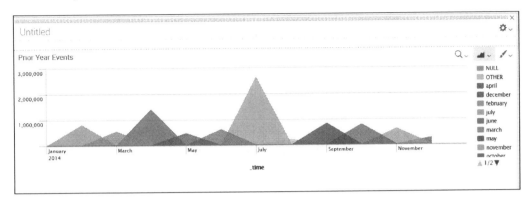

A cool trick

By default, each new panel is added to the bottom of the dashboard, as you can see in the preceding screenshot. You can rearrange your dashboard panels if you like as dashboards allow you to have up to three panels distributed horizontally, which is a great way to show visualizations. If you click on the upper border of your panel, you can drag panels around the page, like so:

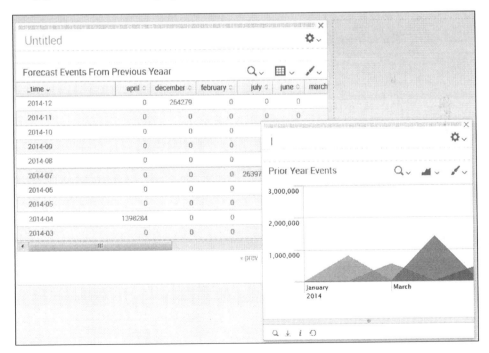

Let's get back to those three icons on our dashboard panels:

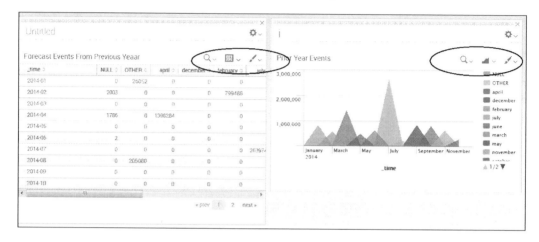

Let's click on the first (leftmost) icon that looks like a magnifying glass:

In our dashboard example, our panels use **INLINE SEARCH** as the base query. An inline search string lets us build a query directly within our dashboard. This is often convenient as many searches will have no purpose but for a particular dashboard, so there is no reason for these searches to appear in the Splunk menus. This also reduces external dependencies, making it easier to move the dashboard to another app.

The options here include: **Edit Title, Edit Search String, Convert to Report,** and **Delete**.

Using these options, you can modify your dashboard panel as you like or remove (delete) it from the dashboard and start again.

Converting the panel to a report

You may want to convert your dashboard panel (that is powered by an inline search) to a Splunk report, so that it can have some of the advantages that report-based panels have over inline-search-powered panels, such as faster loading times due to report acceleration.

In the following screenshot, I have clicked on **Convert to Report** and added a **Report Title** and **Description** on the **Convert to Report** dialog:

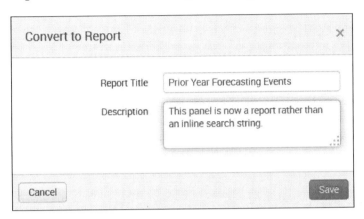

Now our dashboard panel is based upon a Splunk report:

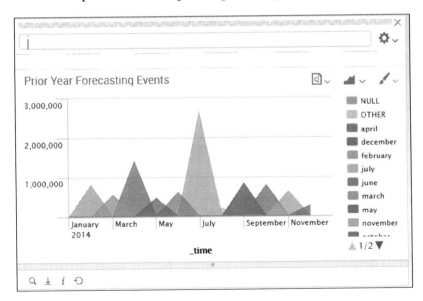

Notice how our magnifying icon has changed? It is not the **Search Report** icon. Let's click on it:

If we select **Prior Year Forecasting Events** (which is what we named the report), we get a confirmation:

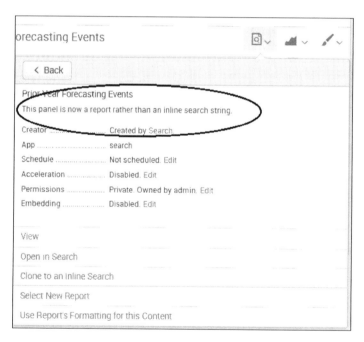

Of course, as you can see, Splunk allows us more options for our dashboard panel, such as: **View**, **Open in Search**, **Clone** (back) **to an Inline Search**, **Select a New Report,** and **Use Report's Formatting for this Content**. Perhaps a favorite is **View** which opens the panel as a full-featured Splunk report:

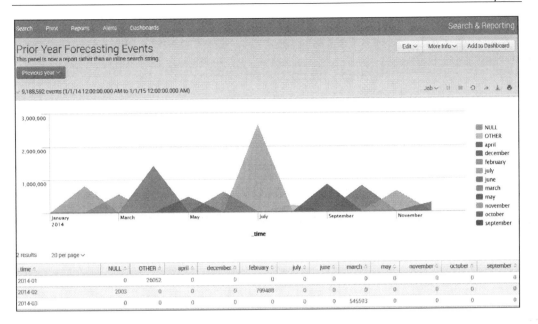

Moving on, we've already touched on the middle icon (when we switched the formatting of our panel from pie to area), so we'll briefly mention here that in addition to reformatting your panel, you have the ability to click on **Events**, which will list the raw events in your panel similar to what you would see if you ran your original search string:

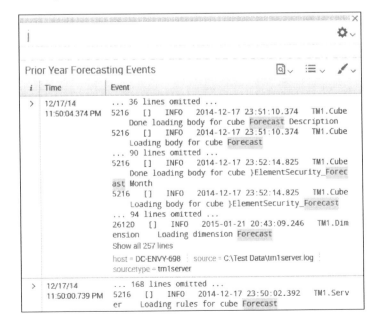

Moving onto the third or the rightmost icon, the one that resembles a paint brush, we see additional options for our panel (formatting options that will be based upon the selected panel's format). For example, our left dashboard panel is formatted as a statistical table, so the following options are selectable:

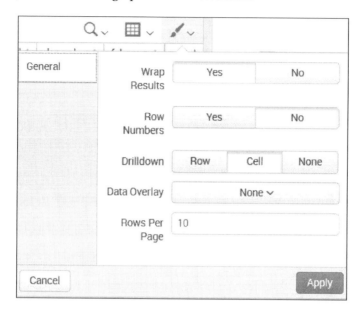

You can experiment with the various selections and click **Apply** to view their particular effect on your panel, until you arrive at what you are happy with.

More options

Also on your panel, in the upper-right corner, you will find an icon resembling a gear (see the next screenshot). Clicking on this icon allows you to rename your panel, convert it to a prebuilt panel, or remove (delete) it from the dashboard.

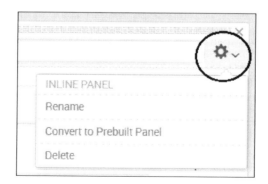

Rename and **Delete** are obvious, so what does **Convert to Prebuilt Panel** mean? Well, up to now our panel has been an inline panel—one that you can edit with the Splunk dashboard editor and Panel Editor (you can also edit the child elements of a panel element by editing the simple XML source code — more on this later in this chapter). A prebuilt panel is a panel that is a simple XML code which can be shared among various dashboards. You cannot edit the title, search, or visualizations of a prebuilt panel from the dashboard reference.

Back to the dashboard

Our dashboard menu includes three selections (in the upper-right corner, as shown in the following screenshot). We have already explored the first (**Add Panel**) in this chapter. Let's now move on to **Add Input**:

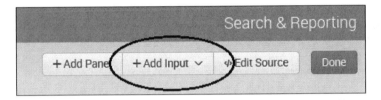

Add input

Adding an input to your dashboard will convert it to a form. All dashboards are actually made up of XML code (we touched a bit on this earlier when we introduced prebuilt panels). In the next section (**Edit Source**), we will dive deep into this topic but for now, understand that the dashboard that we have created is made up of or defined by the XML which Splunk is using, and adding any type of input will modify the underlying XML (in fact, after adding any input, the xml tag **<dashboard>** is changed to **<form>**).

Once you click **Add Input,** you can select an input from the list shown in the following screenshot:

For example, you can select **Text** to add a text field for user input. You can have more than one input on your dashboard, and you can drag inputs to rearrange them on your form (dashboard). You can even drag an input onto a panel within your dashboard and make that input apply only to the panel. Once you are happy with your inputs, you can click **Done** to indicate that you have finished editing. We will go into this in more detail later in this chapter under the section on building forms.

Edit source

Finally, let's go on to our third icon, **Edit Source**. As I have already mentioned, all Splunk dashboards are defined by XML. If you don't have experience with XML, you can create, edit, and maintain dashboards using the dashboard editor (similar to what we've been doing with our examples). However, by using XML, Splunk gives us the ability to create dashboards as complex and robust as we need them to be.

Editing XML directly

Before proceeding, let me take a moment to tip my hat to Splunk for its dashboard editor. There are only a couple of reasons why you would still need to edit simplified XML dashboards: forms and post-processing data. I predict that these reasons will go away in the future as more features are added to the dashboard editor.

The documentation for simplified XML panels can be found by searching `http://www.splunk.com/` for panel reference for simple XML. The following link is a good place to start:

```
http://docs.splunk.com/Documentation/Splunk/latest/Viz/
PanelreferenceforSimplifiedXML
```

UI examples app

Before digging into the XML behind dashboards, it may be a good idea to install the Splunk UI examples app for 4.1+, available at Splunkbase (see *Chapter 8, Working with Apps,* for information about Splunkbase). The examples provided in this app give a good overview of the features available in both simplified XML and advanced XML dashboards.

The simplest way to find this app is from the default Splunk home screen by clicking on Splunk Apps.

Building forms

Forms allow you to make a template that needs one or more pieces of information supplied to run. You can build these directly using raw XML, but I find it simpler to build a simple dashboard and then modify the XML accordingly. The other option is to copy an existing dashboard and modify it to meet your needs. We will touch on a simple use case in the following section.

Creating a form from a dashboard

First, let's think of a use case that we might be able to use with our previous example. How about a form that tells us about the forecast events for a particular year? Let's start with our previous search example:

```
sourcetype="*" Forecast | timechart count as "Forecast Events" by
date_month
```

Since we have already created a dashboard from this query (in the section *Using wizards to build dashboards*), let's look at the XML for our dashboard. As we did earlier, click on **Edit Source** (on the dashboard editor). The XML for our dashboard looks like the following code. Notice the occurrence of two `<panel>` tags within our XML indicating that there are two panels in our dashboard:

```
<dashboard>
 <label>Forecast Events</label>
 <description>This is my wonderful save as dashboard example.</
description>
 <row>
  <panel>
   <table>
    <title>Forecast Events From Previous Year</title>
    <search>
     <query>sourcetype="*" Forecast | timechart count as "Forecast
Events" by date_month</query>
     <earliest>-1y@y</earliest>
     <latest>@y</latest>
    </search>
   </table>
  </panel>
  <panel>
   <chart>
    <title>Prior Year Forecasting Events</title>
    <search ref="Prior Year Forecasting Events"></search>
    <option name="list.drilldown">full</option>
    <option name="list.wrap">1</option>
    <option name="maxLines">5</option>
    <option name="raw.drilldown">full</option>
    <option name="rowNumbers">0</option>
    <option name="table.drilldown">all</option>
    <option name="table.wrap">1</option>
    <option name="type">list</option>
    <fields>["host","source","sourcetype"]</fields>
    <option name="charting.axisLabelsX.majorLabelStyle.
overflowMode">ellipsisNone</option>
    <option name="charting.axisLabelsX.majorLabelStyle.rotation">0</
option>
    <option name="charting.axisTitleX.visibility">visible</option>
    <option name="charting.axisTitleY.visibility">visible</option>
    <option name="charting.axisTitleY2.visibility">visible</option>
    <option name="charting.axisX.scale">linear</option>
    <option name="charting.axisY.scale">linear</option>
    <option name="charting.axisY2.enabled">false</option>
    <option name="charting.axisY2.scale">inherit</option>
    <option name="charting.chart">line</option>
    <option name="charting.chart.bubbleMaximumSize">50</option>
    <option name="charting.chart.bubbleMinimumSize">10</option>
    <option name="charting.chart.bubbleSizeBy">area</option>
```

```
      <option name="charting.chart.nullValueMode">gaps</option>
      <option name="charting.chart.sliceCollapsingThreshold">0.01</
  option>
      <option name="charting.chart.stackMode">default</option>
      <option name="charting.chart.style">shiny</option>
      <option name="charting.drilldown">all</option>
      <option name="charting.layout.splitSeries">0</option>
      <option name="charting.legend.labelStyle.
  overflowMode">ellipsisMiddle</option>
      <option name="charting.legend.placement">right</option>
     </chart>
    </panel>
   </row>
  </dashboard>
```

That's pretty simple. To convert our dashboard into a form, we have to do the following things:

First, change `<dashboard>` to `<form>` within our XML. Don't forget the closing tag `</dashboard>` to `</form>`. Next, create a `<fieldset>` tag with any form elements.

Something like this:

```
<form>
<label>Chapter 5 Build a Form 1</label>
<fieldset>
<input type="text" token="myyear">
<label>MyYear</label>
</input>
</fieldset>
```

Now we add the appropriate variable in `<query>` to reflect the form values.

```
<query>sourcetype="*" Forecast date_year=$myyear$ | timechart
count as "Forecast Events" by date_month</query>
```

When we're through, our XML looks like this:

```
<form>
 <label>Forecast Events</label>
 <description>This is my wonderful save as dashboard example.</
description>
 <label>Chapter 5 Build a Form 1</label>
<fieldset>
<input type="text" token="myyear">
<label>MyYear</label>
</input>
```

```
    </fieldset>
    <row>
     <panel>
      <table>
       <title>Forecast Events From Previous Yeaar</title>
       <search>
        <query>sourcetype="*" Forecast date_year=$myyear$ | timechart
count as "Forecast Events" by date_month</query>
        <earliest>-1y@y</earliest>
        <latest>@y</latest>
       </search>
      </table>
     </panel>
     <panel>
      <chart>
       <title>Prior Year Forecasting Events</title>
       <search ref="Prior Year Forecasting Events"></search>
       <option name="list.drilldown">full</option>
       <option name="list.wrap">1</option>
       <option name="maxLines">5</option>
       <option name="raw.drilldown">full</option>
       <option name="rowNumbers">0</option>
       <option name="table.drilldown">all</option>
       <option name="table.wrap">1</option>
       <option name="type">list</option>
       <fields>["host","source","sourcetype"]</fields>
       <option name="charting.axisLabelsX.majorLabelStyle.
overflowMode">ellipsisNone</option>
       <option name="charting.axisLabelsX.majorLabelStyle.rotation">0</
option>
       <option name="charting.axisTitleX.visibility">visible</option>
       <option name="charting.axisTitleY.visibility">visible</option>
       <option name="charting.axisTitleY2.visibility">visible</option>
       <option name="charting.axisX.scale">linear</option>
       <option name="charting.axisY.scale">linear</option>
       <option name="charting.axisY2.enabled">false</option>
       <option name="charting.axisY2.scale">inherit</option>
       <option name="charting.chart">line</option>
       <option name="charting.chart.bubbleMaximumSize">50</option>
       <option name="charting.chart.bubbleMinimumSize">10</option>
       <option name="charting.chart.bubbleSizeBy">area</option>
       <option name="charting.chart.nullValueMode">gaps</option>
       <option name="charting.chart.sliceCollapsingThreshold">0.01</
option>
```

```
      <option name="charting.chart.stackMode">default</option>
      <option name="charting.chart.style">shiny</option>
      <option name="charting.drilldown">all</option>
      <option name="charting.layout.splitSeries">0</option>
      <option name="charting.legend.labelStyle.
  overflowMode">ellipsisMiddle</option>
      <option name="charting.legend.placement">right</option>
    </chart>
   </panel>
  </row>
 </form>
```

Let's click on **Save** and then search for **Forecast Events** that occurred in a particular year. Now looking at our example dashboard, we notice our input field **MyYear** and a **Submit** button at the top of the panel along with a **Search is waiting for input** message:

We now have a useful form for displaying the forecast events for a particular year.

Driving multiple panels from one form

A single form can also be used to drive multiple panels at once. Earlier, we had our dashboard with two panels—one of which we converted into a report. Let's revisit the dashboard in that state for a moment. If we wanted to (and this would properly make the most sense), we could again edit the (XML) source for the dashboard and this time convert all the searches, as we did in the previous example, to use our form field.

```
<form>
 <label>Forecast Events</label>
 <description>This is my wonderful save as dashboard example.</
description>
 <label>Chapter 5 Build a Form 1</label>
 <fieldset>
  <input type="text" token="myyear">
   <label>MyYear</label>
  </input>
 </fieldset>
 <row>
  <panel>
   <table>
    <title>Forecast Events From Previous Yeaar</title>
    <search>
     <query>sourcetype="*" Forecast date_year=$myyear$ | timechart
count as "Forecast Events" by date_month</query>
     <earliest>-1y@y</earliest>
     <latest>@y</latest>
    </search>
   </table>
  </panel>
 </row>
 <row>
  <panel>
   <chart>
    <title>Forecast Events From Previous Yeaar</title>
    <search>
     <query>sourcetype="*" Forecast date_year=$myyear$ | timechart
count as "Forecast Events" by date_month</query>
```

```
      <earliest>-1y@y</earliest>
      <latest>@y</latest>
    </search>
    <option name="wrap">true</option>
    <option name="rowNumbers">true</option>
    <option name="dataOverlayMode">none</option>
    <option name="count">10</option>
    <option name="charting.axisLabelsX.majorLabelStyle.
overflowMode">ellipsisNone</option>
    <option name="charting.axisLabelsX.majorLabelStyle.rotation">0</
option>
    <option name="charting.axisTitleX.visibility">visible</option>
    <option name="charting.axisTitleY.visibility">visible</option>
    <option name="charting.axisTitleY2.visibility">visible</option>
    <option name="charting.axisX.scale">linear</option>
    <option name="charting.axisY.scale">linear</option>
    <option name="charting.axisY2.enabled">false</option>
    <option name="charting.axisY2.scale">inherit</option>
    <option name="charting.chart">area</option>
    <option name="charting.chart.bubbleMaximumSize">50</option>
    <option name="charting.chart.bubbleMinimumSize">10</option>
    <option name="charting.chart.bubbleSizeBy">area</option>
    <option name="charting.chart.nullValueMode">gaps</option>
    <option name="charting.chart.sliceCollapsingThreshold">0.01</
option>
    <option name="charting.chart.stackMode">default</option>
    <option name="charting.chart.style">shiny</option>
    <option name="charting.drilldown">all</option>
    <option name="charting.layout.splitSeries">0</option>
    <option name="charting.legend.labelStyle.
overflowMode">ellipsisMiddle</option>
    <option name="charting.legend.placement">right</option>
  </chart>
  </panel>
 </row>
</form>
```

After clicking on **Save**, we should be back at the dashboard, which is now a form with our field, which drives both the dashboard panels.

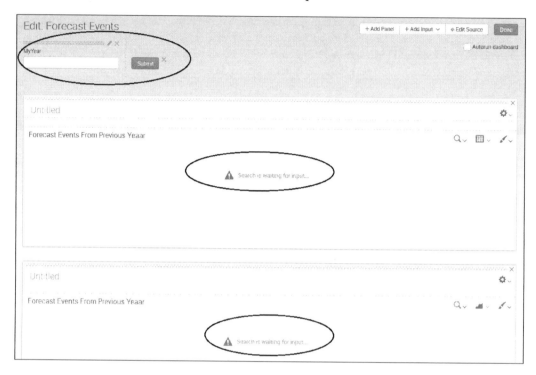

There are several other form elements available, with many options to customize their behavior. To find the official documentation, search `http://www.splunk.com/` for build and edit forms with simple XML. There are also many useful examples in the documentation and in the UI Examples app (see the *UI examples app* section, earlier in this chapter).

Post-processing search results

You may have noticed that, in our previous example, both of our queries started with the same actual query:

```
sourcetype="*" Forecast date_year=$myyear$ | timechart count as
"Forecast Events" by date_month
```

It is, of course, wasteful to run the same query four times. In prior versions of Splunk, using `<searchPostProcess>`, we could run the query once and then run commands on the results for each panel. The first step would be to move the initial query out of the panel to the top level of the XML.

The results from `<searchTemplate>` would be used by a panel if it has no query of its own, or it will be used as the source for `<searchPostProcess>`. One additional piece of information was needed — the fields that are needed by the panels. We could get this by using table, like so:

```
<?xml version='1.0' encoding='utf-8'?>
<form>
<searchTemplate>
sourcetype="*" Forecast date_year=$myyear$ | timechart count as
"Forecast Events" by date_month
</searchTemplate>
```

This technique would work exactly like our previous example but would only run the query once, drawing more quickly, and saving resources for everyone. However, more work is required, as we see in the next section.

Post-processing limitations

When using `<searchPostProcess>`, there is one big limitation and several smaller limitations that often mandate a little extra work:

- Only the first 10,000 results are passed from a raw query. To deal with this, it is necessary to run events through `stats`, `timechart`, or `table`. Transforming commands such as `stats` will reduce the number of rows produced by the initial query, increasing the performance.

- Only fields referenced specifically are passed from the original events. This can be dealt with by using table (as we did in the previous example), or by aggregating results into fewer rows with stats.

- `<searchPostProcess>` elements cannot use form values. If you need the values of form elements, you need to hand them along from the initial query.

- Panels cannot use form values in a `<searchString>` element if they are referenced in the top level `<searchTemplate>` element. This can be accomplished in advanced XML, which we will cover in *Chapter 9, Building Advanced Dashboards*.

The first limitation is the most common item to affect users. The usual solution is to pre-aggregate the events into a superset of what is needed by the panels. To accomplish this, our first task would be to look at the queries and figure out which fields need to be handed along for all queries to work and so on.

Features replaced

Moving along, in Splunk version 6.2, the simple XML `<searchString>`, `<searchTemplate>`, `<searchName>`, and `<searchPostProcess>` elements are replaced by the new `<search>` element.

The following is a (two panel) dashboard using the `<search>` tag and the `stats` command in version 6.2 to deal with post-processing limitations. First, the query (the search) is defined at the dashboard level (not within any panel). This is our base search (notice the search ID):

```
<dashboard>
 <label>Dashboard with post-process search</label>
 <!-- Base search cannot pass more than 10,000 events to post-process
searches-->
 <!—This dashboard uses the stats transforming command -->
 <!-- This limits events passed to post-process search -->
 <search id="baseSearch">
  <query>sourcetype=tm1* dimension | stats count by date_month, date_
wday</query>
 </search>
 <row>
```

Now, within our dashboard panels, the search base is defined along with our additional search strings:

```
   <panel>
    <chart>
     <title>Dimension Events count by Month</title>
     <search base="baseSearch">
      <query>stats sum(count) AS count by date_month</query>
     </search>
     <!-- post-process search -->
     <option name="charting.axisLabelsX.majorLabelStyle.
overflowMode">ellipsisNone</option>
     <option name="charting.axisLabelsX.majorLabelStyle.rotation">0</
option>
     <option name="charting.axisTitleX.visibility">visible</option>
     <option name="charting.axisTitleY.visibility">visible</option>
     <option name="charting.axisTitleY2.visibility">visible</option>
     <option name="charting.axisX.scale">linear</option>
     <option name="charting.axisY.scale">linear</option>
     <option name="charting.axisY2.enabled">false</option>
     <option name="charting.axisY2.scale">inherit</option>
     <option name="charting.chart">column</option>
```

```
    <option name="charting.chart.bubbleMaximumSize">50</option>
    <option name="charting.chart.bubbleMinimumSize">10</option>
    <option name="charting.chart.bubbleSizeBy">area</option>
    <option name="charting.chart.nullValueMode">gaps</option>
    <option name="charting.chart.sliceCollapsingThreshold">0.01</
option>
    <option name="charting.chart.stackMode">default</option>
    <option name="charting.chart.style">shiny</option>
    <option name="charting.drilldown">all</option>
    <option name="charting.layout.splitSeries">0</option>
    <option name="charting.legend.labelStyle.
overflowMode">ellipsisMiddle</option>
    <option name="charting.legend.placement">right</option>
  </chart>
 </panel>
 <panel>
  <chart>
   <title>Dimension Events count by Day</title>
   <search base="baseSearch">
    <query>stats sum(count) AS count by Weekday</query>
   </search>
   <!-- post-process search -->
   <option name="charting.chart">pie</option>
   <option name="charting.axisLabelsX.majorLabelStyle.
overflowMode">ellipsisNone</option>
   <option name="charting.axisLabelsX.majorLabelStyle.rotation">0</
option>
   <option name="charting.axisTitleX.visibility">visible</option>
   <option name="charting.axisTitleY.visibility">visible</option>
   <option name="charting.axisTitleY2.visibility">visible</option>
   <option name="charting.axisX.scale">linear</option>
   <option name="charting.axisY.scale">linear</option>
   <option name="charting.axisY2.enabled">false</option>
   <option name="charting.axisY2.scale">inherit</option>
   <option name="charting.chart.bubbleMaximumSize">50</option>
   <option name="charting.chart.bubbleMinimumSize">10</option>
   <option name="charting.chart.bubbleSizeBy">area</option>
   <option name="charting.chart.nullValueMode">gaps</option>
   <option name="charting.chart.sliceCollapsingThreshold">0.01</
option>
   <option name="charting.chart.stackMode">default</option>
   <option name="charting.chart.style">shiny</option>
   <option name="charting.drilldown">all</option>
   <option name="charting.layout.splitSeries">0</option>
```

```
        <option name="charting.legend.labelStyle.
overflowMode">ellipsisMiddle</option>
        <option name="charting.legend.placement">right</option>
        <option name="wrap">true</option>
        <option name="rowNumbers">false</option>
        <option name="dataOverlayMode">none</option>
        <option name="count">10</option>
        <option name="mapping.data.maxClusters">100</option>
        <option name="mapping.map.center">(0,0)</option>
        <option name="mapping.map.zoom">2</option>
        <option name="mapping.markerLayer.markerMaxSize">50</option>
        <option name="mapping.markerLayer.markerMinSize">10</option>
        <option name="mapping.markerLayer.markerOpacity">0.8</option>
        <option name="mapping.tileLayer.maxZoom">7</option>
        <option name="mapping.tileLayer.minZoom">0</option>
      </chart>
    </panel>
  </row>
</dashboard>
```

The following is the dashboard generated by the preceding XML source:

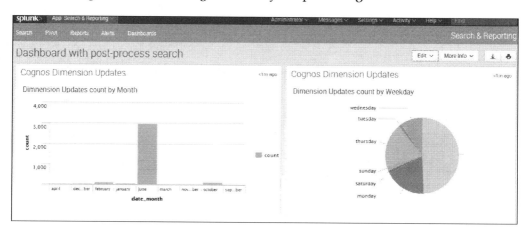

Autorun dashboard

One more important option for your dashboards is the AutoRun setting that is seen in the following screenshot:

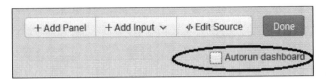

When you add fields to submit values (for the search string in a panel, as we did in our example), the Autorun setting indicates if the search in the panels of your dashboard should be run upon loading the page. The default is *false*. That means that the dashboard will load and wait for the user to enter or select a value and click **Submit**. Suppose you'd rather load your dashboard and show data right away using some default or standard value. To do that, we could modify our XML like this:

```
<fieldset autoRun="true">
  <input type="text" token="myyear"><default>2014</default>
   <label>MyYear</label>
  </input>
 </fieldset>
```

In the preceding code, I've added the Autorun setting to the `<fieldset>` tag and provided the `<default>`. When I save my changes, the dashboard will execute (run) the search using the default value (2014) and my dashboard panels will display the results. Of course, the user still has the ability to change the search value and resubmit the query.

Depending upon a variety of factors, this convenience may or may not be a viable option as it would be foolish to rerun a search every time a dashboard loads if the underlying data is slow to change. In that case, a better option would be to set Autorun to *false* and perhaps use scheduled searches (which we discuss in the next section).

Scheduling the generation of dashboards

As we stepped through the wizard interface to create panels, we accepted the default value of running the search each time the dashboard loads. As we mentioned earlier, this means that the user is penalized each and every time the dashboard is loaded in their web browser. It is silly (and a waste of resources) to rerun perhaps multiple searches that are within a dashboard panel if the data, that the search is based upon, does not change often. For example, if the indexed data is updated every evening, then re-running a search on that data multiple times within the same day will not yield different results and would be a waste of resources.

A more prudent approach would be to convert the dashboard panels to not use inline, real-time searches but reference reports instead (earlier in this chapter, we covered *Convert to Report*) or to use scheduled-queries.

If we use reports or scheduled-queries in our dashboard, when the dashboard is loaded, the results from the last scheduled run will be used.

The dashboard will draw as quickly as the browser can draw the panels. This is particularly useful when multiple users use a dashboard, perhaps in an operations group. If there are no saved results available, the query will simply be run normally.

Be sure to ask yourself just how fresh the data on a dashboard needs to be. If you are looking at a week's worth of data, is up to one hour old data acceptable? What about four hours old? 24 hours old? The less often the search is run, the fewer resources you will use, and the more responsive the system will be for everyone else. As your data volume increases, the searches will take more time to complete. If you notice your installation becoming less responsive, check the performance of your scheduled searches in the **Jobs** or the **Status** dashboards in the **Search** app.

For a dashboard that will be constantly monitored, real-time queries are probably more efficient, particularly if multiple people will be using the dashboard. Real-time queries are first backfilled. For instance, a real-time query watching 24 hours will first run a query against the previous 24 hours and then add new events to the results as they appear. This feature makes real-time queries over fairly long periods practical and useful.

Summary

Once again, we have really only scratched the surface of what is possible, using simplified XML dashboards. I encourage you to dig into the examples in the UI xamples app (see the *UI examples app* section, earlier in this chapter).

When you are ready to make additional customizations or use some of the cool modules available from Splunk and the community, you can use advanced XML features, which we will look at in *Chapter 9, Building Advanced Dashboards*. In *Chapter 6, Advanced Search Examples*, we will dive into advanced search examples, which can be a lot of fun. We'll expose some really powerful features of the search language and go over a few tricks that I've learned over the years.

6

Advanced Search Examples

In this chapter, we will work through a few advanced search examples in great detail. The examples and data shown are fictitious, but will, hopefully, spark some ideas that you can apply to your own data. For a huge collection of examples and help topics, check out Splunk answers at `http://answers.splunk.com`. Our chapter flow will be as follows:

- Using subsearches to find loosely related events
- Using transaction
- Determining concurrency
- Calculating events per slice of time
- Rebuilding top
- Acceleration

Using subsearches to find loosely related events

The number of use cases for subsearches in the real world might be small, but for those situations where they can be applied, subsearches can be a magic bullet. Let's look at an example and then talk about some rules.

Subsearch

Let's start with these events:

```
2015-02-10 12:59:59 msgid=704783 from=tuck@companyx.com to=taylor@
VENDOR1.com
2015-02-10 12:59:59 msgid=171755 from=steve@companyx.com to=lou@
VENDOR1.com
2015-02-10 12:59:59 msgid=668955 from=lou@companyx.com to=steve@
Vendor2.com
2015-02-10 12:59:59 msgid=001404 from=mary@companyx.com to=richard@
Vendor2.com
2015-02-10 12:59:59 msgid=284794 from=ronnie@companyx.com to=toto@
Vendor2.com
2015-02-10 12:59:59 msgid=362127 from=nanette@companyx.com to=sam@
Vendor2.com
2015-02-10 12:59:59 msgid=571419 from=paige@companyx.com
to=ronnie@g&r.com
```

From these events, let's find out who `mary` has sent messages to. In these events, we see that the `from` and `to` values are in different entries. We could use `stats` to pull these events together, and then filter the resulting rows, like this:

```
sourcetype=webmail to OR from
| stats values(from) as from values(to) as to by msgid
| search from=mary@companyx.com
```

The problem is that on a busy mail server, this search might retrieve millions of events, and then throw most of the work away. We want to actually use the index efficiently, and a subsearch can help us do that.

This is how we could tackle this with a subsearch:

```
[search sourcetype=webmail from=mary@companyx.com | fields msgid]
sourcetype=webmail to
```

Let's step through everything that's happening here:

1. The search inside the brackets is run:

    ```
    sourcetype=webmail from=mary@companyx.com
    ```

    Given my sample events, this will locate several events, as seen in the following screenshot:

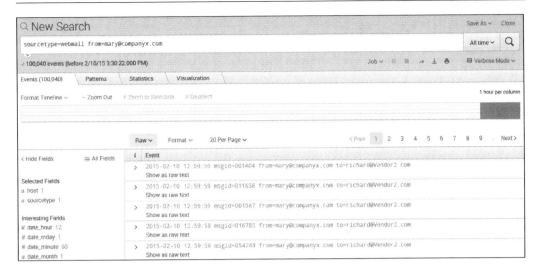

2. The second part of our search string is as follows:| `fields msgid` this instructs the subsearch to only return the field `msgid`.

   Behind the scenes, the subsearch results are essentially added to the outer search as an OR statement, producing this search:

   ```
   ( (msgid=123456) OR (msgid=234567) .).. And so on
   sourcetype=webmail to
   ```

   This will be a much more efficient search, using the index effectively.

3. This new search returns the answer we're looking for (notice the circled `msgid` values. They would be the values that Splunk uses in its internal `msgid=` search):

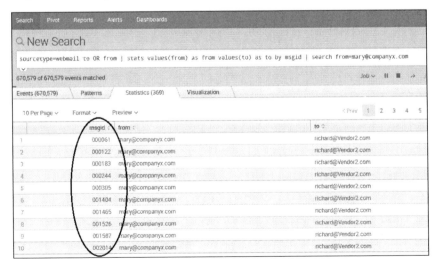

Subsearch caveats

To prevent a subsearch from being too expensive, they are limited by a time and event count:

- The default time limit for the subsearch to complete is 60 seconds. If the subsearch is still running at that point, it is finalized, and only the events located up to that point are added to the outer search.

- Likewise, the default event limit for the subsearch is 1,000. After this point, any further events will be truncated. If either of these limits is reached, there is probably a better way to accomplish the task at hand.

Another consideration is that the fields returned from the subsearch must be searchable. There is a magical field called `search` that will be added to the query as a raw search term, but you have to do a little more work. See search context later in this chapter for an example.

Nested subsearches

Subsearches can also be nested, if needed. With mail server logs, it is sometimes necessary to find all the events related to a particular message. Some fictitious log entries are given, such as:

```
... in=123 msgid=123456 from=mary@companyx.com
... msgid=123456 out=987 subject=Important
... out=987 to=bob@vendor1.co.uk
```

We can see that the first event has the value of `from`, but there is no longer anything in common with the event that contains the `to` field. Luckily, there is an interim event that does contain `out` along with `msgid`, which we have in the first event.

We can write a query like this to find our events:

```
[search sourcetype=WebMailIfoDatas out
[search sourcetype=WebMailIfoDatas from=mary@companyx.com | fields
msgid]
| fields out]
sourcetype=WebMailIfoDatas to
```

The following are the parts of the search, numbered according to the order of execution:

1. `[search sourcetype=WebMailIfoDatas from=mary@companyx.com | fields msgid]`

2. `[search sourcetype=WebMailIfoDatas out | fields out]`

3. `sourcetype=WebMailIfoDatas to`

Let's step through this example:

1. The innermost nested search (1) is run:

    ```
    sourcetype=WebMailIfoDatas from=mary@companyx.com | fields
    msgid
    ```

2. This is attached to the next innermost search (2), like this:

    ```
    sourcetype=WebMailIfoDatas out
    (msgid=123456)
    | fields out
    ```

3. The results of this search are attached to the outermost search (3), like this:

    ```
    (out=987)
    sourcetype=WebMailIfoDatas to
    ```

4. This is the final query, which returns the answer that we are looking for:

    ```
    ... out=987 to=bob@vendor1.co.uk
    ```

Using transaction

The transaction command lets you group events based on their proximity to other events. This proximity is determined either by ranges of time, or by specifying the text contained in the first and/or last event in a transaction.

This is an expensive process, but is sometimes the best way to group certain events. Unlike other transforming commands, when using transaction, the original events are maintained, and are grouped together into multivalued events.

Some rules of thumb for the usage of transaction are as follows:

*   If the question can be answered using `stats`, it will almost always be more efficient.

*   All the events needed for the transaction have to be found in one search.

*   When grouping is based on field values, and all the events need at least one field in common with at least one other event, then it can be considered as part of the transaction. This doesn't mean that every event must have the same field, but that all events should have some field from the list of fields specified.

- When grouping is based solely on `startswith` and `endswith`, it is important that transactions do not interleave in the search results.

- Every effort should be made to reduce the number of open transactions, as an inefficient query can use a lot of resources. This is controlled by limiting the scope of time with `maxspan` and `maxpause`, and/or by using `startswith` and `endswith`.

Let's step through a few possible examples of the transaction command in use.

Using transaction to determine the session's length

Some fictitious events are given as follows. Assuming that this is a busy server, there might be a huge number of events occurring between requests from this particular session:

```
2012-04-27T03:14:31 user=mary GET /foo?q=1 uid=abcdefg
...hundreds of events...
2012-04-27T03:14:46 user=mary GET /bar?q=2 uid=abcdefg
...hundreds of thousands of events...
2012-04-27T06:40:45 user=mary GET /foo?q=3 uid=abcdefg
...hundreds of events...
2012-04-27T06:41:49 user=mary GET /bar?q=4 uid=abcdefg
```

The definition of huge depends on the infrastructure that you have dedicated to Splunk. See *Chapter 12, Advanced Deployments*, for more information about sizing your installation, or contact Splunk support.

Let's build a query to see the transactions belonging to `mary`. We will consider a session complete when there have been no events for five minutes:

```
sourcetype="impl_splunk_web" user=mary | transaction maxpause=5m
user
```

Let's step through everything that's happening here:

1. The initial query is run, simply returning all events for the user mary:

   ```
   sourcetype="impl_splunk_web" user=mary
   ```

2. `| transaction` starts the command.

3. `maxpause=5m` indicates that any transaction that has not seen an event for five minutes will be closed. In a large dataset, this time frame might be too expensive, leaving a huge number of transactions open longer than necessary.

4. `user` is the field to use for linking events together. If events have different values of `user`, a new transaction will start with the new value of `user`.

Given our events, we will end up with four groupings of events:

i	Event
>	2012-11-11T19:26:33 user=mary GET /products/?q=3 uid=abcdefg 2012-11-11T19:27:35 user=mary GET /bar?q=4 uid=abcdefg
>	2012-11-11T16:00:27 user=mary GET /products/index.html?q=1 uid=abcdefg 2012-11-11T16:00:27 user=mary GET /bar?q=2 uid=abcdefg
>	2012-08-25T20:15:30 user=mary GET /bar?q=3 uid=abcdefg 2012-08-25T20:16:31 user=mary GET /bar?q=4 uid=abcdefg
>	2012-08-25T16:49:27 user=mary GET /bar?q=2 uid=abcdefg

Each of these groupings can then be treated like a single event.

A `transaction` command has some interesting properties as follows:

- The field `_time` is assigned the value of `_time` from the first event in the transaction.
- The field `duration` contains the time difference between the first and the last event in the transaction.
- The field `eventcount` contains the number of events in the transaction (based upon how your environment's knowledge objects are set up).
- All fields are merged into unique sets. In this case, the field `user` would only ever contain `mary`, but the field `q` would contain the values `[1,2]`, and `[3,4]` respectively.

With these extra fields, we can render a nice table of transactions belonging to `mary` like this:

```
sourcetype="impl_splunk_web" user=mary
 | transaction maxpause=5m user
 | table _time duration eventcount q
```

This will produce a table like this:

_time	duration	eventcount	q
1 2012-11-11 19:26:33	62	2	3 4
2 2012-11-11 16:00:27	0	2	1 2
3 2012-08-25 20:15:30	61	2	3 4
4 2012-08-25 16:49:27	0	1	2

Combining `transaction` with `stats` or `timechart`, we can generate the statistics about the transactions themselves:

```
sourcetype="impl_splunk_web" user=mary
| transaction maxpause=5m user
| stats avg(duration) avg(eventcount)
```

This would give us a table, as shown in the following screenshot:

avg(duration)	avg(eventcount)	avg(eventcount)
1 30.750000	1.750000	1.750000

Calculating the aggregate of transaction statistics

Using the values added by `transaction`, we can, somewhat naively, answer the questions of how long the users spend on a site and how many pages they view per session.

Let's create sessions based on the `uid` field for all events. Using `stats`, we will then calculate the average `duration` value, the average `eventcount` value, and while we're at it, we will determine the distinct number of `users` and session IDs.

```
sourcetype="impl_splunk_web"
| transaction maxpause=5m uid
| stats avg(duration) avg(eventcount) dc(user) dc(uid)
```

This will give us a table as shown in the following screenshot:

avg(duration)	avg(eventcount)	dc(user)	dc(uid)
1 880.014085	179.471831	6	138

Transactions have an average length of 892 seconds, and 227 events.

For large amounts of web traffic, you will want to calculate transactions over small slices of time into a summary index. We will cover summary indexes in *Chapter 10, Summary Indexes and CSV Files*.

Combining subsearches with transaction

Let's put what we learned about subsearches together with transactions. Let's imagine that q=1 represents a particular entry point into our site, perhaps a link from an advertisement. We can use subsearch to find users that clicked on the advertisement, then use transaction to determine how long these users stayed on our site.

To do this, first we need to locate the sessions initiated from this link. The search can be as simple as:

```
sourcetype="impl_splunk_web" q=1
```

This will return events like the following:

i	Event
>	2012-11-11T19:28:03 user=bobby GET /products/x/?q=1 uid=MjI5NTkwMQ
>	2012-11-11T19:22:36 user=user1 GET /products/y/?q=1 uid=NDU0NTI2Ng
>	2012-11-11T19:20:04 user=user4 GET /about/?q=1 uid=MzQyNzY4MA
>	2012-11-11T19:19:53 user=user3 GET /products/x/?q=1 uid=MTcxNzUyOA
>	2012-11-11T19:18:46 user=bobby GET /products/y/?q=1 uid=MjI5NTkwMQ
>	2012-11-11T19:17:48 user=bobby GET /about/?q=1 uid=MjI5NTkwMQ

In our fictitious logs, the field uid represents a session ID. Let's use stats to return one row per unique uid:

```
sourcetype="impl_splunk_web" q=1
| stats count by uid
```

This will render a table like this (the first 10 rows are shown):

	uid ⬦	count ⬦
1	MTE1NDU0Mw	2
2	MTE3MDg3Mg	2
3	MTE5NTQyNA	1
4	MTEwODE4OQ	2
5	MTEzNDUwNg	2
6	MTI0MTExMA	1
7	MTIzNDE2MA	2
8	MTIzNzU3Nw	2
9	MTM2MTAzOA	2
10	MTM3OTQwNw	4

We need to add one more command, `fields`, to limit the fields that come out of our subsearch:

```
sourcetype="impl_splunk_web" q=1
| stats count by uid
| fields uid
```

Now we feed this back into our outer search:

```
[search
sourcetype="impl_splunk_web" q=1
| stats count by uid
| fields uid
]
sourcetype="impl_splunk_web"
```

After the subsearch runs, the combined query is essentially as follows:

```
( (uid=MTAyMjQ2OA) OR (uid=MTI2NzEzNg) OR (uid=MTM0MjQ3NA) )
sourcetype="impl_splunk_web"
```

From this combined query, we now have every event from every `uid` that clicked a link that contained `q=1` in our time frame. We can now add `transaction`, as we saw earlier, to combine these sessions into groups:

```
[search sourcetype="impl_splunk_web" q=1
| stats count by uid
| fields uid]
sourcetype="impl_splunk_web"
| transaction maxpause=5m uid
```

This gives us a list of transactions (shown, in part, in the following image):

i	Event
>	2012-11-11T19:26:33 user=mary GET /products/?q=3 uid=abcdefg 2012-11-11T19:27:35 user=mary GET /bar?q=4 uid=abcdefg
>	2012-11-11T19:22:34 user=user1 GET /products/y/?q=11925408 uid=NDUONTI2Ng 2012-11-11T19:22:36 user=user1 GET /products/y/?q=1 uid=NDUONTI2Ng 2012-11-11T19:22:46 user=user1 GET /products/y/?q=5262471 uid=NDUONTI2Ng 2012-11-11T19:22:50 user=user1 GET /products/?q=13404385 uid=NDUONTI2Ng 2012-11-11T19:23:09 user=user1 GET /contact/?q=12356362 uid=NDUONTI2Ng Show all 52 lines
>	2012-11-11T19:20:02 user=user4 GET /about/?q=787577 uid=MzQyNzY4MA 2012-11-11T19:20:03 user=user4 GET /products/index.html?q=3836670 uid=MzQyNzY4MA 2012-11-11T19:20:04 user=user4 GET /about/?q=1 uid=MzQyNzY4MA 2012-11-11T19:20:14 user=user4 GET /products/y/?q=6128491 uid=MzQyNzY4MA 2012-11-11T19:20:15 user=user4 GET /products/index.html?q=13136424 uid=MzQyNzY4MA Show all 110 lines
>	2012-11-11T19:10:41 user=user2 GET /products/?q=1 uid=MzMzMjk10Q 2012-11-11T19:10:47 user=user2 GET /about/?q=13197136 uid=MzMzMjk10Q 2012-11-11T19:10:49 user=user2 GET /products/y/?q=5755554 uid=MzMzMjk10Q 2012-11-11T19:10:49 user=user2 GET /contact/?q=8114880 uid=MzMzMjk10Q 2012-11-11T19:10:51 user=user2 GET /foo?q=4180100 uid=MzMzMjk10Q Show all 232 lines

Notice that not all of our transactions start with q=1. This means that this transaction did not start when the user clicked the advertisement. Let's make sure our transactions start from the desired entry point of q=1:

```
[search sourcetype="impl_splunk_web" q=1
| stats count by uid
| fields uid]
sourcetype="impl_splunk_web"
| transaction maxpause=5m
startswith="q=1"
uid
```

The startswith field indicates that a new transaction should start at the time the search term q=1 is found in an event.

The field startswith works only on the field _raw (the actual event text). In this case, startswith="q=1", is looking for the literal phrase "q=1", not the field q.

This will cause any occurrence of `q=1` to start a new transaction. We still have a few transactions that do not contain `q=1` which we will eliminate next.

i	Event
>	2012-11-11T19:28:03 user=bobby GET /products/x/?q=1 uid=MjI5NTkwMQ
	2012-11-11T19:28:04 user=bobby GET /foo?q=327716 uid=MjI5NTkwMQ
	2012-11-11T19:28:17 user=bobby GET /bar?q=7523912 uid=MjI5NTkwMQ
	2012-11-11T19:28:18 user=bobby GET /about/?q=1959605 uid=MjI5NTkwMQ
	2012-11-11T19:28:22 user=bobby GET /contact/?q=4213221 uid=MjI5NTkwMQ
	Show all 14 lines
>	2012-11-11T19:22:36 user=user1 GET /products/y/?q=1 uid=NDU0NTI2Ng
	2012-11-11T19:22:46 user=user1 GET /products/y/?q=5262471 uid=NDU0NTI2Ng
	2012-11-11T19:22:50 user=user1 GET /products/?q=13404385 uid=NDU0NTI2Ng
	2012-11-11T19:23:09 user=user1 GET /contact/?q=12356362 uid=NDU0NTI2Ng
	2012-11-11T19:23:10 user=user1 GET /foo?q=5435855 uid=NDU0NTI2Ng
	Show all 51 lines
>	2012-11-11T19:20:04 user=user4 GET /about/?q=1 uid=MzQyNzY4MA
	2012-11-11T19:20:14 user=user4 GET /products/y/?q=6128491 uid=MzQyNzY4MA
	2012-11-11T19:20:15 user=user4 GET /products/index.html?q=13136424 uid=MzQyNzY4MA
	2012-11-11T19:20:24 user=user4 GET /foo?q=13723991 uid=MzQyNzY4MA
	2012-11-11T19:20:24 user=user4 GET /products/x/?q=11606483 uid=MzQyNzY4MA
	Show all 108 lines
>	2012-11-11T19:19:53 user=user3 GET /products/x/?q=1 uid=MTcxNzUyOA
	2012-11-11T19:19:59 user=user3 GET /products/x/?q=8117707 uid=MTcxNzUyOA
	2012-11-11T19:20:06 user=user3 GET /products/x/?q=5848169 uid=MTcxNzUyOA
	2012-11-11T19:20:14 user=user3 GET /products/y/?q=8692949 uid=MTcxNzUyOA
	2012-11-11T19:20:15 user=user3 GET /products/y/?q=2703345 uid=MTcxNzUyOA
	Show all 113 lines
>	2012-11-11T19:18:46 user=bobby GET /products/y/?q=1 uid=MjI5NTkwMQ
	2012-11-11T19:18:46 user=bobby GET /foo?q=4233491 uid=MjI5NTkwMQ
	2012-11-11T19:18:51 user=bobby GET /products/x/?q=10375985 uid=MjI5NTkwMQ
	2012-11-11T19:19:03 user=bobby GET /products/y/?q=10591079 uid=MjI5NTkwMQ
	2012-11-11T19:19:04 user=bobby GET /bar?q=3826342 uid=MjI5NTkwMQ
	Show all 119 lines
>	2012-11-11T19:17:48 user=bobby GET /about/?q=1 uid=MjI5NTkwMQ
	2012-11-11T19:17:52 user=bobby GET /products/y/?q=1481996 uid=MjI5NTkwMQ
	2012-11-11T19:17:53 user=bobby GET /products/y/?q=7300557 uid=MjI5NTkwMQ
	2012-11-11T19:18:02 user=bobby GET /about/?q=9251424 uid=MjI5NTkwMQ
	2012-11-11T19:18:04 user=bobby GET /contact/?q=9348499 uid=MjI5NTkwMQ
	Show all 12 lines
>	2012-11-11T19:16:45 user=user2 GET /products/x/?q=1 uid=MzMzMjk1OQ
	2012-11-11T19:16:50 user=user2 GET /about/?q=12032899 uid=MzMzMjk1OQ
	2012-11-11T19:16:54 user=user2 GET /bar?q=7172570 uid=MzMzMjk1OQ
	2012-11-11T19:16:54 user=user2 GET /products/x/?q=6262807 uid=MzMzMjk1OQ

To discard the transactions that do not contain `q=1`, add a search command:

```
[search sourcetype="impl_splunk_web" q=1
| stats count by uid
| fields uid]
sourcetype="impl_splunk_web"
| transaction maxpause=5m startswith="q=1" uid
| search q=1
```

Finally, let's add `stats` to count the number of transactions, the distinct values of `uid`, the average `duration` of each transaction, and the average number of clicks per transaction:

```
[search sourcetype="impl_splunk_web" q=1
| stats count by uid
| fields uid]
sourcetype="impl_splunk_web"
| transaction maxpause=5m startswith="q=1" uid
| search q=1
| stats count dc(uid) avg(duration) avg(eventcount)
```

This gives us a table as shown in the following screenshot:

count	dc(uid)	avg(duration)	avg(eventcount)
1	250	132	488.036000	98.808000

We can swap `stats` with `timechart` to see how these statistics change over time:

```
[search sourcetype="impl_splunk_web" q=1
| stats count by uid
| fields uid]
sourcetype="impl_splunk_web"
| transaction maxpause=5m startswith="q=1" uid
| search q=1
| timechart bins=500 avg(duration) avg(eventcount)
```

Determining concurrency

Determining the number of users currently using a system is difficult, particularly if the log does not contain events for both the beginning and the end of a transaction. With web server logs in particular, it is not quite possible to know when a user has left a site. Let's investigate a couple of strategies for answering this question.

Using transaction with concurrency

If the question you are trying to answer is—how many transactions were happening at a time?, you can use transaction to combine related events and calculate the duration of each transaction. We will then use the `concurrency` command to increase a counter when the events start, and decrease when the time has expired for each transaction. Let's start with our searches from the previous section:

```
sourcetype="impl_splunk_web"
| transaction maxpause=5m uid
```

This will return a transaction for every `uid`, assuming that if no requests were made for five minutes, the session is complete. This provides results as shown in the following screenshot:

i	Time	Event
>	11/11/12 7 27 41 000 PM	2012-11-11T19:27:41 user=user1 GET /products/x/?q=6018685 uid=MTAONjI1Ng 2012-11-11T19:27:45 user=user1 GET /bar?q=4533574 uid=MTAONjI1Ng 2012-11-11T19:27:49 user=user1 GET /products/y/?q=4013720 uid=MTAONjI1Ng 2012-11-11T19:27:52 user=user1 GET /about/?q=7566917 uid=MTAONjI1Ng 2012-11-11T19:27:58 user=user1 GET /products/index.html?q=7507807 uid=MTAONjI1Ng Show all 30 lines host = DC-ENVY-698 sourcetype = impl_splunk_web
>	11/11/12 7 26 33 000 PM	2012-11-11T19:26:33 user=mary GET /products/?q=3 uid=abcdefg 2012-11-11T19:27:35 user=mary GET /bar?q=4 uid=abcdefg host = DC-ENVY-698 sourcetype = impl_splunk_web
>	11/11/12 7:22:34.000 PM	2012-11-11T19:22:34 user=user1 GET /products/y/?q=11925408 uid=NDUONTI2Ng 2012-11-11T19:22:36 user=user1 GET /products/y/?q=1 uid=NDUONTI2Ng 2012-11-11T19:22:46 user=user1 GET /products/y/?q=5262471 uid=NDUONTI2Ng 2012-11-11T19:22:50 user=user1 GET /products/?q=13404385 uid=NDUONTI2Ng 2012-11-11T19:23:09 user=user1 GET /contact/?q=12356362 uid=NDUONTI2Ng Show all 52 lines host = DC-ENVY-698 sourcetype = impl_splunk_web
>	11/11/12 7.20:02.000 PM	2012-11-11T19:20:02 user=user4 GET /about/?q=787577 uid=MzQyNzY4MA 2012-11-11T19:20:03 user=user4 GET /products/index.html?q=3836670 uid=MzQyNzY4MA 2012-11-11T19:20:04 user=user4 GET /about/?q=1 uid=MzQyNzY4MA 2012-11-11T19:20:14 user=user4 GET /products/y/?q=6128491 uid=MzQyNzY4MA 2012-11-11T19:20:15 user=user4 GET /products/index.html?q=13136424 uid=MzQyNzY4MA Show all 110 lines host = DC-ENVY-698 sourcetype = impl_splunk_web

By simply adding the `concurrency` command, we can determine the overlap of these transactions, and find out how many transactions were occurring at a time. Let's also add the `table` and `sort` commands to create a table:

```
sourcetype="impl_splunk_web"
 | transaction maxpause=5m uid
 | concurrency duration=duration
 | table _time concurrency duration eventcount
 | sort _time
```

This produces a table as follows:

_time ‹	concurrency ‹	duration ‹	eventcount ‹
1 2012-08-25 16:49:18	1	47	51
2 2012-08-25 16:49:18	2	313	92
3 2012-08-25 16:49:18	3	133	58
4 2012-08-25 16:49:19	4	921	210
5 2012-08-25 16:49:19	5	1633	365
6 2012-08-25 16:49:20	6	5	5
7 2012-08-25 16:49:27	6	0	1
8 2012-08-25 16:50:15	5	968	225
9 2012-08-25 16:51:32	5	852	178
10 2012-08-25 16:54:37	5	64	14

From these results, we can see that as transactions begin, concurrency increases and then levels off as transactions expire. In our sample data, the highest value of concurrency we see is **6**.

Using concurrency to estimate server load

In the previous example, the number of concurrent sessions was quite low since each transaction is counted as one event, no matter how many events make up that transaction. While this provides an accurate picture of the number of concurrent transactions, it doesn't necessarily provide a clear picture of the server load.

Looking at the timeline of our events, we see a large spike of events at the beginning of our log. This did not affect the previous example, because most of these events belong to a single-user session.

Some web logs provide the time it took to serve a request. Our log does not have this duration, so we'll use `eval` to simulate a value for duration per request:

```
sourcetype="impl_splunk_web"
| eval duration=2
| concurrency duration=duration
| timechart max(concurrency)
```

Here we have set the duration of each request to 2 seconds (possibly a reasonable time for an event?). The `concurrency` command will use the value of `duration`, treating each event as if it were a 2-second long transaction.

The timechart looks like this:

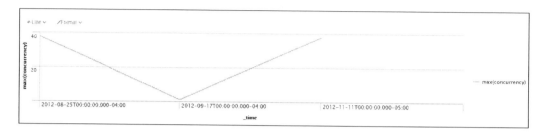

As we can see in our sample data, the large spike of requests at certain times in our log, translates to high concurrency.

Later in this chapter, we will calculate events per some period of time, which will provide a very similar answer, more efficiently. But it will not be quite the same answer, as the count will be fixed by slices of time instead of a running total that changes with each event.

Calculating concurrency with a by clause

One limitation of the `concurrency` command is that there is no way to simultaneously calculate the concurrency for multiple sets of data. For instance, what if you wanted to know the concurrency per host, as opposed to concurrency across your entire environment?

In our sample set of data, we have only one host, but we have multiple values for the network field. Let's use that field for our exercise.

Our fake concurrency example from the previous section looks like this:

```
sourcetype=impl_splunk_gen network="*"
| eval d=2
| concurrency duration=d
| timechart max(concurrency)
```

First, let's rebuild this search using the `streamstats` command. This command will calculate the rolling statistics and attach the calculated values to the events themselves. To accommodate `streamstats`, we will need an event representing the start and end of each transaction. We can accomplish this by creating a multivalued field, essentially an array, and then duplicate our events based on the values in this field.

First, let's create our end time. Remember that `_time` is simply the UTC epoch time at which this event happened, so we can treat it as a number.

```
sourcetype=impl_splunk_gen network="*"
| eval endtime=_time+2
```

Piping that through table `_time` network endtime, we see the following:

i	_time	network ⌄	endtime ⌄
>	11/11/12 5:08:58.000 PM	prod	1352671740
>	11/11/12 5:08:55.000 PM	prod	1352671737
>	11/11/12 5:08:54.000 PM	prod	1352671736
>	11/11/12 5:08:53.000 PM	prod	1352671735
>	11/11/12 5:08:52.000 PM	prod	1352671734
>	11/11/12 5:08:52.000 PM	prod	1352671734
>	11/11/12 5:08:50.000 PM	qa	1352671732
>	11/11/12 5:08:50.000 PM	prod	1352671732
>	11/11/12 5:08:48.000 PM	prod	1352671730
>	11/11/12 5:08:47.000 PM	prod	1352671729
>	11/11/12 5:08:46.000	prod	1352671728

Next, we want to combine `_time` and our endtime into a multivalued field, which we will call t:

```
sourcetype=impl_splunk_gen network="*"
| eval endtime=_time+2
| eval t=mvappend(_time,endtime)
```

Piping that through table _time network t, we see the following output:

i	_time	network ⇅	t ⇅
>	11/11/12 5:08:58.000 PM	prod	1352671738
			1352671740
>	11/11/12 5:08:55.000 PM	prod	1352671735
			1352671737
>	11/11/12 5:08:54.000 PM	prod	1352671734
			1352671736
>	11/11/12 5:08:53.000 PM	prod	1352671733
			1352671735
>	11/11/12 5:08:52.000 PM	prod	1352671732
			1352671734

As you can see, we have our actual _time, which Splunk always draws according to the user's preferences, then our network value, and then the two values for t created using mvappend. Now we can expand each event into two events, so that we have a start and end event:

```
sourcetype=impl_splunk_gen network="*"
| eval endtime=_time+2
| eval t=mvappend(_time,endtime)
| mvexpand t
```

The mvexpand command replicates each event for each value in the field specified. In our case, each event will create two events, as t always contains two values. All other fields are copied into the new event. With the addition of table _time network t, our events now look like this:

i	_time	network ⬦	t ⬦
>	11/11/12 5:08:58.000 PM	prod	1352671738
>	11/11/12 5:08:58.000 PM	prod	1352671740
>	11/11/12 5:08:55.000 PM	prod	1352671735
>	11/11/12 5:08:55.000 PM	prod	1352671737
>	11/11/12 5:08:54.000 PM	prod	1352671734
>	11/11/12 5:08:54.000 PM	prod	1352671736
>	11/11/12 5:08:53.000 PM	prod	1352671733
>	11/11/12 5:08:53.000 PM	prod	1352671735

Now that we have a start and end event, we need to mark the events as such. We will create a field named increment that we can use to create a running total. Start events will be positive, while end events will be negative. As the events stream through streamstats, the positive value will increment our counter, and the negative value will decrement our counter.

Our start events will have the value of _time replicated in t, so we will use eval to test this and set the value of increment accordingly. After setting increment, we will reset the value of _time to the value of t, so that our end events appear to have happened in the future:

```
sourcetype=impl_splunk_gen network="*"
| eval endtime=_time+2
| eval t=mvappend(_time,endtime)
| mvexpand t
| eval increment=if(_time=t,1,-1)
| eval _time=t
```

With the addition of table `_time` network increment, this gives us results as shown in the following screenshot:

i	_time	network ⬍	increment ⬍
>	11/11/12 5:08:58.000 PM	prod	1
>	11/11/12 5:08:07.000 PM	prod	1
>	11/11/12 5:08:07.000 PM	prod	1
>	11/11/12 5:08:07.000 PM	prod	-1
>	11/11/12 5:08:06.000 PM	prod	-1
>	11/11/12 5:08:05.000 PM	prod	1
>	11/11/12 5:08:04.000 PM	prod	1
>	11/11/12 5:08:04.000 PM	prod	-1

The `streamstats` command expects events to be in the order in which you want to calculate your statistics. Currently, our fictitious end events are sitting right next to the start events, but we want to calculate a running total of `increment`, based on the order of `_time`.

The sort command will take care of this for us. The `0` value before the field list defeats the default limit of 10,000 rows.

```
sourcetype=impl_splunk_gen network="*"
| eval endtime=_time+2
| eval t=mvappend(_time,endtime)
| mvexpand t
| eval increment=if(_time=t,1,-1)
| eval _time=t
| sort 0 _time network increment
```

One thing to note at this point is that we have reset several values in this query using commands. We have changed `_time`, and now we have changed `increment`. A field can be changed as many times as is needed, and the last assignment in the chain wins.

Now that our events are sorted by `_time`, we are finally ready for `streamstats`. This command calculates statistics over a rolling set of events, in the order in which the events are seen. In combination with our `increment` field, this command will act just like concurrency, but will keep separate running totals for each of the fields listed after by:

```
sourcetype=impl_splunk_gen network="*"
| eval endtime=_time+2
| eval t=mvappend(_time,endtime)
| mvexpand t
| eval increment=if(_time=t,1,-1)
| eval _time=t
| sort 0 _time network increment
| streamstats sum(increment) as concurrency by network
| search increment="1"
```

The last search statement will eliminate our synthetic end events. Piping the results through table `_time` network `increment` concurrency, we get the following results:

i	_time	network ⇕	increment ⇕	concurrency ⇕
>	11/11/12 4:00:26.000 PM	prod	1	1
>	11/11/12 4:00:29.000 PM	qa	1	1
>	11/11/12 4:00:32.000 PM	prod	1	1
>	11/11/12 4:00:34.000 PM	prod	1	1
>	11/11/12 4:00:34.000 PM	prod	1	2
>	11/11/12 4:00:35.000 PM	prod	1	3
>	11/11/12 4:00:38.000 PM	prod	1	1
>	11/11/12			

With the addition of timechart `max(concurrency)` by network, we see something like the following screenshot:

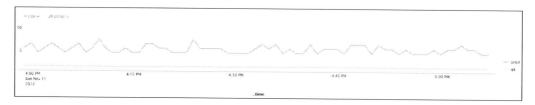

While this has been an interesting exercise, in the real world, you probably wouldn't calculate web server utilization in such a manner. The number of events is often quite large, and the time that each event takes is normally negligible. This approach would be more interesting for longer running processes, such as batch or database processes.

The more common approach for web logs is to simply count events over time. We'll look at several ways to accomplish this next.

Calculating events per slice of time

There are a number of ways to calculate events per some period of time. All these techniques rely on rounding `_time` down to some period of time, and then grouping the results by the rounded buckets of `_time`.

Using timechart

The simplest approach to counting events over time is simply to use `timechart`, like this:

```
sourcetype=impl_splunk_gen network=prod
| timechart span=1m count
```

In the table view, we see the following:

_time ⌃	count ⌃
1	2012-11-11 16:00:00	28
2	2012-11-11 16:01:00	54
3	2012-11-11 16:02:00	54
4	2012-11-11 16:03:00	54
5	2012-11-11 16:04:00	54
6	2012-11-11 16:05:00	54
7	2012-11-11 16:06:00	54
8	2012-11-11 16:07:00	54
9	2012-11-11 16:08:00	52
10	2012-11-11 16:09:00	56

Charts in Splunk do not attempt to show more points than the pixels present on the screen. The user is, instead, expected to change the number of points to graph, using the bins or span attributes. Calculating average events per minute, per hour shows another way of dealing with this behavior.

If we only wanted to know about the minutes that actually had events instead of every minute of the day, we could use bucket and stats, like this:

```
sourcetype=impl_splunk_gen network=prod
| bucket span=1m _time
| stats count by _time
```

The bucket command rounds the _time field of each event down to the minute in which it occurred, which is exactly what timechart does internally. This data will look the same, but any minutes without events will not be included. Another way to accomplish the same thing would be as follows:

```
sourcetype=impl_splunk_gen network=prod
| timechart span=1m count
| where count>0
```

Calculating average requests per minute

If we take our previous queries and send the results through `stats`, we can calculate the average events per minute, like this:

```
sourcetype=impl_splunk_gen network=prod
| timechart span=1m count
| stats avg(count) as "Average events per minute"
```

This gives us exactly one row:

Alternatively, we can use `bucket` to group events by minute, and `stats` to `count` by each minute that has values, as shown in the following code:

```
sourcetype=impl_splunk_gen
| bucket span=1m _time
| stats count by _time
| stats avg(count) as "Average events per minute"
```

We are now presented with a somewhat higher number:

Why? In this case, our fictitious server was down for some time. In our second example, only minutes that actually had events were included in the results, because `stats` does not produce an event for every slice of time, as timechart does. To illustrate this difference, look at the results of two queries:

```
sourcetype=impl_splunk_gen
| timechart span=1h count
```

This query produces the following table:

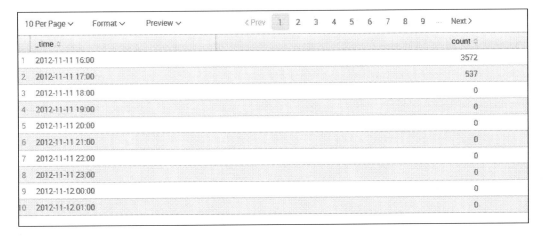

Let's use `bucket` and `stats`, as follows:

```
sourcetype=impl_splunk_gen
| bucket span=1m _time
| stats count by _time
```

We get this table as the output:

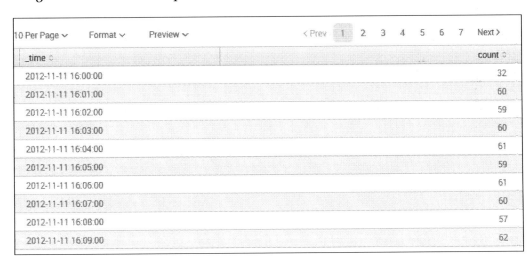

In this case, we used a 1 minute (1m) time slot.

Calculating average events per minute, per hour

One limitation of graphing in Splunk is that only a certain number of events can be drawn, as there are only so many pixels available to draw. When counting or adding values over varying periods of time, it can be difficult to know what timescale is being represented. For example, consider the following query:

```
earliest=-1h sourcetype=impl_splunk_gen
| timechart count
```

Splunk will produce this graph for the preceding query:

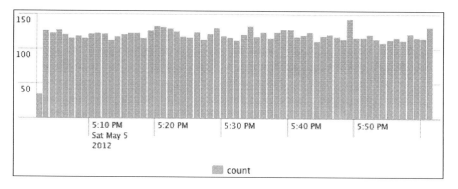

Each of these bars represent one minute. Let's change the time frame to 24 hours:

```
earliest=-24h sourcetype=impl_splunk_gen
| timechart count
```

We are presented with this graph:

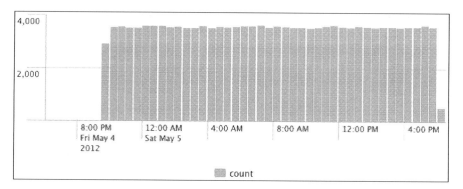

There is no indication as to what period of time is represented by each bar unless you roll over the chart. In this case, each bar represents 30 minutes. This makes the significance of the *y* axis difficult to judge. In both cases, we can add `span=1m` to timechart, and we would know that each bar represents one minute. This would be fine for a chart representing one hour, but a query for 24 hours would produce too many points, and we would see a truncated chart.

Another approach would be to calculate the average events per minute, and then calculate that value over whatever time frame we are looking at. The Splunk `timechart` command provides a convenient function to accomplish this, but we have to do a little extra work.

```
earliest=-24h sourcetype=impl_splunk_gen
| eval eventcount=1
| timechart span=1h per_minute(eventcount)
```

The `per_minute` command calculates the sum of `eventcount` per minute, then finds the average value for the slice of time that each bar represents. In this case, we are seeing the average number of events per hour.

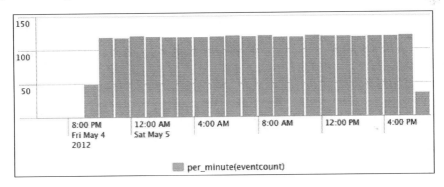

This scale looks in line with our one-hour query, as we are now looking at the event count per minute.

Like in the *Calculating average requests per minute* section, we could also ignore minutes that had no data. We could accomplish that as shown in the following code:

```
earliest=-24h sourcetype=impl_splunk_gen
| bucket span=1m _time
| stats count by _time
| timechart span=1h avg(count)
```

This approach does not penalize incomplete hours, for instance, the current hour.

The graph looks like this:

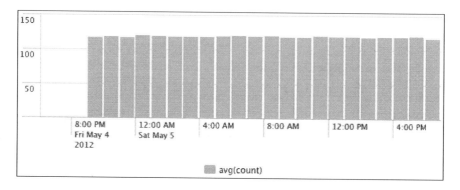

This gives us a better understanding of events for the current hour, but is arguably not entirely truthful about the first hour in the graph.

Rebuilding top

The top command is very simple to use, but is actually doing a fair amount of interesting work. I often start with top, then switch to stats count, but then wish for something that top provides automatically. This exercise will show you how to recreate all the elements, so that you might pick and choose what you need.

Let's recreate the top command by using other commands.

Here is the query that we will replicate:

```
sourcetype="impl_splunk_gen" error
  | top useother=t limit=5 logger user
```

The output looks like this:

	logger ⬍	user ⬍	count ⬍	percent ⬍
1	BarClass	mary	773	18.812363
2	BarClass	jacky	422	10.270139
3	BarClass	bob	394	9.588708
4	BarClass	linda	391	9.515697
5	BarClass	Bobby	381	9.272329
6	OTHER	OTHER	1748	42.540764

To build count, we can use `stats` like this:

```
sourcetype="impl_splunk_gen" error
| stats count by logger user
```

This gets us most of the way towards our final goal:

	logger ⇕	user ⇕	count ⇕
1	AuthClass	Bobby	103
2	AuthClass	bob	68
3	AuthClass	extrauser	33
4	AuthClass	jacky	81
5	AuthClass	linda	79
6	AuthClass	mary	148
7	BarClass	Bobby	381
8	BarClass	bob	394
9	BarClass	extrauser	162
10	BarClass	jacky	422
11	BarClass	linda	391
12	BarClass	mary	773
13	FooClass	Bobby	104
14	FooClass	bob	87
15	FooClass	extrauser	43
16	FooClass	jacky	90
17	FooClass	linda	81
18	FooClass	mary	146
19	LogoutClass	Bobby	88
20	LogoutClass	bob	74
21	LogoutClass	extrauser	28
22	LogoutClass	jacky	82
23	LogoutClass	linda	80
24	LogoutClass	mary	171

To calculate the percentage that `top` includes, we will first need the total number of events. The `eventstats` command lets us add statistics to every row, without replacing the rows.

```
sourcetype="impl_splunk_gen" error
| stats count by logger user
| eventstats sum(count) as totalcount
```

The following adds our `totalcount` column in the result:

	logger ⬍	user ⬍	count ⬍	totalcount ⬍
1	AuthClass	Bobby	103	4109
2	AuthClass	bob	68	4109
3	AuthClass	extrauser	33	4109
4	AuthClass	jacky	81	4109
5	AuthClass	linda	79	4109
6	AuthClass	mary	148	4109
7	BarClass	Bobby	381	4109
8	BarClass	bob	394	4109
9	BarClass	extrauser	162	4109
10	BarClass	jacky	422	4109
11	BarClass	linda	391	4109
12	BarClass	mary	773	4109
13	FooClass	Bobby	104	4109
14	FooClass	bob	87	4109
15	FooClass	extrauser	43	4109
16	FooClass	jacky	90	4109
17	FooClass	linda	81	4109
18	FooClass	mary	146	4109
19	LogoutClass	Bobby	88	4109
20	LogoutClass	bob	74	4109
21	LogoutClass	extrauser	28	4109
22	LogoutClass	jacky	82	4109
23	LogoutClass	linda	80	4109
24	LogoutClass	mary	171	4109

Now that we have our total, we can calculate the percentage for each row.

While we're at it, let's sort the results in a descending order by `count`:

```
sourcetype="impl_splunk_gen" error
| stats count by logger user
| eventstats sum(count) as totalcount
| eval percent=count/totalcount*100
| sort -count
```

This gives us the following output:

logger ⇕	user ⇕	count ⇕	percent ⇕	totalcount ⇕
1 BarClass	mary	773	18.812363	4109
2 BarClass	jacky	422	10.270139	4109
3 BarClass	bob	394	9.588708	4109
4 BarClass	linda	391	9.515697	4109
5 BarClass	Bobby	381	9.272329	4109
6 LogoutClass	mary	171	4.161596	4109
7 BarClass	extrauser	162	3.942565	4109
8 AuthClass	mary	148	3.601850	4109
9 FooClass	mary	146	3.553176	4109
10 FooClass	Bobby	104	2.531029	4109
11 AuthClass	Bobby	103	2.506693	4109
12 FooClass	jacky	90	2.190314	4109
13 LogoutClass	Bobby	88	2.141640	4109
14 FooClass	bob	87	2.117303	4109
15 LogoutClass	jacky	82	1.995619	4109
16 AuthClass	jacky	81	1.971283	4109
17 FooClass	linda	81	1.971283	4109
18 LogoutClass	linda	80	1.946946	4109
19 AuthClass	linda	79	1.922609	4109
20 LogoutClass	bob	74	1.800925	4109
21 AuthClass	bob	68	1.654904	4109
22 FooClass	extrauser	43	1.046483	4109
23 AuthClass	extrauser	33	0.803115	4109
24 LogoutClass	extrauser	28	0.681431	4109

If not for useother=t, we could simply end our query with head 5, which would return the first five rows. To accomplish the other row, we will have to label everything beyond row five with a common value, and collapse the rows using stats. This will take a few steps.

First, we need to create a counter field, which we will call rownum:

```
sourcetype="impl_splunk_gen" error
| stats count by logger user
| eventstats sum(count) as totalcount
| eval percent=count/totalcount*100
| sort -count
| eval rownum=1
```

This gives us the following result (only the first 10 rows are shown):

	logger ⇕	user ⇕	count ⇕	percent ⇕	rownum ⇕	totalcount ⇕
1	BarClass	mary	773	18.812363	1	4109
2	BarClass	jacky	422	10.270139	1	4109
3	BarClass	bob	394	9.588708	1	4109
4	BarClass	linda	391	9.515697	1	4109
5	BarClass	Bobby	381	9.272329	1	4109
6	LogoutClass	mary	171	4.161596	1	4109
7	BarClass	extrauser	162	3.942565	1	4109
8	AuthClass	mary	148	3.601850	1	4109
9	FooClass	mary	146	3.553176	1	4109
10	FooClass	Bobby	104	2.531029	1	4109

Next, using `accum`, we will increment the value of `rownum`:

```
sourcetype="impl_splunk_gen" error
| stats count by logger user
| eventstats sum(count) as totalcount
| eval percent=count/totalcount*100
| sort -count
| eval rownum=1
| accum rownum
```

This gives us the following output (only the first 10 rows are shown):

	logger ⇕	user ⇕	count ⇕	percent ⇕	rownum ⇕	totalcount ⇕
1	BarClass	mary	773	18.812363	1	4109
2	BarClass	jacky	422	10.270139	2	4109
3	BarClass	bob	394	9.588708	3	4109
4	BarClass	linda	391	9.515697	4	4109
5	BarClass	Bobby	381	9.272329	5	4109
6	LogoutClass	mary	171	4.161596	6	4109
7	BarClass	extrauser	162	3.942565	7	4109
8	AuthClass	mary	148	3.601850	8	4109
9	FooClass	mary	146	3.553176	9	4109
10	FooClass	Bobby	104	2.531029	10	4109

Now using `eval`, we can label everything beyond row five as OTHER, and flatten
`rownum` beyond five:

```
sourcetype="impl_splunk_gen" error
| stats count by logger user
| eventstats sum(count) as totalcount
| eval percent=count/totalcount*100
| sort -count
| eval rownum=1
| accum rownum
| eval logger=if(rownum>5,"OTHER",logger)
| eval user=if(rownum>5,"OTHER",user)
| eval rownum=if(rownum>5,6,rownum)
```

Now we get the following output (only the first 10 rows are shown):

	logger	user	count	percent	rownum	totalcount
1	BarClass	mary	773	18.812363	1	4109
2	BarClass	jacky	422	10.270139	2	4109
3	BarClass	bob	394	9.588708	3	4109
4	BarClass	linda	391	9.515697	4	4109
5	BarClass	Bobby	381	9.272329	5	4109
6	OTHER	OTHER	171	4.161596	6	4109
7	OTHER	OTHER	162	3.942565	6	4109
8	OTHER	OTHER	148	3.601850	6	4109
9	OTHER	OTHER	146	3.553176	6	4109
10	OTHER	OTHER	104	2.531029	6	4109

Next, we will recombine the values using `stats`. Events are sorted by the fields listed
after `by`, which will maintain our original order:

```
sourcetype="impl_splunk_gen" error
| stats count by logger user
| eventstats sum(count) as totalcount
| eval percent=count/totalcount*100
| sort -count
| eval rownum=1
| accum rownum
| eval logger=if(rownum>5,"OTHER",logger)
```

```
| eval user=if(rownum>5,"OTHER",user)
| eval rownum=if(rownum>5,6,rownum)
| stats
sum(count) as count
sum(percent) as percent
by rownum logger user
```

This gives us:

rownum ⬍	logger ⬍	user ⬍	count ⬍	percent ⬍
1	BarClass	mary	773	18.812363
2	BarClass	jacky	422	10.270139
3	BarClass	bob	394	9.588708
4	BarClass	linda	391	9.515697
5	BarClass	Bobby	381	9.272329
6	OTHER	OTHER	1748	42.540764

We're almost done. All that's left to do is hide the rownum column. We can use fields for this purpose:

```
sourcetype="impl_splunk_gen" error
| stats count by logger user
| eventstats sum(count) as totalcount
| eval percent=count/totalcount*100
| sort -count
| eval rownum=1
| accum rownum
| eval logger=if(rownum>5,"OTHER",logger)
| eval user=if(rownum>5,"OTHER",user)
| eval rownum=if(rownum>5,6,rownum)
| stats
sum(count) as count
sum(percent) as percent
by rownum logger user
| fields - rownum
```

This finally gives us what we are after:

	logger ⇕	user ⇕	count ⇕	percent ⇕
1	BarClass	mary	773	18.812363
2	BarClass	jacky	422	10.270139
3	BarClass	bob	394	9.588708
4	BarClass	linda	391	9.515697
5	BarClass	Bobby	381	9.272329
6	OTHER	OTHER	1748	42.540764

And we're done. Just a reminder of what we were reproducing:

```
top useother=t limit=5 logger user
```

That is a pretty long query to replicate a one liner. While completely recreating `top` is not something that is practically needed, hopefully this example sheds some light on how to combine commands in interesting ways.

Acceleration

With Splunk, you can search through enormous volumes of data (proportional to the ever growing number of events to summarize as well as the number of users accessing the data), potentially increasing the amount of time it takes to complete beyond acceptable lengths.

Big data - summary strategy

Generally speaking, you create summaries of the data to report on big data. These summaries are created by background runs of the search upon which your report is based. When a user runs a report against data that has been (pre-) summarized, it runs considerably faster because the summaries it uses are much smaller bites of the total number of events to be searched.

This concept (of pre-summarizing events) can be used with your reports, data models, and indexes. Right now, we will focus on report summary acceleration.

Report acceleration

As we've already stated, summary acceleration uses summaries of events to speed up completion times for certain kinds of reports, and report summary acceleration uses, automatically created by (Splunk) summaries. You can tell Splunk to create these summaries by enabling report acceleration for an eligible existing report by performing the following steps:

On the **Reports** page, you can select a report and click **Edit** to open the **Edit Acceleration** dialog which is seen in the next screenshot:

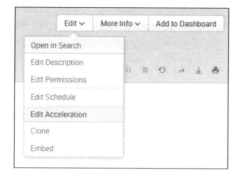

If this report qualifies for acceleration (and your permissions allow for report acceleration), the **Edit Acceleration** dialog will display a checkbox labeled **Accelerate Report**. Select it. The **Summary Range** field should appear (see the following screenshot):

Select the range of time over which you plan to run the report, then click **Save**. Now Splunk will create a summary of the events (consisting of events only within the selected time range) that the report will run against, which reduces the amount of data that the report needs to process and thus, accelerate the report.

Another method for accelerating a report is to go to **Settings**, then **Searches, reports, and alerts**:

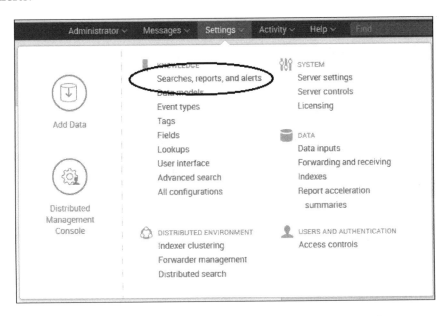

From the **Searches, reports, and alerts** page, you can select a report (which opens the detail page for that report), click **Accelerate this search** and then set a **Summary range**:

Accelerated reports are indicated on the **Searches, reports, and alerts** page with a lightning bolt graphic as shown in the following screenshot:

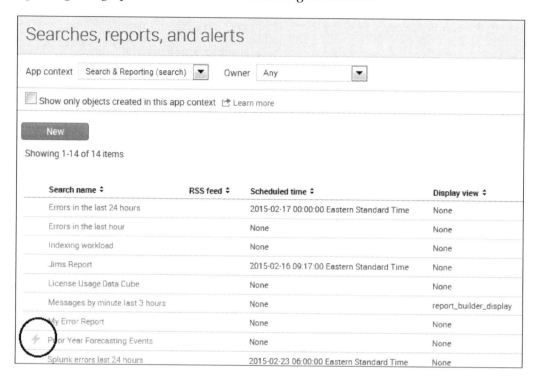

Report acceleration availability

Report acceleration should always be on your mind while designing reports. However, not all your reports can be accelerated. You can't accelerate your report in the following cases:

- It was created via pivot.
- Your permissions do not enable you to accelerate searches (you require the schedule_search and accelerate_search capabilities), or WRITE is not granted to you for the report.
- The underlying search uses the verbose search mode.

Summary

I hope this chapter was enlightening, and has sparked some ideas that you can apply to your own data. As stated in the introduction, Splunk Answers (`http://answers.splunk.com`) is a fantastic place to find examples and help in general. You can ask your questions there, and contribute answers back to the community.

In the next chapter, we will use more advanced features of Splunk to help extend the search language, and enrich data at search time.

7
Extending Search

In this chapter, we will look at some of the features that Splunk provides beyond its already powerful search language. We will cover the following, along with the help of examples:

- Tags and event types that help you categorize events, for both search and reporting
- Lookups that allow you to add external fields to events as though they were part of the original data
- Macros that let you reuse snippets of search in powerful ways
- Workflow actions that let you build searches and links based on the field values in an event
- External commands that allow you to use Python code to work with search results

In this chapter, we will investigate a few of the many commands included in Splunk. We will write our own commands in *Chapter 13, Extending Splunk*.

Using tags to simplify search

Tags allow you to attach a marker to the fields and event types in Splunk. You can then search and report on these tags later. Let's attach a tag to a couple of users who are administrators. Start with the following search:

```
sourcetype="impl_splunk_gen"
| top user
```

This search gives us a list of our users such as **ronnie**, **tuck**, **jarde**, **shelby**, and so on:

	user ⇕	count ⇕	percent ⇕
1	ronnie	100046	10.004600
2	tuck	100044	10.004400
3	jarde	100036	10.003600
4	shelby	100031	10.003100
5	natile	99980	9.998000
6	nanette	99976	9.997600
7	steve	99975	9.997500
8	mary	99972	9.997200
9	paige	99971	9.997100
10	lou	99969	9.996900

Let's say that in our group, **shelby** and **steve** are administrators. Using a standard search, we can simply search for these two users like this:

```
sourcetype="impl_splunk_gen" (user=shelby OR user=steve)
```

Searching for these two users while going forward will still work. However if we search for the tag value, we can avoid being forced to update multiple saved queries in the future.

To create a tag, we first need to locate the field.

```
>   2015-02-27 12:59:59 req_time=4203 msgid=420340 INFO Hello World user=shelby network=green ip=54.202.139.178
    Show as raw text
```

If the **user** field isn't already visible, click on it in the field picker, and then click on
Select and show in results:

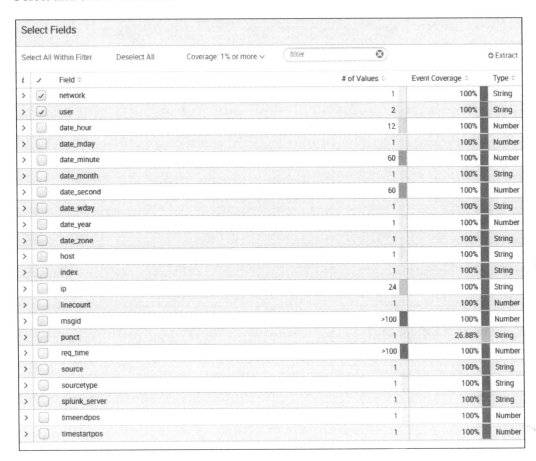

From our listed events, you can select an event and click on the arrow in the
column **i**:

Next, we can click the **Actions** arrow for the field to create a tag for, and select **Edit Tags**:

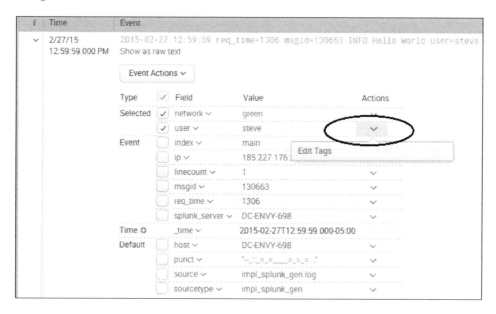

This opens the **Create Tags** dialog as shown in the following image:

Let's tag **user=steve** with `admin`:

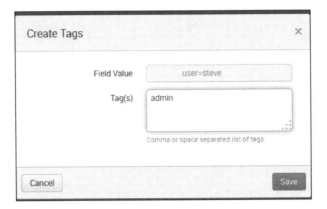

We now see our tag next to the field, **user**:

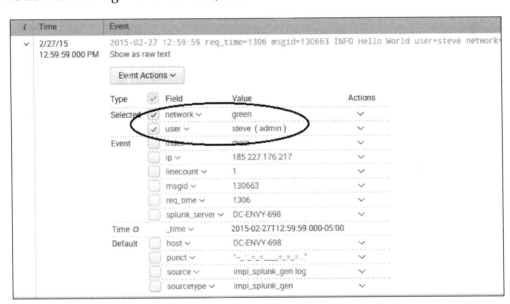

Once this is done, follow the same steps for `user=shelby`. With these two users tagged, we can search for the tag value instead of the actual usernames:

```
sourcetype="impl_splunk_gen" tag::user="admin"
```

Under the covers, this query is unrolled into exactly the same query that we started with. The advantage is that if this tag is added to new values or removed from existing ones, no queries have to be updated.

Some other interesting features of tags are as follows:

- Tags can be searched globally simply by using `tag=tag_name`; in this case `tag=admin`. Using this capability, you can apply any tag to any field or event type, and simply search for the tag. This is commonly used in security applications to tag hosts, users, and event types that need special monitoring.

- Any field or event type can have any number of tags. Simply choose the tag editor and enter multiple tag values separated by spaces.

- To remove a tag, simply edit the tags again and remove the value(s) you want to remove.

- Tags can also be edited in **Settings** at **Settings | Tags**.

Using event types to categorize results

An event type is essentially a simple search definition, with no pipes or commands.

To define an event type, first make a search. Let's search for the following:

```
sourcetype="impl_splunk_gen_SomeMoreLogs" logger=AuthClass
```

Let's say these events are login events. To make an event type, choose **Settings** and then **Event types**, as shown in the following screenshot:

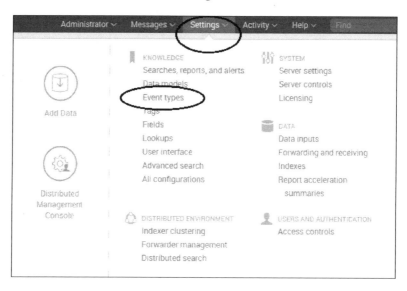

This presents us with the **Event types** page where we view existing event types and, as we want to do here, create a new event:

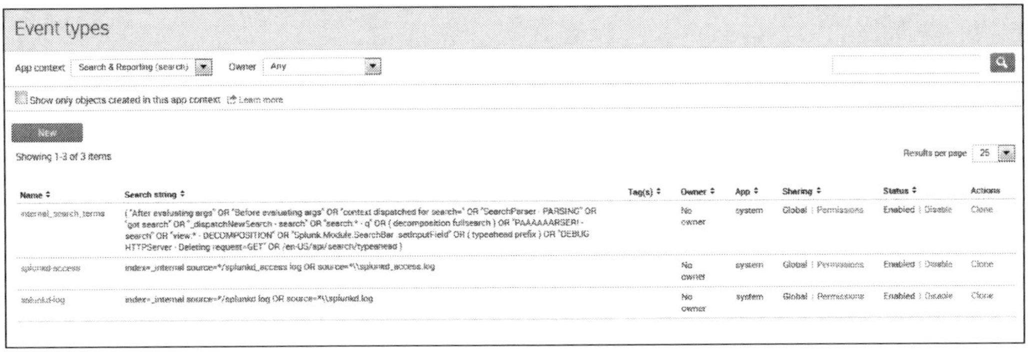

Image showing the Splunk Event Types page listing existing event types

First, click the button labeled **New**. Splunk will display the **Add New** page:

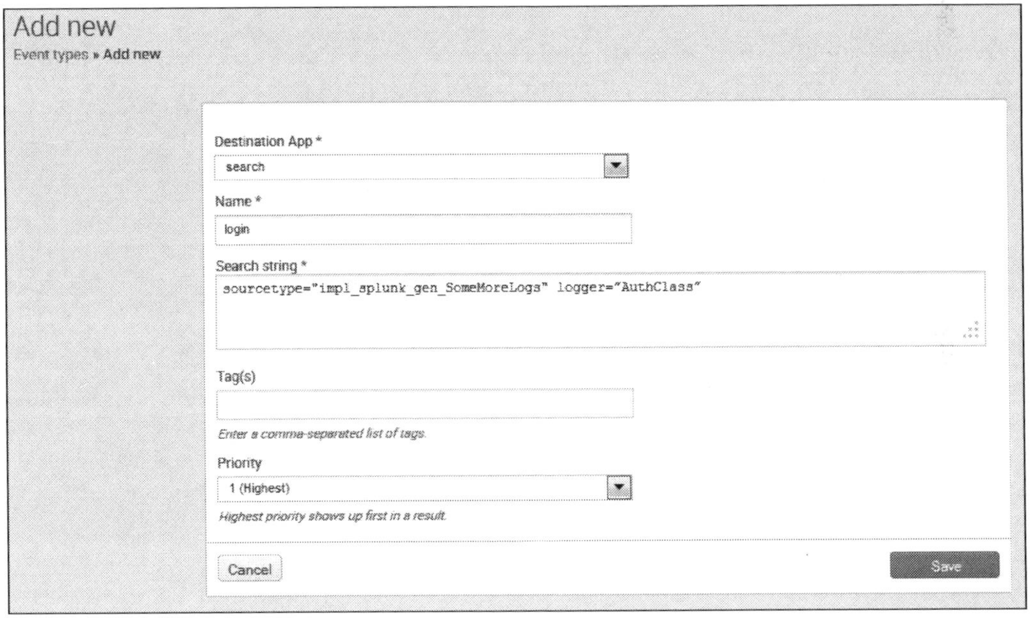

Let's name our event type `login`.

We can now search for the same events using the event type:

```
eventtype=login
```

Event types can be used as part of another search, as follows:

```
eventtype=login loglevel=error
```

Event type definitions can also refer to other event types. For example, let's assume that all login events that have a `loglevel` value of `error` are in fact failed logins. We can now save this into another event type using the same steps as mentioned previously. Let's call it `failed_login`. We can now search for these events using the following:

```
eventtype="failed_login"
```

Now, let's combine this event type with the users that we tagged as `admin` in the previous section:

```
eventtype="failed_login" tag::user="admin"
```

This will find all failed logins for administrators. Let's now save this as yet another event type, `failed_admin_login`. We can now search for these events, as follows:

```
eventtype="failed_admin_login"
```

As a final step, let's tag this event type. First, make sure that the field `eventtype` is visible. Your events should look like this:

Image showing a sample of a single event

Notice the three values of `eventtype` in this case. We are searching only for `eventtype=failed_admin_login`, but this event also matches the definitions of `eventtype=failed_login` and `eventtype=login`. Also notice our tagged user.

We are not searching for the **admin** tag, but **steve** matches `tag::user=admin`, so the value is tagged accordingly.

Following the steps in the previous section, tag `eventtype=failed_admin_login` with the value `actionable`:

We can now search for these events with the following query:

```
tag::eventtype="actionable"
```

This technique is very useful for building up definitions of events that should appear in alerts and reports. For example, consider the following query:

```
sourcetype="impl_splunk_gen_SomeMoreLogs"
tag::eventtype="actionable" | table _time eventtype user
```

This will now give us a very useful report, shown as follows:

_time	eventtype	user
1 2015-02-28 12:59:59	login Login failed_admin_login failed_login	steve
2 2015-02-28 12:59:59	login Login failed_admin_login failed_login	shelby
3 2015-02-28 12:59:59	login Login failed_admin_login failed_login	steve
4 2015-02-28 12:59:59	login Login failed_admin_login failed_login	shelby
5 2015-02-28 12:59:59	login Login failed_admin_login failed_login	shelby
6 2015-02-28 12:59:59	login Login failed_admin_login failed_login	shelby
7 2015-02-28 12:59:59	login	steve

Think about the ways that these event types are being used in this seemingly simple query:

- **Search**: An event type definition is defined as a search, so it seems only natural that you can search for events that match an event type definition.
- **Categorization**: As events are retrieved, if the events match the definition of any event type, those events will have the name of that event type added to the eventtype field.
- **Tagging**: Since event types can also be tagged, tag values assigned to certain event types can be used for both search and categorization. This is extremely powerful for assigning common tags to varied sets of results; for instance, events that belong in a report or should cause an alert.

For clarity, let's unroll this query to see what Splunk is essentially doing under the covers.

The query is expanded from the tag and event type definitions, as follows:

```
tag::eventtype="actionable"
eventtype="failed_admin_login"
eventtype="failed_login" tag::user="admin"
(eventtype=login loglevel=error) tag::user="admin"
((sourcetype="impl_splunk_gen" logger="AuthClass")
loglevel=error) tag::user="admin"
((sourcetype="impl_splunk_gen" logger="AuthClass")
loglevel=error) (user=steve OR user=shelby)
```

Let's explain what happens at each step:

1. The initial search.
2. All event types that are tagged actionable, are substituted. In this case, we only have one, but if there were multiple, they would be combined with OR.
3. The definition of the event type `failed_admin_login` is expanded.
4. The definition of `failed_login` is expanded.
5. The definition of `login` is expanded.
6. All values of user with the tag `admin` are substituted, separated by OR.

Any changes to tagged values or event type definitions will be reflected the next time they are used in any search or report.

Using lookups to enrich data

Sometimes, information that would be useful for reporting and searching is not located in the logs themselves, but is available elsewhere. Lookups allow us to enrich data, and even search against the fields in the lookup as if they were part of the original events.

The source of data for a lookup can be either a **Comma Separated Values (CSV)** file or a script. We will cover the most common use of a CSV lookup in the next section. We will cover scripted lookups in *Chapter 13, Extending Splunk*.

There are three steps for fully defining a lookup: creating the file, defining the lookup definition, and optionally wiring the lookup to run automatically.

Defining a lookup table file

A lookup table file is simply a CSV file. The first line is treated as a list of field names for all the other lines.

Lookup table files are managed at **Settings | Lookups | Lookup table files**. Simply upload a new file and give it a filename, preferably ending in `.csv`. An example lookup file (`users.csv`) is shown as follows:

```
user,city,department,state
steve,Dallas,HR,TX
shelby,Dallas,IT,TX
mary,Houston,HR,TX
nanette,Houston,IT,TX
tuck,Chicago,HR,IL
```

With this file uploaded, we can immediately use it with the `lookup` command. In the simplest case, the format of the lookup command is as follows:

```
lookup [lookup definition or file name] [matching field]
```

An example of its usage is as follows:

```
sourcetype=" impl_splunk_gen_SomeMoreLogs"
| lookup users.csv user
```

We can now see all the fields from the lookup file as if they were in the events:

We can use these fields in reports:

```
sourcetype=" impl_splunk_gen_SomeMoreLogs"
| lookup users.csv user
| stats count by user city state department
```

This will produce results as shown in the following screenshot:

	user ⌄	city ⌄	state ⌄	department ⌄	count ⌄
1	mary	Houston	TX	HR	99964
2	nanette	Houston	TX	IT	99971
3	shelby	Dallas	TX	IT	100035
4	steve	Dallas	TX	HR	99979
5	tuck	Chicago	IL	HR	100024

This is all that is required to use a CSV lookup to enrich data, but if we do a little more configuration work, we can make the lookup even more useful.

Defining a lookup definition

Though you can access a lookup immediately by the filename, defining the lookup allows you to set other options, reuse the same file, and later make the lookup run automatically. Creating a definition also eliminates a warning message that appears when simply using the filename.

Navigate to **Settings | Lookups | Lookup definitions** and click on the **New** button.

Stepping through these fields, we have the following:

- **Destination app**: This is where the lookup definition will be stored. This matters because you may want to limit the scope of a lookup to a particular application for performance reasons.

- **Name**: This is the name that you will use in search strings.

- **Type**: The options here are **File-based** or **External**. We will cover **External**, or scripted, in *Chapter 13, Extending Splunk*.

- **Lookup file**: We have chosen `users.csv` in this case.

- **Configure time-based lookup**: Using a time-based lookup, you can have a value that changes at certain points in time while going forward. For instance, if you built a lookup for the versions of software deployed to the various hosts at different times, you could generate a report on errors or response times by the software version.

- **Advanced options**: This simply exposes the remaining fields.

- **Minimum matches**: This defines the number of items in the lookup that must be matched. With a value of 1, the value of **Default matches** will be used if no match is found.

- **Maximum matches**: This defines the maximum number of matches before stopping. For instance, if there were multiple entries for each user in our lookup file, this value would limit the number of rows that would be applied to each event.

- **Default matches**: This value will be used to populate all fields from the lookup when no match is found, and **Minimum matches** is greater than 0. After clicking on **Save**, we can use our new lookup in the following manner:

```
sourcetype="impl_splunk_gen_SomeMoreLogs"
| lookup userslookup user
| stats count by user city state department
```

This will produce results as shown in the following screenshot:

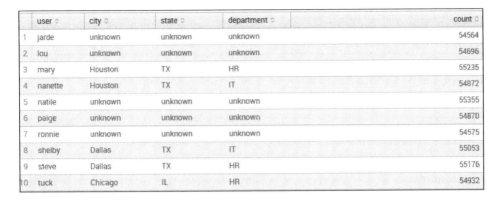

	user ⬦	city ⬦	state ⬦	department ⬦		count ⬦
1	jarde	unknown	unknown	unknown		54564
2	lou	unknown	unknown	unknown		54696
3	mary	Houston	TX	HR		55235
4	nanette	Houston	TX	IT		54872
5	natile	unknown	unknown	unknown		55355
6	paige	unknown	unknown	unknown		54870
7	ronnie	unknown	unknown	unknown		54575
8	shelby	Dallas	TX	IT		55053
9	steve	Dallas	TX	HR		55176
10	tuck	Chicago	IL	HR		54932

Lookup tables have other features, including wildcard lookups, CIDR lookups, and temporal lookups. We will use those features in later chapters.

Defining an automatic lookup

Automatic lookups are, in this author's opinion, one of the coolest features in Splunk. Not only are the contents of the lookup added to events as if they were always there, but you can also search against the fields in the lookup file as if they were part of the original event.

To define the automatic lookup, navigate to **Settings** | **Lookups** | **Automatic lookups** and click on the **New** button:

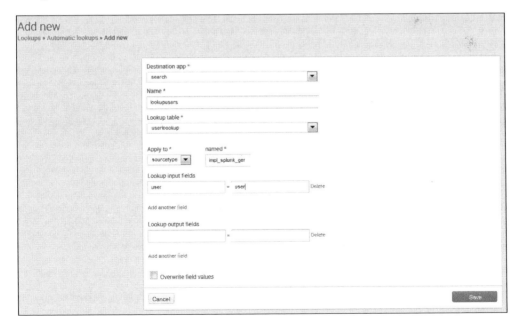

Let's step through the fields in this definition:

- **Destination app**: This is the application where the definition will live. We'll discuss the implications of this choice in *Chapter 8, Working with Apps*.

- **Name**: This name is used in the configuration. It should not contain spaces or special characters. We will discuss its significance in *Chapter 11, Configuring Splunk*.

- **Lookup table**: This is the name of the lookup definition.

- **Apply to**: This lets us choose which events are acted upon. The usual case is **sourcetype**, which must match a **sourcetype** name exactly. Alternatively, you can specify **source** or **host**, with or without wildcards.

- **Lookup input fields**: This defines the fields that will be queried in the lookup file. One field must be specified, but multiple fields can also be specified. Think of this as a join in a database. The left side is the name of the field in the lookup file. The right side is the name of the existing field in our events.

- **Lookup output fields**: This section lets you decide what columns to include from the lookup file and optionally overrides the names of those fields. The left side is the name of the field in the lookup file. The right side is the field to be created in the events. If left blank, the default behavior is to include all fields from the lookup, using the names defined in the lookup file.

- **Overwrite field values**: If this option is selected, any existing field values in an event will be overwritten by a value with the same name from the lookup file.

After clicking on **Save**, we see the listing of **Automatic lookups**. Initially, the **Sharing** option is **Private**, which will cause problems if you want to share searches with others. To share the lookup, first click on **Permissions**.

Image showing the Automatic Lookups page

This presents us with the **Permissions** page. Change the value of `Object` should appear in to **All apps**. We will discuss these permissions in greater detail in *Chapter 11, Configuring Splunk*.

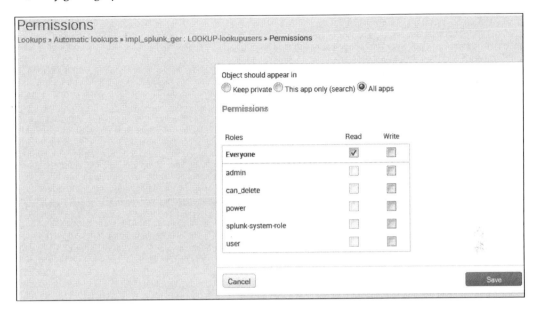

We now have a fully automatic lookup, enriching our sourcetype based on the value of **user** in each event. To show the power of this lookup, let's search for a field in the lookup file, as if it were part of the events:

```
sourcetype="impl_splunk_gen_SomeMoreLogs" department="HR" | top user
```

Even though `department` isn't in our events at all, Splunk will reverse `lookup`, find the values of **user** that are in `department`, and run the search for those users.

This returns the following result:

user ⌄	count ⌄	percent ⌄
1 steve	20690	33.462720
2 tuck	20570	33.268640
3 mary	20570	33.268640

Let's combine this search with an event type that we defined earlier. To find the most recent failed login for each member of HR, we can run the following code:

```
sourcetype="impl_splunk_gen_SomeMoreLogs" department="HR"
eventtype="failed_login"
| dedup user
| table _time user department city state
```

This returns the following:

The purpose of the `dedup` command is simply to keep only one event for each value of **user**. As events are returned in the *most recent first* order, this query will return the most recent `login` for each user. We will configure more advanced lookups in later chapters.

Troubleshooting lookups

If you are having problems with a lookup, very often the cause lies within permissions. Check permissions at all three of these paths:

- **Settings | Lookups | Lookup table files**
- **Settings | Lookups | Lookup definitions**
- **Settings | Lookups | Automatic lookups**

Once permissions are squared away, be sure to keep the following points in mind:

- Check your spelling of the fields.
- By default, lookup values are case sensitive.
- If your installation is using multiple indexers, it may take some time for the lookup files and definitions to be distributed to your indexers, particularly if the lookup files are large or you have installed many apps that have assets to be distributed.
- A rule of thumb is that a lookup file should not have more than two million rows. If a lookup is too large, an external lookup script may be required

Using macros to reuse logic

A macro serves the purpose of replacing bits of search language with expanded phrases (additionally, macros have other uses, such as assisting in workflow creation).

Using macros can help you reuse logic and greatly reduce the length of queries.

Let's use the following as our example case:

```
sourcetype="impl_splunk_gen_SomeMoreLogs" user=mary
 | transaction maxpause=5m user
 | stats avg(duration) avg(eventcount)
```

Creating a simple macro

Let's take the last two lines of our query and convert them to a macro. First, navigate to **Settings** | **Advanced search** | **Advanced search** | **Search macros** and click on **New**.

Walking through our fields, we have the following:

- **Destination app**: This is where the macro will live.
- **Name**: This is the name we will use in our searches.

- **Definition**: This is the text that will be placed in our search.
- **Use eval-based definition?**: If checked, the **Definition** string is treated as an `eval` statement instead of the raw text. We'll use this option later.

The remaining fields are used if arguments are specified. We will use these in our next example.

After clicking on **Save**, our macro is now available for use. We can use it like this:

```
sourcetype="impl_splunk_gen_SomeMoreLogs" user=mary
`webtransactions`
```

The phrase `webtransactions` is enclosed by backticks. This is similar to the usage of backticks on a Unix command line, where a program can be executed to generate an argument. In this case, `` `webtransactions` `` is simply replaced with the raw text defined in the macro, recreating the query that we started with.

Creating a macro with arguments

Let's collapse the entire search into a macro that takes two arguments, the `user` and a value for `maxpause`.

Be sure to remove newlines from your search definition. Macros do not appear to work with embedded newlines.

Walking through our fields, we have the following:

- **Name**: This is the name we will use in our searches. The parentheses and integer (2) specify how many arguments this macro expects.
- **Definition**: We have defined the entire query in this case. The variables are defined as $user$ and $maxpause$. We can use these names because we have defined the variables under `Arguments`.
- **Arguments**: This list assigns variable names to the values handed in to the macro.

After clicking on **Save**, our macro is now available for use. We can use it like this:

```
webtransactions_user_maxpause(mary,5m)
```

or

```
`webtransactions_user_maxpause("mary","5m")`
```

 We will use this feature in conjunction with a workflow action later in this chapter. See the *Building a workflow action to show field context* section later in this chapter.

Creating workflow actions

Workflow actions allow us to create custom actions based on the values in search results. The two supported actions either run a search or link to a URL.

Running a new search using values from an event

To build a workflow action, navigate to **Settings | Fields | Workflow actions** and click on **New**. You are presented with a form as seen in the following screenshot:

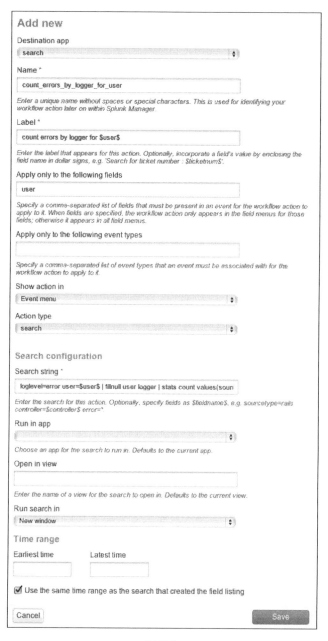

Let's walk through the following fields:

- **Destination app**: This is the app where the workflow action definition will live.
- **Name**: This is the name used in configuration files. This name cannot contain spaces, but underscores are fine.
- **Label**: This is what will appear in the menu. It can contain variables. In this case, we have included `$user$`, which will be populated with the value of the user field from the event.
- **Apply only to the following fields**: This workflow action will only appear on an event if all the fields specified in this list have a value. **Show action in** will determine which menus can contain the workflow action.
- **Apply only to the following event types**: Only shows this workflow action for events that match a particular event type. For instance, if you defined an event type called login, you might want a custom workflow action to search for all logins for this particular user over the last week.
- **Show action in**: The three options are **Event menu**, **Fields menus**, and **Both**.
  - The **Event menu** option is to the left of the event. If **Apply only to the following fields** is not empty, the workflow action will only be present if all the fields specified are present in the event.
  - The **Fields menus** option falls to the right of each field under the events. If **Apply only to the following fields** is not empty, only the fields listed will contain the workflow action. Both will show the workflow action at both places, following the same rules.
  - **Action type**: The choices here are **search** or **link**. We have chosen search.

  We will try link in the next section.

- **Search string**: This is the search template to run. You will probably use field values here, but it is not required.
- **Run in app**: If left blank, the current app will be used, otherwise the search will be run in the app that is specified. You would usually want to leave this blank.
- **Open in view**: If left blank, the current view will be used. If you expect to use an events listing panel on dashboards, you probably want to set this to **flashtimeline**.
- **Run search in**: The choices here are **New window** or **Current window**.

- **Time range**: You can specify a specific time range here, either in epoch time or relative time. Leaving **Latest time** empty will search to the latest data available.

- **Use the same time range as the search that created the field listing**: In most cases, you will either check this checkbox or provide a value in at least **Earliest time**. If you do not, the query will run over all time, which is not usually what you want. It is also possible to specify the time frame in our query.

After we click on **Save**, we now see our action in the event workflow action menu like this:

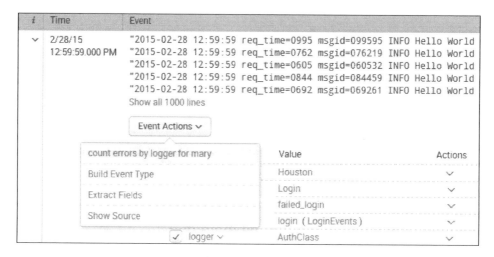

After we choose the option, a new window appears with our results, like this:

Image showing the results in 3 columns: user, logger and count

Linking to an external site

A workflow action can also link to an external site, using information from an event.

Let's imagine that your organization has some other web-based tool. If that tool can accept arguments via GET or POST requests, then we can link directly to it from the Splunk results.

Create a new workflow action as we did in the previous example, but change **Action type** to link. The options change to those shown in the following screenshot:

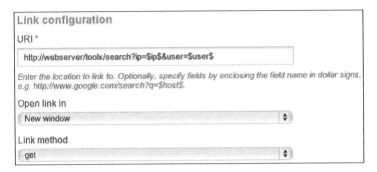

Splunk will encode any variables in the URL so that special characters survive. If you need a variable to not be encoded—for instance, if the value is actually part of the URL—add an exclamation point before the variable name, like this:

```
$!user$
```

If **Link method** is set to POST, then more input fields appear, allowing you to specify post arguments like this:

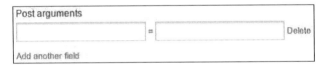

Choosing this workflow action will open a new window with the URL that we specified, either in the current window or in a new window, according to the value of **Open link in**.

The fields used by a workflow action can also come from automatic lookups. This is useful in cases where the external tool needs some piece of information that is not in your events, but can be derived from your events.

Building a workflow action to show field context

Show Source is available as a workflow action on all events. When chosen, it runs a query that finds events around the current event for the same source and host. While this is very useful, sometimes it would be nice to see events that have something else in common besides the source, and to see those events in the regular search interface, complete with the timeline and field picker.

To accomplish this, we will make a workflow action and macro that work in tandem to build the appropriate query. This example is fairly advanced, so don't be alarmed if it doesn't make a lot of sense.

Building the context workflow action

First, let's build our workflow action. As before, make a workflow action with **Action type** set to **search** as seen in the following screenshot:

Name *

context_1m_5m

Enter a unique name without spaces or special characters. This is used for identifying your workflow action later on within Splunk Manager.

Label *

Context for $@field_name$=$@field_value$, -1m thru 5m

Enter the label that appears for this action. Optionally, incorporate a field's value by enclosing the field name in dollar signs, e.g. "Search for ticket number : $ticketnum$".

Apply only to the following fields

*

Specify a comma-separated list of fields that must be present in an event for the workflow action to apply to it. When fields are specified, the workflow action only appears in the field menus for those fields; otherwise it appears in all field menus.

Apply only to the following event types

Specify a comma-separated list of event types that an event must be associated with for the workflow action to apply to it.

Show action in

Fields menus

Action type

search

Search configuration

Search string *

`context("$@field_name$", "$@field_value$", "$_time$", "-1m", "+5m")`

Enter the search for this action. Optionally, specify fields as $fieldname$, e.g. sourcetype=rails controller=$controller$ error=.*

Run in app

Choose an app for the search to run in. Defaults to the current app.

Open in view

flashtimeline

Enter the name of a view for the search to open in. Defaults to the current view.

Run search in

New window

Time range

Earliest time   Latest time

☐ Use the same time range as the search that created the field listing

Let's step through our values, which are as follows:

- **Name**: This can be anything. Let's name it after our time frame.

- **Label**: This is what will appear in the menu. You may notice two special fields, `@field_name` and `@field_value`. These two fields only make sense when **Show action in is set to Fields menus**.

  There are a number of `@variables` available to workflow actions. Search `http://docs.splunk.com/` for *Create workflow actions in Splunk* to find the complete documentation.

- **Apply only to the following fields**: This can be blank or * to indicate all fields.

- **Show action in**: We have chosen **Fields menus** in this case.

- **Action type**: We are running a search. It's a fairly strange search, as we are using a macro, but it is still technically a search.

- **Search string**: The fact that this query is a macro doesn't matter to the workflow action, `` `context("$@field_name$", "$@field_value$", "$_time$", "-1m", "+5m")` ``. We will create the context macro next.

- **Run in app**: With nothing chosen, this macro will execute the search in the current app.

- **Open in view**: We want to make sure that our query executes in **flashtimeline**, so we set it explicitly.

- **Run search in**: We choose **New window**.

- **Time**: Contrary to the previous advice, we have left the time frame unspecified. We will be overriding the search times in the search itself. Anything specified here will be replaced.

After clicking on **Save**, the workflow action is available on all the field menus.

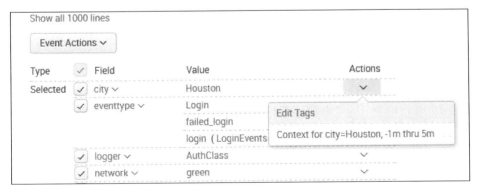

Choosing the above menu item generates this search:

```
'context("ip", "1.22.3.3", "2012-05-16T20:23:59-0500", "-1m", "+5m")'
```

Let us consider our query definition:

```
'context("$@field_name$", "$@field_value$", "$_time$", "-1m", "+5m")'
```

We can see that the variables were simply replaced, and the rest of the query was left unchanged. The variable _time is not in the format I would expect (I would have expected the epoch value), but we can work with it.

Building the context macro

When searching, you can specify the time ranges in the query itself. There are several fields that allow us to specify the time. They are as follows:

- **earliest**: This is the earliest time, inclusive. It can be specified as either a relative time or an epoch time in seconds.

- **latest**: This is the latest time, exclusive. Only events with a date before this time will be returned. This value can be specified as either a relative time or an epoch time in seconds.

- **now**: Using this field, you can redefine the relative values in earliest and latest that are calculated against. It must be defined as epoch time in seconds.

Now, given our inputs, let's define our variable names:

- field_name = ip
- field_value = 1.22.3.3
- event_time = 2012-05-16T20:23:59-0500
- earliest_relative = -1m
- latest_relative = +5m

The query we want to run looks like this:

```
earliest=-1m latest=+5m now=[epoch event time] ip=1.22.3.3
```

The only value we don't have is now. To calculate this, there is a function available to eval called strptime. To test this function, let's use |stats to create an event, build an event_time field, and parse the value. Consider the following code:

```
|stats count
| eval event_time="2012-05-16T20:23:59-0500"
| eval now=strptime(event_time,"%Y-%m-%dT%H:%M:%S%z")
```

This gives us the following table:

count ⬍	event_time ⬍	now ⬍
1 0	2012-05-16T20:23:59-0500	1337217839.000000

Good references for `strptime` formats can be found on modern Linux systems by running man `strptime` or man `date`, or by searching http://www.google.com. Splunk has several special extensions to `strptime` that can be found by searching for enhanced `strptime()` support at http://docs.splunk.com/.

Now that we have our epoch value for `now`, we can build and test our query like this:

```
earliest=-1m latest=+5m now=1337217839 ip=1.22.3.3
```

This gives us a normal event listing, from one minute before our event to five minutes after our selected event, only showing events that have the field in common.

Now that we have our search, and our `eval` statement for converting the value of now, we can actually build our macro in **Settings | Advanced search | Search macros | Add new**.

Name *

Enter the name of the macro. If the search macro takes an argument, indicate this by appending the number of arguments to the name. For example: mymacro(2)

```
context(5)
```

Definition *

Enter the string the search macro expands to when it is referenced in another search. If arguments are included, enclose them in dollar signs. For example: $arg1$

```
"now=" + strptime("$event_time$","%Y-%m-%dT%H:%M:%S%Z") + "
earliest=$earliest_relative$ latest=$latest_relative$ $field_name$=\"$field_value$\""
```

☑ Use eval-based definition?

Arguments

Enter a comma-delimited string of argument names. Argument names may only contain alphanumeric, '_' and '-' characters.

```
field_name,field_value,event_time,earliest_relative,latest_relative
```

This macro is using a few interesting features, as follows:

- Macros can take arguments. The number of arguments is specified in the name of the macro by appending (`[argument count]`) to the name of the macro. In this case, we are expecting five arguments.

- The definition of a macro can actually be an `eval` statement. This means we can use `eval` functions to build our query based on some value handed to the macro. In this case, we are using `strptime`. Things to note about this feature are as follows:

  The `eval` statement is expected to return a string. If your statement fails to return a string , for some reason, the user will see an error.

  The variable names specified are replaced before the `eval` statement is executed. This means that there may be issues with escaping the values in the variables, so some care is required to make sure whether your value contains quotes or not as is expected.

- **Use eval-based definition?** is checked to indicate that this macro is expected to be parsed as an `eval` statement.

- In the **Arguments** field, we specify the names for the arguments handed in.

These are the names we refer to in the **Definition** field. After clicking on **Save**, we have a working macro. You might make adjustments to this workflow action to better suit your needs. Let's change the definition to sort events by ascending time, and prevent searching across indexes. Change the workflow action definition **Search string** to:

```
'context("$@field_name$", "$@field_value$", "$_time$", "-1m",
"+5m")'
index=$index$ | reverse
```

Let's expand this just for clarity, like this:

```
'context("$@field_name$", "$@field_value$", "$_time$", "-1m", "+5m")'
index=$index$ | reverse
'context("ip", "1.22.3.3", "2012-05-16T20:23:59-0500", "-1m", "+5m")'
index=implsplunk | reverse
earliest=-1m latest=+5m now=1337217839 ip=1.22.3.3
index=implsplunk | reverse
```

You can create multiple workflow actions that specify different time frames, or include other fields; for instance, `host`.

Using external commands

The Splunk search language is extremely powerful, but at times, it may be either difficult or impossible to accomplish some piece of logic by using nothing but the search language. To deal with this, Splunk allows external commands to be written in Python. A number of commands ship with the product, and a number of commands are available in apps at `http://splunk-base.splunk.com/`.

Let's try out a few of the included commands. The documentation for the commands is included with other search commands at `http://docs.splunk.com/`. You can find a list of all included commands, both internal and external, by searching for `All search commands`. We will write our own commands in *Chapter 13, Extending Splunk*.

Extracting values from XML

Fairly often, machine data is written in XML format. Splunk will index this data without any issue, but it has no native support for XML. Though XML is not an ideal logging format, it can usually be parsed simply enough. Two commands are included in the search app that can help us pull fields out of XML.

xmlkv

`xmlkv` uses regular expressions to create fields from tag names. For instance, given the following XML:

```
<doc><a>foo</a><b>bar</b></doc>
```

`xmlkv` will produce the fields `a=foo` and `b=bar`. To test, try this:

```
|stats count
| eval _raw="<doc><a>foo</a><b>bar</b></doc>"
| xmlkv
```

This produces a table, as shown in the following screenshot:

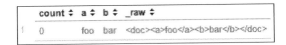

As this command is using regular expressions, its advantage is that malformed or incomplete XML statements will still produce results.

Using an external command is significantly slower than using the native search language, particularly if you are dealing with large sets of data. If it is possible to build the required fields using `rex` or `eval`, it will execute faster and it will introduce a smaller load on your Splunk servers. For instance, in the previous example, the fields could be extracted using:

```
| rex "<a.*?>(?<a>.*?)<" | rex "<b.*?>(?<b>.*?)<"
```

XPath

XPath is a powerful language for selecting values from an XML document. Unlike xmlkv, which uses regular expressions, XPath uses an XML parser. This means that the event must actually contain a valid XML document.

For example, consider the following XML document:

```
<d>
<a x="1">foo</a>
<a x="2">foo2</a>
<b>bar</b>
</d>
```

If we wanted the value for a tag whose x attribute equals 2, the XPath code would look like this:

```
//d/a[@x='2']
```

To test this, let's use our |stats trick to generate a single event and execute the xpath statement:

```
|stats count
| eval _raw="<d><a x='1'>foo</a><a x='2'>foo2</a><b>bar</b></d>"
| xpath outfield=a "//d/a[@x='2']"
```

This generates an output, as shown in the following screenshot:

count ⇕	a ⇕	_raw ⇕
0	foo2	<d><a x="1">foo</a><a x="2">foo2</a>bar</d>

The xpath command will also retrieve multivalue fields. For instance, this xpath statement simply instructs to find any field:

```
|stats count
| eval _raw="<d><a x='1'>foo</a><a x='2'>foo2</a><b>bar</b></d>"
| xpath outfield=a "//a"
```

The result of this query is as shown:

count ⇕	a ⇕	_raw ⇕
0	foo foo2	<d><a x="1">foo</a><a x="2">foo2</a>bar</d>

There are many XPath references available online. My favorite quick reference is at the *Mulberry Technologies* website: `http://www.mulberrytech.com/quickref/xpath2.pdf`

Using Google to generate results

External commands can also act as data generators, similar to the `stats` command that we used to create test events. There are a number of these commands, but let's try a fun example, google (some organizations may not have an internet connection for use in your Splunk apps, but we'll assume you do have access for these examples). This command takes one argument, a search string, and returns the results as a set of events. Let's execute a search for Splunk:

```
|google "splunk"
```

This produces a table, as shown in the following screenshot:

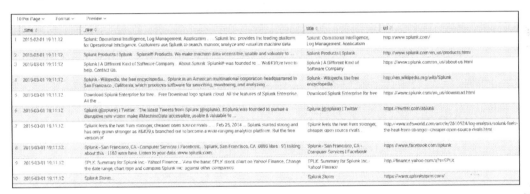

Image showing the results of our search listing various titles and Web URL's in a result table

This example may not be terribly useful, but you can probably think of external sources that you would like to query as a starting point, or even to populate a subsearch for another Splunk query. We'll write an example data generator in *Chapter 13, Extending Splunk*.

Summary

In this chapter, we quickly covered tags, event types, lookups, macros, workflow actions, and external commands. I hope these examples and discussions will serve as a starting point for your apps. More examples can be found in the official Splunk documentation at `http://docs.splunk.com/` and at `http://splunk-base.splunk.com/`.

In the next chapter, we will dive into creating and customizing our own apps.

8
Working with Apps

Splunk apps are what the industry calls knowledge objects. A knowledge object is a prearrangement of configurations within Splunk, based upon some logic, agreed upon consideration or need. With Splunk, you have the ability to create these apps to extend or customize the users' Splunk experience. In this chapter, we will explore what makes up a Splunk app. We will:

- Inspect included apps
- Install apps from Splunkbase
- Build our own app
- Customize app navigation
- Customize the look and feel of apps

Defining an app

In the strictest sense, an app is a directory of configurations and, sometimes, code. The directories and files inside have a particular naming convention and structure.

All configurations are in plain text, and can be edited using your choice of text editor. Apps generally serve one or more of the following purposes:

- **Act as a container for searches, dashboards, and related configurations**: This is what most users will do with apps. This is not only useful for logical grouping, but also for limiting what configurations are applied and at what time. This kind of app usually does not affect other apps.

- **Providing extra functionality**: Many objects can be provided in an app for use by other apps. These include field extractions, lookups, and external commands, saved searches, workflow actions, and even dashboards. These apps often have no user interface at all; instead, they add functionality to other apps.

- **Configuring a Splunk installation for a specific purpose**: In a distributed deployment, there are several different purposes that are served by the multiple installations of Splunk. The behavior of each installation is controlled by its configuration, and it is convenient to wrap those configurations into one or more apps. These apps completely change the behavior of a particular installation.

Included apps

Without apps, Splunk has no user interface, rendering it essentially useless. Luckily, Splunk comes with a few apps to get us started. We'll now take a look at a few of these apps.

The Splunk (Web) Framework is not really an app, but a framework for developers who want to create experiences using Splunk and its analytical capabilities. The Splunk Web Framework lets you quickly create custom apps by using prebuilt components, styles, templates, and reusable samples, and by adding your own custom logic, interactions, reusable components, and UI.

- **Introspection_generator_addon**: refers to the data that Splunk Enterprise logs and uses to populate the `_introspection` index. It generates data about your Splunk instance and environment, and writes that data to log files to aid in reporting on system resource utilization and troubleshooting problems.

- **Distributed Management Console**: provides the ability to view detailed performance information about your Splunk Enterprise deployment.

- **gettingstarted**: This app provides the help screens that you can access from the launcher. There are no searches, only a single dashboard that simply includes an HTML page.

- **Search & Reporting**: This is the app where users spend most of their time. It contains the main search dashboard that can be used from any app, external search commands that can be used from any app, admin dashboards, custom navigation, custom CSS, a custom app icon, a custom app logo, and many other useful elements.

- **splunk_datapreview**: This app provides the data preview functionality in the admin interface. It is built entirely using JavaScript and custom REST endpoints.

- **SplunkDeploymentMonitor**: This app provides searches and dashboards to help you keep track of your data usage and the health of your Splunk deployment. It also defines indexes, saved searches, and summary indexes. It is a good source for more advanced search examples.

- **SplunkForwarder and SplunkLightForwarder**: These apps, which are disabled by default, simply disable portions of a Splunk installation so that the installation is lighter in weight. We will discuss these in greater detail in *Chapter 12, Advanced Deployments*. If you never create or install another app, and instead simply create saved searches and dashboards in the app search, you can still be quite successful with Splunk. Installing and creating more apps, however, allows you to take advantage of others' work, organize your own work, and ultimately share your work with others.

Installing apps

Apps can either be installed from Splunkbase or uploaded through the admin interface. To get started, from the Splunk Home page, you can click on **Splunk Apps** (shown in the following screenshot):

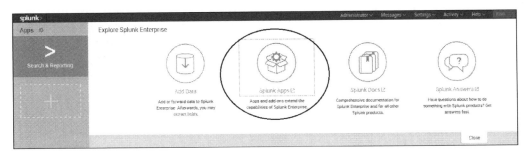

Installing apps from Splunkbase

If your Splunk server has direct access to the Internet, you can install apps from Splunkbase with just a few clicks. After clicking on Splunk Apps, the most popular apps will be listed as follows:

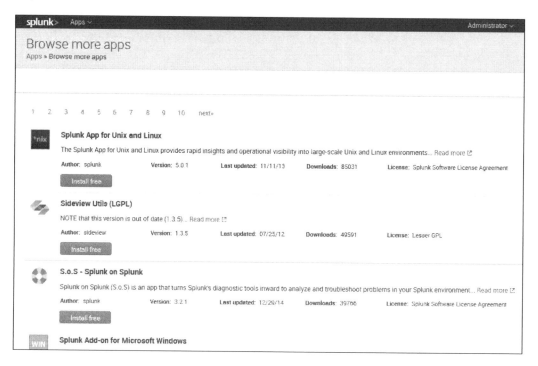

Let's install a pair of apps and have a little fun. First, install **Geo Location Lookup Script** (powered by MAXMIND) by clicking on the **Install free** button (you may have to scroll through the list of apps to find it). You will be prompted for your `http://www.splunk.com` login. This is the same login that you created when you downloaded Splunk. If you don't have an account, you will need to create one.

You can also locate the app using your web browser by going to `http://apps.splunk.com` and searching for the app by name, downloading it as a file, and then uploading it into Splunk:

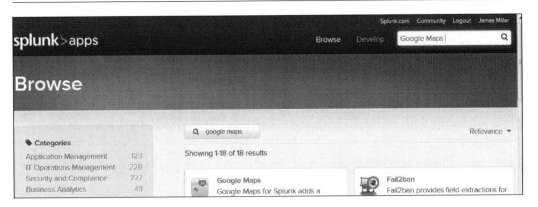

Next, install the **Google Maps** app. This app was built by a Splunk customer and contributed back to the Splunk community. This app will prompt you to restart Splunk.

Once you have restarted and logged back in, check the menu:

Google Maps is now visible, but where is Geo Location Lookup Script? Remember that not all apps have dashboards; nor do they necessarily have any visible components at all.

Using Geo Location Lookup Script

Geo Location Lookup Script is a lookup script to provide geolocation information for IP addresses. Looking at the documentation, we see this example:

```
eventtype=firewall_event | lookup geoip clientip as src_ip
```

You can find the documentation for any Splunkbase app by searching for it at `http://splunkbase.com`, or by clicking on **View details** on Splunk Apps (next to any installed app), by clicking on Apps and viewing the **Apps** page.

Let's go through the arguments of the lookup command:

`geoip`—this is the name of the lookup provided by Geo Location Lookup Script.

You can see the available lookups by going to **Settings | Lookups | Lookup definitions**.

- **clientip**: This is the name of the field in the lookup that we are matching against.

- **as src_ip**: This says to use the value of `src_ip` to populate the field before it; in this case, clientip. I personally find this wording confusing. In my mind, I read this as *using* instead of *as*.

Included in the *Implementing Splunk Data Generator* app (available at `http://packtpub.com/support`), is a `sourcetype` instance named `impl_splunk_ips`, which looks like this:

```
2012-05-26T18:23:44 ip=64.134.155.137
```

The IP addresses in this fictitious log are from one of my websites. Let's see some information about these addresses:

```
sourcetype="impl_splunk_ips" | lookup geoip clientip AS ip | top
client_country
```

This gives us a table similar to the one shown in the following screenshot (note that after running the command, new fields are added, such as **client_country**):

	client_country ⇕	count ⇕	percent ⇕
1	United States	447	71.634615
2	China	90	14.423077
3	Russian Federation	39	6.250000
4	Slovenia	15	2.403846
5	United Kingdom	14	2.243590
6	Ukraine	9	1.442308
7	South Africa	3	0.480769
8	Germany	2	0.320513
9	United Arab Emirates	1	0.160256
10	Turkey	1	0.160256

That's interesting. I wonder who is visiting my site from **Slovenia**.

Using Google Maps

Now let's do a similar search in the **Google Maps** app. Choose **Google Maps** from the **App** menu. The interface looks like the standard search interface, but with a map instead of an event listing. Let's try this remarkably similar (but not identical) query using a lookup provided in the **Google Maps** app:

```
sourcetype="impl_splunk_ips"
| lookup geo ip
```

The map generated looks like this:

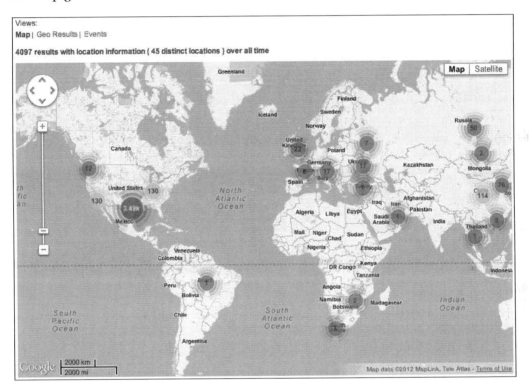

Unsurprisingly, most of the traffic to this little site came from the author's house in Austin, Texas. We'll use the Google Maps app for something more interesting in *Chapter 9, Building Advanced Dashboards*.

Installing apps from a file

It is not uncommon for Splunk servers to not have access to the Internet, particularly in a datacenter. In this case, follow these steps:

1. Download the app from `http://www.splunkbase.com`. The file will have a `.spl` or `.tgz` extension.
2. Navigate to Splunk Apps (then to the **Apps** page).
3. Click on **Install app** from file.
4. Upload the downloaded file using the form provided.
5. Restart if the app requires it.
6. Configure the app if required.

That's it. Some apps have a configuration form. If this is the case, you will see a **Setup** link next to the app when you go to **Manager | Apps**. If something goes wrong, contact the author of the app.

If you have a distributed environment, in most cases the app only needs to be installed on your search head. The components that your indexers need will be distributed automatically by the search head. Check the documentation for the app.

Building your first app

For our first app, we will use one of the templates provided with Splunk. To get started, navigate to the Splunk **Apps** page (as we described earlier in this chapter), and then click on **Create app**. The following page will open:

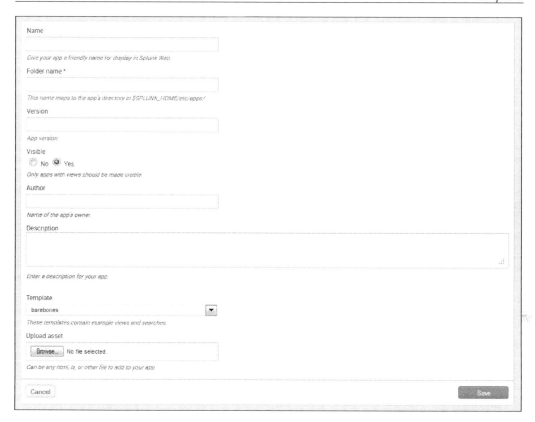

Set the fields as follows:

- Set **Name** to `Implementing Splunk App One`. This name will be visible on the home screen, in the **App** menu, and in the app banner on the upper-left side of the window.

- Set **Folder name** to `is_app_one`. This value will be the name of the app directory on the filesystem, so you should limit your name to letters, numbers, and underscores.

- Set **Version** to `1.0` (it's our first version of the app!).

- Set **Visible** to **Yes**. If your app simply provides resources for other apps to use, there may be no reason for it to be visible.

- Fill in the **Author** (your name!) and **Description** (describe your app).

- Set **Template** to **barebones**. The **barebones** template contains sample navigation and the minimal configuration required by an app. The `sample_ app` template contains many example dashboards and configurations.

- **Upload asset** you can leave alone for now (we'll touch on this later).

After clicking on **Save**, we can now visit our app by going to back to the Splunk **Apps** page or, by returning to our home page. Look at the following screenshot and you will notice that we can see the apps we've installed thus far (**Google Maps**, **MAXMIND**, and **Implementing Splunk App One**):

Now that we have our app, we can create searches and dashboards, and maintain them in our app. The simplest way to ensure that your objects end up in your app is to verify that the app banner is correct before creating objects or before entering the Splunk Manager. Our app banner looks like this:

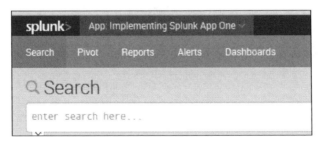

Create a dashboard called **Errors** using the following searches (refer to *Chapter 5, Simple XML Dashboards*, for detailed instructions):

```
error sourcetype="impl_splunk_gen" | timechart count by user
error sourcetype="impl_splunk_gen" | top user
error sourcetype="impl_splunk_gen" | top logger
```

This produces the following result:

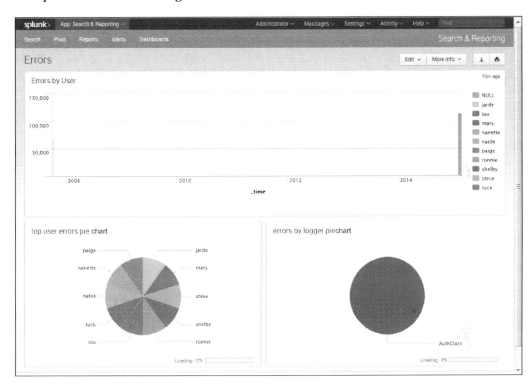

Our new dashboard appears in the navigation menu under **Dashboards**:

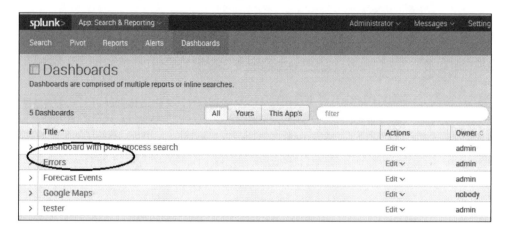

Editing navigation

Navigation is controlled by an XML file that can be accessed by going to **Settings | User interface | Navigation menus**:

Nav name ‡	Owner ‡	App ‡	Sharing ‡	Status ‡
default	No owner	is_app_one	App	Permissions	Enabled

There can only be one active navigation file per app, and it is always called **default**.

After clicking on the name, we see the XML provided by the barebones template:

```
<nav search_view="search" color="#65A637">
 <view name="search" default='true' />
 <view name="data_models" />
 <view name="reports" />
 <view name="alerts" />
 <view name="dashboards" />
</nav>
```

Note that if you check the navigation for another app (*search*) you will notice the same XML.

The structure of the XML is essentially the following:

```
nav
view
saved
collection
view
a href
saved
divider
collection
```

The logic of navigation is probably best absorbed by simply editing it and seeing what happens. You should keep a backup, as this XML is somewhat fragile, and Splunk does not provide any kind of version control. Here are some general details about `nav`:

- Children of `nav` appear in the navigation bar.

- `collection`: Children of `collection` tags appear in a menu or submenu. If the child tags do not produce any results, the menu will not appear. The `divider` tag always produces a result, so it can be used to ensure that a menu appears.

- `view`: This tag represents a dashboard, with the following attributes:

  - `name` is the name of the dashboard filename, without the `.xml` extension.

  - The first view element with the attribute `default='true'` will load automatically when the app is selected.

  - The label of each `view` is based on the contents of the label tag in the dashboard XML, not the name of the dashboard `filename`.

  - `match="dashboard"` selects all dashboards whose filename contains dashboard. If you want to group dashboards, you may want to follow a naming convention to make grouping more predictable.

  - `source="unclassified"` essentially means *all views that have not been previously associated to a menu*. In other words, this will match dashboards that were not explicitly referenced by name or matched using the match attribute or a different view tag.

- `a href`: You can include standard HTML links of the form `<a href="http://a.b/c">`.

  The link is untouched and passed along as written.

- `saved`: This tag represents a saved search, with the following attributes:

  - `name` is equal to the name of a saved search.
  - `match="report"` selects all the saved searches that have report in their names.
  - `source="unclassified"` essentially means *all searches that have not yet been previously associated to a menu*. In other words, this will match searches that were not explicitly referenced by name or matched using the `match` attribute or a different saved tag.

Let's customize our navigation. We'll make a few changes like these:

- Create an entry specifically for our errors dashboard
- Add `default='true'` so that this dashboard loads by default
- Simplify the `Views` and `Searches` collections

These changes are reflected in the following code:

```
<nav>
<view name="errors" default='true' />
<view name="flashtimeline" />
<collection label="Views">
<view source="unclassified" />
</collection>
<collection label="Searches">
<saved source="unclassified" />
</collection>
</nav>
```

Our navigation now looks like this screenshot:

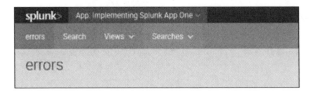

With this navigation in place, all new dashboards will appear under **Views**, and all new saved searches will appear under **Searches**. Notice that **Advanced Charting** and **Google Maps** appear under **Views**. Neither of these dashboards are part of our app, but are visible because of the permissions in their respective apps. We will discuss permissions in more detail in the *Object permissions* section.

Customizing the appearance of your app

It is helpful to further customize the appearance of your application, if for no other reason than to make it more obvious which app is currently active.

Customizing the launcher icon

The launcher icon is seen both in the `Home` app and in Splunkbase, if you decide to share your app. The icon is a 36 x 36 PNG file named `appIcon.png`. I have created a simple icon for our sample app (please don't judge my art skills):

To use the icon follow these steps:

1. Navigate to **Apps | Manage Apps**.
2. Click on **Edit properties** next to our app, `Implementing Splunk App One`.
3. Click on **Upload asset** and select the file.
4. Click on **Save**.

Our icon will now appear on the launcher screen, like in the following screenshot:

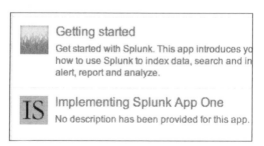

Using custom CSS

In earlier versions of Splunk, you could utilize CSS stylesheets to override the default look of a Splunk application. One common element to change was the application icon in the application bar. You could follow these steps to do just that:

1. First, create a file named `application.css`. This file will be loaded on every dashboard of the application containing it. The CSS is listed later in this section. As of Splunk Version 4.3.2, the first time `application.css` is added to an app of Version 4.3.2, a restart is required before the file is served to the users. Subsequent updates do not require a restart.

2. Next, create a file named `appLogo.png`. This file can be called anything, as we will reference it explicitly in our CSS file.

3. For each file, follow the same steps as for uploading the launcher icon:

   1. Navigate to **Apps | Manage Apps**.
   2. Click on **Edit properties** next to our app, `Implementing Splunk App One`.
   3. Click on **Upload asset** and select the file.
   4. Click on **Save**.

In Splunk version 6.2, this feature is currently not supported. You should check back to `http://www.splunk.com` for updates on this feature.

Using custom HTML

In some apps, you will see static HTML blocks. This can be accomplished using both simple and complex dashboards.

Custom HTML in a simple dashboard

In a simple dashboard, you can simply insert an `<html>` element inside a `<row>` element (inside a `dashboard` tag, of course), and include static HTML inline. For example, after uploading an image named `graph.png`, the following block can be added to any dashboard:

```
<dashboard>
<row>
<html>
<table>
<tr>
<td><img src="/static/app/is_app_one/graph.png" /></td>
<td>
<p>Lorem ipsum ...</p>
<p>Nulla ut congue ...</p>
<p>Etiam pharetra ...</p>
</td>
</tr>
</table>
</html>
</row>
<dashboard>
```

The XML would render this panel:

This approach has the advantage that no other files are needed. The disadvantage, however, is that you cannot build the HTML document in an external program and upload it untouched.

You could also reference custom CSS using this method by adding classes to application.css, and then referencing those classes in your HTML block.

Using server-side include in a complex dashboard

You can also develop static pages as HTML documents, referencing other files in the same directory. Let's build a slightly more complicated page using `graph.png`, but also a style from `application.css` as follows:

1. Place `graph.png` and `application.css` into a directory.
2. Create a new HTML file. Let's name it `intro.html`.
3. Add any styles for your page to `application.css`.
4. Upload the new HTML file and the modified CSS file.
5. Create the dashboard referencing the HTML file.

Starting with the HTML from our previous example, let's make it a complete document. Move the image to a CSS style and add a class to our text, like this:

```
<html>
<head>
<link rel="stylesheet" type="text/css"
href="application.css" />
</head>
<body>
<table>
<tr>
<td class="graph_image"></td>
<td>
<p class="lorem">Lorem ipsum ...</p>
<p class="lorem">Nulla ut congue ...</p>
<p class="lorem">Etiam pharetra ...</p>
</td>
</tr>
</table>
</body>
</html>
```

Maintaining the classes for the navigation bar, add our page classes to the application CSS, like this:

```
.appHeaderWrapper h1 {
display: none;
}
```

```
.appLogo {
height: 43px;
width: 155px;
padding-right: 5px;
float: left;
background: url(appLogo.png) no-repeat 0 0;
}
.appHeaderWrapper {
background: #612f00;
}
.lorem {
font-style:italic;
background: #CCCCCC;
padding: 5px;
}
.graph_image {
height: 306px;
width: 235px;
background: url(graph.png) no-repeat 0 0;
}
```

We can now open this file in a browser. Clipped for brevity, the page looks like this:

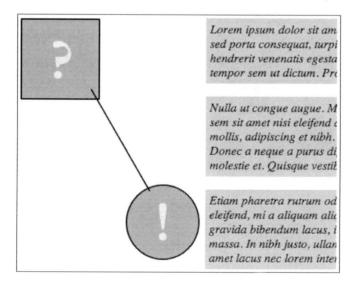

To include this external HTML document, we have to use advanced XML. We will cover advanced XML more thoroughly in *Chapter 9, Building Advanced Dashboards*.

First, build a minimal dashboard like this:

```
<view template="dashboard.html">
<label>Included</label>
<!-- chrome here -->
<module
name="ServerSideInclude"
layoutPanel="panel_row1_col1">
<param name="src">intro.html</param>
</module>
</view>
```

All simple XML dashboards are converted to advanced XML behind the scenes. We will take advantage of this later.

Now upload our files as we did earlier under the *Customizing the launcher icon* section. The page should render nearly identically as the file did in the browser, with the addition of the border around the panel:

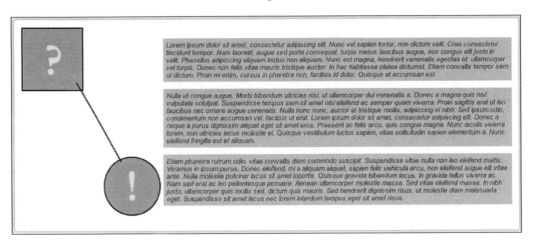

A few things to note from this overly simplified example are as follows:

1. Your CSS classes may end up merging with styles included by Splunk in unexpected ways. Using the developer tools in any modern browser will help greatly.

2. The navigation and dashboard title were excluded for brevity. They would normally go where we see `<!-- chrome here -->`. This is interesting because there are cases where you would want to exclude the navigation; something that cannot be done with simple XML.

3. The static files, such as `application.css`, can be edited directly on the filesystem, and the changes will be seen immediately. This is not true of the dashboard XML file. We will cover these locations later in the *App directory structure* section.

Object permissions

Almost all objects in Splunk have permissions associated with them. The permissions essentially have the following three options:

- **Private**: Only the user that created the search can see or use the object, and only in the app where it was created

- **App**: All users that have permission to read an object may use that object in the context of the app that contains the object

- **Global**: All users that have permission to read an object may use that object in any app

How permissions affect navigation

To see a visible instance of permissions in action, let's look at our navigation.

In our application, `Implementing Splunk App One`, our navigation looks like this:

If you recall the navigation XML which we built earlier, this menu is controlled by the following XML:

```
<collection label="Views">
<view source="unclassified" />
</collection>
```

There is no mention of any of these dashboards. This is where they are coming from:

- **Advanced Charting** is inherited from the **Search** app. Its permissions are set to Global.

- **Included** is from this app. Its permissions are set to **App**.

- Google Maps is inherited from the **Google Maps** app. Its permissions are set to **Global**.

If the permissions of a dashboard or search are set to **Private**, a green dot appears next to the name in the navigation.

Dashboards or searches shared from other apps can also be referenced by name.

For example, most apps, including ours, will include a link to flashtimeline, which appears as **Search**, the label in that dashboard's XML:

```
<view name="flashtimeline" />
```

This allows us to use this dashboard in the context of our app, so that all the other objects that are scoped solely to our app will be available.

How permissions affect other objects

Almost everything you create in Splunk has permissions. To see all objects, navigate to **Settings | All configurations**.

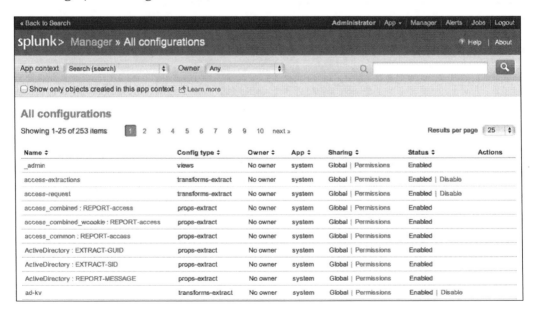

Everything with the value system in the **App** column, ships with Splunk. These items live in the `$SPLUNK_HOME/etc/system` directory. We will cover these different configuration types in *Chapter 11, Configuring Splunk*, but the important takeaway is that the **Sharing** settings affect nearly everything.

When you create new objects and configurations, it is important to share all related objects. For instance, in *Chapter 7, Extending Search*, we created lookups.

It is important that all three parts of the lookup definition are shared appropriately, or users will be presented with error messages.

Correcting permission problems

If you see errors about permissions, it is more than likely that some object still has **Sharing** set to **Private**, or is shared at the **App** level but needs to be **Global**.

A common point of confusion is when an app is created within the Splunk search app, but with the expectation that they will be visible within another app.

Follow these steps to find the object:

1. Navigate to **Settings | All configurations**.
2. Change **App** context to **All**.
3. Sort by using the **Sharing** status. Click twice so that **Private** objects come to the top.
4. If there are too many items to look through, filter the list by adding terms to the search field in the upper-right corner, or changing the **App context** value.
5. Fix the permissions appropriately. In most cases, the permissions you want will look like this:

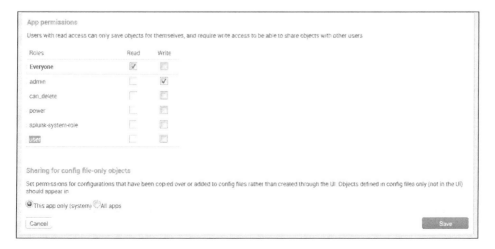

You should choose **All apps** with care. For instance, when building a lookup, it is common to share the lookup table file and lookup definition across all apps. This allows the lookup to be used in searches by other apps. It is less common to share the *Automatic lookup*, as this can affect the performance in other apps in unforeseen ways.

The app directory structure

If you do much beyond building searches and dashboards, sooner or later you will need to edit files in the filesystem directly. All apps live in `$SPLUNK_HOME/etc/apps/`. On Unix systems, the default installation directory is `/opt/splunk`. On Windows, the default installation directory is `C:\Program Files\Splunk`.

This is the value that `$SPLUNK_HOME` will inherit on startup.

Stepping through the most common directories, we have:

- **appserver**: This directory contains files that are served by the Splunk web app. The files that we uploaded in earlier sections of this chapter are stored in `appserver/static`.

- **bin**: This is where command scripts belong. These scripts are then referenced in `commands.conf`. This is also a common location for scripted inputs to live, though they can live anywhere.

- **default and local**: These two directories contain the vast majority of the configurations that make up an app.

    We will discuss these configurations and how they merge in *Chapter 11, Configuring Splunk*.

    Here is a brief look:

    ○ Newly created, unshared objects live in:

        `$SPLUNK_HOME/etc/users/USERNAME/APPNAME/local`.

    ○ Once an object is shared at the **App** or **Global** level, the object is moved to the following path:

        `$SPLUNK_HOME/etc/APPNAME/local`.

    ○ Files in the local directory take precedence over its equivalent value in default.

    ○ Dashboards live in `(default|local)/data/ui/views`.

    ○ Navigations lives in `(default|local)/data/ui/nav`.

When editing files by hand, my general rule of thumb is to place configurations in the local directory unless the app is going to be redistributed. We'll discuss this in more detail in the *Adding your app to Splunkbase* section.

- **lookups**: Lookup files belong in this directory. They are then referenced in (default|local)/transforms.conf.

- **metadata**: The files default.meta and local.meta in this directory tell Splunk how configurations in this app should be shared. It is generally much easier to edit these settings through the **Settings** interface.

Let's look at the contents of our is_app_one app, which we created earlier:

```
appserver/static/appIcon.png
appserver/static/application.css
appserver/static/appLogo.png
appserver/static/graph.png
appserver/static/intro.html
bin/README
default/app.conf
default/data/ui/nav/default.xml
default/data/ui/views/README
local/app.conf
local/data/ui/nav/default.xml
local/data/ui/views/errors.xml
local/data/ui/views/included.xml
local/savedsearches.conf
local/viewstates.conf
metadata/default.meta
metadata/local.meta
```

The file metadata/default.meta, and all files in default/, were provided in the template app. We created all the other files. With the exception of the PNG files, all files are plain text.

Adding your app to Splunkbase

Splunkbase (https://apps.splunk.com/) is a wonderful community-supported site that Splunk put together for users and Splunk employees alike to share the Splunk apps. The apps on Splunkbase are a mix of fully realized apps, add-ons of various sorts, and just example code.

Preparing your app

Before we upload our app, we need to make sure that all our objects are shared properly, move our files to default, and configure `app.conf`.

Confirming sharing settings

To see sharing settings for all our objects, navigate to **Settings | All configurations**, and set the **App context** option:

In the case of a self-contained app like ours, all objects should probably be set to **App** under **Sharing**. If you are building an app to share lookups or commands, the value should be **Global**.

Cleaning up our directories

When you upload an app, you should move everything out of `local` and into `default`. This is important because all changes that a user makes will be stored in `local`.

When your app is upgraded, all files in the app will be replaced, and the user's changes will be lost. The following Unix commands illustrate what needs to be done:

1. First, let's copy our app to another location, perhaps `/tmp`:

   ```
   cp -r $SPLUNK_HOME/etc/apps/is_app_one /tmp/
   ```

2. Next, let's move everything from `local` to `default`. In the case of `.xml` files, we can simply move the files; but `.conf` files are a little more complicated, and we need to merge them manually. The following command does this:

   ```
   cd /tmp/is_app_one
   mv local/data/ui/nav/*.xml default/data/ui/nav/
   mv local/data/ui/views/*.xml default/data/ui/views/
   #move conf files, but don't replace conf files in default
   mv -n local/*conf default/
   ```

3. Now we need to merge any .conf files that remain in `local`. The only
    configuration we have left is `app.conf`:

```
local/app.conf default/app.conf
[ui]
[launcher]
[package]
check_for_updates = 1
[install]
is_configured = 0
[ui]
is_visible = 1
label = Implementing Splunk
App One
[launcher]
author =
description =
version = 1.0
```

Configuration merging is additive, with any values from `local` added
to the values in `default`. In this case, the merged configuration would
be as follows:

```
[install]
is_configured = 0
[ui]
Working with Apps
[ 198 ]
is_visible = 1
label = Implementing Splunk App One
[launcher]
author =
description =
version = 1.0
[package]
check_for_updates = 1
```

4. Place this merged configuration in `default/app.conf` and delete `local/`
    `app.conf`.

We will cover configuration merging extensively in *Chapter 11, Configuring Splunk*.

Packaging your app

To package an app, we need to be sure that there are a few values in `default/app.conf`, and only then build the archive.

First, edit `default/app.conf` like this:

```
[install]
is_configured = 0
build = 1
[ui]
is_visible = 1
label = Implementing Splunk App One
[launcher]
author = My name
description = My great app!
version = 1.0
[package]
check_for_updates = 1
id = is_app_one
```

The identifier build is used in all URLs, so it should be incremented to defeat browser caching and (the identifier) id should be a unique value in Splunkbase—you will be alerted if the value is not unique.

Next, we need to build a tar file compressed with `gzip`. With a modern version of `tar`, the command is simply the following:

```
cd /tmp
tar -czvf is_app_one.tgz is_app_one
#optionally rename as spl
mv is_app_one.tgz is_app_one.spl
```

The Splunk documentation (`http://docs.splunk.com/Documentation/Splunklatest/AdvancedDev/PackageApp`) covers this extensively, including Mac and Windows procedures.

Uploading your app

Now that we have our archive, all we have to do is send it up to Splunkbase. In version 6.2, submitting Apps is done by pointing your browser to `https://apps.splunk.com/` and following the directions there.

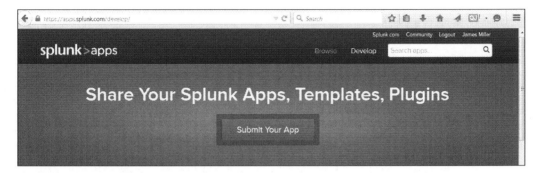

If your app meets the rigid criteria and once the Splunk personnel approve your app, it will appear in Splunkbase, ready for others to download.

Summary

In this chapter, we covered installing, building, customizing, and sharing apps. Apps are a loose concept in Splunk, with many different purposes served by a simple directory of files. Hopefully, we have covered the basics well enough for you to get started on your own great apps. In later chapters, we will build even more complicated object types, as well as custom code to extend Splunk in unique ways.

In the next chapter, we will dig into advanced dashboards, covering what can be done with Splunk alone, and what can be done with the help of a few popular apps.

9
Building Advanced Dashboards

In *Chapter 5, Simple XML Dashboards*, we covered building dashboards using simple XML. We first used the wizards provided in Splunk and then edited the resultant XML code. When you reach the limits of what can be accomplished with simple XML, one option is to dive into Splunk's advanced XML.

In this chapter, we will explore advanced XML practices while also discussing the following topics:

- The pipe symbol
- Using `top` to show common field values
- Using `stats` to aggregate values
- Using `chart` to turn data
- Using `timechart` to show values over time
- Working with fields

Reasons for working with advanced XML

Here are a few reasons to use advanced XML:

- **More control over layout**: With advanced XML, you have better control over where form elements and chromes appear and somewhat improved control over the placement of the output.
- **Custom drilldowns**: It is only possible to create custom drilldowns from tables and charts using advanced XML.

- **Access to more parameters**: The modules in simple XML actually use advanced XML modules, but many parameters are not exposed. Sometimes, the desire is actually to disable features, and this is only possible using advanced XML.

- **Access to more modules**: There are many modules that are not available when we are using simple XML, for example, the search bar itself. All extra modules provided by the apps at Splunkbase, for example, Google Maps, are for use in advanced XML.

Reasons for not working with advanced XML

There are also a number of reasons not to work with advanced XML:

- **Steep learning curve**: Depending on what technologies you are comfortable working with and, possibly, on how well the rest of this chapter is written, the learning curve for advanced XML can be steep.

- **No direct control over HTML**: If there is a particular HTML that you want to produce from search results, this may not be as simple as you had hoped. Short of writing your own module, you must work within the bounds of the options provided to the existing modules, modify CSS with application. CSS, or modify the HTML code using JavaScript.

- **No direct control over logic**: If you need specific things to happen when you click on specific table cells, particularly based on other values in the same row, this can only be accomplished by modifying the document using JavaScript. This is possible, but it is not well documented. Examples can be found at http://splunkbase.com, both in answer posts and sample applications. Check out *customBehaviors* in the third-party app called **Sideview Utils** for an alternative.

If you have specific layout or logic requirements, you can be better served using one of the Splunk APIs available at http://dev.splunk.com and writing applications in your favorite language.

The development process

When building dashboards, my approach is generally as follows:

1. Create the required queries.

2. Add the queries to a simple XML dashboard. Use the GUI tools to tweak the dashboard as much as possible. If possible, finish all graphical changes at this stage.

3. If form elements are needed, convert the simple XML dashboard to a form. If possible, make all logic work with simple XML.

4. Convert the simple XML dashboard to an advanced XML dashboard. There is no reverse conversion possible, so this should be done as late as possible and only if needed.

5. Edit the advanced XML dashboard accordingly.

The idea is to take advantage of the Splunk GUI tools as much as possible, letting the simple XML conversion process add all of the advanced XML that you would have to otherwise find yourself. We covered steps 1–3 in the previous chapters. Step 4 is covered in the *Converting simple XML to advanced XML* section.

The advanced XML structure

Before we dig into the modules provided, let's look at the structure of XML itself and cover a couple of concepts.

The tag structure of an advanced XML document is essentially as follows:

```
view
module
param
...
module
...
```

The main concept of Splunk's XML structure is that the effects of modules flow downstream to child modules.

This is a vital concept to understand. The XML structure has almost nothing to do with layout and everything to do with the flow of data.

Let's look at the following simple example:

```
<view
template="dashboard.html">
<label>Chapter 9, Example 1</label>
<module
name="HiddenSearch"
layoutPanel="panel_row1_col1"
autoRun="True">
```

```
<param name="earliest">-99d</param>
<param name="search">error | top user</param>
<module name="SimpleResultsTable"></module>
</module>
</view>
```

This document produces the following sparse dashboard with one panel:

	user ⬍	count ⬍	percent ⬍
1	ronnie	114372	10.007525
2	tuck	114352	10.005775
3	shelby	114324	10.003325
4	jarde	114310	10.002100
5	lou	114294	10.000700
6	paige	114266	9.998250
7	steve	114256	9.997375
8	mary	114242	9.996150
9	natile	114238	9.995800
10	nanette	114206	9.993000

Let's look through this example line by line:

- `<view`: This opens the outer tag. This tag begins all advanced XML dashboards.
- `template="dashboard.html">`: This sets the base HTML template. Dashboard layout templates are stored in the following path:

    `$SPLUNK_HOME/share/splunk/search_mrsparkle/templates/view/`

    Among other things, the templates define the panels available for use in `layoutPanel`.

- `<label>Chapter 9, Example 1</label>`: This sets the label used for navigation.
- `<module`: This begins our first module declaration.
- `name="HiddenSearch"`: This is the name of the module to use. `HiddenSearch` runs a search but displays nothing, relying instead on child modules to render the output.

- `layoutPanel="panel_row1_col1"`: This states where in the dashboard to display our panel. It seems strange to give this attribute to a module that displays nothing, but `layoutPanel` must be specified on every immediate child of `view`. See the *Understanding layoutPanel* section for more details.

- `autoRun="True">`: Without this attribute, the search does not run when the dashboard loads and, instead, waits for user interaction from form elements. Since we have no form elements, we need this attribute to see the results.

- `<param name="earliest">-99d</param>`: It is very important to specify a value at the earliest as the query will, by default, run over. All the `param` values affect only the module tag they are nested directly inside.

- `<param name="search">error | top user</param>`: This is the actual query to run.

- `<module name="SimpleResultsTable"></module>`: This module simply displays a table of the events produced by a parent module. Since there are no `param` tags specified, the defaults for this module are used.

- `</module>`: Close the `HiddenSearch` module. This is required for valid XML, but it also implies that the scope of influence of this module is closed. To reiterate, only the downstream modules of the `HiddenSearch` module receives the events it produces.

- `</view>`: This closes the document.

This is a very simple dashboard. It lacks navigation, form elements, job status, and drilldowns. Adding all of these things is initially somewhat complicated to understand. Luckily, you can build a dashboard in simple XML, convert it to advanced XML, and then modify the provided XML as needed.

Converting simple XML to advanced XML

Let's go back to one of the dashboards we created in *Chapter 5*, *Simple XML Dashboards*, `errors_user_form`.

We built this before our app, so it still lives in the **Search** app.

Just to refresh your memory, the simple XML code behind this dashboard looks as follows:

```
<?xml version='1.0' encoding='utf-8'?>
<form>
<fieldset>
<input type="text" token="user">
<label>User</label>
</input>
```

```
<input type="time" />
</fieldset>
<label>Errors User Form</label>
<row>
<chart>
<searchString>
sourcetype="impl_splunk_gen" loglevel=error user="$user$" | timechart
count as "Error count" by network
</searchString>
<title>
Dashboard - Errors - errors by network timechart
</title>
<option name="charting.chart">line</option>
</chart>
</row>
<row>
<chart>
<searchString>
sourcetype="impl_splunk_gen" loglevel=error user="$user$" | bucket
bins=10 req_time | stats count by req_time
</searchString>
<title>
Error count by req_times
</title>
<option name="charting.chart">pie</option>
</chart>
<chart>
<searchString>
sourcetype="impl_splunk_gen" loglevel=error user="$user$" | stats
count by logger
</searchString>
<title>Errors by logger</title>
<option name="charting.chart">pie</option>
</chart>
</row>
<row>
<event>
<searchString>
sourcetype="impl_splunk_gen" loglevel=error user="$user$"
</searchString>
<title>Error events</title>
<option name="count">10</option>
<option name="displayRowNumbers">true</option>
<option name="maxLines">10</option>
```

```
<option name="segmentation">outer</option>
<option name="softWrap">true</option>
</event>
</row>
</form>
```

In simple XML, the layout and logic flow are tied together. Before simple XML is rendered to the user, Splunk first dynamically converts it to advanced XML in memory. We can access advanced XML by appending `?showsource= advanced` to any URL, as follows:

```
http://localhost:8000/en-US/app/is_app_one/errors?showsource=advanced
```

This produces a page (somewhat different than the earlier version of Splunk when you used `showsource=1`) similar to this:

View source: errors (None)

Properties

- *label*: None
- *isVisible*: True
- *stylesheet*: None
- *displayView*: None
- *hasRowGrouping*: False
- *refresh*: -1
- *template*: dashboard.html
- *objectMode*: SimpleDashboard
- *onunloadCancelJobs*: True
- *autoCancelInterval*: 90

Module tree

Collapse all | Expand all | Toggle all

- AccountBar_0_0_0 *appHeader*
  - AccountBar config
- AppBar_0_0_1 *navigationHeader*
  - AppBar config
- Message_0_0_2 *messaging*
  - Message config
- DashboardTitleBar_0_0_3 *viewHeader*
  - DashboardTitleBar config
- Message_1_0_4 *navigationHeader*
  - Message config

This is followed by a textbox containing raw XML, as shown here:

```
XML source

<view autoCancelInterval="90" isVisible="true" objectMode="SimpleDashboard" onunloadCancelJobs="true"
refresh="-1" template="dashboard.html">
  <label/>
  <module name="AccountBar" layoutPanel="appHeader"/>
  <module name="AppBar" layoutPanel="navigationHeader"/>
  <module name="Message" layoutPanel="messaging">
    <param name="filter">*</param>
    <param name="clearOnJobDispatch">False</param>
    <param name="maxSize">1</param>
  </module>
  <module name="DashboardTitleBar" layoutPanel="viewHeader"/>
  <module name="Message" layoutPanel="navigationHeader">
    <param name="level">warn</param>
    <param name="filter">splunk.search.job</param>
    <param name="clearOnJobDispatch">True</param>
    <param name="maxSize">1</param>
  </module>
</view>
```

An abbreviated version of the advanced XML version of `errors_user_form` follows:

```
<view
... template="dashboard.html">
<label>Errors User Form</label>
<module name="AccountBar" layoutPanel="appHeader"/>
<module name="AppBar" layoutPanel="navigationHeader"/>
<module name="Message" layoutPanel="messaging">
...<module name="Message" layoutPanel="messaging">
...<module name="TitleBar" layoutPanel="viewHeader">
...<module name="ExtendedFieldSearch" layoutPanel="viewHeader">
<param name="replacementMap">
<param name="arg">
<param name="user"/>
</param>
</param>
<param name="field">User</param>
<param name="intention">
... <module name="TimeRangePicker">
<param name="searchWhenChanged">False</param>
<module name="SubmitButton">
<param name="allowSoftSubmit">True</param>
<param name="label">Search</param>
<module
```

```
name="HiddenSearch"
layoutPanel="panel_row1_col1"
group="Dashboard - Errors - errors by network timechart"
autoRun="False">
<param name="search">
sourcetype="impl_splunk_gen"
loglevel=error user="$user$"
| timechart count as "Error count" by network
</param>
<param name="groupLabel">
Dashboard - Errors - errors by network timechart
</param>
<module name="ViewstateAdapter">
<param name="suppressionList">
<item>charting.chart</item>
</param>
<module name="HiddenFieldPicker">
<param name="strictMode">True</param>
<module name="JobProgressIndicator">
<module name="EnablePreview">
<param name="enable">True</param>
<param name="display">False</param>
<module name="HiddenChartFormatter">
<param name="charting.chart">line</param>
<module name="JSChart">
<param name="width">100%</param>
<module name="Gimp"/>
<module name="ConvertToDrilldownSearch">
<module name="ViewRedirector">
... </module>
<module name="ViewRedirectorLink">
... </module>
<module
name="HiddenSearch"
layoutPanel="panel_row2_col1"
group="Error count by req_times"
autoRun="False">
<param name="search">
sourcetype="impl_splunk_gen" loglevel=error
user="$user$"
| bucket bins=10 req_time | stats count by req_time
</param>
<param name="groupLabel">Error count by req_times</param>
... </module>
```

```
<module
name="HiddenSearch"
layoutPanel="panel_row2_col2"
group="Errors by logger"
autoRun="False">
<param name="search">
sourcetype="impl_splunk_gen"
loglevel=error user="$user$"
| stats count by logger
</param>
<param name="groupLabel">Errors by logger</param>
... </module>
<module
name="HiddenSearch"
layoutPanel="panel_row3_col1"
group="Error events"
autoRun="False">
<param name="search">
sourcetype="impl_splunk_gen"
loglevel=error
user="$user$"
</param>
<param name="groupLabel">Error events</param>
<module name="ViewstateAdapter">
... <module name="HiddenFieldPicker">
... <module name="JobProgressIndicator"/>
<module name="Paginator">
<param name="count">10</param>
... <module name="EventsViewer">
... <module name="Gimp"/>
... </module>
...
</view>
```

This XML code is more verbose than we actually need, but, luckily, it is easier to delete code than to create it.

Module logic flow

The main concept of nested modules is that parent (upstream) modules affect child (downstream) modules. Looking at the first panel, the full module flow is as follows:

```
<module name="ExtendedFieldSearch">
<module name="TimeRangePicker">
```

```
<module name="SubmitButton">
<module name="HiddenSearch">
<module name="ViewstateAdapter">
<module name="HiddenFieldPicker">
<module name="JobProgressIndicator">
<module name="EnablePreview">
<module name="HiddenChartFormatter">
<module name="JSChart">
<module name="ConvertToDrilldownSearch">
<module name="ViewRedirector">
<module name="ViewRedirectorLink">
```

A reference to the modules installed in your instance of Splunk is available at `/modules`. In my case, the full URL is as follows:

`http://localhost:8000/en-US/modules`

Let's step through these modules in turn and discuss what they each accomplish:

- **ExtendedFieldSearch**: This provides a textbox for entry. The parameters for this module are complicated and represent arguably the most complicated aspect of advanced XML—intentions. Intentions affect child modules, specifically `HiddenSearch`. We will this cover in the *Using intentions* section.

- **TimeRangePicker**: This provides the standard time picker. It affects child `HiddenSearch` modules that do not have times specified either using `param` values or in the query itself. The precedence of times used in a query is as follows:

    ○ Times specified in the query itself

    ○ Times specified via the earliest and latest `param` values to the search module

    ○ A value provided by `TimeRangePicker`

- **SubmitButton**: This draws the **Search** button and fires off any child search modules when clicked on.

- **HiddenSearch**: As we saw before, this runs a query and produces events for downstream modules. In this case, `autoRun` is set to `false` so that the query waits for the user.

- **ViewstateAdapter**: A viewstate describes what settings a user has selected in the GUI, for instance, sort order, page size, or chart type. Anytime you change a chart setting or pick a time range, you create a viewstate that is saved by Splunk. This module is used to access an existing viewstate or to suppress specific viewstate settings. By suppressing specific settings, the default or specified values of child modules will be used instead. This module is rarely needed unless you are using a saved search with an associated viewstate.

- **HiddenFieldPicker**: This module limits what fields are accessible to downstream modules. This is useful when we run a query that produces many fields but only certain fields are needed. This affects the fields shown below events in an events listing or the columns displayed in a table view. This module is rarely needed.

- **JobProgressIndicator**: This module displays a progress bar until the job is completed. In this case, because of the placement of the module in XML, it appears above the results. This module does not affect downstream modules, so it can be listed on its own.

- **EnablePreview**: This module allows you to specify whether searches should refresh with incomplete results while the query is running.

  The default appears to be true for Splunk-provided modules, but this module allows you to control this behavior. This module does not affect downstream modules, so it can be listed on its own.

  Disabling the preview can improve the performance dramatically but provides no information until the query is complete, which is less visually appealing, particularly during a long-running query.

- **HiddenChartFormatter**: This module is where the chart settings are specified. These settings affect any child modules that draw charts.

- **JSChart**: This draws a chart using JavaScript. Prior to Splunk 4.3, all charts were drawn using Flash. The `FlashChart` module is still included for backward compatibility.

- **ConvertToDrilldownSearch**: This module takes the values from a click on a parent module and produces a query based on the query that produced the results. This usually works, but not always, depending on the complexity of the query. We will build a custom drilldown search later.

- **ViewRedirector**: This module accepts the query from its upstream module and redirects the user to use `viewTarget` with the query specified in the URL. Usually, `flashtimeline` is specified as `viewTarget param`, but it could be any dashboard. The query affects a `HiddenSearch` or `SearchBar` module.

- **ViewRedirectorLink**: This module sends the user to a new search page with the search results for this module.

Thinking about what we have seen in this flow, we could say that modules can do the following things:

- Generate events
- Modify a query
- Modify the behavior of a downstream module
- Display an element on the dashboard
- Handle actions produced by clicks

It is also possible for a module to do the following:

- Post process the events produced by a query
- Add custom JavaScript to the dashboard

Understanding layoutPanel

In an advanced XML dashboard, the value of the `layoutPanel` attribute determines which panel a module is drawn to. This separation of logic and layout can be useful—for instance, allowing you to reuse data generated by a query with multiple modules—but displays the results on different parts of the page.

A few rules about this attribute are as follows:

- The `layoutPanel` attribute must appear on all immediate children of `<view>`.
- The `layoutPanel` attribute can appear on descendant child module tags.
- If a module does not have a `layoutPanel` attribute, it will inherit the value from the closest upstream module that does.
- Modules that have visible output are added to their respective `layoutPanel` attributes in the order they appear in the XML.
- Modules flow in the panel they are placed. Most modules take the entire width of the panel, but some do not, and flow from left to right before wrapping.

Looking through our XML, we find these elements with the `layoutPanel` attribute, as shown here:

```
<module name="AccountBar" layoutPanel="appHeader"/>
<module name="AppBar" layoutPanel="navigationHeader"/>
<module name="Message" layoutPanel="messaging">
<module name="TitleBar" layoutPanel="viewHeader">
<module name="ExtendedFieldSearch" layoutPanel="viewHeader">
<module name="TimeRangePicker">
<module name="SubmitButton">
<module name="HiddenSearch" layoutPanel="panel_row1_col1">...
<module name="HiddenSearch" layoutPanel="panel_row2_col1">...
<module name="HiddenSearch" layoutPanel="panel_row2_col2">...
<module name="HiddenSearch" layoutPanel="panel_row3_col1">
...
```

The first set of `layoutPanel` values are panels included in the chrome of the page. This displays the account information, navigation, and messages to the user. The second set of modules makes up the title and form elements. Notice that `TimeRangePicker` and `SubmitButton` have no `layoutPanel` value but inherit from `ExtendedFieldSearch`.

The results panels all begin with a `HiddenSearch` module. All of the children of each of these modules inherit this `layoutPanel` value.

Panel placement

For your dashboard panels, you will almost always use a `layoutPanel` value of the `panel_rowX_colY` form.

A simple visualization of the layout produced by our modules would look similar to the following image:

In our simple XML version of this dashboard, the layout was tied directly to the order of the XML, as shown here:

```
<row>
<chart></chart>
</row>
<row>
```

```
<chart></chart>
<chart></chart>
</row>
<row>
<event></event>
</row>
```

Just to reiterate, the simple XML structure translates to the following code:

```
<row>
<chart></chart> == panel_row1_col1
</row>
<row>
<chart></chart> == panel_row2_col1
<chart></chart> == panel_row2_col2
</row>
<row>
<event></event> == panel_row3_col1
</row>
```

There is another extension available, _grp1, that allows you to create columns inside a panel. We will try that out in the *Creating a custom drilldown* section later.

Reusing a query

One example of separating layout from data would be using a single query to populate both a table and a chart.

The advanced XML for this could look like the following code:

```
<view template="dashboard.html">
<label>Chapter 9 - Reusing a query</label>
<module
name="StaticContentSample"
layoutPanel="panel_row1_col1">
<param name="text">Text above</param>
</module>
<module
name="HiddenSearch"
layoutPanel="panel_row1_col1"
autoRun="True">
<param name="search">
sourcetype="impl_splunk_gen" loglevel=error | top user
</param>
<param name="earliest">-99d</param>
```

```
<module name="HiddenChartFormatter">
<param name="charting.chart">pie</param>
<module name="JSChart"></module>
<module
name="StaticContentSample"
layoutPanel="panel_row1_col1">
<!-- this layoutPanel is unneeded, but harmless -->
<param name="text">Text below</param>
</module>
</module>
<module name="SimpleResultsTable"
layoutPanel="panel_row1_col2"></module>
</module>
</view>
```

This XML renders a dashboard similar to the following screenshot:

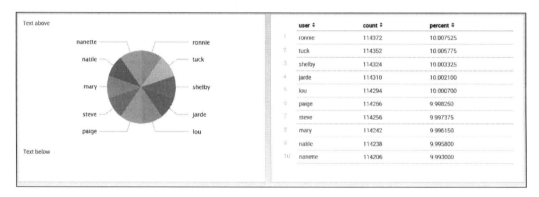

There are some things to notice in this XML:

- The data produced by `HiddenSearch` is used by both child modules.
- JSChart inherits `layoutPanel="panel_row1_col1"` from `HiddenSearch`.
- `SimpleResultsTable` has its own `layoutPanel` attribute set to `panel_row1_col2`, so the table draws to the right.
- Both `StaticContentSample` modules specify `layoutPanel="panel_row1_col1"` and, therefore, appear in the same panel as the chart. Even though they are at different depths in the XML, the order drawn follows the order seen in the XML.

Using intentions

Intentions allow you to affect downstream searches using values provided by other modules, for instance, form fields or the results of a click. There are a number of available intention types, but we will cover the two most common ones, `stringreplace` and `addterm`. You can see examples of other types of intentions in the UI Examples app available at `http://splunkbase.com`.

stringreplace

This is the most common intention to use and maps directly to the only available action in simple XML—variable replacement. Let's look at our search field from our advanced XML example:

```
<module name="ExtendedFieldSearch" layoutPanel="viewHeader">
<param name="replacementMap">
<param name="arg">
<param name="user"/>
</param>
</param>
<param name="field">User</param>
<param name="intention">
<param name="name">stringreplace</param>
<param name="arg">
<param name="user">
<param name="fillOnEmpty">True</param>
</param>
</param>
</param>
```

Stepping through the `param` instances, we have the following terms and their descriptions:

- `field`: This is the label for the field displayed in the dashboard.

- `replacementMap`: This parameter names the variable that the `ExtendedFieldSearch` module is creating. I have been told that the nested nature means nothing, and we should simply copy and paste the entire block of XML, changing nothing but the value of the deepest `param` tag—in this case to `user`.

- `intention`: Intentions have specific structures that build blocks of query from a structured XML. In the case of `stringreplace` (which is the most common use case), we can essentially copy the entire XML and, once again, change nothing but the value of the third-level `param`, which is currently `user`. The `fillOnEmpty` value determines whether to make the substitution when the `user` variable is empty.

- All of this code simply tells us to replace `$user$` in any searches with the value of the input field. Our first `HiddenSearch` value looks like the following:

```
<module name="HiddenSearch" ...
<param name="search">
sourcetype="impl_splunk_gen"
loglevel=error user="$user$"
| timechart count as "Error count" by network
</param>
```

The value of `$user$` will be replaced and the query will be run.

If you want to see exactly what is happening, you can insert a `SearchBar` module as a child of the form elements, and it will render the resulting query. For example, see the code of the `drilldown_chart1` dashboard in the *UI examples app* available at `http://splunkbase.com`.

addterm

This intention is useful for adding search terms to a query with or without user interaction. For example, let's say you always want to ensure that a particular value of the field source is queried. You can then modify the query that will be run, appending a search term. Here is an example: `https://epic.packtpub.com/index.php?action=DetailView&module=oss_Chapters&record=498f4042-7a34-1cff-c73e-547c2ca548f9&offset=2&stamp=143651240309334330e` from the `advanced_lister_with_` dashboard.

The searchbar in the *UI examples app* is available at `http://splunkbase.com`. The following code encapsulates this discussion:

```
<module name="HiddenIntention">
<param name="intention">
<param name="name">addterm</param>
<param name="arg">
<param name="source">*metrics.log</param>
</param>
<!-- tells the addterm intention to put our term in the first search
clause no matter what. -->
```

```
<param name="flags"><list>indexed</list></param>
</param>
```

Stepping through the `param` instances, we have the following terms and their descriptions:

- `name`: This parameter sets the type of intention—in this case, `addterm`.
- `arg`: This is used to set the field to add to the query.

  The nested `param` tag sets the fieldname and value to use in the query.

  In this case, `source="*metrics.log"` is added to the query.

  Variables can be used in either the `name` attribute or body of this nested `param` tag. We will see an example of this in the *Creating a custom drilldown* section.

- `flags`: Every example of `addterm` that I can find includes this attribute exactly as written. It essentially says that the term to be added to the search should be added before the first pipe symbol and not at the end of the full query.

  For example, consider the following query:

  ```
  error | top logger
  ```

  This `param` tag would amend our query like this:

  ```
  error source="*metrics.log" | top logger
  ```

Creating a custom drilldown

A drilldown is a query built using values from a previous query. The `ConvertToDrilldownSearch` module will build a query automatically from the table or graph that it is nested inside. Unfortunately, this only works well when the query is fairly simple and when you want to see raw events. To build a custom drilldown, we will combine intentions and the nested nature of modules.

Building a drilldown to a custom query

Looking back at our chart in the *Reusing a query* section, let's build a custom drilldown that shows the top instances of another field when it is clicked on.

Here is an example dashboard that draws a chart and then runs a custom query when clicked on:

```
<view template="dashboard.html">
<label>Chapter 9 - Drilldown to custom query</label>
<!-- chrome -->
```

```
<module
name="HiddenSearch"
layoutPanel="panel_row1_col1"
autoRun="True"
group="Errors by user">
<param name="search">
sourcetype=* loglevel=error | top user
</param>
<param name="earliest">-99d</param>
<!-- draw the chart -->
<module name="HiddenChartFormatter">
<param name="charting.chart">pie</param>
<module name="JSChart">
<!-- nested modules are invoked on click -->
<!-- create a new query -->
<module name="HiddenSearch">
<param name="search">
sourcetype=* loglevel=error
| top logger
</param>
<!-- create an intention using the value from the chart.
Use addterm to add a user field to the query. -->
<module name="ConvertToIntention">
<param name="intention">
<param name="name">addterm</param>
<param name="arg">
<param name="user">$click.value$</param>
</param>
<param name="flags">
<item>indexed</item>
</param>
</param>
<!-- Send the user to flashtimeline
with the new query. -->
<module name="ViewRedirector">
<param name="viewTarget">flashtimeline</param>
</module>
</module>
</module>
</module>
</module>
</module>
</view>
```

Everything should look very similar up until the `JSChart` module. Inside this module, we find a `HiddenSearch` module. The idea is that the downstream modules of display modules are not invoked until the display module is clicked on.

`HiddenSearch` is used to build a query in this case, but instead of the query being handed to a display module, it is handed to the `ViewRedirector` module.

The magical field in all of this is `click.value`. This field contains the value that was clicked on in the chart.

Let's look at what this dashboard renders:

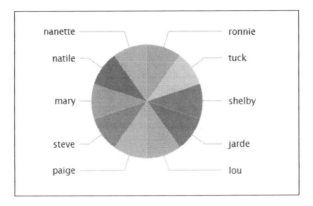

The resulting query when we click on the slice of the pie for the user `shelby` looks like the following screenshot:

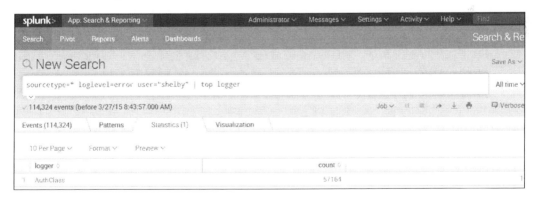

Look back to the *addterm* section for more details about how this intention works.

Building a drilldown to another panel

Another option for a drilldown is to draw a new panel on the same dashboard. This lets you create various drilldowns without redrawing the screen, which might be less jarring to the user. Here is the XML code:

```xml
<?xml version="1.0"?>
<view template="dashboard.html">
<label>Chapter 9 - Drilldown to new graph</label>
<!-- chrome should go here -->
<module
name="HiddenSearch"
layoutPanel="panel_row1_col1"
autoRun="True"
group="Errors by user">
<param name="search">
sourcetype=impl_splunk_gen_more error loglevel=error | top user
</param>
<param name="earliest">-99d</param>
<module name="HiddenChartFormatter">
<param name="charting.chart">pie</param>
<!-- draw the first chart -->
<module name="JSChart">
<!-- the modules inside the chart will wait for
interaction from the user -->
<module name="HiddenSearch">
<param name="earliest">-99d</param>
<param name="search">
Sourcetypeimpl_splunk_gen_more error loglevel=error
user=$user$ | timechart count by logger
</param>
<module name="ConvertToIntention">
<param name="intention">
<param name="name">stringreplace</param>
<param name="arg">
<param name="user">
<param name="value">$click.value$</param>
</param>
</param>
</param>
<!-- print a header above the new chart -->
<module name="SimpleResultsHeader">
<param name="entityName">results</param>
<param name="headerFormat">
Errors by logger for $click.value$
```

```
</param>
</module>
<!-- draw the chart. We have not specified another
layoutPanel, so it will appear below the first
chart -->
<module name="HiddenChartFormatter">
<param name="charting.chart">area</param>
<param name="chart.stackMode">stacked</param>
<module name="JSChart"/>
</module>
</module>
</module>
</module>
</module>
</module>
</view>
```

Here's what the dashboard looks like after clicking on shelby in the pie chart:

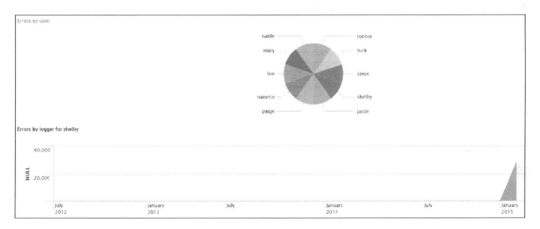

Building a drilldown to multiple panels using HiddenPostProcess

Taking the last dashboard further, let's build a number of panels from a single custom drilldown query. As we covered in *Chapter 5, Simple XML Dashboards*, search results can be post processed, allowing you to use the same query results in multiple ways. In advanced XML, this is accomplished by using the HiddenPostProcess module.

We will also add the chrome for our first complete dashboard. Here is an abbreviated example. The complete dashboard is in the `Chapter9_drilldown_to_new_graph_with_postprocess.xml` file in the `Implementing Splunk App One` app:

```
<view template="dashboard.html">
<Label>Chapter 9 - Drilldown to new graph with postprocess</label>
<!-- The chrome at the top of the dashboard
containing navigation and the app header -->
<module name="AccountBar" layoutPanel="appHeader"/>
<module name="AppBar" layoutPanel="navigationHeader"/>
<module name="Message" layoutPanel="messaging">
<param name="filter">*</param>
<param name="clearOnJobDispatch">False</param>
<param name="maxSize">1</param>
</module>
<module name="DashboardTitleBar" layoutPanel="viewHeader"/>
<module name="Message" layoutPanel="navigationHeader">
<param name="filter">splunk.search.job</param>
<param name="clearOnJobDispatch">True</param>
<param name="maxSize">1</param>
<param name="level">warn</param>
</module>
<! -- Begin our initial search
which will populate our pie chart -->
<module
name="HiddenSearch" layoutPanel="panel_row1_col1"
autoRun="True" group="Errors by user">
<param name="search">
sourcetype="impl_splunk_gen" loglevel=error | top user
</param>
<param name="earliest">-99d</param>
<module name="HiddenChartFormatter">
<param name="charting.chart">pie</param>
<module name="JSChart">
<!-- Initially, only the pie chart will be drawn
After a click on a user wedge, this nested query will run -->
<module name="HiddenSearch">
<param name="earliest">-24h</param>
<param name="search">
sourcetype="impl_splunk_gen" loglevel=error
user="$user$" | bucket span=30m _time
| stats count by logger _time
</param>
<module name="ConvertToIntention">
```

```
<param name="intention">
<param name="name">stringreplace</param>
<param name="arg">
<param name="user">
<param name="value">$click.value$</param>
...
<!-- The remaining modules are downstream from the pie chart
and are invoked when a pie wedge is clicked -->
<module name="SimpleResultsHeader"
layoutPanel="panel_row2_col1">
<param name="entityName">results</param>
<param name="headerFormat">
Errors by logger for $click.value$
</param>
</module>
<!-- The SingleValue modules -->
<module name="HiddenPostProcess">
<param name="search">
stats sum(count) as count by logger
| sort -count | head 1
| eval f=logger + " is most common (" + count + ")" |
table f </param>
<module name="SingleValue"
layoutPanel="panel_row2_col1"></module>
</module>
...
<!-- The chart -->
<module name="HiddenPostProcess">
<param name="search">
timechart span=30m sum(count) by logger
</param>
<module name="HiddenChartFormatter">
<param name="charting.chart">area</param>
<param name="chart.stackMode">stacked</param>
<module
name="JSChart"
layoutPanel="panel_row4_col1_grp1"/>
</module>
</module>
<!-- The table -->
<module name="HiddenPostProcess">
<param name="search">
stats sum(count) as count by logger
</param>
```

```
<module name="SimpleResultsTable"
layoutPanel="panel_row4_col1_grp2"/>
</module>
...
</module>
</view>
```

This dashboard contains the chrome, which is very useful as it displays the errors in your intentions and query statements.

Let's step through the new queries. The initial query is the same and is shown here:

```
sourcetype="impl_splunk_gen" loglevel=error | top user
```

The next query may seem strange, but there's a good reason for this:

```
sourcetype="impl_splunk_gen" loglevel=error user="$user$"
| bucket span=30m _time
| stats count by logger _time
```

If you look back at *Chapter 6, Advanced Search Examples*, we used buckets and stats to slice events by _time and other fields. This is a convenient way to break down events for post processing, where one or more of the post-process queries use timechart. This query produces a row with the field count for every unique value of logger in each 30-minute period.

Post processing has a limit of 10,000 events. To accommodate this limit, all aggregation possible should be done in the initial query. Ideally, only what is needed by all child queries should be produced by the initial query. It is also important to note that all fields needed by post-process queries must be returned by the initial query.

The first HiddenPostProcess value builds a field for a module we haven't used yet, SingleValue, which takes the first value it sees and renders that value in a rounded rectangle. The following code shows this:

```
stats sum(count) as count by logger
| sort -count
| head 1
| eval f=logger + " is most common (" + count + ")"
| table f
The query is additive, so the full query for this module is
essentially:
sourcetype="impl_splunk_gen" loglevel=error user="bob"
| bucket span=30m _time
| stats count by logger _time
| stats sum(count) as count by logger
| sort -count
```

```
| head 1
| eval f=logger + " is most common (" + count + ")"
| table f
```

The remaining `SingleValue` modules do similar work to find the count of unique loggers, the maximum errors per hour, and the average errors per hour. To step through these queries, simply copy each piece and add it to a query in the search bar.

Other things to notice in this dashboard are as follows:

- `grp` builds columns inside a single panel, for instance, in `layoutPanel="panel_row4_col1_grp2"`

- `SingleValue` modules do not stack vertically but rather flow horizontally, overflowing onto the next line when the window width is reached

- `span` is used in the bucket statement and is the minimum needed by any post-process statements but as large as possible to minimize the number of events returned

Third-party add-ons

There are many excellent apps available at `http://splunkbase.com`, a number of which provide custom modules. We will cover two of the most popular, Google Maps and Sideview Utils.

Google Maps

As we saw in *Chapter 8, Working with Apps*, the Google Maps app provides a dashboard and lookup to draw results on a map. The underlying module is also available to use in your own dashboards.

Here is a very simple dashboard that uses the `GoogleMaps` module:

```
<?xml version="1.0"?>
<view template="search.html">
<!-- chrome -->
<label>Chapter 9 - Google Maps Search</label>
<module name="AccountBar" layoutPanel="appHeader"/>
<module name="AppBar" layoutPanel="navigationHeader"/>
<module name="Message" layoutPanel="messaging">
<param name="filter">*</param>
<param name="clearOnJobDispatch">False</param>
<param name="maxSize">1</param>
</module>
```

```
<!-- search -->
<module name="SearchBar" layoutPanel="splSearchControls-inline">
<param name="useOwnSubmitButton">False</param>
<module name="TimeRangePicker">
<param name="selected">Last 60 minutes</param>
<module name="SubmitButton">
<!-- map -->
<module
name="GoogleMaps"
layoutPanel="resultsAreaLeft"
group="Map" />
</module>
</module>
</module>
</view>
```

This code produces a search bar with a map under it, as seen here in the following screenshot:

When using the GoogleMaps module, you would usually convert a set of values to geographic coordinates. This is usually accomplished using the geoip lookup (for examples, see *Chapter 8, Working with Apps*) to convert IP addresses to locations or by using a custom lookup of some sort.

Just to show that the data can come from anywhere, let's make a graph by setting the `_geo` field on events from one of our example source types:

```
sourcetype="impl_splunk_gen_more" req_time
| eventstats max(req_time) as max
| eval lat=(req_time/max*360)-180
| eval lng=abs(lat)/2-15
| eval _geo=lng+","+lat
```

This query produces a *V* from our random `req_time` field, as shown in the following screenshot. See the map documentation at `http://www.splunkbase.com` for more information about the `_geo` field:

This is a very simplistic example that uses the default settings for nearly everything.

For a more complete example, see the Google Maps dashboard included with the Google Maps app. You can see the source code in the manager or by using the `showsource` attribute. On my server, that URL is `http://localhost:8000/en-US/app/maps/maps?showsource=advanced`.

Sideview Utils

Sideview Utils is a third-party app for Splunk that provides an alternative set of modules for most of what you need to build an interactive Splunk dashboard. These modules remove the complexity of intentions and make it much easier to build forms, make it possible to use variables in HTML, and make it much simpler to handle values between panels and dashboards.

We will use a few of the modules to build forms and link multiple dashboards together based on URL values.

An older, but still functional version of SideviewUtils, is available through Splunkbase. You can download the latest version from `http://sideviewapps.com/`, which adds a number of features, including a visual editor to assemble dashboards.

The Sideview search module

Let's start with a simple search:

```
<?xml version="1.0"?>
<view template="dashboard.html">
<!-- add sideview -->
<module layoutPanel="appHeader" name="SideviewUtils"/>
<!-- chrome -->
<label>Chapter 9 - Sideview One</label>
<module name="AccountBar" layoutPanel="appHeader"/>
<module name="AppBar" layoutPanel="navigationHeader"/>
<module name="Message" layoutPanel="messaging">
<param name="filter">*</param>
<param name="clearOnJobDispatch">False</param>
<param name="maxSize">1</param>
</module>
<!-- search -->
<module
name="Search"
autoRun="True"
group="Chapter 9 - Sideview One"
layoutPanel="panel_row1_col1">
<param name="earliest">-99d</param>
<param name="search">source="impl_splunk_gen_more" | top user</param>
<!-- chart -->
<module name="HiddenChartFormatter">
<param name="charting.chart">pie</param>
<module name="JSChart"/>
</module>
</module>
</view>
```

This dashboard renders identically to the first panel, previously described in the *Building a drilldown to a custom query* section. There are two things to notice in this example:

- The SideviewUtils module is needed to include the code needed by all Sideview Utils apps
- We use the alternative Search module as a replacement for the HiddenSearch module to illustrate our first SideviewUtils module

In this simplistic example, HiddenSearch still works.

Linking views with Sideview

Starting from our simple dashboard, let's use the `Redirector` module to build a link. This link could be to anything, but we will link to another Splunk dashboard, which we will build next. Here's the XML code:

```
...
<module name="JSChart">
<module name="Redirector">
<param name="arg.user">$click.value$</param>
<param name="url">chapter_9_sideview_2</param>
</module>
</module>
...
```

After clicking on shelby, a new URL is built using the user value. In my case, the URL is:

```
http://localhost:8000/en-US/app/is_app_one/chapter_9_
sideview_2?user=shelby
```

The dashboard referenced does not exist yet, so this URL returns an error.

Let's create the second dashboard now.

Sideview URLLoader

The `URLLoader` module provides us with the ability to set variables from the query string of a URL—a very useful feature. For our next dashboard, we will draw a table showing the error counts for the user value provided in the URL:

```
<view template="dashboard.html">
<!-- add sideview -->
<module name="SideviewUtils" layoutPanel="appHeader"/>
<!-- chrome -->
 <Label>Chapter 9 - Sideview Two</Label>
<module name="AccountBar" layoutPanel="appHeader"/>
<module name="AppBar" layoutPanel="navigationHeader"/>
<module name="Message" layoutPanel="messaging">
<param name="filter">*</param>
<param name="clearOnJobDispatch">False</param>
<param name="maxSize">1</param>
</module>
<!-- search -->
<module
name="URLLoader"
```

```
      layoutPanel="panel_row1_col1"
      autoRun="True">
      <module name="HTML">
      <param name="html"><![CDATA[
      <h2>Errors by logger for $user$.</h2>
      ]]>
      </param>
      </module>
      <module name="Search" group="Chapter 9 - Sideview Two">
      <param name="earliest">-199d</param>
      <param name="search">
      sourcetype="*" user="$user$" | top user
      </param>
      <!-- table -->
      <module name="SimpleResultsTable">
      <param name="drilldown">row</param>
      <module name="Redirector">
      <param name="url">chapter_9_sideview_3</param>
      <param name="arg.logger">
      $click.fields.logger.rawValue$
      </param>
      <param name="arg.user">$user$</param>
      <param name="arg.earliest">
      $search.timeRange.earliest$
      </param>
      </module>
      </module>
      </module>
      </module>
      </view>
```

It is very important that autoRun="true" be placed in one module—most likely
URLLoader—and that it exists only in a single module.

With the value of the user as shelby in our URL, this dashboard (using my data) creates the simple view (notice the logged errors for shelby seem to be of only one type), as shown in the following screenshot:

Looking at the modules in this example that are of interest, we have the following terms and their descriptions:

- **SideviewUtils**: This module is required to use any of the other Sideview modules. It is invisible to the user but is still required.

- **URLLoader**: This module takes any values specified in the URL query string and turns them into variables to be used by the descendant modules. Our URL contains user=mary, so $user$ is replaced with the value mary.

- **HTML**: This module draws a snippet of HTML inline. Variables from URLLoader and from form elements are replaced.

- **Search**: This replacement for HiddenSearch understands variables from URLLoader and form elements. This completely obviates the need for intentions. In our case, $user$ is replaced.

- **Redirector**: In this example, we are going to hand along two values to the next dashboard—user from URLLoader and logger from the table itself.

Notice the following code terms and their descriptions:

- logger is populated with $click.fields.logger.rawValue$.

- When a table is clicked on, the variable called click.fields contains all fields from the row of the table clicked on.

- rawValue makes sure that an unescaped value is returned. As the Sideview documents say:

  > *"Rule of Thumb for displaying in headers and sending via redirects, use $foo.rawValue$. For searches, use foo."*

This rule applies to values in `Redirector` and not in display.

- `search.timeRange` contains information about the times used by this search as to whether it comes from the URL, a `TimeRangePicker`, or `params` to the `Search` module. `arg.earliest` adds the value to the URL.

With a click on the table row for `LogoutClass`, we are taken to the following URL:

```
http://localhost:8000/en-US/app/is_app_one/chapter_9_sideview_3? user
=mar&ylogger=LogoutClass&earliest=1344188377
```

We will create the dashboard at this URL in the next section.

Sideview forms

For our final dashboard using Sideview modules, we will build a dashboard with a form that can be prefilled from a URL and allows the changing of the time range. The advantage of this dashboard is that it can be used as a destination of a click without being linked to from elsewhere. If the user accesses this dashboard directly, the default values specified in the dashboard will be used instead. Let's look at the code:

```xml
<?xml version="1.0"?>
<view template="dashboard.html">
<!-- add sideview -->
<module name="SideviewUtils" layoutPanel="appHeader"/>
<!-- chrome -->
<label>Chapter 9 - Sideview Three</label>
<module name="AccountBar" layoutPanel="appHeader"/>
<module name="AppBar" layoutPanel="navigationHeader"/>
<module name="Message" layoutPanel="messaging">
<param name="filter">*</param>
<param name="clearOnJobDispatch">False</param>
<param name="maxSize">1</param>
</module>
<!-- URLLoader -->
<module
name="URLLoader"
layoutPanel="panel_row1_col1"
autoRun="True">
<!-- form -->
<!-- user dropdown -->
<module name="Search" layoutPanel="panel_row1_col1">
```

```
<param name="search">
source="impl_splunk_gen" user user="*"
| top user
</param>
<param name="earliest">-24h</param>
<param name="latest">now</param>
<module name="Pulldown">
<param name="name">user</param>
<!-- use valueField in SideView 2.0 -->
<param name="searchFieldsToDisplay">
<list>
<param name="value">user</param>
<param name="label">user</param>
</list>
</param>
<param name="label">User</param>
<param name="float">left</param>
<!-- logger textfield -->
<module name="TextField">
<param name="name">logger</param>
<param name="default">*</param>
<param name="label">Logger:</param>
<param name="float">left</param>
<module name="TimeRangePicker">
<param name="searchWhenChanged">True</param>
<param name="default">Last 24 hours</param>
<!-- submit button -->
<module name="SubmitButton">
<param name="allowSoftSubmit">True</param>
<!-- html -->
<module name="HTML">
<param name="html"><![CDATA[
<h2>Info for user $user$, logger $logger$.</h2>
]]></param>
</module>
<!-- search 1 -->
<module
name="Search"
group="Chapter 9 - Sideview Three">
<param name="search">
source="impl_splunk_gen" user="$user$"
```

```
logger="$logger$"
| fillnull value="unknown" network
| timechart count by network
</param>
<!-- JobProgressIndicator -->
<module name="JobProgressIndicator"/>
<!-- chart -->
<module name="HiddenChartFormatter">
<param name="charting.chart">area</param>
<param name="charting.chart.stackMode">
stacked
</param>
<module name="JSChart"/>
</module>
</module>
<!-- search 2 -->
<module
name="Search"
group="Chapter 9 - Sideview Three">
<param name="search">
source="impl_splunk_gen" user="$user$"
logger="$logger$"
| fillnull value="unknown" network
| top network
</param>
<!-- table -->
<module name="SimpleResultsTable"/>
</module>
</module>
</module>
</module>
</module>
</module>
</module>
</view>
```

This draws a dashboard that is similar to the following screenshot:

There are quite a few things to cover in this example, so let's step through portions of the XML.

Include SideviewUtils to enable the other `Sideview` modules. In this case, `URLLoader`, `HTML`, `Pulldown`, `Search`, and `TextField` are `Sideview` modules. This is done using the following code:

```
<module layoutPanel="appHeader" name="SideviewUtils"/>
```

Wrap everything in `URLLoader` so that we get values from the URL:

```
<module
name="URLLoader"
layoutPanel="panel_row1_col1"
autoRun="True">
```

Start a search to populate the user dropdown. This query will find all the users who have been active in the last 24 hours:

```
<module name="Search" layoutPanel="panel_row1_col1">
<param name="search">
source="impl_splunk_gen" user user="*"
| top user
</param>
<param name="earliest">-24h</param>
<param name="latest">now</param>
```

Using a query to populate a dropdown can be very expensive, particularly as your data volumes increase. You may need to precalculate these values, either storing the values in a CSV using `outputcsv` and `inputcsv` or using a summary index. For examples of summary indexing and using CSV files for transient data, see *Chapter 10, Summary Indexes and CSV Files*.

This module draws the user selector. The menu is filled by the `Search` module, but notice that the value selected is from our URL value:

```
<module name="Pulldown">
<!-- use valueField in SideView 2.0 -->
<param name="searchFieldsToDisplay">
<list>
<param name="value">user</param>
<param name="label">user</param>
</list>
</param>
<param name="name">user</param>
<param name="label">User</param>
<param name="float">left</param>
```

Next is a text field for our logger. This is a Sideview version of `ExtendedFieldSearch`. It will prepopulate using upstream variables:

```
<module name="TextField">
<param name="name">logger</param>
<param name="default">*</param>
<param name="label">Logger:</param>
<param name="float">left</param>
```

The `TimeRangePicker` module honors the earliest and latest values in the URL. Note that `searchWhenChanged` must be `True` to work properly in this case. As a rule of thumb, `searchWhenChanged` should always be `True`:

```
<module name="TimeRangePicker">
<param name="searchWhenChanged">True</param>
<param name="default">Last 24 hours</param>
```

The `SubmitButton` module kicks off a search when values are changed. `allowSoftSubmit` allows outer modules to start the query either by choosing a value or hitting *return* in a text field:

```
<module name="SubmitButton">
<param name="allowSoftSubmit">True</param>
```

The following are two `Search` modules, each containing an output module:

```
<module
name="Search"
group="Chapter 9 - Sideview Three">
<param name="search">
source="impl_splunk_gen" user="$user$"
logger="$logger$"
| fillnull value="unknown" network
| timechart count by network
</param>
<!-- JobProgressIndicator -->
<module name="JobProgressIndicator"/>
<!-- chart -->
<module name="HiddenChartFormatter">
<param name="charting.chart">area</param>
<param name="charting.chart.stackMode">
stacked
</param>
<module name="JSChart"/>
</module>
</module>
<!-- search 2 -->
<module
group="Chapter 9 - Sideview Three"
name="Search">
<param name="search">
source="impl_splunk_gen" user="$user$"
logger="$logger$"
| fillnull value="unknown" network
| top network
</param>
<!-- table -->
<module name="SimpleResultsTable">
<param name="drilldown">row</param>
</module>
```

For greater efficiency, these two searches can be combined into one query and the `PostProcess` module can be used.

Summary

We have covered an enormous amount of ground in this chapter. The toughest concepts we touched on were module nesting, `layoutPanel`, intentions, and an alternative to intentions with Sideview Utils. As with many skills, the best way to become proficient is to dig in and, hopefully, have some fun along the way! The examples in this chapter should give you a head start.

In the next chapter, we will cover summary indexing, a powerful part of Splunk that can improve the efficiency of your queries greatly.

10
Summary Indexes and CSV Files

As the number of events retrieved by a query increases, performance decreases linearly. Summary indexing allows you to calculate the statistics in advance and then run reports against these roll ups, dramatically increasing performance.

In this chapter, we will cover the following topics:

- Understanding summary indexes
- When to use a summary index
- When not to use a summary index
- Populating summary indexes with saved searches
- Using summary index events in a query
- Using `sistats`, `sitop`, and `sitimechart`
- How latency affects summary queries
- How and when to backfill summary data
- Reducing summary index size
- Calculating `top` for a large time frame
- Using CSV files to store transient data
- Speeding up queries and backfilling

Understanding summary indexes

A summary index is a place to store events calculated by Splunk. Usually, these events are aggregates of raw events broken up over time, for instance, the number of errors that occurred per hour. By calculating this information on an hourly basis, it is cheap and fast to run a query over a longer period of time, for instance, days, weeks, or months.

A summary index is usually populated from a saved search with summary indexing enabled as an action. This is not the only way, but is certainly the most common.

On disk, a summary index is identical to any other Splunk index. The difference is solely the source of data. We create the index through configuration or through the GUI like any other index, and we manage the index size in the same way.

Think of an index like a table or possibly a tablespace, in a typical SQL database. Indexes are capped by size and/or time much like a tablespace, but all the data is stored together much like a table. We will discuss index management in *Chapter 11, Configuring Splunk*.

Creating a summary index

To create an index, navigate to **Settings** | **Indexes** | **New**.

Index settings

Index name *

summary_impl_splunk

Set index name (e.g., INDEX_NAME). Search using index=INDEX_NAME.

Home path

Hot/warm db path. Leave blank for default ($SPLUNK_DB/INDEX_NAME/db).

Cold path

Cold db path. Leave blank for default ($SPLUNK_DB/INDEX_NAME/colddb).

Thawed path

Thawed/resurrected db path. Leave blank for default ($SPLUNK_DB/INDEX_NAME/thaweddb).

Max size (MB) of entire index

500000

Maximum target size of entire index.

Max size (MB) of hot/warm/cold bucket

auto

Maximum target size of buckets. Enter 'auto_high_volume' for high-volume indexes.

Frozen archive path

Frozen bucket archive path. Set this if you want Splunk to automatically archive frozen buckets.

Cancel   Save

For now, let's simply give our new index a name and accept the default values.

We will discuss these settings under the `indexes.conf` section in *Chapter 11, Configuring Splunk*. I like to put the word `summary` at the beginning of any summary index but the name does not matter. I would suggest you follow some naming convention that makes sense to you.

Now that we have an index to store events in, let's do something with it.

When to use a summary index

When the question you want to answer requires looking at all or most events for a given source type, the number of events can become huge very quickly. This is what is generally referred to as a *dense search*.

For example, if you want to know how many page views happened on your website, the query to answer this question must inspect every event. Since each query uses a processor, we are essentially timing how fast our disk can retrieve the raw data and how fast a single processor can decompress that data. Doing a little math, we get the following:

1,000,000 hits per day /

10,000 events processed per second =

100 seconds

If we use multiple indexers or possibly buy much faster disks, we can cut this time but only linearly. For instance, if the data is evenly split across four indexers, without changing disks, this query will take roughly 25 seconds.

If we use summary indexing, we should be able to improve our time dramatically.

Let's assume we have calculated the hit counts per five minutes. Now doing the math:

*24 hours * 60 minutes per hour / 5 minute slices =*

288 summary events

If we then use those summary events in a query, the math looks like the following:

288 summary events /

10,000 events processed per second =

.0288 seconds

This is a significant increase in performance. In reality, we would probably store more than 288 events. For instance, let's say we want to count the events by their HTTP response code. Assuming that there are 10 different status codes we see on a regular basis, we have:

*24 hours * 60 minutes per hour / 5 minute slices * 10 codes = 2880 events*

The math then looks as follows:

2,880 summary events /

10,000 events processed per second =

.288 seconds

That's still a significant improvement over 100 seconds.

When not to use a summary index

There are several cases where summary indexes are either inappropriate or inefficient. Consider the following:

- When you need to see the original events: In most cases, summary indexes are used to store aggregate values. A summary index could be used to store a separate copy of events but this is not usually the case. The more events you have in your summary index, the less advantage it has over the original index.

- When the possible number of categories of data is huge: For example, if you want to know the top IP addresses seen per day, it may be tempting to simply capture a count of every IP address seen. This can still be a huge amount of data, and may not save you a lot of search time, if any. Likewise, simply storing the top 10 addresses per slice of time may not give an accurate picture over a long period of time. We will discuss this scenario under the *Calculating top for a large time frame* section.

- When it is impractical to slice the data across sufficient dimensions: If your data has a large number of dimensions or attributes and it is useful to slice the data across a large number of these dimensions, then the resulting summary index may be sufficiently smaller than your original index not to bother with.

- When it is difficult to know the acceptable time slice: As we set up a few summary indexes, we have to pick the slice of time to which we aggregate. If you think that one hour is an acceptable time slice, and you find out later that you really need 10 minutes of resolution, it is not the easiest task to recalculate the old data into these 10-minute slices. It is, however, very simple to later change your 10-minute search to one hour, as the 10-minute slices should still work for your hourly reports.

Populating summary indexes with saved searches

A search to populate a summary index is much like any other saved search (see *Chapter 2, Understanding Search,* for more details on creating saved searches).

The differences are that this search will run periodically, and the results will be stored in the summary index.

So let's build a simple summary search by following these steps:

1. Start with a search that produces some statistic:

   ```
   source="impl_splunk_gen" | stats count by user
   ```

2. Save this search as **summary - count by user**.

3. Edit the search in **Settings** by navigating to **Settings | Searches, reports and alerts | summary – count by user**.

4. Set the appropriate times. This is a somewhat complicated discussion. See the *How latency affects summary queries* section discussed later.

This is continued as shown in the following screenshot:

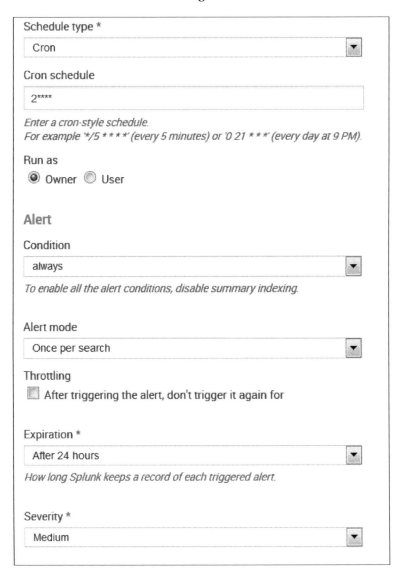

And finally:

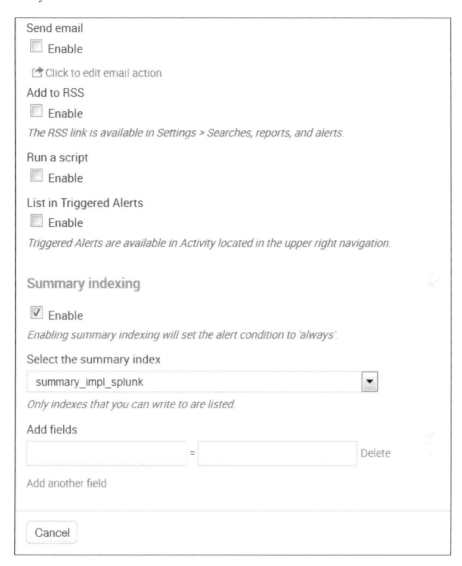

Let's look at the following fields:

- **Search**: `source="impl_splunk_gen" | stats count by user`: This is our query. Later we will use `sistats`, a special summary index version of stats.

- **Start time**: `-62m@m`: It may seem strange that we didn't simply say `-60m@m`, but we need to take latency into account. See the *How latency affects summary queries* section discussed later for more details.

- **Finish time**: -2m@m

- **Schedule and Alert | Schedule this search**: This checkbox needs to be checked for the query to run on a schedule.

- **Schedule type**: Cron

- **Cron schedule**: 2 * * * *: This indicates that the query runs on minute 2 of every hour, every day. To accommodate for latency, the Cron schedule is shifted after the beginning of the hour, along with the start and finish times. See the *How latency affects summary queries* section discussed later for more details.

- **Summary indexing | Enable**: This checkbox enables writing of the output to another index.

- **Select the summary index: summary_impl_splunk** This is the index to write our events to.

  Non-admin users are only allowed to write to the index summary. This ability is controlled by the indexes_edit capability, which only the admin role has enabled by default. See *Chapter 11, Configuring Splunk* for a discussion on roles and capabilities.

- **Add fields**: Using these fields, you can store extra pieces of information in your summary index. This can be used to group results from multiple summary results, or to tag results.

Using summary index events in a query

After the query to populate the summary index has run for some time, we can use the results in other queries.

If you're in a hurry or need to report against slices of time before the query was created, you will need to backfill your summary index. See the *How and when to backfill summary data* section for details about calculating the summary values for past events.

First, let's look at what actually goes into the summary index:

```
08/15/2012 10:00:00, search_name="summary - count by user",
search_now=1345046520.000, info_min_time=1345042800.000, info_max_
time=1345046400.000, info_search_time=1345050512.340, count=17,
user=mary
```

Breaking this event down, we have the following:

- `08/15/2012 10:00:00`: This is the time at the beginning of this block of data. This is consistent with how `timechart` and `bucket` work.
- `search_name="summary - count by user"`: This is the name of the search. This is usually the easiest way to find the results you are interested in.
- `search_now ... info_search_time`: These are informational fields about the summary entry and are generally not useful to users.
- `count=17, user=mary`: The rest of the entry will be whatever fields were produced by the populating query.

There will be one summary event per row produced by the populating query.

Now let's build a query against this data. To start the query, we need to specify the name of the index and the name of the search:

```
index="summary_impl_splunk" search_name="summary - count by user"
```

Originally, on my machine (different data will of course yield different results), this query loads 48 events as compared to the 22,477 original events.

Using `stats`, we can quickly find the statistics by `user`:

```
index="summary_impl_splunk" | stats sum(count) count by user
```

This produces a very simple table, similar to the following screenshot:

	user ⬍	sum(count) ⬍	count ⬍
1	Bobby	12113	16
2	bob	11845	16
3	extrauser	3612	16
4	jacky	12158	16
5	linda	12057	16
6	mary	24092	16

We are calculating the **sum(count)** and **count** in this query, which you might expect to produce the same number, but they are doing very different things:

- **sum(count)**: If you look back at our raw event, count contains the number of times that a user appeared in that slice of time. We are storing the raw value in this count field. See the *Using sistats, sitop, and sitimechart* section for a completely different approach.
- **count**: This actually represents the number of events in the summary index.

The generator that is producing these events is not very random, so all users produce at least one event per hour. Producing a timechart is no more complicated:

```
index="summary_impl_splunk" | timechart span=1h sum(count) by user
```

This produces our graph as shown in the following screenshot:

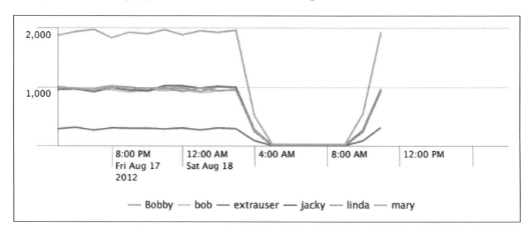

The main thing to remember here is that we cannot make a graph more detailed than the schedule of our populating query. In this case, the populating query uses a span of one hour. An hour is granular enough for most daily reports and certainly fine for weekly or monthly reports, but it may not be granular enough for an operations dashboard.

The following are a few other interesting queries you could make with this simple set of data:

```
index="summary_impl_splunk" search_name="summary - count by user"
| stats avg(count) as "Average events per hour"
```

The previous code snippet tells us the average number of events per slice of time (which we know is one hour). Adding `bucket` and another `stats` command, we can calculate for a custom period of time, as follows:

```
index="summary_impl_splunk" search_name="summary - count by user"
| bucket span=4h _time
| stats sum(count) as count by _time
| stats avg(count) as "Average events per 4 hours"
```

This query would give us the user with the maximum number of events in a given hour and the hour that it occurred in:

```
index="summary_impl_splunk" search_name="summary - count by user"
| stats first(_time) as _time max(count) as max by user
| sort -max
| head 1
| rename max as "Maximum events per hour"
```

Using sistats, sitop, and sitimechart

First, let's define some new functions:

- `Sistats`: `sistats` is the summary indexing version of the stats command, which calculates the aggregate statistics over the dataset.

- `Sitop`: `sitop` is the summary indexing version of the `top` command, which returns the most frequent value of a field or a combination of fields.

- `Sitimechart`: `sitimechart` is the summary indexing version of the `timechart` command, which creates a time-series chart visualization with the corresponding table of statistics.

So far, we have used the `stats` command to populate our summary index. While this works perfectly well, the `si*` variants have a couple of advantages:

- The remaining portion of the query does not have to be rewritten. For instance, `stats count` still works as if you were counting the raw events.

- The `stats` functions that require more data than what happened in that slice of time, will still work. For example, if your time slices each represent an hour, it is not possible to calculate the average value for a day using the average of each hour. The `sistats function` holds enough information to make this work.

There are also a few fairly serious disadvantages to be aware of:

- The query using the summary index must use a subset of the functions and split fields that were in the original populating query. If the subsequent query strays from what is in the original `sistats` data, the results may be unexpected and difficult to debug. For example, see the following code:

```
source="impl_splunk_gen"
| sitimechart span=1h avg(req_time) by user
| stats avg(req_time)
```

The following code returns unpredictable and wildly incorrect values:

```
source="impl_splunk_gen"
| sitimechart span=1h avg(req_time) by user
| stats max(req_time)
```

Notice that `avg` went into `sistats`, but we tried to calculate `max` from the results.

- Using **dc** (**distinct count**) with `sistats` can produce huge events. This happens because to accurately determine unique values over slices of time all original values must be kept. One common use case is to find the top IP addresses that hit a public-facing server. See the *Calculating top for a large time frame* section for alternate approaches to this problem.

- The contents of the summary index are quite difficult to read as they are not meant to be used by humans.

To see how all this works, let's build a few queries. We start with a simple stats query as follows:

```
sourcetype=impl_splunk_gen
| stats count max(req_time) avg(req_time) min(req_time) by user
```

This produces results like you would expect:

user ◇	count ◇	max(req_time) ◇	avg(req_time) ◇	min(req_time) ◇
jarde	100036	9999	9499.569375	9000
lou	99969	6999	6499.373436	6000
mary	99972	999	499.552025	0
nanette	99976	3999	3499.401536	3000
natile	99980	8999	8499.562032	8000
paige	99971	5999	5499.620750	5000
ronnie	100046	2999	2499.403714	2000
shelby	100031	4999	4499.556048	4000
steve	99975	1999	1499.321360	1000
tuck	100044	7999	7499.468754	7000

Now we could save this and send it straight to the summary index, but the results are not terribly nice to use and the average of the average would not be accurate.

On the other hand, we can use the `sistats` variant as follows:

```
sourcetype=impl_splunk_gen
| sistats count max(req_time) avg(req_time) min(req_time) by user
```

The results have a lot of extra information not meant for humans, as shown in the following screenshot:

psrsvd_ct_req_time ⇕	psrsvd_gc ⇕	psrsvd_nc_req_time ⇕	psrsvd_nn_req_time ⇕	psrsvd_nx_req_time ⇕	psrs
8609	11459	8609	1	12239	528
8531	11294	8531	2	12237	521
3464	3464	3464	6	12239	212
8674	11473	8674	1	12236	532
8505	11375	8505	2	12237	519
17282	23098	17282	1	12239	105

Splunk knows how to deal with these results and can use them in combination with the **stats** functions as if they were the original results. You can see how `sistats` and `stats` work together by chaining them together, as follows:

```
sourcetype=impl_splunk_gen
| sistats
count max(req_time) avg(req_time) min(req_time)
by user
| stats count max(req_time) avg(req_time) min(req_time) by user
```

Even though the `stats` function is not receiving the original events, it knows how to work with these `sistats` summary events. We are presented with exactly the same results as the original query, as shown in the following screenshot:

jarde	100036	9999	9499.569375	9000
lou	99969	6999	6499.373436	6000
mary	99972	999	499.552025	0
nanette	99976	3999	3499.401536	3000
natile	99980	8999	8499.562032	8000
paige	99971	5999	5499.620750	5000
ronnie	100046	2999	2499.403714	2000
shelby	100031	4999	4499.556048	4000
steve	99975	1999	1499.321360	1000
tuck	100044	7999	7499.468754	7000

`sitop` and `sitimechart` work in the same fashion.

Let's walk through the procedure to set up summary searches as follows:

1. Save the query using `sistats`:

    ```
    sourcetype=impl_splunk_gen
    | sistats count max(req_time) avg(req_time) min(req_time) by
    user
    ```

2. Set the times accordingly, as we saw previously in the *Populating summary indexes with saved searches* section. See the *How latency affects summary queries* section for more information.

3. Build a query that queries the summary index, as we saw previously in the *Using summary index events in a query* section. Assuming that we saved this query as a testing `sistats`, the query would be:

    ```
    index="summary_impl_splunk"
    search_name="testing sistats".
    ```

4. Use the original `stats` function against the results, as follows:

    ```
    index="summary_impl_splunk" search_name="testing sistats"
    | stats count max(req_time) avg(req_time) min(req_time) by
    user
    ```

This should produce exactly the same results as the original query.

The `si*` variants still seem somewhat magical to me, but they work so well that it is in your own best interest to dive in and trust the magic. Be very sure that your functions and fields are a subset of the original.

How latency affects summary queries

Latency is the difference between the time assigned to an event (usually parsed from the text) and the time it was written to the index. Both times are captured in `_time` and `_indextime`, respectively.

This query will show us what our latency is:

```
sourcetype=impl_splunk_gen
| eval latency = _indextime - _time
| stats min(latency) avg(latency) max(latency)
```

In my case, these statistics look as shown in the following screenshot:

min(latency) ⬍	avg(latency) ⬍	max(latency) ⬍
-0.465	31.603530	72.390

The latency in this case is exaggerated because the script behind `impl_splunk_gen` is creating events in chunks. In most production Splunk instances, the latency is usually just a few seconds. If there is any slowdown, perhaps because of network issues, the latency may increase dramatically and so it should be accounted for.

This query will produce a table showing the time for every event:

```
sourcetype=impl_splunk_gen
| eval latency = _indextime - _time
| eval time=strftime(_time,"%Y-%m-%d %H:%M:%S.%3N")
| eval indextime=strftime(_indextime,"%Y-%m-%d %H:%M:%S.%3N")
| table time indextime latency
```

The previous query produces the following table:

	time ⬍	indextime ⬍	latency ⬍
51	2012-08-22 21:38:11.107	2012-08-22 21:38:33.000	21.893
52	2012-08-22 21:38:11.011	2012-08-22 21:38:33.000	21.989
53	2012-08-22 21:38:10.546	2012-08-22 21:38:33.000	22.454
54	2012-08-22 21:38:10.433	2012-08-22 21:38:33.000	22.567
55	2012-08-22 21:38:10.419	2012-08-22 21:38:33.000	22.581
56	2012-08-22 21:38:09.588	2012-08-22 21:38:33.000	23.412
57	2012-08-22 21:38:08.955	2012-08-22 21:38:33.000	24.045
58	2012-08-22 21:38:08.502	2012-08-22 21:38:33.000	24.498
59	2012-08-22 21:38:07.867	2012-08-22 21:38:33.000	25.133

To deal with this latency, you should add enough delay in your query that populates the summary index. The following are a few examples:

```
Confidence Time slice Earliest Latest cron
2 minutes 1 hour -62m@m -2m@m 2 * * * *
15 minutes 1 hour -1h@h -0h@h 15 * * * *
5 minutes 5 minutes -10m@m -5m@m */5 * * * *
1 hour 15 minutes -75m@m -60m@m */15 * * * *
1 hour 24 hours -1d@d -0d@d 0 1 * * * *
```

Sometimes you have no idea when your logs will be indexed, as when they are delivered in batches on unreliable networks.

This is what I would call *unpredictable latency*. For one possible solution, take a look at the app `indextime search` available at `http://splunkbase.com`.

How and when to backfill summary data

If you are building reports against summary data, you need enough time represented in your summary index. If your report represents only a day or two, then you can probably just wait for the summary to have enough information. If you need the report to work sooner rather than later, or the time frame is longer, then you can backfill your summary index.

Using fill_summary_index.py to backfill

The `fill_summary_index.py` script allows you to backfill the summary index for any time period that you like. It does this by running the saved searches which you have defined to populate your summary indexes, but only for the time periods you specify.

To use the script, follow the given procedure:

1. Create your scheduled search, as detailed previously in the *Populating summary indexes with saved searches* section.

2. Log in to the shell on your Splunk instance. If you are running a distributed environment, log in to the search head.

3. Change directories to the Splunk bin directory:

   cd $SPLUNK_HOME/bin.

   $SPLUNK_HOME is the root of your Splunk installation. The default installation directory is `/opt/splunk` on Unix operating systems, and `c:\ProgramFiles\Splunk` on Windows.

4. Run the `fill_summary_index` command. An example from inside the script is as follows:

   ```
   ./splunk cmd python fill_summary_index.py -app is_app_one -name
   "summary - count by user" -et -30d -lt now -j 8 -dedup true -auth
   admin:changeme
   ```

Let's break down these arguments in the following manner:

- `./splunk cmd`: This essentially sets the environment variables so that whatever runs next has the appropriate settings to find the Splunk libraries and included Python modules.

- `python fill_summary_index.py`: This runs the script itself using the Python executable and the modules included with the Splunk distribution.

- `-app is_app_one`: This is the name of the app that contains the summary populating queries in question.

- `-name "summary - count by user"`: This is the name of the query to run. `*` will run all summary queries contained in the app specified.

- `-et -30d`: This is the earliest time to consider. The appropriate times are determined and used to populate the summary index.

- `-lt now`: This is the latest time to consider.

- `-j 8`: This determines how many queries to run simultaneously.

- `-dedup true`: This is used to determine whether there are results already for each slice of time. Without this flag, you could end up with duplicate entries in your summary index. For some statistics this wouldn't matter, but for most it would.

  If you are concerned that you have summary data that is incomplete, perhaps because summary events were produced while an indexer was unavailable, you should investigate the `delete` command to remove these events first. The `delete` command is not efficient and should be used sparingly, if at all.

- `-auth admin:changeme`: The `auth` to run the query (the admin default or if they were changed, the new credentials).

  When you run this script, it will run the query with the appropriate times as if the query had been run at those times in the past. This can be a very slow process, particularly if the number of slices is large. For instance, slices every five minutes for a month would be *30 * 24 * (60/5) = 8,640 queries.*

Using collect to produce custom summary indexes

If the number of events destined for your summary index could be represented in a single report, we can use the `collect` function to create our own summary index entries directly. This has the advantage that we can build our index in one shot. That could be much faster than running the `backfill` script, which must run one search per slice of time. For instance, if you want to calculate 15-minute slices over a month, the script will fire off 2,880 queries.

If you dig into the code that actually produces summary indexes, you will find that it uses the `collect` command to store events into the specified index. The `collect` command is available to us and with a little knowledge we can use it directly.

First, we need to build a query that slices our data by buckets of time as follows:

```
source="impl_splunk_gen"
| bucket span=1h _time
| stats count by _time user
```

This gives us a simple table as shown in the following screenshot:

	_time ⬍	user ⬍	count ⬍
1	8/22/12 8:00:00.000 PM	Bobby	549
2	8/22/12 8:00:00.000 PM	bob	565
3	8/22/12 8:00:00.000 PM	extrauser	168
4	8/22/12 8:00:00.000 PM	jacky	551
5	8/22/12 8:00:00.000 PM	linda	588
6	8/22/12 8:00:00.000 PM	mary	1115
7	8/22/12 9:00:00.000 PM	Bobby	960
8	8/22/12 9:00:00.000 PM	bob	979
9	8/22/12 9:00:00.000 PM	extrauser	294
10	8/22/12 9:00:00.000 PM	jacky	942

Notice that there is a row per slice of time and for each user that produced events during that slice of time.

Let's add a few more fields to make it more interesting:

```
source="impl_splunk_gen"
| bucket span=1h _time
| eval error=if(loglevel="ERROR",1,0)
| stats count avg(req_time) dc(ip) sum(error) by _time user
```

This gives us a table as shown in the following screenshot:

	_time ⇕	user ⇕	count ⇕	avg(req_time) ⇕	dc(ip) ⇕	sum(error) ⇕
1	8/22/12 8:00:00.000 PM	Bobby	549	5918.018913	6	144
2	8/22/12 8:00:00.000 PM	bob	565	6002.448357	6	117
3	8/22/12 8:00:00.000 PM	extrauser	168	6125.517857	6	40
4	8/22/12 8:00:00.000 PM	jacky	551	6005.267123	6	143
5	8/22/12 8:00:00.000 PM	linda	588	6215.339326	6	130
6	8/22/12 8:00:00.000 PM	mary	1115	6039.061078	6	292
7	8/22/12 9:00:00.000 PM	Bobby	960	6144.366255	6	227
8	8/22/12 9:00:00.000 PM	bob	979	6413.421622	6	229
9	8/22/12 9:00:00.000 PM	extrauser	294	6129.421769	6	88
10	8/22/12 9:00:00.000 PM	jacky	942	6115.462518	6	227

Now, to get ready for our summary index, we switch to `sistats` and add a `search_name` field as the saved search would. Use `testmode` to make sure that everything is working as expected, in the following manner:

```
source="impl_splunk_gen"
| bucket span=1h _time
| eval error=if(loglevel="ERROR",1,0)
| sistats count avg(req_time) dc(ip) sum(error) by _time user
| eval search_name="summary - user stats"
| collect index=summary_impl_splunk testmode=true
```

The results of this query show us what will actually be written to the summary index but as this is not designed for humans, let's simply test the round trip by adding the original stats statement at the end, as follows:

```
source="impl_splunk_gen"
| bucket span=1h _time
| eval error=if(loglevel="ERROR",1,0)
| sistats count avg(req_time) dc(ip) sum(error) by _time user
| eval search_name="summary - hourly user stats - collect test"
| collect index=summary_impl_splunk testmode=true
| stats count avg(req_time) dc(ip) sum(error) by _time user
```

If we have done everything correctly, the results should be identical to the original table:

	_time ⬍	user ⬍	count ⬍	avg(req_time) ⬍	dc(ip) ⬍	sum(error) ⬍
1	8/22/12 8:00:00.000 PM	Bobby	549	5918.018913	6	144
2	8/22/12 8:00:00.000 PM	bob	565	6002.448357	6	117
3	8/22/12 8:00:00.000 PM	extrauser	168	6125.517857	6	40
4	8/22/12 8:00:00.000 PM	jacky	551	6005.267123	6	143
5	8/22/12 8:00:00.000 PM	linda	588	6215.339326	6	130
6	8/22/12 8:00:00.000 PM	mary	1115	6039.061078	6	292
7	8/22/12 9:00:00.000 PM	Bobby	960	6144.366255	6	227
8	8/22/12 9:00:00.000 PM	bob	979	6413.421622	6	229
9	8/22/12 9:00:00.000 PM	extrauser	294	6129.421769	6	88
10	8/22/12 9:00:00.000 PM	jacky	942	6115.462518	6	227

To actually run this query, we simply remove `testmode` from collect, as follows:

```
source="impl_splunk_gen"
| bucket span=1h _time
| eval error=if(loglevel="ERROR",1,0)
| sistats count avg(req_time) dc(ip) sum(error) by _time user
| eval search_name="summary - user stats"
| collect index=summary_impl_splunk
```

Beware that you will end up with duplicate values if you use the `collect` command over a time frame that already has results in the summary index. Either use a custom time frame to ensure that you do not produce duplicates, or investigate the `delete` command, which as mentioned earlier is not efficient and should be avoided if possible.

No results will be available until the query is complete and the file created behind the scenes is indexed. On my installation, querying one month of data, the query inspected 2.2 million events in 173 seconds producing 2,619 summary events.

Let's use the summary data now:

```
index=summary_impl_splunk
search_name="summary - hourly user stats - collect test"
 | timechart sum(error) by user
```

This will give us a neat graph as shown in the following screenshot:

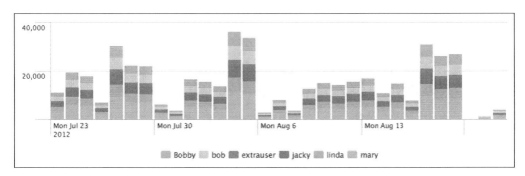

Because this is created from the summary instead of three minutes, this query completes in 1.5 seconds.

In this specific case, using `collect` was four times faster than using the `fill_summary_index.py` script. That said, it is much easier to make a mistake so be very careful. Rehearse with collect `testmode=true` and a trailing stats or `timechart` command.

Reducing summary index size

If the saved search populating a summary index produces too many results, the summary index is less effective at speeding up searches. This usually occurs because one or more of the fields used for grouping has more unique values than expected.

One common example of a field that can have many unique values is the URL in a web access log. The number of URL values might increase in instances where:

- The URL contains a session ID
- The URL contains search terms
- Hackers are throwing URLs at your site trying to break in
- Your security team runs tools looking for vulnerabilities

On top of this, multiple URLs can represent exactly the same resource, as follows:

- `/home/index.html`
- `/home/`
- `/home/index.html?a=b`
- `/home/?a=b`

We will cover a few approaches to flatten these values. These are just examples and ideas and your particular case may require a different approach.

Using eval and rex to define grouping fields

One way to tackle this problem is to make up a new field from the URL using `rex`.

Perhaps you only really care about the hits by directories. We can accomplish this with `rex`, or if needed multiple `rex` statements.

Looking at the fictional source type `impl_splunk_web`; we see results that look like the following:

```
2012-08-25T20:18:01 user=bobby GET /products/x/?q=10471480
uid=Mzg2NDc0OA
2012-08-25T20:18:03 user=user3 GET /bar?q=923891 uid=MjY1NDI5MA
2012-08-25T20:18:05 user=user3 GET /products/index.html?q=9029891
uid=MjY1NDI5MA
2012-08-25T20:18:08 user=user2 GET /about/?q=9376559 uid=MzA4MTc5OA
```

URLs are tricky, as they might or might not contain certain parts of the URL. For instance, the URL may or may not have a query string, may or may not have a page, and may or may not have a trailing slash. To deal with this, instead of trying to make an all- encompassing regular expression, we will take advantage of the behavior of `rex`, which is to make no changes to the event if the pattern does not match.

Consider the following query:

```
sourcetype="impl_splunk_web"
| rex "\s[A-Z]+\s(?P<url>.*?)\s"
| rex field=url "(?P<url>.*)\?"
| rex field=url "(?P<url>.*/)"
| stats count by url
```

In our case, this will produce the following report:

url ‡	count ‡
1 /	5741
2 /about/	2822
3 /contact/	2847
4 /products/	5653
5 /products/x/	5637
6 /products/y/	2786

Stepping through these `rex` statements, we have:

* `rex "\s[A-Z]+\s(?P<url>.*?)\s"`:

  This pattern matches a space followed by uppercase letters followed by a space, and then captures all characters until a space into the field `url`. The field `attribute` is not defined, so the `rex` statement matches against the `_raw` field. The values extracted look like the following:

  ◦ `/products/x/?q=10471480`
  ◦ `/bar?q=923891`
  ◦ `/products/index.html?q=9029891`
  ◦ `/about/?q=9376559`

* `rex field=url "(?P<url>.*)\?"`:

  Searching the field `url`, this pattern matches all characters until a question mark. If the pattern matches, the result replaces the contents of the field `url`. If the pattern doesn't match, `url` stays the same. The values of `url` will now be as follows:

  ◦ `/products/x/`
  ◦ `/bar`
  ◦ `/products/index.html`
  ◦ `/about/`

- `rex field=url "(?P<url>.*/)":`

  Once again, while searching the field `url`, this pattern matches all characters until and including the last slash.

  The values of `url` are then as follows:

    o   `/products/x/`

    o   `/`

    o   `/products/`

    o   `/about/`

  This should effectively reduce the number of possible URLs, and hopefully make our summary index more useful and efficient. It may be that you only want to capture up to three levels of depth. You could accomplish that with the following `rex` statement:

- `rex field=url "(?P<url>/(?:[^/]/){,3})"`

The possibilities are endless. Be sure to test as much data as you can when building your summary indexes.

Using a lookup with wildcards

Splunk lookups also support wildcards, which we can use in this case.

One advantage is that we can define arbitrary fields for grouping, independent of the values of `url`.

For a lookup wildcard to work, first we need to set up our `url` field and the lookup:

1. Extract the `url` field. The `rex` pattern we used before should work:

    `\s[AZ]+\s(?P<url>.*?)\s`. See *Chapter 3, Tables, Charts, and Fields*, for detailed instructions on setting up a field extraction. Don't forget to set permissions on the extraction.

2. Create our lookup file. Let's call the lookup file `flatten_summary_lookup.csv`. Use the following contents for our example log:

    ```
    url,section
    /about/*,about
    /contact/*,contact
    /*/*,unknown_non_root
    /*,root
    *,nomatch
    ```

    If you create your lookup file in Excel on a Mac, be sure to save the file using the format Windows comma separated values (.csv).

3. Upload the lookup table file and create our lookup definition and automatic lookup. See the *Using lookups to enrich data section* in *Chapter 7, Extending Search*, for detailed instructions. The automatic lookup definition should look like the following screenshot (the value of *Name* doesn't matter):

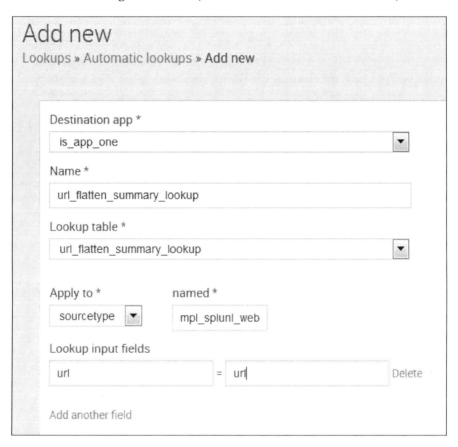

4. Set the permissions on all the objects. I usually opt for **All Apps** for **Lookup table** files and **Lookup definitions**, and **This app** only for **Automatic lookups**. See *Chapter 7, Extending Search*, for details.

5. Edit transforms.conf. In this version (actually as of Splunk 4.3), not all the features of lookups can be defined through the admin interface. To access these features, the configuration files that actually drive Splunk must be edited manually.

We will cover configuration files in greater detail in *Chapter 11, Configuring Splunk*, but for now let's add two lines to one file and move on:

1. Edit `$SPLUNK_HOME/etc/apps/is_app_one/local/transforms.conf`. The name of the directory `is_app_one` may be different depending on what app was active when you created your lookup definition. If you can't find this file, check your permissions and the App column in the admin interface.

2. You should see these two lines, or something similar, depending on what you named your **Lookup table** file and **Lookup definition** instances:

   ```
   [flatten_summary_lookup]
   filename = flatten_summary_lookup.csv
   ```

   If you do not see these lines in this file, check your permissions.

3. Add two more lines below `filename`:

   ```
   match_type = WILDCARD(url)
   max_matches = 1
   ```

   These two lines effectively say the following:

   ○ `match_type = WILDCARD(url)`: When evaluating the field `url`, honor wildcard characters. Without this setting, matches are always exact.

   ○ `max_matches = 1`: Stop searching after the first match. By default, up to 10 matches are allowed. We want to match only the first line that matches, effectively using the lookup like a case statement.

If everything is wired up properly, we should now be able to run the search:

```
sourcetype=impl_splunk_web | stats count by section
```

This should give us the following simple report:

	section ‡	count ‡
1	about	2822
2	contact	2847
3	root	5741
4	unknown_non_root	14076

To see in greater detail what is really going on, let's try the following search:

```
sourcetype=impl_splunk_web
| rex field=url "(?P<url>.*)\?"
| stats count by section url
```

The `rex` statement is included to remove the query string from the value of `url` created by our extracted field. This gives us the following report:

section ↕	url ↕	count ↕
1 about	/about/	2822
2 contact	/contact/	2847
3 root	/bar	2847
4 root	/foo	2894
5 unknown_non_root	/products/	5653
6 unknown_non_root	/products/x/	5637
7 unknown_non_root	/products/y/	2786

Looking back at our lookup file, our matches appear to be as follows:

```
url pattern section
/about/ /about/* about
/contact/ /contact/* contact
/bar /* root
/foo /* root
/products/ /*/* unknown_non_root
/products/x/ /*/* unknown_non_root
/products/y/ /*/* unknown_non_root
```

If you read the lookup file from top to bottom, the first pattern that matches wins.

Using event types to group results

Another approach for grouping results to reduce the summary index size would be to use event types in creative ways. For a refresher on event types, see *Chapter 7, Extending Search*.

This approach has the following advantages:

- All definitions are defined through the web interface
- It is possible to create arbitrarily complex definitions
- You can easily search for only those events that have defined section names
- You can place events in multiple groups if desired

The disadvantages to this approach are as follows:

- This is a non-obvious approach.
- It is inconvenient to not place events in multiple groups if more than one event type matches. For instance, if you want a page to match /product/x/* but not **/product/***, it is not convenient to do so.

The following is the procedure to create these event types:

1. For each section, create an event type as follows:

2. Set the permissions to either **This app only** or **Global**, depending on the scope.

3. Repeat this for each section that you want to summarize. The clone link in manager makes this process much faster.

With our event types in place, we can now build queries. The `Tag` value that we included means we can search easily for only those events that match a section, like the following:

```
tag::eventtype="summary_url" | top eventtype
```

The previous code returns a table as shown in the following screenshot:

	eventtype ⇕	count ⇕	percent ⇕
1	bogus	19745	100.000000
2	url_products	14076	71.288934
3	url_contact	2847	14.418840
4	url_about	2822	14.292226

Our results contain the new event types that we created, along with an unwanted event type, **bogus**. Remember that all event type definitions that match an event are attached. This is very powerful but sometimes is not what you expect. The **bogus** event type definition is *, which means it matches everything. The **bogus** event type was added purely to illustrate the point and has no practical use.

Let's create a new field from our summary event type name, then aggregate based on the new field:

```
tag::eventtype="summary_url"
| rex field=eventtype "url_(?P<section>.*)"
| stats count by section
```

The previous code gives us the results that we are looking for, as shown in the following screenshot:

	section ⇕	count ⇕
1	about	2822
2	contact	2847
3	products	14076

This search finds only the events that have defined event types, which may be what you want. To group all other results into an other group, we instead need to search for all events in the following manner:

```
sourcetype=impl_splunk_web
| rex field=eventtype "url_(?P<section>.*)"
| fillnull value="other" section
| stats count by section
```

The previous code then produces the following report:

	section ↕	count ↕
1	about	2822
2	contact	2847
3	other	5741
4	products	14076

Hopefully, these examples will be food for thought when it comes to collapsing your results into more efficient summary results.

Calculating top for a large time frame

One common problem is to find the top contributors out of some huge set of unique values. For instance, if you want to know what IP addresses are using the most bandwidth in a given day or week, you may have to keep track of the total of request sizes across millions of unique hosts to definitively answer this question. When using summary indexes, this means storing millions of events in the summary index, quickly defeating the point of summary indexes.

Just to illustrate, let's look at a simple set of data:

```
Time 1.1.1.1 2.2.2.2 3.3.3.3 4.4.4.4 5.5.5.5 6.6.6.6
12:00 99 100 100 100
13:00 99 100 100 100
14:00 99 100 101 100
15:00 99 99 100 100
16:00 99 100 100 100
total 495 300 299 401 400 100
```

If we only stored the top three IPs per hour, our data set would look like the following:

```
Time 1.1.1.1 2.2.2.2 3.3.3.3 4.4.4.4 5.5.5.5 6.6.6.6
12:00 100 100 100
13:00 100 100 100
14:00 100 101 100
15:00 99 100 100
16:00 100 100 100
total 300 299 401 400 100
```

According to this data set, our top three IP addresses are 4.4.4.4, 5.5.5.5, and 2.2.2.2. The actual largest value was for 1.1.1.1, but it was missed because it was never in the top three.

To tackle this problem we need to keep track of more data points for each slice of time. But how many?

Using our generator data, let's count a random number and see what kind of results we see. In my data set, it is the following query:

```
source="impl_splunk_gen" | top req_time
```

When run over a week, this query gives me the following results:

	req_time ⬍	count ⬍	percent ⬍
1	10	402	0.072102
2	34	383	0.068694
3	15	377	0.067618
4	118	374	0.067080
5	26	373	0.066901
6	21	370	0.066362
7	18	366	0.065645
8	46	365	0.065466
9	140	365	0.065466
10	291	363	0.065107

How many unique values were there? The following query will tell us that:

```
source="impl_splunk_gen" | stats dc(req_time)
```

This tells us there are (based on my data) 12,239 unique values of req_time. How many different values are there per hour? The following query will calculate the average unique values per hour:

```
source="impl_splunk_gen"
| bucket span=1h _time
| stats dc(req_time) as dc by _time
| stats avg(dc)
```

This tells us that each hour there are an average of (again, given my data) 3,367 unique values of req_time.

So if we stored every count of every `req_time` for a week, we will store *3,367 * 24 * 7 = 565,656 values*. How many values would we have to store per hour to get the same answer which we received before?

The following is a query that attempts to answer that question:

```
source="impl_splunk_gen"
| bucket span=1h _time
| stats count by _time req_time
| sort 0 _time -count
| streamstats count as place by _time
| where place<50
| stats sum(count) as count by req_time
| sort 0 -count
| head 10
```

Breaking this query down, we have:

- `source="impl_splunk_gen"`: This finds the events.
- `| bucket span=1h _time`: This floors our `_time` field to the beginning of the hour. We will use this to simulate hourly summary queries.
- `| stats count by _time req_time`: This generates a `count` per `req_time` per hour.
- `| sort 0 _time -count`: This sorts and keeps all events (that's what `0` means), first ascending by `_time` and then descending by `count`.
- `| streamstats count as place by _time`: This loops over the events, incrementing `place`, and starting the count over when `_time` changes. Remember that we flattened `_time` to the beginning of each hour.
- `| where place<50`: This keeps the first 50 events per hour. These will be the largest 50 values of count per hour, since we sorted descending by count.
- `| stats sum(count) as count by req_time`: This adds up what we have left across all hours.
- `| sort 0 -count`: This sorts the events in descending order by count.
- `| head 10`: This shows the first 10 results.

How did we do? Keeping the top 50 results per hour, my results look as shown in the following screenshot:

	req_time ↕	count ▾
1	10	139
2	257	125
3	101	109
4	103	109
5	140	107
6	46	107
7	15	98
8	21	98
9	24	97
10	211	96

That really isn't close. Let's try this again. We'll try where *place<1000*. This gives us the following results:

	req_time ↕	count ▾
1	10	401
2	34	367
3	15	361
4	26	356
5	101	354
6	118	351
7	18	350
8	21	349
9	46	345
10	291	344

That is much closer but we're still not quite there. After experimenting a little more, place<2000 was enough to get the expected top 10. This is better than storing 3,367 rows per hour. This may not seem like a big enough difference to bother about, but increase the number of events by 10 or 100 and it can make a huge difference.

To use these results in a summary index, you would simply eliminate the results going into your dataset. One way to accomplish this might be as follows:

```
source="impl_splunk_gen"
| sitop req_time
| streamstats count as place
| where place<2001
```

The first row produced by `sitop` contains the total value.

Another approach, using a combination of `eventstats` and `sistats`, is as follows:

```
source="impl_splunk_gen"
| eventstats count by req_time
| sort 0 -req_time
| streamstats count as place
| where place<2001
| sistats count by req_time
```

Luckily, this is not a terribly common problem, so most of this complexity can be avoided. For another option, see the *Storing a running calculation* section.

Summary index searches

You can use established summary indexes for just about any saved search or report. Using Splunk Web, summary indexing is an alert option for scheduled reports. To leverage a summary index for a saved report:

1. Navigate to **Settings > Searches, Reports, and Alerts**.
2. Select the name of your report.
3. Under **Schedule and alert**, select **Schedule**.
4. Schedule the report. (http://www.splunk.com states that, *searches that populate summary indexes should run on a fairly frequent basis in order to create statistically accurate final reports*).
5. Under **Alert**, set **Condition** to **Always**.
6. Set **Alert mode** to **Once per search**.
7. Under summary indexing, select **Enable**.
8. Select the name of the summary index that the report populates from the **Select the summary index list**.

That's it! Your search or report will now use your summary index.

Using CSV files to store transient data

Sometimes it is useful to store small amounts of data outside a Splunk index. Using the `inputcsv` and `outputcsv` commands, we can store tabular data in CSV files on the filesystem.

Pre-populating a dropdown

If a dashboard contains a dynamic dropdown, you must use a search to populate the dropdown. As the amount of data increases, the query to populate the dropdown will run more and more slowly, even from a summary index. We can use a CSV file to store just the information needed, simply adding new values when they occur.

First, we build a query to generate the CSV file. This query should be run over as much data as possible:

```
source="impl_splunk_gen"
| stats count by user
| outputcsv user_list.csv
```

Next, we need a query to run periodically and append any new entries to the file. Schedule this query to run periodically as a saved search:

```
source="impl_splunk_gen"
| stats count by user
| append [inputcsv user_list.csv]
| stats sum(count) as count by user
| outputcsv user_list.csv
```

To then use this in our dashboard, our populating query will simply be:

```
|inputcsv user_list.csv
```

A simple dashboard XML using this query would look like the following:

```
<input type="dropdown" token="sourcetype">
<label>User</label>
<populatingSearch fieldForValue="user" fieldForLabel="user">
|inputcsv user_list.csv
</populatingSearch>
</input>
```

Creating a running calculation for a day

If the number of events per day is in millions or tens of millions, querying all events for that day can be extremely expensive. For that reason, it makes sense to do part of the work in smaller periods of time.

Using a summary index to store these interim values can sometimes be an overkill if those values are not needed for long. In the *Calculating top for a large time frame* section, we ended up storing thousands of values every few minutes. If we simply wanted to know the top 10 per day, this might be seen as a waste. To cut down on the noise in our summary index, we can use a CSV as cheap interim storage.

The steps are essentially to:

1. Periodically query recent data and update the CSV.
2. Capture top values in summary at the end of the day.
3. Empty the CSV file.

Our periodic query looks like the following:

```
source="impl_splunk_gen"
| stats count by req_time
| append [inputcsv top_req_time.csv]
| stats sum(count) as count by req_time
| sort 10000 -count
| outputcsv top_req_time.csv
```

Let's break down the query line by line:

- `source="impl_splunk_gen"`: This is the query to find the events for this slice of time.
- `| stats count by req_time`: This helps calculate the count by `req_time`.
- `| append [inputcsv top_req_time.csv]`: This loads the results generated so far from the CSV file, and adds the events to the end of our current results.
- `| stats sum(count) as count by req_time`: This uses `stats` to combine the results from our current time slice and the previous results.
- `| sort 10000 -count`: This sorts the results descending by `count`. The second term, `10,000`, specifies that we want to keep the first 10,000 results.
- `| outputcsv top_req_time.csv`: This overwrites the CSV file.

Schedule the query to run periodically, perhaps every 15 minutes. Follow the same rules about latency as discussed in the *How latency affects summary queries* section.

When the rollup is expected, perhaps each night at midnight, schedule two more queries a few minutes apart, as follows:

- `| inputcsv top_req_time.csv | head 100`: Save this as a query adding to a summary index, as in the *Populating summary indexes with saved searches* section

- `| stats count |outputcsv top_req_time.csv`: This query will simply overwrite the CSV file with a single line

Summary

In this chapter, we have explored the use of summary indexes and the commands surrounding them. While summary indexes are not always the answer, they can be very useful for particular problems. We also explored alternative approaches by using CSV files for interim storage.

In our next chapter, we will dive into the configuration files that drive Splunk.

11
Configuring Splunk

Everything that controls Splunk lives in its configuration files sitting in the filesystem of each instance of Splunk. These files are unencrypted, easily readable, and easily editable. Almost all of the work that we have done so far has been accomplished through the web interface, but everything actually ends up in these configuration files.

While the web interface does a lot, there are many options that are not represented in the admin interface. There are also some things that are simply easier to accomplish by editing the files directly.

In this chapter, we will cover the following topics:

- Locating configuration files
- Merging configurations
- Debugging configurations
- Common configurations and their parameters

Locating Splunk configuration files

Splunk's configuration files live in `$SPLUNK_HOME/etc`. This is reminiscent of Unix's `/etc` directory but is instead contained within Splunk's directory structure.

This has the advantage that the files don't have to be owned by root. In fact, the entire Splunk installation can run as an unprivileged user (assuming you don't need to open a port below 1024 or read files only readable by another user).

The directories that contain configurations are as follows:

- **$SPLUNK_HOME/etc/system/default**: These are the default configuration files that ship with Splunk. Never edit these files as they will be overwritten each time you upgrade.

- **$SPLUNK_HOME/etc/system/local**: This is the location of the global configuration overrides specific to this host. There are very few configurations that need to live here—most configurations that do live here are created by Splunk itself. In almost all cases, you should make your configuration files inside an app.

- **$SPLUNK_HOME/etc/apps/$app_name/default**: This is the proper location for configurations in an app that will be shared either through Splunkbase or otherwise.

- **$SPLUNK_HOME/etc/apps/$app_name/local**: This is where most configurations should live and where all the nonprivate configurations created through the web interface will be placed.

- **$SPLUNK_HOME/etc/users/$user_name/$app_name/local**: When a search configuration is created through the web interface, it will have a permission setting of *Private* and will be created in a user- or app-specific configuration file. Once permissions are changed, the configuration will move to the corresponding directory named `$app_name/local`.

There are a few more directories that contain files that are not `.conf` files. We'll talk about those later in this chapter, under the *User interface resources* section.

The structure of a Splunk configuration file

The `.conf` files used by Splunk look very similar to `.ini` files. A simple configuration looks as follows:

```
#settings for foo
[foo]
bar=1
la = 2
```

Let's look at the following couple of definitions:

- **stanza**: A stanza is used to group attributes. Our stanza in this example is
  [foo]. A common synonym for this is "section". Keep in mind the following
  key points:
  - ° A stanza name must be unique in a single file
  - ° The order does not matter

- **attribute**: An attribute is a name-value pair. Our attributes in this example
  are bar and la. A common synonym is parameter. Keep in mind the
  following key points:
  - ° The attribute name must not contain a whitespace or the equals sign.
  - ° Each attribute belongs to the stanza defined previously; if the
    attribute appears before all stanzas, the attribute belongs to the stanza
    [default].
  - ° The attribute name must be unique in a single stanza but not in a
    configuration.
  - ° Each attribute must have its own line and can only use one line.
    Spaces around the equals sign do not matter.

These are a few rules that may not apply in other implementations:

- Stanza and property names are case sensitive
- The comment character is #
- Bare attributes at the top of a file are added to the [default] stanza
- Any attributes in the [default] stanza are added to all stanzas that do not
  have an attribute with that name already

The configuration merging logic

Configurations in different locations merge behind the scenes into one super
configuration. Luckily, the merging happens in a predictable way, is fairly easy
to learn, and there is a tool to help us preview this merging.

The merging order

The merging order is slightly different depending on whether the configuration is being used by the search engine or another part of Splunk. The difference is whether there is an active user and app.

The merging order outside of search

Configurations being used outside of search are merged in a fairly simple order. These configurations include the files to read, the indexed fields to create, the indexes that exist, deployment server and client configurations, and other settings. These configurations merge in this order:

1. `$SPLUNK_HOME/etc/system/default`: This directory contains the base configurations that ship with Splunk.

    Never make changes in `$SPLUNK_HOME/etc/system/default` as your changes will be lost when you upgrade Splunk.

2. `$SPLUNK_HOME/etc/apps/*/default`: Configurations are overlaid in the reverse ASCII order by app directory name, that is, *a beats z*.

3. `$SPLUNK_HOME/etc/apps/*/local`

4. `$SPLUNK_HOME/etc/system/local`

    ◦ The configurations in this directory are applied last.

    ◦ Outside of search, these configurations cannot be overridden by an app configuration. Apps are a very convenient way to compartmentalize control and distribute configurations. This is particularly relevant if you use the deployment server, which we will cover in *Chapter 12, Advanced Deployments*.

Don't edit configurations in `$SPLUNK_HOME/etc/system/local`—even if you have a very specific reason. An app is almost always the correct place for configuration.

A little pseudo code to describe this process might look as follows:

```
$conf = new Configuration('$SPLUNK_HOME/etc/')
$conf.merge( 'system/default/$conf_name' )
for $this_app in reverse(sort(@all_apps)):
$conf.merge( 'apps/$this_app/default/$conf_name' )
for $this_app in reverse(sort(@all_apps)):
$conf.merge( 'apps/$this_app/local/$conf_name' )
$conf.merge( 'system/local/$conf_name' )
```

The merging order when searching

When you are searching, configuration merging is slightly more complicated. When you are running a search, there is always an active user and app, and they come into play. The logical order looks like this:

1. `$SPLUNK_HOME/etc/system/default`
2. `$SPLUNK_HOME/etc/system/local`
3. `$SPLUNK_HOME/etc/apps/not app`
   - Each app, other than the current app, is looped through in the ASCII order of the directory name (not the visible app name). Unlike merging outside of search, here *z beats a*.
   - All configuration attributes that are shared globally are applied, first from default and then from local.
4. `$SPLUNK_HOME/etc/apps/app`

   All configurations from default and then local are merged.

5. `$SPLUNK_HOME/etc/users/user/app/local`

   Maybe a little pseudo code would make this clearer:

```
$conf = new Configuration('$SPLUNK_HOME/etc/')
$conf.merge( 'system/default/$conf_name' )
$conf.merge( 'system/local/$conf_name' )
for $this_app in sort(@all_apps):
if $this_app != $current_app:
$conf.merge_shared( 'apps/$this_app/default/$conf_name' )
$conf.merge_shared( 'apps/$this_app/local/$conf_name' )
$conf.merge( 'apps/$current_app/default/$conf_name' )
$conf.merge( 'apps/$current_app/local/$conf_name' )
$conf.merge( 'users/$current_user/$current_app/local/$conf_name' )
```

The configuration merging logic

Now that we know which configurations will merge in what order, let's cover the logic for how they actually merge. The logic is fairly simple:

- The configuration name, stanza name, and attribute name must match exactly
- The last configuration added wins

The best way to understand configuration merging is through examples.

Configuration merging – example 1

Say we have the base configuration `default/sample1.conf`:

```
[foo]
bar=10
la=20
```

And, say we merge a second configuration, `local/sample1.conf`:

```
[foo]
bar=15
```

The resulting configuration would be as follows:

```
[foo]
bar=15
la=20
```

The things to notice here are as follows:

- The second configuration does not simply replace the prior configuration
- The value of `bar` is taken from the second configuration
- The lack of a `la` property in the second configuration does not remove the value from the final configuration

Configuration merging – example 2

Say we have the `default/sample2.conf` base configuration:

```
[foo]
bar = 10
la=20
[pets]
cat = red
Dog=rex
```

And say we merge a second configuration, `local/sample2.conf`:

```
[pets]
cat=blue
dog=fido
fish = bubbles
  [foo]
bar= 15
[cars]
ferrari =0
```

The resulting configuration would be as follows:

```
[foo]
bar=15
la=20
[pets]
cat=blue
dog=rex
Dog=fido
fish=bubbles
[cars]
ferrari=0
```

The things to notice in this example are as follows:

- The order of the stanzas does not matter
- The spaces around the equals sign do not matter
- Dog does not override dog as all stanza names and property names are case sensitive
- The cars stanza is added fully

Configuration merging – example 3

Let's do a little exercise, merging four configurations from different locations.

In this case, we are not in search, so we will use the rules from the *Merging order outside of search* section.

Let's walk through a few sample configurations:

For $SPLUNK_HOME/etc/apps/d/default/props.conf, we have the following code:

```
[web_access]
MAX_TIMESTAMP_LOOKAHEAD = 25
TIME_PREFIX = ^\[
[source::*.log]
BREAK_ONLY_BEFORE_DATE = true
```

For $SPLUNK_HOME/etc/system/local/props.conf, we have the following code:

```
BREAK_ONLY_BEFORE_DATE = false
[web_access]
TZ = CST
```

For `$SPLUNK_HOME/etc/apps/d/local/props.conf`, we have the following code:

```
[web_access]
TZ = UTC
[security_log]
EXTRACT-<name> = \[(?P<user>.*?)\]
```

For `$SPLUNK_HOME/etc/apps/b/default/props.conf`, we have the following code:

```
[web_access]
MAX_TIMESTAMP_LOOKAHEAD = 20
TIME_FORMAT = %Y-%m-%d $H:%M:%S
[source::*/access.log]
BREAK_ONLY_BEFORE_DATE = false
```

I've thrown a bit of a curveball here by placing the files out of merging order.

These configurations would actually merge in this order:

```
$SPLUNK_HOME/etc/apps/d/default/props.conf
$SPLUNK_HOME/etc/apps/b/default/props.conf
$SPLUNK_HOME/etc/apps/d/local/props.conf
$SPLUNK_HOME/etc/system/local/props.conf
```

Walking through each merge, the configuration would look as follows:

1. We will start with `$SPLUNK_HOME/etc/apps/d/default/props.conf`:
    ```
    [web_access]
    MAX_TIMESTAMP_LOOKAHEAD = 25
    TIME_PREFIX = ^\[
    [source::*.log]
    BREAK_ONLY_BEFORE_DATE = true
    ```

2. We will then merge `$SPLUNK_HOME/etc/apps/b/default/props.conf`:
    ```
    [web_access]
    MAX_TIMESTAMP_LOOKAHEAD = 30
    TIME_PREFIX = ^\[
    TIME_FORMAT = %Y-%m-%d $H:%M:%S
      [source::*.log]
    BREAK_ONLY_BEFORE_DATE = true
    [source::*/access.log]
    BREAK_ONLY_BEFORE_DATE = false
    ```

Even though [source::*.log] and [source::*/access.log] both match a file called access.log, they will not merge in the configuration because the stanza names do not match exactly. This logic is covered later in the *Stanza types* section under the *props.conf* heading.

3. Then, we will merge $SPLUNK_HOME/etc/apps/d/local/props.conf:

```
[web_access]
MAX_TIMESTAMP_LOOKAHEAD = 30
TIME_PREFIX = ^\[
TIME_FORMAT = %Y-%m-%d $H:%M:%S
TZ = UTC
[source::*.log]
BREAK_ONLY_BEFORE_DATE = true
[source::*/access.log]
BREAK_ONLY_BEFORE_DATE = false
[security_log]
EXTRACT-<name> = \[(?P<user>.*?)\]
```

4. We will finally merge the globally overriding $SPLUNK_HOME/etc/system/ configuration:

```
local/props.conf file:
[default]
BREAK_ONLY_BEFORE_DATE = false
[web_access]
MAX_TIMESTAMP_LOOKAHEAD = 25
TIME_PREFIX = ^\[
TIME_FORMAT = %Y-%m-%d $H:%M:%S
TZ = CST
BREAK_ONLY_BEFORE_DATE = false
[source::*.log]
BREAK_ONLY_BEFORE_DATE = true
[source::*/access.log]
Configuring Splunk
[ 288 ]
BREAK_ONLY_BEFORE_DATE = false
[security_log]
EXTRACT-<name> = \[(?P<user>.*?)\]
BREAK_ONLY_BEFORE_DATE = false
```

The setting with the biggest impact here is the BREAK_ONLY_BEFORE_DATE = false bare attribute. It is first added to the [default] stanza and then added to all stanzas that do not already have any value.

As a general rule, avoid using the [default] stanza and bare word attributes. The final impact may not be what you expect.

Configuration merging – example 4

In this case, we are in search, so we will use the more complicated merging order.

Assuming that we are currently working in the d app, let's merge the same configurations again. For simplicity, we are assuming that all attributes are shared globally. We will merge the same configurations listed previously in *Configuration merging – example 3*.

With d as our current app, we will now merge in this order:

```
$SPLUNK_HOME/etc/system/local/props.conf
$SPLUNK_HOME/etc/apps/b/default/props.conf
$SPLUNK_HOME/etc/apps/d/default/props.conf
$SPLUNK_HOME/etc/apps/d/local/props.conf
```

Walking through each merge, the configuration will look as follows:

1. We will start with $SPLUNK_HOME/etc/system/local/props.conf:

    ```
    BREAK_ONLY_BEFORE_DATE = false
    [web_access]
    TZ = CST
    ```

2. Now, we will merge the default for apps other than our current app (which, in this case, is only one configuration): $SPLUNK_HOME/etc/apps/b/default/props.conf:

    ```
    BREAK_ONLY_BEFORE_DATE = false
    [web_access]
    MAX_TIMESTAMP_LOOKAHEAD = 20
    TIME_FORMAT = %Y-%m-%d $H:%M:%S
    TZ = CST
      [source::*/access.log]
    BREAK_ONLY_BEFORE_DATE = false
    ```

3. Next, we will merge the default of our current app: $SPLUNK_HOME/etc/apps/d/default/props.conf:

    ```
    BREAK_ONLY_BEFORE_DATE = false
    [web_access]
    MAX_TIMESTAMP_LOOKAHEAD = 25
    TIME_PREFIX = ^\[
    TIME_FORMAT = %Y-%m-%d $H:%M:%S
    ```

```
TZ = CST
[source::*/access.log]
BREAK_ONLY_BEFORE_DATE = false
[source::*.log]
BREAK_ONLY_BEFORE_DATE = true
```

4. Now, we will merge our current app local `$SPLUNK_HOME/etc/apps/d/`
   `local/props.conf`:

```
BREAK_ONLY_BEFORE_DATE = false
[web_access]
MAX_TIMESTAMP_LOOKAHEAD = 25
TIME_PREFIX = ^\[
TIME_FORMAT = %Y-%m-%d $H:%M:%S
TZ = UTC
[source::*/access.log]
BREAK_ONLY_BEFORE_DATE = false
[source::*.log]
BREAK_ONLY_BEFORE_DATE = true
[security_log]
EXTRACT-<name> = \[(?P<user>.*?)\]
```

5. And finally, we will apply our default stanza to stanzas that don't already
   have the attribute:

```
BREAK_ONLY_BEFORE_DATE = false
  [web_access]
MAX_TIMESTAMP_LOOKAHEAD = 25
TIME_PREFIX = ^\[
TIME_FORMAT = %Y-%m-%d $H:%M:%S
TZ = UTC
BREAK_ONLY_BEFORE_DATE = false
[source::*/access.log]
BREAK_ONLY_BEFORE_DATE = false
[source::*.log]
BREAK_ONLY_BEFORE_DATE = true
[security_log]
EXTRACT-<name> = \[(?P<user>.*?)\]
BREAK_ONLY_BEFORE_DATE = false
```

I know this is fairly confusing, but with practice, it will make sense. Luckily, **btool**, which we will cover in the next section, makes it easier to see this.

Using btool

To help preview merged configurations, we call on btool, a command-line tool that prints the merged version of configurations. The Splunk site has one of my favorite documentation notes of all time, as follows:

> *btool is not tested by Splunk and is not officially supported or guaranteed. That said, it's what our Support team uses when trying to troubleshoot your issues.*

With that warning in mind, btool has never steered me wrong. The tool has a number of functions, but the only one I have ever used is list, as follows:

```
$SPLUNK_HOME/bin/splunk cmd btool props list
```

This produces 5,277 lines of output, which I won't list here. Let's list the `impl_splunk_gen` stanza by adding it to the end of the command line, as shown here:

```
/opt/splunk/bin/splunk cmd btool props list impl_splunk_gen
```

This will produce an output such as this:

```
[impl_splunk_gen]
ANNOTATE_PUNCT = True
BREAK_ONLY_BEFORE =
BREAK_ONLY_BEFORE_DATE = True
... truncated ...
LINE_BREAKER_LOOKBEHIND = 100
LOOKUP-lookupusers = userslookup user AS user OUTPUTNEW
MAX_DAYS_AGO = 2000
... truncated ...
TRUNCATE = 10000
TZ = UTC
maxDist = 100
```

Our configuration file at `$SPLUNK_HOME/etc/apps/ImplementingSplunkDataGenerator/local/props.conf` contains only the following lines:

```
[impl_splunk_web]
LOOKUP-web_section = flatten_summary_lookup url AS url OUTPUTNEW
EXTRACT-url = \s[A-Z]+\s(?P<url_from_app_local>.*?)\s
EXTRACT-foo = \s[A-Z]+\s(?P<url_from_app>.*?)\s
```

So, where did the rest of this configuration come from? With the use of the -debug flag, we can get more details:

```
/opt/splunk/bin/splunk cmd btool props list impl_splunk_gen -debug
```

This produces the following query:

```
Implementi [impl_splunk_gen]
system ANNOTATE_PUNCT = True
system BREAK_ONLY_BEFORE =
system BREAK_ONLY_BEFORE_DATE = True
... truncated ...
system LINE_BREAKER_LOOKBEHIND = 100
Implementi LOOKUP-lookupusers = userslookup user AS user OUTPUTNEW
system MAX_DAYS_AGO = 2000
... truncated ...
system TRUNCATE = 10000
Implementi TZ = UTC
system maxDist = 100
```

The first column, truncated though it is, tells us what we need to know. The vast majority of these lines are defined in the system, most likely in system/default/props.conf.

The remaining items from our file are labeled Implementi, which is the beginning of our app directory, ImplementingSplunkDataGenerator. If you ever have a question about where some setting is coming from, btool will save you a lot of time. Also, check out the *Splunk on Splunk* app at Splunkbase for access to btool from the Splunk web interface.

An overview of Splunk .conf files

If you have spent any length of time in the filesystem investigating Splunk, you must have seen many different files ending in .conf. In this section, we will give you a quick overview of the most common .conf files. The official documentation is the best place to look for a complete reference to files and attributes.

The quickest way to find the official documentation is with your favorite search engine by searching for splunk filename.conf. For example, a search for splunk props.conf pulled up (and will pull up) the Splunk documentation for props.conf first in every search engine I tested.

props.conf

The stanzas in `props.conf` define which events to match based on host, source, and sourcetype. These stanzas are merged into the master configuration based on the uniqueness of stanza and attribute names, as with any other configuration, but there are specific rules governing when each stanza is applied to an event and in what order. Stated as simply as possible, attributes are sorted by type, then by priority, and then by the ASCII value.

We'll cover those rules under the *Stanza types* section. First, let's look at common attributes.

Common attributes

The full set of attributes allowed in `props.conf` is vast. Let's look at the most common attributes and try to break them down by the time when they are applied.

Search-time attributes

The most common attributes that users will make in `props.conf` are field extractions. When a user defines an extraction through the web interface, it ends up in `props.conf`, as shown here:

```
[my_source_type]
EXTRACT-foo = \s(?<bar>\d+)ms
EXTRACT-cat = \s(?<dog>\d+)s
```

This configuration defines the fields bar and dog for the `my_source_type` source type. Extracts are the most common search-time configurations. Any of the stanza types listed under the *Stanza types* section can be used, but the source type is definitely the most common one.

Other common search-time attributes include:

- `REPORT-foo = bar`: This attribute is a way to reference stanzas in `transforms.conf`, but apply them at search time instead of index time. This approach predates `EXTRACT` and is still useful in a few special cases.

  We will cover this case later under the *transforms.conf* section.

- `KV_MODE = auto`: This attribute allows you to specify whether Splunk should automatically extract fields in the form of `key=value` from events. The default value is auto. The most common change is to disable automatic field extraction for performance reasons by setting the value to none. Other possibilities are multi, JSON, and XML.

- `LOOKUP-foo = mylookup barfield`: This attribute lets you wire up a lookup to automatically run for a set of events. The lookup itself is defined in `transforms.conf`.

Index-time attributes

As discussed in *Chapter 3, Tables, Charts, and Fields*, it is possible to add fields to the metadata of events. This is accomplished by specifying a transform in `transforms.conf`, and an attribute in `props.conf`, to tie the transformation to specific events.

The attribute in `props.conf` looks as follows: `TRANSFORMS-foo = bar1,bar2`.

This attribute references stanzas in `transforms.conf` by name, in this case, `bar1` and `bar2`. These transform stanzas are then applied to the events matched by the stanza in `props.conf`.

Parse-time attributes

Most of the attributes in `props.conf` actually have to do with parsing events. To successfully parse events, a few questions need to be answered, such as these:

- When does a new event begin? Are events multiline? Splunk will make fairly intelligent guesses, but it is best to specify an exact setting. Attributes that help with this include:

    ◦ `SHOULD_LINEMERGE = false`: If you know that your events will never contain the newline character, setting this to `false` will eliminate a lot of processing.

    ◦ `BREAK_ONLY_BEFORE = ^\d\d\d\d-\d\d-\d\d`: If you know that new events always start with a particular pattern, you can specify it using this attribute.

    ◦ `TRUNCATE = 1024`: If you are certain you only care about the first *n* characters of an event, you can instruct Splunk to truncate each line. What is considered a line can be changed with the next attribute.

    ◦ `LINE_BREAKER = ([\r\n]+)(?=\d{4}-\d\d-\d\d)`: This is the most efficient approach to multiline events is to redefine what Splunk considers a line. This example says that a line is broken on any number of newlines followed by a date of the form `1111-11-11`. The big disadvantage to this approach is that, if your log changes, you will end up with garbage in your index until you update your configuration. Try the props helper app available at Splunkbase for help in making this kind of configuration.

- Where is the date? If there is no date, see DATETIME_CONFIG further down this bullet list. The relevant attributes are as follows:

  ○ TIME_PREFIX = ^\[: By default, dates are assumed to fall at the beginning of the line. If this is not true, give Splunk some help and move the cursor past the characters preceding the date. This pattern is applied to each line, so if you have redefined LINE_BREAKER correctly, you can be sure only the beginnings of actual multiline events are being tested.

  ○ MAX_TIMESTAMP_LOOKAHEAD = 30: Even if you change no other setting, you should change this one. This setting says how far after TIME_PREFIX to test for dates. With no help, Splunk will take the first 150 characters of each line and then test regular expressions to find anything that looks like a date. The default regular expressions are pretty lax, so what it finds may look more like a date than the actual date. If you know that your date is never more than *n* characters long, set this value to n or n+2. Remember that the characters retrieved come after TIME_PREFIX.

- What does the date look like? These attributes will be of assistance here:

  ○ TIME_FORMAT = %Y-%m-%d %H:%M:%S.%3N %:z: If this attribute is specified, Splunk will apply strptime to the characters immediately following TIME_PREFIX. If this matches, then you're done. This is, by far, the most efficient and least error-prone approach. Without this attribute, Splunk actually applies a series of regular expressions until it finds something that looks like a date.

  ○ DATETIME_CONFIG = /etc/apps/a/custom_datetime.xml: As mentioned, Splunk uses a set of regular expressions to determine the date. If TIME_FORMAT is not specified, or won't work for some strange reason, you can specify a different set of regular expressions or disable time extraction completely by setting this attribute to CURRENT (the indexer clock time) or NONE (file modification time, or if there is no file, clock time). I personally have never had to resort to a custom datetime.xml file, though I have heard of it being done.

- The Data preview function available when you are adding data through the manager interface builds a good, usable configuration. The configuration generated does not use LINE_BREAKER, which is definitely safer but less efficient.

  Here is a sample stanza that uses LINE_BREAKER for efficiency:

  ```
  [mysourcetype]
  TIME_FORMAT = %Y-%m-%d %H:%M:%S.%3N %:z
  ```

```
MAX_TIMESTAMP_LOOKAHEAD = 32
TIME_PREFIX = ^\[
SHOULD_LINEMERGE = False
LINE_BREAKER = ([\r\n]+)(?=\[\d{4}-\d{1,2}-\d{1,2}\s+\
d{1,2}:\d{1,2}:\d{1,2})
TRUNCATE = 1024000
```

This configuration would apply to log messages that looked like this:

```
[2011-10-13 13:55:36.132 -07:00] ERROR Interesting message.
More information.
And another line.
[2011-10-13 13:55:36.138 -07:00] INFO All better.
[2011-10-13 13:55:37.010 -07:00] INFO More data
and another line.
```

Let's walk through how these settings affect the first line of this sample configuration:

- `LINE_BREAKER` states that a new event starts when one or more newline characters are followed by a bracket and series of numbers and dashes in the `[1111-11-11 11:11:11]` pattern.

- `SHOULD_LINEMERGE=False` tells Splunk not to bother trying to recombine multiple lines.

- `TIME_PREFIX` moves the cursor to the character after the `[` character.

- `TIME_FORMAT` is tested against the characters at the current cursor location. If it succeeds, we are done.

- If `TIME_FORMAT` fails, `MAX_TIMESTAMP_LOOKAHEAD` characters are read from the cursor position (after `TIME_PREFIX`) and the regular expressions from `DATE_CONFIG` are tested.

- If the regular expressions fail against the characters returned, the time last parsed from an event is used. If there is no last time parsed, the modification date from the file would be used, if known; otherwise, the current time would be used.

This is the most efficient and precise way to parse events in Splunk, but also the most brittle. If your date format changes, you will almost certainly have junk data in your index. Only use this approach if you are confident the format of your logs will not change without your knowledge.

Input-time attributes

There are only a couple of attributes in `props.conf` that matter at the input stage, but they are generally not needed:

- `CHARSET = UTF-16LE`: When reading data, Splunk has to know the character set used in the log. Most applications write their logs using either `ISO-8859-1 or UTF-8` is handled by the default settings just fine. Some Windows applications write logs in 2-byte Little Endian, which is indexed as garbage. `Setting CHARSET = UTF-16LE` takes care of the problem. Check the official documentation for a list of supported encodings.

- `NO_BINARY_CHECK = true`: If Splunk believes that a file is binary, it will not index the file at all. If you find that you have to change this setting to convince Splunk to read your files, it is likely that the file is in an unexpected character set. You might try other `CHARSET` settings before enabling this setting.

Stanza types

Now that we have looked at common attributes, let's talk about the different types of stanzas in `props.conf`. Stanza definitions can take the following three forms:

- `[foo]`
  - This is the exact name of a source type and is the most common type of stanza to be used; the source type of an event is usually defined in `inputs.conf`
  - Wildcards are not allowed

- `[source::/logs/.../*.log]`
  - This matches the source attribute, which is usually the path to the log where the event came from
  - `*` matches a file or directory name
  - `...` matches any part of a path

- `[host::*nyc*]`
  - This matches the host attribute, which is usually the value of the hostname on a machine running Splunk Forwarder
  - `*` is allowed

Types follow this order in taking precedence:

1. Source.

2. Host.

3. Source type.

For instance, say an event has the following fields:

```
sourcetype=foo_type
source=/logs/abc/def/gh.log
host=dns4.nyc.mycompany.com
```

Given this configuration snippet and our preceding event, we have the following code:

```
[foo_type]
TZ = UTC
[source::/logs/.../*.log]
TZ = MST
[host::*nyc*]
TZ = EDT
```

`TZ = MST` would be used during parsing because the source stanza takes precedence.

To extend this example, say we have this snippet:

```
[foo_type]
TZ = UTC
TRANSFORMS-a = from_sourcetype
[source::/logs/.../*.log]
TZ = MST
BREAK_ONLY_BEFORE_DATE = True
TRANSFORMS-b = from_source
[host::*nyc*]
TZ = EDT
BREAK_ONLY_BEFORE_DATE = False
TRANSFORMS-c = from_host
```

The attributes applied to our event would, therefore, be as shown here:

```
TZ = MST
BREAK_ONLY_BEFORE_DATE = True
TRANSFORMS-a = from_sourcetype
TRANSFORMS-b = from_source
TRANSFORMS-c = from_host
```

Priorities inside a type

If there are multiple source or host stanzas that match a given event, the order in which settings are applied also comes into play. A stanza with a pattern has a priority of 0, while an exact stanza has a priority of 100. Higher priorities win. For instance, say we have the following stanza:

```
[source::/logs/abc/def/gh.log]
TZ = UTC
[source::/logs/.../*.log]
TZ = CDT
```

Our TZ value will be UTC since the exact match of source::/logs/abc/def/gh.log has a higher priority.

When priorities are identical, stanzas are applied by the ASCII order. For instance, say we have this configuration snippet:

```
[source::/logs/abc/.../*.log]
TZ = MST
[source::/logs/.../*.log]
TZ = CDT
```

The attribute TZ=CDT would win because /logs/.../*.log is first in the ASCII order.

This may seem counterintuitive since /logs/abc/.../*.log is arguably a better match. The logic for determining what makes a better match, however, can quickly become fantastically complex, so the ASCII order is a reasonable approach.

You can also set your own value of priority, but luckily, it is rarely needed.

Attributes with class

As you dig into configurations, you will see attribute names of the FOO-bar form.

The word after the dash is generally referred to as the class. These attributes are special in a few ways:

- Attributes merge across files as with any other attribute
- Only one instance of each class will be applied according to the rules described previously
- The final set of attributes is applied in the ASCII order by the value of the class. Once again, say we are presented with an event with the following fields:
  ```
  sourcetype=foo_type
  source=/logs/abc/def/gh.log
  host=dns4.nyc.mycompany.com
  ```

And, say that this is the configuration snippet:

```
[foo_type]
TRANSFORMS-a = from_sourcetype1, from_sourcetype2
[source::/logs/.../*.log]
TRANSFORMS-c = from_source_b
[source::/logs/abc/.../*.log]
TRANSFORMS-b = from_source_c
[host::*nyc*]
TRANSFORMS-c = from_host
The surviving transforms would then be:
TRANSFORMS-c = from_source_b
TRANSFORMS-b = from_source_c
TRANSFORMS-a = from_sourcetype1, from_sourcetype2
```

To determine the order in which the transforms are applied to our event, we will sort the stanzas according to the values of their classes, in this case, c, b, and a. This gives us:

```
TRANSFORMS-a = from_sourcetype1, from_sourcetype2
TRANSFORMS-b = from_source_c
TRANSFORMS-c = from_source_b
```

The transforms are then combined into a single list and executed in this order:

```
from_sourcetype1, from_sourcetype2, from_source_c, from_source_b
```

The order of transforms usually doesn't matter, but it is important to understand it if you want to chain transforms and create one field from another. We'll try this later, in the *transforms.conf* section.

inputs.conf

This configuration, as you might guess, controls how data makes it into Splunk.

By the time this data leaves the input stage, it still isn't an event but has some basic metadata associated with it: `host`, `source`, `sourcetype`, and optionally `index`. This basic metadata is then used by the parsing stage to break the data into events according to the rules defined in `props.conf`:

Input types can be broken down into files, network ports, and scripts. First, we will look at attributes that are common to all inputs.

Common input attributes

These common bits of metadata are used in the parsing stage to pick the appropriate stanzas in `props.conf`.

- `host`: By default, `host` will be set to the hostname of the machine producing the event. This is usually the correct value, but it can be overridden when appropriate.
- `source`: This field is usually set to the path, file, or network port that an event came from, but this value can be hardcoded.
- `sourcetype`: This field is almost always set in `inputs.conf` and is the primary field to determine which set of parsing rules in `props.conf` to apply to these events.

 It is very important to set `sourcetype`. In the absence of a value, Splunk will create automatic values based on the source, which can easily result in an explosion of `sourcetype` values.

- `index`: This field says what index to write events to. If it is omitted, the default `index` will be used.

All of these values can be modified using transforms, the only caveat being that these transforms are applied after the parsing step. The practical consequence of this is that you cannot apply different parsing rules to different events in the same file, for instance, different time formats on different lines.

Files as inputs

The vast majority of events in Splunk come from files. Usually, these events are read from the machine where they are produced and as the logs are written. Very often, the entire input's stanza will look as follows:

```
[monitor:///logs/interesting.log*]
sourcetype=interesting
```

This is often all that is needed. This stanza says:

- Read all logs that match the `/logs/interesting.log*` pattern, and going forward, watch them for new data
- Name the source type "interesting"
- Set the source to the name of the file in which the log entry was found
- Default the host to the machine where the logs originated
- Write the events to the default index

These are usually perfectly acceptable defaults. If `sourcetype` is omitted, Splunk will pick a default source type based on the filename, which you don't want—your source type list will get very messy very fast.

Using patterns to select rolled logs

You may notice that the previous stanza ended in `*`. This is important because it gives Splunk a chance to find events that were written to a log that has recently rolled. If we simply watch `/logs/interesting.log`, it is likely that events will be missed at the end of the log when it rolls, particularly on a busy server.

There are specific cases where Splunk can get confused, but in the vast majority of cases, the default mechanisms do exactly what you would hope for. See the *When to use crcSalt* section further on for a discussion about special cases.

Using blacklist and whitelist

It is also possible to use a blacklist and whitelist pattern for more complicated patterns. The most common use case is to blacklist files that should not be indexed, for instance, `gz` and `zip` files. This can be done as follows:

```
[monitor:///opt/B/logs/access.log*]
sourcetype=access
blacklist=.*.gz
```

This stanza would still match `access.log.2012-08-30`, but if we had a script that compressed older logs, Splunk would not try to read `access.log.2012-07-30.gz`.

Conversely, you can use a whitelist to apply very specific patterns, as shown here:

```
[monitor:///opt/applicationserver/logs]
sourcetype=application_logs
whitelist=(app|application|legacy|foo)\.log(\.\d{4})?
blacklist=.*.gz
```

This whitelist would match `app.log`, `application.log`, `legacy.log.2012-08-13`, and `foo.log`, among others. The blacklist will negate any `gz` files.

Since a log is a directory, the default behavior will be to recursively scan that directory.

Selecting files recursively

The layout of your logs or your application may dictate a recursive approach.

For instance, say we have these stanzas:

```
[monitor:///opt/*/logs/access.log*]
sourcetype=access
[monitor:///opt/.../important.log*]
sourcetype=important
```

The character * will match a single file or directory, while . . . will match any depth. This will match the files you want, with the caveat that all of /opt will continually be scanned.

Splunk will continually scan all directories from the first wildcard in a monitor path.

If /opt contains many files and directories, which it almost certainly does, Splunk will use an unfortunate amount of resources scanning all directories for matching files, constantly using memory and CPU. I have seen a single Splunk process watching a large directory structure use 2 gigabytes of memory. A little creativity can take care of this, but it is something to be aware of.

The takeaway is that if you know the possible values for *, you are better off writing multiple stanzas. For instance, assuming our directories in /opt are A and B, the following stanzas will be far more efficient:

```
[monitor:///opt/A/logs/access.log*]
sourcetype=access
[monitor:///opt/B/logs/access.log*]
sourcetype=access
```

It is also perfectly acceptable to have stanzas matching files and directories that simply don't exist. This causes no errors, but be careful not to include patterns that are so broad that they match unintended files.

Following symbolic links

When scanning directories recursively, the default behavior is to follow symbolic links. Often this is very useful, but it can cause problems if a symbolic link points to a large or slow filesystem. To control this behavior, simply do this:

```
followSymlink = false
```

It's probably a good idea to put this on all of your monitor stanzas until you know you need to follow a symbolic link.

Setting the value of the host from the source

The default behavior of using the hostname from the machine forwarding the logs is almost always what you want. If, however, you are reading logs for a number of hosts, you can extract the hostname from the source using host_regex or host_segment. For instance, say we have the path:

```
/nfs/logs/webserver1/access.log
```

To set host to webserver1, you could use:

```
[monitor:///nfs/logs/*/access.log*]
sourcetype=access
host_segment=3
```

You could also use:

```
[monitor:///nfs/logs/*/access.log*]
sourcetype=access
host_regex=/(.*?)/access\.log
```

The host_regex variable could also be used to extract the value of the host from the filename. It is also possible to reset the host using a transform, with the caveat that this will occur after parsing, which means any settings in props.conf that rely on matching the host will already have been applied.

Ignoring old data at installation

It is often the case that, when Splunk is installed, months or years of logs are sitting in a directory where logs are currently being written. Logs that are appended to infrequently may also have months or years of events that are no longer interesting and would be wasteful to index.

The best solution is to set up archive scripts to compress any logs older than a few days, but in a large environment, this may be difficult to do. Splunk has two settings that help ignore older data, but be forewarned: once these files have been ignored, there is no simple way to change your mind later. If, instead, you compress older logs and blacklist the compressed files as explained in the *Using blacklist and whitelist* section, you can simply decompress, at a later stage, any files you would like to index. Let's look at a sample stanza:

```
[monitor:///opt/B/logs/access.log*]
sourcetype = access
ignoreOlderThan = 14d
```

In this case, `ignoreOlderThan` says to ignore, forever, all events in any files, the modification date of which is older than 14 days. If the file is updated in the future, any new events will be indexed.

The `followTail` attribute lets us ignore all events written until now, instead starting at the end of each file. Let's look at an example:

```
[monitor:///opt/B/logs/access.log*]
sourcetype = access
followTail = 1
```

Splunk will note the length of files matching the pattern, but `TailfollowTail` instructs Splunk to ignore everything currently in these files. Any new events written to the files will be indexed. Remember that there is no easy way to alter this if you change your mind later.

It is not currently possible to say *ignore all events older than x*, but since most logs roll on a daily basis, this is not commonly a problem.

When to use crcSalt

To keep track of what files have been seen before, Splunk stores a checksum of the first 256 bytes of each file it sees. This is usually plenty as most files start with a log message, which is almost guaranteed to be unique. This breaks down when the first 256 bytes are not unique on the same server.

I have seen two cases where this happens, as follows:

1. The first case is when logs start with a common header containing information about the product verion, for instance:

```
================================================================
== Great product version 1.2 brought to you by Great company ==
== Server kernel version 3.2.1 ==
```

2. The second case is when a server writes many thousands of files with low time resolution, for instance:

```
12:13:12 Session created
12:13:12 Starting session
```

To deal with these cases, we can add the path to the log to the checksum, or salt our crc. This is accomplished as shown here:

```
[monitor:///opt/B/logs/application.log*]
sourcetype = access
crcSalt = <SOURCE>
```

It says to include the full path to this log in the checksum.

This method will only work if your logs have a unique name. The easiest way to accomplish this is to include the current date in the name of the log when it is created. You may need to change the pattern for your log names so that the date is always included and the log is not renamed.

Do not use **crcSalt** if your logs change names!

If you enable crcSalt in an input where it was not already enabled, you will re-index all the data! You need to ensure that the old logs are moved aside or uncompressed and blacklisted before enabling this setting in an existing configuration.

Destructively indexing files

If you receive logfiles in batches, you can use the batch input to consume `logs` and then delete them. This should only be used against a copy of the logs.

See the following example:

```
[batch:///var/batch/logs/*/access.log*]
sourcetype=access
host_segment=4
move_policy = sinkhole
```

This stanza would index the files in the given directory and then delete the files. Make sure this is what you want to do!

Network inputs

In addition to reading files, Splunk can listen to network ports. The stanzas take the following form:

```
[protocol://<remote host>:<local port>]
```

The remote host portion is rarely used, but the idea is that you can specify different input configurations for specific hosts. The usual stanzas look as follows:

* `[tcp://1234]`: This specifies that we will listen to port 1234 for TCP connections. Anything can connect to this port and send data in.
* `[tcp-ssl://importanthost:1234]`: This listens on TCP using SSL, and we can apply this stanza to the `importanthost` host. Splunk will generate self-signed certificates the first time it is launched.
* `[udp://514]`: This is generally used to receive `syslog` events. While this does work, it is generally considered a best practice to use a dedicated syslog receiver, such as `rsyslog` or `syslogng`. See *Chapter 12, Advanced Deployments*, for a discussion on this subject.

- `[splunktcp://9997]` or `[splunktcp-ssl://9997]`: In a distributed environment, your indexers will receive events on the specified port. It is a custom protocol used between Splunk instances. This stanza is created for you when you use the **Manager** page at **Manager | Forwarding and receiving | Receive data**.

For TCP and UDP inputs, the following attributes apply:

- `source`: If it is not specified, the source will default to `protocol:port`, for instance, `udp:514`.

- `sourcetype`: If it is not specified, `sourcetype` will also default to `protocol:port`, but this is generally not what you want. It is best to specify a source type and create a corresponding stanza in `props.conf`.

- `connection_host`: With network inputs, what value to capture for `host` is somewhat tricky. Your options essentially are:

  - `connection_host = dns` uses reverse DNS to determine the hostname from the incoming connection. When reverse DNS is configured properly, this is usually your best bet. This is the default setting.

  - `connection_host = ip` sets the host field to the IP address of the remote machine. This is your best choice when reverse DNS is unreliable.

  - `connection_host = none` uses the hostname of the Splunk instance receiving the data. This option can make sense when all traffic is going to an interim host.

  - `host = foo` sets the hostname statically.

  - It is also common to reset the value of the host using a transform, for instance, with syslog events. This happens after parsing, though, so it is too late to change things such as time zone based on the host.

- `queueSize`: This value specifies how much memory Splunk is allowed to set aside for an input queue. A common use for a queue is to capture spikey data until the indexers can catch up.

- `persistentQueueSize`: This value specifies a persistent queue that can be used to capture data to the disk if the in-memory queue fills up. If you find yourself building a particularly complicated setup around network ports, I would encourage you to talk to Splunk support as there may be a better way to accomplish your goals.

Native Windows inputs

One nice thing about Windows is that system logs and many application logs go to the same place.

Unfortunately, that place is not a file, so native hooks are required to access these events. Splunk makes those inputs available using stanzas of the `[WinEventLog:LogName]`. form. For example, to index the `Security` log, the stanza simply looks like this:

```
[WinEventLog:Security]
```

There are a number of supported attributes, but the defaults are reasonable. The only attribute I have personally used is `current_only`, which is the equivalent of `followTail` for monitor stanzas. For instance, this stanza says to monitor the `Application` log, but also to start reading from now:

```
[WinEventLog:Application]
current_only = 1
```

This is useful when there are many historical events on the server.

The other input available is **Windows Management Instrumentation (WMI)**. With WMI, you can accomplish the following:

- Monitor native performance metrics as you would find in Windows Performance Monitor
- Monitor the Windows Event Log API
- Run custom queries against the database behind WMI
- Query remote machines

Even though it is theoretically possible to monitor many Windows servers using WMI and a few Splunk forwarders, this is not advised. The configuration is complicated, does not scale well, introduces complicated security implications, and is not thoroughly tested. Also, reading Windows Event Logs via WMI produces different output than the native input, and most apps that expect Windows events will not function as expected.

The simplest way to generate the `inputs.conf` and `wmi.conf` configurations needed for Windows Event Logs and WMI is to install Splunk for Windows on a Windows host and then configure the desired inputs through the web interface. See the official Splunk documentation for more examples.

Scripts as inputs

Splunk will periodically execute processes and capture the output. For example, here is input from the ImplementingSplunkDataGenerator app:

```
[script://./bin/implSplunkGen.py 2]
interval=60
sourcetype=impl_splunk_gen_sourcetype2
source=impl_splunk_gen_src2
host=host2
index=implSplunk
```

Things to notice in this example are as follows:

- The present working directory is the root of the app that contains inputs. conf.
- Files that end with .py will be executed using the Python interpreter included with Splunk. This means the Splunk Python modules are available.

  To use a different Python module, specify the path to Python in the stanza.

- Any arguments specified in the stanza will be handed to the script as if it was executed at the command line.
- The interval specifies how often, in seconds, this script should be run:
    ◦ If the script is still running, it will not be launched again.
    ◦ Long-running scripts are fine. Since only one copy of a script will run at a time, the interval will instead indicate how often to check whether the script is still running.
    ◦ This value can also be specified in the cron format.

Any programming language can be used as long as it can be executed at the command line. Splunk simply captures the standard output from whatever is executed.

Included with Splunk for Windows are scripts to query WMI. One sample stanza looks as follows:

```
[script://$SPLUNK_HOME\bin\scripts\splunk-wmi.path]
```

The things to note are as follows:

- Windows paths require backslashes instead of slashes
- $SPLUNK_HOME will expand properly

transforms.conf

The `transforms.conf` configuration is where we specify transformations and lookups that can then be applied to any event. These transforms and lookups are referenced by name in `props.conf`.

For our examples in the later subsections, we will use this event:

```
2012-09-24T00:21:35.925+0000 DEBUG [MBX] Password reset called.
[old=1234, new=secret, req_time=5346]
```

We will use it with these metadata values:

```
sourcetype=myapp
source=/logs/myapp.session_foo-jA5MDkyMjEwMTIK.log
host=vlbmba.local
```

Creating indexed fields

One common task accomplished with `transforms.conf` is the creation of new indexed fields. Indexed fields are different than extracted fields in that they must be created at index time and can be searched for whether the value is in the raw text of the event or not. It is usually preferable to create extracted fields instead of indexed fields. See *Chapter 3, Tables, Charts, and Fields*, for a deeper discussion about when indexed fields are beneficial.

Indexed fields are only applied to events that are indexed after the definition is created. There is no way to backfill a field without re-indexing.

Creating a loglevel field

The format of a typical stanza in `transforms.conf` looks as follows:

```
[myapp_loglevel]
REGEX = \s([A-Z]+)\s
FORMAT = loglevel::$1
WRITE_META = True
```

This will add to our events the field `loglevel=DEBUG`. This is a good idea if the values of `loglevel` are common words outside of this location, for instance `ERROR`.

Walking through this stanza, we have the following:

- `[myapp_loglevel]`: The stanza can be any unique value, but it is in your best interest to make the name meaningful. This is the name referenced in `props.conf`.

- `REGEX = \s([A-Z]+)\s`: This is the pattern to test against each event that is handed to us. If this pattern does not match, this transform will not be applied.

- `FORMAT = loglevel::$1`: Create the `loglevel`. Under the hood, all indexed fields are stored using a :: delimiter, so we have to follow that form.

- `WRITE_META = True`: Without this attribute, the transform won't actually create an indexed field and store it with the event.

Creating a session field from the source

Using our event, let's create another field, session, which appears only to be in the value of the source:

```
[myapp_session]
SOURCE_KEY = MetaData:Source
REGEX = session_(.*?)\.log
FORMAT = session::$1
WRITE_META = True
```

Note the `SOURCE_KEY`.attribute. The value of this field can be any existing metadata field or another indexed field that has already been created. See the *Attributes with class* subsection within the *props.conf* section for a discussion about the transform execution order. We will discuss these fields in the `Modifying metadata fields` subsection.

Creating a tag field

It is also possible to create fields simply to tag events that would be difficult to search for otherwise. For example, if we wanted to find all events that were slow, we could search for:

```
sourcetype=myapp req_time>999
```

Without an indexed field, this query would require parsing every event that matches `sourcetype=myapp` over the time that we are interested in. The query would then discard all events whose `req_time` value was 999 or less.

If we know ahead of time that a value of `req_time>999` is bad, and we can come up with a regular expression to specify what "bad" is, we can tag these events for quicker retrieval. Say we have this `transforms.conf` stanza:

```
[myapp_slow]
REGEX = req_time=\d{4,}
FORMAT = slow_request::1
WRITE_META = True
```

This `REGEX` will match any event containing `req_time=` followed by four or more digits.

After adding `slow_request` to `fields.conf` (see the *fields.conf* section), we can search for `slow_request=1` and find all slow events very efficiently. This will not apply to events that were indexed before this transform existed. If the events that are slow are uncommon, this query will be much faster.

Creating host categorization fields

It is common to have parts of a hostname mean something in particular. If this pattern is well known and predictable, it may be worthwhile to pull the value out into fields. Working from our fictitious host value, `vlbmba.local` (which happens to be my laptop), we might want to create fields for the owner and the host type. Our stanza might look similar to this:

```
[host_parts]
SOURCE_KEY = MetaData:Host
REGEX = (...)(...)\.
FORMAT = host_owner::$1 host_type::$2
WRITE_META = True
```

With our new fields, we can now easily categorize errors by whatever information is encoded into the hostname. Another approach would be to use a lookup, which has the advantage of being retroactive. This approach has the advantage of faster searches for the specific fields.

Modifying metadata fields

It is sometimes convenient to override the main metadata fields. We will look at one possible reason for overriding each base metadata value.

Remember that transforms are applied after parsing, so changing metadata fields via transforms cannot be used to affect which `props.conf` stanzas are applied for date parsing or line breaking.

For instance, with `syslog` events that contain the hostname, you cannot change the time zone because the date has already been parsed before the transforms are applied. The keys provided by Splunk include:

- `_raw` (this is the default value for `SOURCE_KEY`)
- `MetaData:Source`
- `MetaData:Sourcetype`
- `MetaData:Host`
- `_MetaData:Index`

Overriding the host

If your hostnames are appearing differently from different sources: for instance, `syslog` versus Splunk Forwarders, you can use a transform to normalize these values. Given our hostname `vlbmba.local`, we may want to only keep the portion to the left of the first period. The stanza would look as follows:

```
[normalize_host]
SOURCE_KEY = MetaData:Host
DEST_KEY = MetaData:Host
REGEX = (.*?)\.
FORMAT = host::$1
```

This will replace our hostname with `vlbmba`. Note these two things:

- `WRITE_META` is not included because we are not adding to the metadata of this event; we are instead overwriting the value of a core metadata field
- `host::` must be included at the beginning of the format

Overriding the source

Some applications will write a log for each session, conversation, or transaction. One problem this introduces is an explosion of source values. The values of the source will end up in `$SPLUNK_HOME/var/lib/splunk/*/db/Sources.data`—one line per unique value of the source. This file will eventually grow to a huge size, and Splunk will waste a lot of time updating it, causing unexplained pauses. A new setting in `indexes.conf`, called `disableGlobalMetadata`, can also eliminate this problem.

To flatten this value, we could use a stanza such as this:

```
[myapp_flatten_source]
SOURCE_KEY = MetaData:Source
DEST_KEY = MetaData:Source
REGEX = (.*session_).*.log
FORMAT = source::$1x.log
```

This would set the value of source to /logs/myapp.session_x.log, which would eliminate our growing source problem. If the value of session is useful, the transform in the *Creating a session field from source* section could be run before this transform to capture the value. Likewise, a transform could capture the entire value of the source and place it into a different metadata field.

A huge number of logfiles on a filesystem introduces a few problems, including running out of nodes and the memory used by the Splunk process of tracking all of the files. As a general rule, a cleanup process should be designed to archive older logs.

Overriding sourcetype

It is not uncommon to change the sourcetype field of an event based on the contents of the event, particularly from syslog. In our fictitious example, we want a different source type for events that contain [MBX] after the log level so that we can apply different extracts to these events. The following examples will do this work:

```
[mbx_sourcetype]
DEST_KEY = MetaData:Sourcetype
REGEX = \d+\s[A-Z]+\s\([MBX\])
FORMAT = sourcetype::mbx
```

Use this functionality carefully as it easy to go conceptually wrong, and this is difficult to fix later.

Routing events to a different index

At times, you may want to send events to a different index, either because they need to live longer than other events or because they contain sensitive information that should not be seen by all users. This can be applied to any type of event from any source, whether it be a file, network, or script.

All that we have to do is match the event and reset the index.

```
[contains_password_1]
DEST_KEY = _MetaData:Index
REGEX = Password reset called
FORMAT = sensitive
```

The things to note are as follows:

- In this scenario, you will probably make multiple transforms, so make sure to make the name unique
- DEST_KEY starts with an underscore

- FORMAT does not start with index::
- The index sensitive must exist on the machine indexing the data, or else the event will be lost

Lookup definitions

A simple lookup simply needs to specify a filename in transforms.conf, as shown here:

```
[testlookup]
filename = test.csv
```

Assuming that test.csv contains the user and group columns and our events contain the field user, we can reference this lookup using the lookup command in search, as follows:

```
* | lookup testlookup user
```

Otherwise, we can wire this lookup to run automatically in props.conf, as follows:

```
[mysourcetype]
LOOKUP-testlookup = testlookup user
```

That's all you need to get started, and this probably covers most cases. See the *Using lookups to enrich data* section in *Chapter 7, Extending Search*, for instructions on creating lookups.

Wildcard lookups

In *Chapter 10, Summary Indexes and CSV Files*, we edited transforms.conf but did not explain what was happening. Let's take another look. Our transform stanza looks as follows:

```
[flatten_summary_lookup]
filename = flatten_summary_lookup.csv
match_type = WILDCARD(url)
max_matches = 1
```

Walking through what we added, we have the following terms and their descriptions:

- match_type = WILDCARD(url): This says that the value of the url field in the lookup file may contain wildcards. In our example, the URL might look like / contact/* in our CSV file.
- max_matches = 1: By default, up to 10 entries that match in the lookup file will be added to an event, with the values in each field being added to a multivalue field. In this case, we only want the first match to be applied.

CIDR wildcard lookups

CIDR wildcards look very similar to text-based wildcards but use Classless Inter-Domain Routing (CIDR) rules to match lookup rows against an IP address.

Let's try an example.

Say we have this lookup file:

```
ip_range,network,datacenter
10.1.0.0/16,qa,east
10.2.0.0/16,prod,east
10.128.0.0/16,qa,west
10.129.0.0/16,prod,west
```

It has this corresponding definition in `transforms.conf`:

```
[ip_address_lookup]
filename = ip_address_lookup.csv
match_type = CIDR(ip_range)
max_matches = 1
```

And, there are a few events such as these:

```
src_ip=10.2.1.3 user=mary
src_ip=10.128.88.33 user=bob
src_ip=10.1.35.248 user=bob
```

We could use `lookup` to enrich these events as follows:

```
src_ip="*"
| lookup ip_address_lookup ip_range as src_ip
| table src_ip user datacenter network
```

This would match the appropriate IP address and give us a table such as this one:

src_ip ‡	user ‡	datacenter ‡	network ‡
1 10.2.1.3	mary	east	prod
2 10.128.88.33	bob	west	qa
3 10.1.35.248	bob	east	qa

The query also shows that you could use the same lookup for different fields using the `as` keyword in the `lookup` call.

Using time in lookups

A temporal lookup is used to enrich events based on when the event happened. To accomplish this, we specify the beginning of a time range in the lookup source and then specify a format for this time in our lookup configuration. Using this mechanism, lookup values can change over time, even retroactively.

Here is a very simple example to attach a version field based on time. Say we have the following CSV file:

```
sourcetype,version,time
impl_splunk_gen,1.0,2012-09-19 02:56:30 UTC
impl_splunk_gen,1.1,2012-09-22 12:01:45 UTC
impl_splunk_gen,1.2,2012-09-23 18:12:12 UTC
```

We then use the lookup configuration in transforms.conf to specify which field in our lookup will be tested against the time in each event, and what the format of the time field will be:

```
[versions]
filename = versions.csv
time_field = time
time_format = %Y-%m-%d %H:%M:%S %Z
```

With this in place, we can now use our lookup in search, as shown here:

```
sourcetype=impl_splunk_gen error
| lookup versions sourcetype
| timechart count by version
```

This would give us a chart of errors (by version) over time, as shown here:

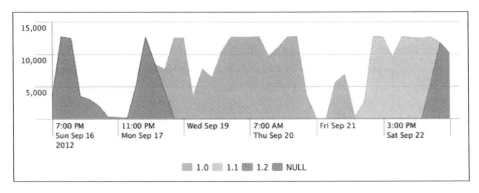

Other use cases include tracking deployments across environments and tracking activity from disabled accounts.

Using REPORT

Attributes of the format `REPORT-foo` in `props.conf` call stanzas in `transforms.conf` at search time, which means that they cannot affect metadata fields. `EXTRACT` definitions are more convenient to write as they live entirely in a single attribute in `props.conf`, but there are a couple of things that can only be done using a `REPORT` attribute paired with a transform defined in `transforms.conf`.

Creating multivalue fields

Assuming some value might occur multiple times in a given event, an `EXTRACT` definition can only match the first occurrence. For example, say we have the event:

```
2012-08-25T20:18:09 action=send a@b.com c@d.com e@f.com
```

We could pull the first e-mail address using the following extraction:

```
EXTRACT-email = (?i)(?P<email>[a-zA-Z0-9._]+@[a-zA-Z0-9._]+)
```

This would set the field `email` to `a@b.com`. Using a `REPORT` attribute and the transform stanza, we can capture all of the e-mail addresses using the `MV_ADD` attribute. The props stanza would look as follows:

```
REPORT-mvemail = mvemail
```

The `transforms.conf` stanza would then look as follows:

```
[mvemail]
REGEX = (?i)([a-zA-Z0-9._]+@[a-zA-Z0-9._]+)
FORMAT = email::$1
MV_ADD = true
```

The `MV_ADD` attribute also has the effect that, if some other configuration has already created the email field, all values that match will be added to the event.

Creating dynamic fields

Sometimes, it can be useful to dynamically create fields from an event. For instance, say we have an event, such as:

```
2012-08-25T20:18:09 action=send from_335353("a@b.com") to_223523("c@d.com") cc_39393("e@f.com") cc_39394("g@h.com")
```

It would be nice to pull from, to, and cc as fields, but we may not know all of the possible field names. This stanza in `transforms.conf` would create the fields we want, dynamically:

```
[dynamic_address_fields]
REGEX=\s(\S+)_\S+\("(.*?)"\)
```

```
FORMAT = $1::$2
MV_ADD=true
```

While we're at it, let's put the numeric value after the field name into a value:

```
[dynamic_address_ids]
REGEX=\s(\S+)_(\S+)\("
FORMAT = $1::$2
MV_ADD=true
```

This gives us multivalue fields such as the ones in the following screenshot:

action ⬍	cc ⬍	from ⬍	to ⬍
send	e@f.com g@h.com 39393 39394	a@b.com 335353	c@d.com 223523

One thing that we cannot do is add extra text to the FORMAT attribute. For instance, in the second case, it would be nice to use a FORMAT attribute such as this one:

```
FORMAT = $1_id::$2
```

Unfortunately, this will not function as we hope and will instead create the field id.

Chaining transforms

As covered before in the *Attributes with class* section, transforms are executed in a particular order. In most cases, this order does not matter, but there are occasions when you might want to chain transforms together, with one transform relying on a field created by a previous transform.

A good example is the source flattening that we used previously in the *Overriding source* section. If this transform happened before our transform in the *Creating a session field from source* section, our session field would always have the value x.

Let's reuse two transforms from the previous sections and then create one more transform. We will chain them to pull the first part of session into yet another field. Say we have these transforms:

```
[myapp_session]
SOURCE_KEY = MetaData:Source
REGEX = session_(.*?)\.log
FORMAT = session::$1
WRITE_META = True
[myapp_flatten_source]
```

```
SOURCE_KEY = MetaData:Source
DEST_KEY = MetaData:Source
REGEX = (.*session_).*.log
FORMAT = source::$1x.log
[session_type]
SOURCE_KEY = session
REGEX = (.*?)-
FORMAT = session_type::$1
WRITE_META = True
```

To ensure that these transforms run in order, the simplest thing would be to place them in a single TRANSFORMS attribute in props.conf, as shown here:

```
[source:*session_*.log]
TRANSFORMS-s = myapp_session,myapp_flatten_source,session_type
```

We can use the source from our sample event specified inside tranforms.conf as follows:

```
source=/logs/myapp.session_foo-jA5MDkyMjEwMTIK.log
```

Walking though the transforms, we have the following terms and their descriptions:

- myapp_session: Reading from the metadata field, source, this creates the indexed field session with the foo-jA5MDkyMjEwMTIK value

- myapp_flatten_source: This resets the metadata field, source, to /logs/ myapp.session_x.log

- session_type: Reading from our newly indexed field, session, this creates the session_type field with the value foo

This same ordering logic can be applied at search time using the EXTRACT and REPORT stanzas. This particular case needs to be calculated as indexed fields if we want to search for these values since the values are part of a metadata field.

Dropping events

Some events are simply not worth indexing. The hard part is figuring out which ones these are and making very sure you're not wrong. Dropping too many events can make you blind to real problems at critical times and can introduce more problems than tuning Splunk to deal with the greater volume of data in the first place.

With that warning stated, if you know what events you do not need, the procedure for dropping events is pretty simple. Say we have an event such as this one:

```
2012-02-02 12:24:23 UTC TRACE Database call 1 of 1,000. [...]
```

I know absolutely that, in this case and for this particular source type, I do not want to index TRACE level events.

In props.conf, I will create a stanza for my source type, as shown here:

```
[mysourcetype]
TRANSFORMS-droptrace=droptrace
```

Then, I will create the following transform in transforms.conf:

```
[droptrace]
REGEX=^\d{4}-\d{2}-\d{2}\s+\d{1,2}:\d{2}:\d{1,2}\s+[A-Z]+\sTRACE
DEST_KEY=queue
FORMAT=nullQueue
```

Splunk compares nullQueue to nulldevice, which (according to the product documentation) tells Splunk not to forward or index the filtered data.

This REGEX attribute is purposely as strict as I can make it. It is vital that I do not accidentally drop other events, and it is better for this brittle pattern to start failing and to let through TRACE events rather than for it to do the opposite.

fields.conf

We need to add to fields.conf any indexed fields we create, or else they will not be searched efficiently, or may even not function at all. For our examples in the *transforms.conf* section, fields.conf would look as follows:

```
[session_type]
INDEXED = true
[session]
INDEXED = true
[host_owner]
INDEXED = true
[host_type]
INDEXED = true
[slow_request]
INDEXED = true
[loglevel]
INDEXED = true
```

These stanzas instruct Splunk not to look in the body of the events for the value being queried. Take, for instance, the following search:

```
host_owner=vlb
```

Without this entry, the actual query would essentially be:

```
vlb | search host_owner=vlb
```

With the expectation that the value vlb is in the body of the event, this query simply won't work. Adding the entry to `fields.conf` fixes this. In the case of loglevel, since the value is in the body, the query will work, but it will not take advantage of the indexed field, instead only using it to filter events after finding all events that contain the bare word.

outputs.conf

This configuration controls how Splunk will forward events. In the vast majority of cases, this configuration exists on Splunk Forwarders, which send their events to Splunk indexers. An example would look similar to this:

```
[tcpout]
defaultGroup = nyc
[tcpout:nyc]
autoLB = true
server = 1.2.3.4:9997,1.2.3.6:9997
```

It is possible to use transforms to route events to different server groups, but it is not commonly used as it introduces a lot of complexity that is generally not needed.

indexes.conf

Put simply, `indexes.conf` determines where data is stored on the disk, how much is kept, and for how long. An index is simply a named directory with a specific structure. Inside this directory structure, there are a few metadata files and subdirectories; the subdirectories are called buckets and actually contain the indexed data.

A simple stanza looks as follows:

```
[implSplunk]
homePath = $SPLUNK_DB/implSplunk/db
coldPath = $SPLUNK_DB/implSplunk/colddb
thawedPath = $SPLUNK_DB/implSplunk/thaweddb
```

Let's walk through these attributes:

- `homePath`: This is the location for recent data.
- `coldPath`: This is the location for older data.
- `thawedPath`: This is a directory where buckets can be restored. It is an unmanaged location. This attribute must be defined, but I for one, have never actually used it.

An aside about the terminology of buckets is probably in order. It is as follows:

- `hot`: This is a bucket that is currently open for writing. It lives in `homePath`.
- `warm`: This is a bucket that was created recently but is no longer open for writing. It also lives in `homePath`.
- `cold`: This is an older bucket that has been moved to `coldPath`. It is moved when `maxWarmDBCount` has been exceeded.
- `frozen`: For most installations, this simply means deleted. For customers who want to archive buckets, `coldToFrozenScript` or `coldToFrozenDir` can be specified to save buckets.
- `thawed`: A thawed bucket is a frozen bucket that has been brought back. It is special in that it is not managed, and it is not included in all time queries. When using `coldToFrozenDir`, only the raw data is typically kept, so Splunk rebuild will need to be used to make the bucket searchable again.

How long data stays in an index is controlled by these attributes:

- `frozenTimePeriodInSecs`: This setting dictates the oldest data to keep in an index. A bucket will be removed when its newest event is older than this value. The default value is approximately 6 years.
- `maxTotalDataSizeMB`: This setting dictates how large an index can be. The total space used across all hot, warm, and cold buckets will not exceed this value. The oldest bucket is always frozen first. The default value is 500 gigabytes. It is generally a good idea to set both of these attributes. `frozenTimePeriodInSecs` should match what users expect. `maxTotalDataSizeMB` should protect your system from running out of disk space.

Less commonly used attributes include:

- `coldToFrozenDir`: If specified, buckets will be moved to this directory instead of being deleted. This directory is not managed by Splunk, so it is up to the administrator to make sure that the disk does not fill up.

- `maxHotBuckets`: A bucket represents a slice of time and will ideally span as small a slice of time as is practical. I would never set this value to less than 3, but ideally, it should be set to 10.

- `maxDataSize`: This is the maximum size for an individual bucket. The default value is set by the processor type and is generally acceptable. The larger a bucket, the fewer the buckets to be opened to complete a search, but the more the disk space needed before a bucket can be frozen. The default is auto, which will never top 750 MB. The setting `auto_high_volume`, which equals 1 GB on 32-bit systems and 10 GB on 64-bit systems, should be used for indexes that receive more than 10 GB a day.

We will discuss sizing multiple indexes in *Chapter 12, Advanced Deployments*.

authorize.conf

This configuration stores definitions of capabilities and roles. These settings affect search functions and the web interface. They are generally managed through the interface at **Manager | Access controls**, but a quick look at the configuration itself may be useful.

A role stanza looks as follows:

```
[role_power]
importRoles = user
schedule_search = enabled
rtsearch = enabled
srchIndexesAllowed = *
srchIndexesDefault = main
srchDiskQuota = 500
srchJobsQuota = 10
rtSrchJobsQuota = 20
```

Let's walk through these settings:

- `importRoles`: This is a list of roles to import capabilities from. The set of capabilities will be the merging of capabilities from imported roles and added capabilities.

- `schedule_search` and `rtsearch`: These are two capabilities enabled for the role power that were not necessarily enabled for the imported roles.

- `srchIndexesAllowed`: This determines which indexes this role is allowed to search. In this case, all are allowed.

- `srchIndexesDefault`: This determines the indexes to search by default. This setting also affects the data shown in **Search | Summary**. If you have installed the `ImplementingSplunkDataGenerator` app, you will see the `impl_splunk_*` source types on this page even though this data is actually stored in the `implsplunk` index.

- `srchDiskQuota`: Whenever a search is run, the results are stored on the disk until they expire. The expiration can be set explicitly when creating a saved search, but the expiration is automatically set for interactive searches. Users can delete old results from the **Jobs** view.

- `srchJobsQuota`: Each user is limited to a certain number of concurrently running searches. The default is three. Users with the power role are allowed 10, while those with the admin role are allowed 50.

- `rtSrchJobsQuota`: Similarly, this is the maximum number of concurrently running real-time searches. The default is six.

savedsearches.conf

This configuration contains saved searches and is rarely modified by hand.

times.conf

This configuration holds definitions for time ranges that appear in the time picker.

commands.conf

This configuration specifies commands provided by an app. We will use this in *Chapter 13, Extending Splunk*.

web.conf

The main settings changed in this file are the port for the web server, the SSL certificates, and whether to start the web server at all.

User interface resources

Most Splunk apps consist mainly of resources for the web application. The app layout for these resources is completely different from all other configurations.

Views and navigation

Like `.conf` files, view and navigation documents take precedence in the following order:

- `$SPLUNK_HOME/etc/users/$username/$appname/local`: When a new dashboard is created, it lands here. It will remain here until the permissions are changed to **App** or **Global**.

- `$SPLUNK_HOME/etc/apps/$appname/local`: Once a document is shared, it will be moved to this directory.

- `$SPLUNK_HOME/etc/apps/$appname/default`: Documents can only be placed here manually. You should do this if you are going to share an app. Unlike `.conf` files, these documents do not merge.

Within each of these directories, views and navigation end up under the directories `data/ui/views` and `data/ui/nav`, respectively. So, given a view `foo`, for the user `bob`, in the app `app1`, the initial location for the document will be as follows:

`$SPLUNK_HOME/etc/users/bob/app1/local/data/ui/views/foo.xml`

Once the document is shared, it will be moved to the following location:

`$SPLUNK_HOME/etc/apps/app1/local/data/ui/views/foo.xml`

Navigation follows the same structure, but the only navigation document that is ever used is called `default.xml`, for instance:

`$SPLUNK_HOME/etc/apps/app1/local/data/ui/nav/default.xml`

You can edit these files directly on the disk instead of through the web interface, but Splunk will probably not realize the changes without a restart—unless you use a little trick. To reload changes to views or navigation made directly on the disk, load the URL `http://mysplunkserver:8000/debug/refresh`, replacing `mysplunkserver` appropriately. If all else fails, restart Splunk.

Appserver resources

Outside of views and navigation, there are a number of resources that the web application will use. For instance, applications and dashboards can reference CSS and images, as we did in *Chapter 8, Working with Apps*. These resources are stored under `$SPLUNK_HOME/etc/apps/$appname/appserver/`. There are a few directories that appear under this directory, as follows:

- `static`: Any static files that you would like to use in your application are stored here. There are a few magic documents that Splunk itself will use, for instance, `appIcon.png`, `screenshot.png`, `application.css`, and `application.js`. Other files can be referenced using includes or templates. See the *Using ServerSideInclude in a complex dashboard* section in *Chapter 8, Working with Apps*, for an example of referencing includes and static images.

- `event_renderers`: Event renderers allow you to run special display code for specific event types. We will write an event renderer in *Chapter 13, Extending Splunk*.

- `templates`: It is possible to create special templates using the *mako* template language. It is not commonly done.

- `modules`: This is where new modules that are provided by apps are stored. Examples of this include the Google Maps and Sideview Utils modules. See `http://dev.splunk.com` for more information about building your own modules or use existing modules as an example.

Metadata

Object permissions are stored in files located at `$SPLUNK_HOME/etc/apps/$appname/metadata/`. The two possible files are `default.meta` and `local.meta`.

These files have certain properties:

- They are only relevant to the resources in the app where they are contained
- They do merge, with entries in `local.meta` taking precedence
- They are generally controlled by the admin interface
- They can contain rules that affect all configurations of a particular type, but this entry must be made manually

In the absence of these files, resources are limited to the current app.

Let's look at `default.meta` for `is_app_one`, as created by Splunk:

```
# Application-level permissions
[]
access = read : [ * ], write : [ admin, power ]
### EVENT TYPES
[eventtypes]
export = system
### PROPS
[props]
export = system
### TRANSFORMS
[transforms]
export = system
### LOOKUPS
[lookups]
Chapter 10
[ 329 ]
export = system
### VIEWSTATES: even normal users should be able to create shared
viewstates
[viewstates]
access = read : [ * ], write : [ * ]
export = system
```

Walking through this snippet, we have the following terms and their descriptions:

- The `[]` stanza states that all users should be able to read everything in this app but that only users with the admin or power roles should be able to write to this app.

- The `[eventtypes]`, `[props]`, `[transforms]`, and `[lookups]` states say that all configurations of each type in this app should be shared by all users in all apps, by default. `export=system` is equivalent to `Global` in the user interface.

- The `[viewstates]` stanza gives all users the right to share `viewstates` globally. A viewstate contains information about dashboard settings made through the web application, for instance, chart settings. Without this, chart settings applied to a dashboard or saved search would not be available.

Looking at `local.meta`, we see settings produced by the web application for the configurations we created through the web application.

```
[indexes/summary_impl_splunk]
access = read : [ * ], write : [ admin, power ]
[views/errors]
access = read : [ * ], write : [ admin, power ]
export = system
owner = admin
version = 4.3
modtime = 1339296668.151105000
[savedsearches/top%20user%20errors%20pie%20chart]
export = none
owner = admin
version = 4.3
modtime = 1338420710.720786000
[viewstates/flashtimeline%3Ah2v14xkb]
owner = nobody
version = 4.3
modtime = 1338420715.753642000
[props/impl_splunk_web/LOOKUP-web_section]
access = read : [ * ]
export = none
owner = admin
version = 4.3
modtime = 1346013505.279379000
```

Hopefully, you get the idea. The web application will make very specific entries for each object created. When distributing an application, it is generally easier to make blanket permissions in `metadata/default.meta` as appropriate for the resources in your application.

For an application that simply provides dashboards, no metadata at all will be needed as the default for all resources (apps) will be acceptable. If your application provides resources to be used by other applications, for instance, lookups or extracts, your `default.meta` file might look like this:

```
### PROPS
[props]
export = system
### TRANSFORMS
[transforms]
export = system
### LOOKUPS
[lookups]
export = system
```

This states that everything in your `props.conf` and `transforms.conf` files, and all lookup definitions, are merged into the logical configuration of every search.

Summary

This chapter provided an overview of how configurations work and a commentary on the most common aspects of Splunk configuration. This is by no means a complete reference for these configurations, which I will leave to the official documentation. I find that the easiest way to get to the official documentation for a particular file is to query your favorite search engine for splunk `configname.conf`. In *Chapter 12, Advanced Deployments*, we will dig into distributed deployments and look at how they are efficiently configured. What you have learned in this chapter will be vital to understanding what is considered to be a best practice.

12
Advanced Deployments

When you first started Splunk, you probably installed it on one machine, imported some logs, and got to work searching. It is wonderful that you can try out the product so easily, but once you move into testing and production, things can get much more complicated, and a bit of planning will save you from trouble later.

In this chapter, we will discuss the following topics:

- Getting data
- The different parts of a distributed deployment
- Distributed configuration management
- Sizing your installation
- Security concerns
- Backup strategies

Planning your installation

The following are a few questions that you need to answer in order to determine how many Splunk instances will be involved in your deployment:

- How much data will be indexed per day? How much data will be kept? The rule of thumb is 100 gigabytes per day per Splunk indexer, assuming that you have fast disks. See the *Sizing indexers* section for more information.
- How many searches will be running simultaneously? This number is probably smaller than you think. This is not the number of users who may be using Splunk, but the number of queries that are running simultaneously. This varies by the type of queries that your group runs.

- What are the sources of data? Where your data comes from can definitely affect your deployment. Planning for all the possible data that you might want to consume can save you from trouble later. See the *Common data sources* section for examples.

- How many data centers do you need to monitor? Dealing with servers in multiple locations introduces another level of complexity, to which there is no single answer. See *Deploying the Splunk binary* section for a few example deployments.

- How will you deploy the Splunk binary?

- How will you distribute configurations?

We will touch on these topics and more.

Splunk instance types

In a distributed deployment, different Splunk processes will serve different purposes. There are four stages of processing that are generally spread across two to four layers. The stages of processing include:

- **input**: This stage consumes raw data from log files, ports, or scripts.

- **parsing**: This stage splits the raw data into events, parses time, sets base metadata, runs transforms, and so on.

- **indexing**: This stage stores the data and optimizes the indexes.

- **searching**: This stage runs queries and presents the results to the user. All these different stages ca be accomplished in one process, but splitting them across servers can improve performance as the log volumes and search load increase.

Splunk forwarders

Each machine that contains the log files generally runs a Splunk forwarder process. The job of this process is to read the logs on that machine or to run scripted inputs.

This installation is either of the following:

- A full installation of Splunk, configured to forward data instead of indexing it

- **Splunk Universal Forwarder**, which is essentially Splunk with everything needed for indexing or searching removed

- With a full installation of Splunk, the process can be configured as one of two kinds of forwarder:

    ° A light forwarder is configured not to parse events but, instead, to forward the raw stream of data to the indexers. This installation has the advantages that it uses very few resources on the machine running the forwarder (unless the number of files being scanned is very large) and that the configuration is simple. It has the disadvantage that the indexers will do more work. If this is what you need, it is recommended that you use the Splunk Universal Forwarder.

    ° A heavy forwarder is configured to parse events, forwarding these parsed or cooked events to the indexers. This has the advantage that the indexer does less work, but the disadvantage that more configurations need to be pushed to the forwarders. This configuration also uses approximately double the CPU and memory as that required for a light forwarder configuration. For most customers, the Splunk Universal Forwarder is the right answer.

The most important configurations to a forwarder installation are:

- `inputs.conf`: This defines what files to read, network ports to listen to, or scripts to run.
- `outputs.conf`: This defines which indexer(s) should receive the data.
- `props.conf`: As discussed in *Chapter 11, Configuring Splunk*, very little of this configuration is relevant to the input stage, but much of it is relevant to the parse stage. The simplest way to deal with this complexity is to send `props.conf` everywhere so that whatever part of the configuration is needed is available. We will discuss this further in the *Using apps to organize configuration* section in this chapter.
- `default-mode.conf`: This configuration is used to disable the processing modules. Most modules are disabled in the case of a light forwarder.
- `limits.conf`: The main setting here is maxKBps, which controls how much bandwidth each forwarder will use.

The default setting for a light forwarder is very low to prevent flooding the network or overtaxing the forwarding machine. This value can usually be increased safely. It is often increased to the limits of the networking hardware.

We will discuss deploying the forwarder under the *Deploying the Splunk binary* section in this chapter.

Splunk indexer

In most deployments, indexers handle both the parsing and indexing of events. If there is only one Splunk indexer, the search is typically handled on this server as well. An indexer, as the name implies, indexes the data. It needs direct access to fast disks, whether they are local disks, SANs, or network volumes.

In my experience, **Network File System (NFS)** does not work reliably for storing Splunk indexes or files. Splunk expects its disks to act like a local disk, which, at times, NFS does not. It is fine to read logs from NFS. **Internet Small Computer System Interface (iSCSI)** works very well for indexers, as does SAN.

The configurations that typically matter to a Splunk indexer are:

- `inputs.conf`: This configuration typically has exactly one input, [`splunktcp://9997`]. This stanza instructs the indexer to listen for connections from the Splunk forwarders on port `9997`.

- `indexes.conf`: This configuration specifies where to place indexes and how long to keep the data. By default:

  - all data will be written to `$SPLUNK_HOME/var/lib/splunk`.

  - the index will grow to a maximum size of 500 gigabytes before dropping the oldest events.

  - the index will retain events for a maximum of six years before dropping the oldest events.

  - Events will be dropped when either limit is reached. We will discuss changing these values under the *Sizing indexers* section.

  - `props.conf` and `transforms.conf`: If the indexer handles parsing, these configurations control how the data stream is broken into events, how the date is parsed, and what indexed fields are created, if any.

  - `server.conf`: This contains the license server address. See the *Sizing indexers* section for a discussion on how many indexers you might need.

Splunk search

When there is only one Splunk server, search happens along with indexing. Until the log volumes increase beyond what one server can handle easily, this is fine. In fact, splitting off the search instance might actually hurt performance as there is more overhead involved in running a distributed search.

Most configurations pertaining to search are managed through the web interface. The configuration specifically concerning distributed search is maintained at **Manager | Distributed search**.

Common data sources

Your data may come from a number of sources; these can be files, network ports, or scripts. Let's walk through a few common scenarios.

Monitoring logs on servers

In this scenario, servers write their logs to a local drive, and a forwarder process monitors these logs. This is the typical Splunk installation.

The advantages of this approach include:

- This process is highly optimized. If the indexers are not overworked, events are usually searchable within a few seconds.

- Slowdowns caused by network problems or indexer overload are handled gracefully. The forwarder process will pick up where it left off when the slowdown is resolved.

- The agent is light, typically using less than 100 megabytes of RAM and a few percent of one CPU. These values go up with the amount of new data written and the number of files being tracked. See `inputs.conf` in *Chapter 11, Configuring Splunk*, for details.

- Logs without a time zone specified will inherit the time zone of the machine running the forwarder. This is almost always what you want.

- The hostname will be picked up automatically from the host. This is almost always what you want.

The disadvantages of this approach include:

- The forwarder must be installed on each server. If you have a system for distributing software already, this is not a problem. We will discuss strategies under the *Deploying the Splunk binary* section.

- The forwarder process must have read rights to all the logs to be indexed.

This is usually not a problem but does require some planning. This typical deployment looks like the following figure:

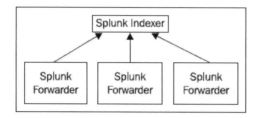

If your log volume exceeds 100 gigabytes of logs produced each day, you need to think about multiple indexers. We will talk about this further in the *Sizing indexers* section.

Monitoring logs on a shared drive

Some customers configure all the servers to write their logs to a network share, NFS or otherwise. This setup can be made to work, but it is not ideal.

The advantages of this approach include:

- A forwarder does not need to be installed on each server that is writing its logs to the share
- Only the Splunk instance reading these logs needs rights to the logs

The disadvantages of this approach include:

- The network share can become overloaded and can become a bottleneck.
- If a single file has more than a few megabytes of unindexed data, the Splunk process will only read this one log until all the data is indexed. If there are multiple indexers in play, only one indexer will be receiving data from this forwarder. In a busy environment, the forwarder may fall behind.
- Multiple Splunk forwarder processes do not share information about what files have been read. This makes it very difficult to manage a failover for each forwarder process without a SAN.
- Splunk relies on the modification time to determine whether the new events have been written to a file. File metadata may not be updated as quickly on a share.

- A large directory structure will cause the Splunk process reading logs to use a lot of RAM and a large percentage of the CPU. A process to move away the old logs would be advisable so as to minimize the number of files that Splunk must track.

This setup often looks like the following figure:

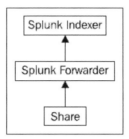

This configuration may look simple, but unfortunately, it does not scale easily.

Consuming logs in batch

Another less common approach is to gather logs periodically from the servers, after the logs have rolled. This is very similar to monitoring logs on a shared drive, except that the problems of scale are possibly even worse.

The advantages of this approach include:

- A forwarder does not need to be installed on each server that is writing its logs to the share.

The disadvantages of this approach include:

- When new logs are dropped, if the files are large, the Splunk process will only read events from one file at a time.
- When this directory is on an indexer, this is fine, but when a forwarder is trying to distribute events across multiple indexers, only one indexer will receive events at a time.
- The oldest events in the rolled log will not be loaded until the log is rolled and copied.
- An active log cannot be copied, as events may be truncated during the copy, or Splunk may be confused and believe that the update file is a new log, indexing the entire file again.

Sometimes this is the only approach possible, and in those cases, you should follow a few rules:

- Only copy complete logs to the watched directory.
- If possible, use batch stanzas instead of monitor stanzas in `inputs.conf,`, so that Splunk can delete files after indexing them.
- If possible, copy sets of logs to different Splunk servers, either to multiple forwarders that then spread the logs across multiple indexers, or possibly directly to watched directories on the indexers. Be sure not to copy the same log to multiple machines as Splunk has no mechanism for sharing the file position information across instances.

Receiving syslog events

Another common source of data is `syslog`, usually from devices that have no filesystem or no support for installing software. These sources are usually devices or appliances, and usually send those events using UDP packets. Syslog management deserves a book of its own, so we will only discuss how to integrate syslog with Splunk at a high level.

Receiving events directly on the Splunk indexer

For very small installations, it may be acceptable to have your Splunk server listen directly for syslog events. This installation looks essentially like the following figure:

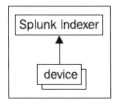

On the Splunk indexer, you would create an input for `syslog`, listening on `udp` or `tcp`. The inputs.conf configuration would look like:

```
[udp://514]
sourcetype = syslog
```

The advantage of this approach is its simplicity. The major caveat is that, if the Splunk process is down or busy for some reason, you will lose messages. Reasons for dropped events could include a heavy system load, large queries, a slow disk, network problems, or a system upgrade.

If your syslog events are important to you, it is worth the trouble to at least use a native syslog receiver on the same hardware, but you should ideally use separate hardware.

Using a native syslog receiver

The best practice is to use a standalone syslog receiver to write events to the disk. Examples of syslog receivers include `syslog-ng` or `rsyslog`. Splunk is then configured to monitor the directories written by the syslog receiver.

Ideally, the `syslog` receiver should be configured to write one file or directory per host. `inputs.conf` can then be configured to use `host_segment` or `host_regex` to set the value of the host. This configuration has the advantage that `props.conf` stanzas can be applied by host, for instance, setting `TZ` by hostname pattern. This is not possible if the host is parsed out of the log messages, as is commonly the case with syslog.

The advantages of a standalone process include the following:

- A standalone process has no other tasks to accomplish, and is more likely to have the processor time to retrieve events from the kernel buffers before the data is pushed out of the buffers
- The interim files act as a buffer so that, in case of a Splunk slowdown or outage, events are not lost
- The syslog data is on disk, so it can be archived independently or queried with other scripts, as appropriate
- If a file is written for each host, the hostname can be extracted from the path to the file, and different parsing rules (for instance time zone) can be applied at that time

A small installation would look like the following figure:

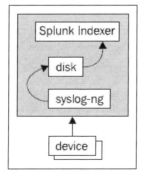

Since the configuration of the native syslog process is simple and unlikely to change, simply using another process on your single Splunk instance will add some level of protection from losing messages. A slow disk, high CPU load, or memory pressure can still cause problems, but you at least won't have to worry about restarting the Splunk process.

The next level of protection would be to use separate hardware to receive the syslog events and to use a Splunk forwarder to send the events to one or more Splunk indexers. That setup looks like the following figure:

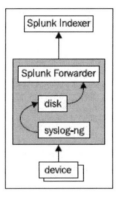

This single machine is still a single point of failure, but it has the advantage that the Splunk server holding the indexes can be restarted at will, and will not affect the instance receiving the syslog events.

The next level of protection is to use a load balancer or a dynamic DNS scheme to spread the syslog data across multiple machines receiving the syslog events, which then forwards the events to one or more Splunk indexers. That setup looks somewhat like the following figure:

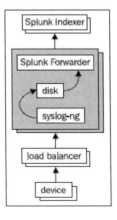

This setup is complicated but very resilient, as only a large network failure will cause loss of events.

Receiving syslog with a Splunk forwarder

It is also possible to use Splunk instances to receive the syslog events directly, which then forwards the forwarders to the Splunk indexers. This setup might look somewhat like the following figure:

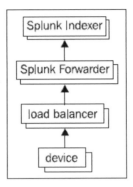

These interim Splunk forwarder processes can be configured with a large input buffer, using the `queueSize` and `persistentQueueSize` settings in `inputs.conf`. Note that these interim forwarders cannot be light forwarders. There are a few advantages to this approach that I can think of:

- If these Splunk forwarder processes are in the data center with the device producing the events, the forwarder process will set the time zone of the events. If you have devices in data centers in multiple time zones, this can be very helpful.
- The work of parsing the events will be handled at this stage, offloading some work from the indexers.

One disadvantage is that any parsing rules that are relevant to the events parsed by these interim forwarders must be installed at this layer, which may require a restart when there are changes.

Consuming logs from a database

Some applications are built to store their logs in a database. This has the advantage that the logs are centralized, but the disadvantage that it is difficult to scale beyond the limits of the database server. If the logs are pulled into Splunk, it is possible to take advantage of the Splunk interface and correlate these events with other logs.

The process to consume database logs is essentially as follows:

1. Build the query to retrieve the appropriate events; use something such as the following code:

```
select date, id, log from log_table
```

2. Identify the field that you will use as your pointer. This is usually either an ID field or a date field.

3. Modify the query to use this pointer field; use something such as the following code:

```
select date,id,log from log_table where id>4567
```

4. Use scripted input to run this query, capture the pointer field, and print the results. There are a number of applications in a number of languages available at `http://splunkbase.com` to get you started, but you can use any language and any tool that you like. The app I know best is the JDBC scripted input, which uses Java and a user-provided JDBC driver. Just to quickly illustrate how it is used, perform the following steps:

   1. Ensure Java 1.5 or greater is installed.

   2. Download the app.

   3. Copy your JDBC driver JAR to `bin/lib`.

   4. Duplicate `bin/example` to `bin/myapp`.

   5. Modify `bin/myapp/query.properties` to look something like the following code:

```
driverClass=com.mysql.jdbc.Driver
connectionString=jdbc:mysql://mydb:3306/
myapp?user=u&password=p
iteratorField=id
query=select date,id,log from entries where id>${id} order
by id
```

   6. Add a matching stanza to `inputs.conf`.

```
[script://./bin/run.sh myapp]
interval = 60
sourcetype = myapp
source = jdbc
```

That should be it. `iteratorField` is not needed if your query handles not retrieving duplicate data through some other way.

Using scripts to gather data

A scripted input in Splunk is simply a process that outputs text. Splunk will run the script periodically, as configured in `inputs.conf`. Let's make a simple example.

The configuration `inputs.conf` inside your app would contain an entry as follows:

```
[script://./bin/user_count.sh]
interval = 60
sourcetype = user_count
```

The script in `bin/user_count.sh` could contain something as follows:

```
#!/bin/sh
DATE=$(date "+%Y-%m-%d %H:%M:%S")
COUNT=$(wc -l /etc/passwd | awk '{print "users="$1}')
echo $DATE $COUNT
```

This would produce an output such as this:

```
2012-10-15 19:57:02 users=84
```

Good examples of this type of script are available in the Unix app, available at `http://www.splunkbase.com`.

Please note that:

- New to Splunk 4.3: an interval can be a `cron` schedule.
- If the name of the script ends in `.py`, Splunk will use its own copy of Python. Remember that there is no Python included with Universal Forwarder.
- Use `props.conf` to control event breaking as if this output was being read from a file.
- Set `DATETIME_CONFIG` to `CURRENT` if there is no date in the output.
- Set an appropriate `BREAK_ONLY_BEFORE` pattern if the events are multiline.
- Set `SHOULD_LINEMERGE` to `False` if the events are not multiline.
- Only one copy of each input stanza will run at a time. If a script should run continually, set interval to `-1`

Sizing indexers

There are a number of factors that affect how many Splunk indexers you will need, but starting with a model system with typical usage levels, the short answer is 100 gigabytes of raw logs per day per indexer. In the vast majority of cases, the disk is the performance bottleneck, except in the case of very slow processors.

The measurements mentioned next assume that you will spread the events across your indexers evenly, using the autoLB feature of the Splunk forwarder. We will talk more about this under Indexer load balancing.

The model system looks like this:

- 8 gigabytes of RAM

- If more memory is available, the operating system will use whatever Splunk does not use for the disk cache.

- Eight fast physical processors. On a busy indexer, two cores will probably be busy most of the time, handling indexing tasks. It is worth noting the following:

  ° More processors won't hurt but will probably not make much of a difference to an indexer as the disks holding the indexes will probably not keep up with the increased search load. More indexers, each with its own disks, will have more impact.

  ° Virtualized slices of cores or oversubscribed virtual hosts do not work well, as the processor is actually used heavily during search, mostly decompressing the raw data.

  ° Slow cores designed for highly threaded applications do not work well. For instance, you should avoid older Sun SPARC processors or slices of cores on AIX boxes.

- Disks performing 800 random **IOPS (input/output operations per second)**

  This is the value considered fast by Splunk engineering. Query your favorite search engine for Splunk bonnie++ for discussions on how to measure this value. The most important thing to remember when testing your disks is that you must test enough data to defeat disk cache. Remember, if you are using shared disks, that the indexers will share the available IOPS.

- No more than four concurrent searches. Please note the following:

  ○ Most queries are finished very quickly

  ○ This count includes interactive queries and saved searches

  ○ Summary indexes and saved searches can be used to reduce the workload of common queries

  ○ Summary queries are simply saved searches

To test your concurrency on an existing installation, try this query:

```
index=_audit search_id action=search
| transaction maxpause=1h search_id
| concurrency duration=duration
| timechart span="1h" avg(concurrency)
max(concurrency)
```

A formula for a rough estimate (assuming eight fast processors and 8 gigabytes of RAM per indexer) might look like this:

```
indexers needed =
[your IOPs] / 800 *
[gigs of raw logs produced per day] / 100 *
[average concurrent queries] / 4
```

The behavior of your systems, network, and users make it impossible to reliably predict performance without testing. These numbers are a rough estimate at best.

Let's say you work for a mid-sized company producing about 80 gigabytes of logs per day. You have some very active users, so you might expect four concurrent queries on an average. You have good disks, which bonnie++ has shown to pull a sustained 950 IOPS. You are also running some fairly heavy summary indexing queries against your web logs, and you expect at least one to be running pretty much all the time. This gives us the following output:

```
950/800 IOPS *
80/100 gigs *
(1 concurrent summary query + 4 concurrent user queries) / 4
= 1.1875 indexers
```

You cannot really deploy 1.1875 indexers, so your choices are either to start with one indexer and see how it performs or to go ahead and start with two indexers.

My advice would be to start with two indexers, if possible. This gives you some fault tolerance, and installations tend to grow quickly as more data sources are discovered throughout the company. Ideally, when crossing the 100-gigabyte mark, it may make sense to start with three indexers and spread the disks across them. The extra capacity gives you the ability to take one indexer down and still have enough capacity to cover the normal load. See the discussion in the *Planning redundancy* section.

If we increase the number of average concurrent queries, increase the amount of data indexed per day, or decrease our IOPS, the number of indexers needed should scale more or less linearly.

If we scale up a bit more, say 120 gigabytes a day, 5 concurrent queries, and two summary queries running on an average, we grow as follows:

```
950/800 IOPS *
120/100 gigs *
(2 concurrent summary query + 5 concurrent user queries) / 4
= 2.5 indexers
```

Three indexers would cover this load, but if one indexer is down, we will struggle to keep up with the data from the forwarders. Ideally, in this case, we should have four or more indexers.

Planning redundancy

The term redundancy can mean different things, depending on your concern. Splunk has features to help with some of these concerns, but not others. In a nutshell, up to and including Version 4.3, Splunk is excellent at making sure that data is captured but in the earlier versions, it provided no tangible mechanism for reliably replicating data across multiple indexers. Starting with Splunk version 5, Splunk added data replication features that can eliminate most of these concerns. Let's take a quick look at the topic now.

The replication factor

When setting up a Splunk indexer cluster, you stipulate the number of copies of data that you want the cluster to maintain. Peer nodes store incoming data in buckets, and the cluster maintains multiple copies of each bucket. The cluster stores each bucket copy on a separate peer node. The number of copies of each bucket (that the cluster maintains) is known as the Splunk replication factor.

Let's try to explain this concept (of the replication factor) with a highly simplified example.

Keep in mind that a cluster (of indexes) can tolerate a failure of 1 less than your total replication factor. So, if you have configured 3 peer indexes, you have a replication factor of 3, so your failure tolerance is 2.

By configuring additional peer nodes, you are telling Splunk to store identical copies of each bucket (of indexed data) on separate nodes, and therefore, increase your failure tolerance (that is, concurrent failures). For the most part, this seems logical and straightforward; more the peer nodes – higher is the failure tolerance.

The trade-off is that you need to store and process all those copies of data.

> *"Although the replicating activity doesn't consume much processing power as the replication factor increases, you need to run more indexers and provision more storage for the indexed data"* – Splunk.com.

Of course, in reality, a Splunk environment is nearly never so simplistic. In most production Splunk environments, the following should be considered:

In most clusters, each of the peer nodes would be functioning as both source and target peers, receiving external data from a forwarder as well as replicated data from other peers.

To accommodate horizontal scaling, a cluster with a replication factor of 3 could consist of many more peers than three. At any given time, each source peer would be streaming copies of its data to two target peers, but each time it started a new hot bucket, its set of target peers could potentially change.

Configuring your replication factors

Of course, as mentioned in the preceding section, it is not often that you deal with a single Splunk replication factor. Typically, you'll have a multisite index clustering model, so you'll need to calculate a full-site replication factor. This replaces the previously explained replication factor, which is specific a single-site environment.

The features are specified on the master node, as part of the basic configuration of the cluster. They provide site-level (`global`) control over the location of bucket copies, in addition to providing control over the total number of copies across the entire cluster. To configure a site-level replication factor, you must set `multisite=true`.

Following are the features of full-site replication factors:

Syntax

You configure the site replication factor with the `site_replication_factor` attribute, which resides in the master `server.conf` file. This attribute resides in the `[clustering]` stanza, in place of the single-site `replication_factor` attribute. For example:

```
[clustering]
mode = master
multisite=true
available_sites=site1,site2
site_replication_factor = origin:2,total:3
site_search_factor = origin:1,total:2
```

Here is the actual syntax required:

```
site_replication_factor = origin:<n>, [site1:<n>,] [site2:<n>,]
..., total:<n>
```

where:

- `<n>` (positive integer indicating the number of copies of a bucket)
- `origin:<n>` (sets the minimum number of copies of a bucket that will be held on the site originating the data in that bucket)
- `site1:<n>, site2:<n>, ...,` (specifies the minimum number of copies that will be held at each specified site)
- `total:<n>` (states the total number of copies of each bucket across all sites in the cluster)

There is a different logic for calculating a `site_replication_factor` (than for single-site replication factors). Obviously, the official documentation, which can be found at

`http://docs.splunk.com/Documentation/Splunk/6.2.0/Indexer/Sitereplicationfactor` is the recommended place to start.

Indexer load balancing

Splunk forwarders are responsible for load balancing across indexers. This is accomplished most simply by providing a list of indexers in `outputs.conf`, as shown in the following code:

```
[tcpout:nyc]
server=nyc-splunk-index01:9997,nyc-splunk-index02:9997
```

If an indexer is unreachable, the forwarder will simply choose another indexer in the list. This scheme works very well and powers most Splunk deployments. If the DNS entry returns multiple addresses, Splunk will balance between the addresses on the port specified.

By default, the forwarder will use auto load balancing, specified by `autoLB=true`. Essentially, the forwarder will switch between indexers on a timer. This is the only option available for the Universal Forwarder and a light forwarder.

On a heavy forwarder, the setting `autoLB=false` will load balance by event. This is less efficient and can cause results to be returned in a non-deterministic manner, since the original event order is not maintained across multiple indexers.

Understanding typical outages

With a single Splunk instance, an outage—perhaps for an operating system upgrade—will cause events to queue on the Splunk forwarder instances. If there are multiple indexers, the forwarders will continue to send events to the remaining indexers.

Let's walk through a simplified scenario. Given these four machines, with the forwarders configured to load balance their output across two indexers, as shown in the following figure:

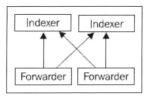

While everything is running, half of the events from each forwarder data will be sent to each indexer. If one indexer is down, we are left with only one indexer, as shown in the figure:

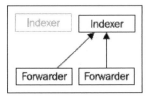

A few things happen in this case:

- All events will be sent to the remaining indexer.
- All events stored on our unavailable indexer will not be included in the search results. Splunk can help with this problem, at the cost of extra disks.
- Queries for recent events will work because these events will be stored on the remaining indexer, assuming that one indexer can handle the entire workload.

If our data throughput is more than what a single indexer can handle, it will fall behind; this makes us essentially blind to new events until the other indexer comes back and we catch up.

As the size of our deployment increases, we can see that the impact of one indexer outage affects our results less, as shown in the following figure:

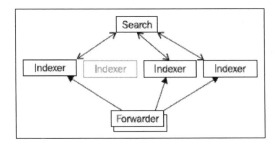

In this case, we have lost only 25 percent of our indexing capacity, and have lost access to only 25 percent of our historical data. As long as three indexers can handle our indexing workload, our indexers will not fall behind and we will continue to have timely access to new events. As the number of indexers increases, the impact of one failed indexer affects us less.

Working with multiple indexes

An index in Splunk is a storage pool for events, capped by size, time, or both. By default, all events will go to the index specified by `defaultDatabase`, which is called main but lives in a directory called `defaultdb`.

The directory structure of an index

Each index occupies a set of directories on the disk. By default, these directories live in `$SPLUNK_DB`, which, by default, is located in `$SPLUNK_HOME/var/lib/splunk`.

Look at the following stanza for the `main` index:

```
[main]
homePath = $SPLUNK_DB/defaultdb/db
coldPath = $SPLUNK_DB/defaultdb/colddb
thawedPath = $SPLUNK_DB/defaultdb/thaweddb
maxHotIdleSecs = 86400
maxHotBuckets = 10
maxDataSize = auto_high_volume
```

If our Splunk installation lives at `/opt/splunk`, the index main is rooted at the path `/opt/splunk/var/lib/splunk/defaultdb`.

To change your storage location, either modify the value of `SPLUNK_DB` in `$SPLUNK_HOME/etc/splunk-launch.conf` or set absolute paths in `indexes.conf`.

`splunk-launch.conf` cannot be controlled from an app, which means it is easy to forget when adding indexers. For this reason, and for legibility, I would recommend using absolute paths in `indexes.conf`.

The `homePath` directories contain index-level metadata, hot buckets, and warm buckets. `coldPath` contains cold buckets, which are simply warm buckets that have aged out. See the upcoming sections *The lifecycle of a bucket* and *Sizing an index* for details.

When to create more indexes

There are several reasons for creating additional indexes. If your needs do not meet one of these requirements, there is no need to create more indexes. In fact, multiple indexes may actually hurt performance if a single query needs to open multiple indexes.

Testing data

If you do not have a test environment, you can use test indexes for staging new data. This then allows you to easily recover from mistakes by dropping the test index. Since Splunk will run on a desktop, it is probably best to test new configurations locally, if possible.

Differing longevity

It may be the case that you need more history for some source types than others. The classic example here is security logs, as compared to web access logs. You may need to keep security logs for a year or more, but need the web access logs for only a couple of weeks.

If these two source types are left in the same index, security events will be stored in the same buckets as web access logs and will age out together. To split these events up, you will need to perform the following steps:

1. Create a new index called security, for instance.
2. Define different settings for the security index.
3. Update inputs.conf to use the new index for security source types.

For one year, you might make an indexes.conf setting such as this:

```
[security]
homePath = $SPLUNK_DB/security/db
coldPath = $SPLUNK_DB/security/colddb
thawedPath = $SPLUNK_DB/security/thaweddb
#one year in seconds
frozenTimePeriodInSecs = 31536000
```

For extra protection, you should also set maxTotalDataSizeMB, and possibly coldToFrozenDir.

If you have multiple indexes that should age together, or if you will split homePath and coldPath across devices, you should use volumes. See the upcoming section, *Using volumes to manage multiple indexes*, for more information.

Then, in inputs.conf, you simply need to add an index to the appropriate stanza as follows:

```
[monitor:///path/to/security/logs/logins.log]
sourcetype=logins
index=security
```

Differing permissions

If some data should only be seen by a specific set of users, the most effective way to limit access is to place this data in a different index, and then limit access to that index by using a role. The steps to accomplish this are essentially as follows:

1. Define the new index.
2. Configure `inputs.conf` or `transforms.conf` to send these events to the new index.
3. Ensure that the user role does not have access to the new index.
4. Create a new role that has access to the new index.
5. Add specific users to this new role. If you are using LDAP authentication, you will need to map the role to an LDAP group and add users to that LDAP group.

To route very specific events to this new index, assuming you created an index called sensitive, you can create a transform as follows:

```
[contains_password]
REGEX = (?i)password[=:]
DEST_KEY = _MetaData:Index
FORMAT = sensitive
```

You would then wire this transform to a particular sourcetype or source index in `props.conf`. See *Chapter 11, Configuring Splunk,* for examples.

Using more indexes to increase performance

Placing different source types in different indexes can help increase performance, if those source types are not queried together. The disks will spend less time seeking, when accessing the source type in question.

If you have access to multiple storage devices, placing indexes on different devices can help increase the performance even more by taking advantage of different hardware for different queries. Likewise, placing `homePath` and `coldPath` on different devices can help performance.

However, if you regularly run queries that use multiple source types, splitting those source types across indexes may actually hurt performance. For example, let's imagine you have two source types called `web_access` and `web_error`.

We have the following line in `web_access`:

```
2012-10-19 12:53:20 code=500 session=abcdefg url=/path/to/app
```

And we have the following line in `web_error`:

```
2012-10-19 12:53:20 session=abcdefg class=LoginClass
```

If we want to combine these results, we could run a query such as the following:

```
(sourcetype=web_access code=500) OR sourcetype=web_error
| transaction maxspan=2s session
| top url class
```

If `web_access` and `web_error` are stored in different indexes, this query will need to access twice as many buckets and will essentially take twice as long.

The lifecycle of a bucket

An index is made up of buckets, which go through a specific life cycle. Each bucket contains events from a particular period of time.

As touched on in *Chapter 11, Configuring Splunk*, the stages of this lifecycle are *hot*, *warm*, *cold*, *frozen*, and *thawed*. The only practical difference between hot and other buckets is that a hot bucket is being written to, and has not necessarily been optimized. These stages live in different places on the disk and are controlled by different settings in `indexes.conf`:

- `homePath` contains as many hot buckets as the integer value of `maxHotBuckets`, and as many warm buckets as the integer value of `maxWarmDBCount`. When a hot bucket rolls, it becomes a warm bucket. When there are too many warm buckets, the oldest warm bucket becomes a cold bucket.

- Do not set `maxHotBuckets` too low. If your data is not parsing perfectly, dates that parse incorrectly will produce buckets with very large time spans. As more buckets are created, these buckets will overlap, which means all buckets will have to be queried every time, and performance will suffer dramatically. A value of five or more is safe.

- `coldPath` contains cold buckets, which are warm buckets that have rolled out of `homePath` once there are more warm buckets than the value of `maxWarmDBCount`. If `coldPath` is on the same device, only a move is required; otherwise, a copy is required.

- Once the values of `frozenTimePeriodInSecs`, `maxTotalDataSizeMB`, or `maxVolumeDataSizeMB` are reached, the oldest bucket will be frozen. By default, frozen means deleted. You can change this behavior by specifying either of the following:
    ○ `coldToFrozenDir`: This lets you specify a location to move the buckets once they have aged out. The index files will be deleted, and only the compressed raw data will be kept. This essentially cuts the disk usage by half. This location is unmanaged, so it is up to you to watch your disk usage.
    ○ `coldToFrozenScript`: This lets you specify a script to perform some action when the bucket is frozen. The script is handed the path to the bucket that is about to be frozen.

- `thawedPath` can contain buckets that have been restored. These buckets are not managed by Splunk and are not included in All time searches. To search these buckets, their time range must be included explicitly in your search.

I have never actually used this directory. Search `http://splunk.com` for restore archived to learn the procedures.

Sizing an index

To determine how much disk space is needed for an index, use the following formula: *(gigabytes per day) * .5 * (days of retention desired)*

Likewise, to determine how many days you can store an index, the formula is essentially:

*(device size in gigabytes) / ((gigabytes per day) * .5)*

The .5 represents a conservative compression ratio. The log data itself is usually compressed to 10 percent of its original size. The index files necessary to speed up search brings the size of a bucket closer to 50 percent of the original size, though it is usually smaller than this.

If you plan to split your buckets across devices, the math gets more complicated unless you use volumes. Without using volumes, the math is essentially as follows:

```
homePath = (maxWarmDBCount + maxHotBuckets) * maxDataSize
coldPath = maxTotalDataSizeMB - homePath
```

For example, say we are given these settings:

```
[myindex]
homePath = /splunkdata_home/myindex/db
coldPath = /splunkdata_cold/myindex/colddb
thawedPath = /splunkdata_cold/myindex/thaweddb
maxWarmDBCount = 50
maxHotBuckets = 6
maxDataSize = auto_high_volume #10GB on 64-bit systems
maxTotalDataSizeMB = 2000000
Filling in the preceding formula, we get these values:
homePath = (50 warm + 6 hot) * 10240 MB = 573440 MB
coldPath = 2000000 MB - homePath = 1426560 MB
```

If we use volumes, this gets simpler and we can simply set the volume sizes to our available space and let Splunk do the math.

Using volumes to manage multiple indexes

Volumes combine pools of storage across different indexes so that they age out together. Let's make up a scenario where we have five indexes and three storage devices.

The indexes are as follows:

```
Name Data per day Retention required Storage needed
web 50 GB no requirement ?
security 1 GB 2 years 730 GB * 50 percent
app 10 GB no requirement ?
chat 2 GB 2 years 1,460 GB * 50
percent
web_summary 1 GB 1 years 365 GB * 50 percent
```

Now let's say we have three storage devices to work with, mentioned in the following table:

```
Name Size
small_fast 500 GB
big_fast 1,000 GB
big_slow 5,000 GB
```

We can create volumes based on the retention time needed. Security and chat share the same retention requirements, so we can place them in the same volumes. We want our hot buckets on our fast devices, so let's start there with the following configuration:

```
[volume:two_year_home]
#security and chat home storage
path = /small_fast/two_year_home
maxVolumeDataSizeMB = 300000
[volume:one_year_home]
#web_summary home storage
path = /small_fast/one_year_home
maxVolumeDataSizeMB = 150000
```

For the rest of the space needed by these indexes, we will create companion volume definitions on `big_slow`, as follows:

```
[volume:two_year_cold]
#security and chat cold storage
path = /big_slow/two_year_cold
maxVolumeDataSizeMB = 850000 #([security]+[chat])*1024 - 300000
[volume:one_year_cold]
#web_summary cold storage
path = /big_slow/one_year_cold
maxVolumeDataSizeMB = 230000 #[web_summary]*1024 - 150000
```

Now for our remaining indexes, whose timeframe is not important, we will use big_fast and the remainder of `big_slow`, like so:

```
[volume:large_home]
#web and app home storage
path = /big_fast/large_home
maxVolumeDataSizeMB = 900000 #leaving 10% for pad
[volume:large_cold]
#web and app cold storage
path = /big_slow/large_cold
maxVolumeDataSizeMB = 3700000
#(big_slow - two_year_cold - one_year_cold)*.9
```

Given that the sum of `large_home` and `large_cold` is 4,600,000 MB, and a combined daily volume of web and app is 60,000 MB approximately, we should retain approximately 153 days of web and app logs with 50 percent compression.

In reality, the number of days retained will probably be larger. With our volumes defined, we now have to reference them in our index definitions:

```
[web]
homePath = volume:large_home/web
coldPath = volume:large_cold/web
thawedPath = /big_slow/thawed/web
[security]
homePath = volume:two_year_home/security
coldPath = volume:two_year_cold/security
thawedPath = /big_slow/thawed/security
coldToFrozenDir = /big_slow/frozen/security
[app]
homePath = volume:large_home/app
coldPath = volume:large_cold/app
thawedPath = /big_slow/thawed/app
[chat]
homePath = volume:two_year_home/chat
coldPath = volume:two_year_cold/chat
thawedPath = /big_slow/thawed/chat
coldToFrozenDir = /big_slow/frozen/chat
[web_summary]
homePath = volume:one_year_home/web_summary
coldPath = volume:one_year_cold/web_summary
thawedPath = /big_slow/thawed/web_summary
thawedPath cannot be defined using a volume and must be specified for
Splunk to start.
```

For extra protection, we specified `coldToFrozenDir` for the indexes' security and chat. The buckets for these indexes will be copied to this directory before deletion, but it is up to us to make sure that the disk does not fill up. If we allow the disk to fill up, Splunk will stop indexing until space is made available.

This is just one approach to using volumes. You could overlap in any way that makes sense to you, as long as you understand that the oldest bucket in a volume will be frozen first, no matter which index put the bucket in that volume.

Deploying the Splunk binary

Splunk provides binary distributions for Windows and a variety of Unix operating systems. For all Unix operating systems, a compressed tar file is provided. For some platforms, packages are also provided.

If your organization uses packages, such as deb or rpm, you should be able to use the provided packages in your normal deployment process. Otherwise, installation starts by unpacking the provided tar to the location of your choice.

The process is the same, whether you are installing the full version of Splunk or the Splunk Universal Forwarder.

The typical installation process involves the following steps:

1. Installing the binary.
2. Adding a base configuration.
3. Configuring Splunk to launch at boot.
4. Restarting Splunk.

Having worked with many different companies over the years, I can honestly say that none of them used the same product or even methodology for deploying software. Splunk takes a hands-off approach to fit in as easily as possible into customer workflows.

Deploying from a tar file

To deploy from a tar file, the command depends on your version of tar. With a modern version of tar, you can run the following command:

```
tar xvzf splunk-4.3.x-xxx-Linux-xxx.tgz
```

Older versions may not handle gzip files directly, so you may have to run the following command:

```
gunzip -c splunk-4.3.x-xxx-Linux-xxx.tgz | tar xvf -
```

This will expand into the current directory. To expand into a specific directory, you can usually add -C, depending on the version of tar, as follows:

```
tar -C /opt/ -xvzf splunk-4.3.x-xxx-Linux-xxx.tgz
```

Deploying using msiexec

In Windows, it is possible to deploy Splunk using msiexec. This makes it much easier to automate deployment on a large number of machines. To install silently, you can use the combination of AGREETOLICENSE and /quiet, as follows:

```
msiexec.exe /i splunk-xxx.msi AGREETOLICENSE=Yes /quiet
```

If you plan to use a deployment server, you can specify the following value:

```
msiexec.exe /i splunk-xxx.msi AGREETOLICENSE=Yes
DEPLOYMENT_SERVER="deployment_server_name:8089" /quiet
```

Or, if you plan to overlay an app that contains `deploymentclient.conf`, you can forego starting Splunk until that app has been copied into place, as follows:

```
msiexec.exe /i splunk-xxx.msi AGREETOLICENSE=Yes LAUNCHSPLUNK=0 /quiet
```

There are options available to start reading data immediately, but I would advise deploying input configurations to your servers, instead of enabling inputs via installation arguments.

Adding a base configuration

If you are using the Splunk deployment server, this is the time to set up `deploymentclient.conf`. This can be accomplished in several ways, as follows:

- On the command line, by running the following code:
  ```
  $SPLUNK_HOME/bin/splunk set deploy-poll
  deployment_server_name:8089
  ```

- By placing a deploymentclient.conf in
  ```
  $SPLUNK_HOME/etc/system/local/
  ```

- By placing an app containing deploymentclient.conf in
  ```
  $SPLUNK_HOME/etc/apps/
  ```

The third option is the one I would recommend because it allows overriding this configuration, via a deployment server, at a later time. We will work through an example later in the *Using Splunk deployment server* section.

If you are deploying configurations in some other way, for instance with puppet, be sure to restart the Splunk forwarder processes after deploying the new configuration.

Configuring Splunk to launch at boot

On Windows machines, Splunk is installed as a service that will start after installation and on reboot.

On Unix hosts, the Splunk command line provides a way to create startup scripts appropriate for the operating system that you are using. The command looks like this:

```
$SPLUNK_HOME/bin/splunk enable boot-start
```

To run Splunk as another user, provide the flag `-user`, as follows:

```
$SPLUNK_HOME/bin/splunk enable boot-start -user splunkuser
```

The `startup` command must still be run as root, but the startup script will be modified to run as the user provided.

If you do not run Splunk as root user, and you shouldn't if you can avoid it, be sure that the Splunk installation and data directories are owned by the user specified in the enable boot-start command. You can ensure this by using `chmod`, such as in `chmod -R splunkuser $SPLUNK_HOME`

On Linux, you could then start the command using `service splunk start`.

Using apps to organize configuration

When working with a distributed configuration, there are a number of ways to organize these configurations. The most obvious approach might be to organize configurations by machine type. For instance, put all configurations needed by web servers into one app and all configurations needed by database servers in another app. The problem with this approach is that any changes that affect both types of machines must be made in both apps, and it is most likely that mistakes will be made.

The less fragile but more complicated approach is to normalize your configurations, ensuring that there is only one copy of each configuration spread into multiple apps.

Separate configurations by purpose

Stepping through a typical installation, you would have configuration apps named like the following:

- **inputs-sometype**: For some logical set of inputs, you would create an app. You could use machine purpose, source type, location, operating system, or whatever makes sense in your situation. Normally, I would expect machine purpose or source type.

- **props-sometype**: This grouping should correspond to the grouping of the inputs, more or less. You may end up with props apps for more than one type, for instance machine type and location.

- **outputs-datacenter**: When deploying across data centers, it is common to place Splunk indexers in each data center. In this case, you would need an app per data center.

- **indexerbase**: Assuming that your indexers are configured similarly, it is handy to put all indexer configurations into an app and deploy it like any other app.

All these configurations are completely separate from search concerns, which should be stored in separate apps, built and maintained through the Splunk web interface.

Let's imagine we have a distributed deployment across two data centers, east and west. Each data center has web servers, app servers, and database servers.

In each data center we have two Splunk indexers. The apps for this setup could be as follows:

- inputs-web, inputs-app, and inputs-db

  ◦ `inputs.conf` specifies the appropriate logs to monitor.

- Each app should be distributed to each machine that is serving that purpose. If there are some machines that serve more than one purpose, they should receive all appropriate apps.

- props-web, props-app, and props-db

  ◦ `props.conf` specifies how to parse the logs.

  ◦ `transforms.conf` is included if there are relevant transforms.

  ◦ Different portions of `props.conf` are needed at different stages of processing. Since it is difficult to know what stage is happening where, it is generally easiest to distribute these source type props apps everywhere.

- props-west, and props-east

  ◦ Sometimes it is necessary to make configuration changes by location, for instance, configuring time zone on machines that are not set up properly. This can be accomplished by using the `TZ` setting in `props.conf` and sending this app to the appropriate data centers.

- outputs-west, and outputs-east

  ◦ These would contain nothing but the `outputs.conf` configuration for the appropriate data center.

- indexerbase

  ○ Assuming that all indexers are configured the same way, this app would contain a standard `indexes.conf` configuration, an `inputs.conf` configuration specifying the `splunktcp` port to listen to connections from Splunk forwarders, and `server.conf` specifying the address of the Splunk license server.

Let's look through an abbreviated listing of all these files:

- For forwarders, we will need these apps:

```
inputs-web
local/inputs.conf
[monitor:///path/to/web/logs/access*.log]
sourcetype = web_access
index = web
[monitor:///path/to/web/logs/error*.log]
sourcetype = web_error
index = web
inputs-app
local/inputs.conf
[monitor:///path/to/app1/logs/app*.log]
sourcetype = app1
index = app
[monitor:///path/to/app2/logs/app*.log]
sourcetype = app2
index = app
inputs-db
local/inputs.conf
[monitor:///path/to/db/logs/error*.log]
sourcetype = db_error
outputs-west
local/outputs.conf
[tcpout:west]
server=spl-idx-west01.foo.com:9997,spl-idx-west02.foo.com:9997
#autoLB=true is the default setting
outputs-east
local/outputs.conf
[tcpout:east]
server=spl-idx-east01.foo.com:9997,spl-idx-east02.foo.com:9997
```

- All instances should receive these apps:

```
props-web
local/props.conf
[web_access]
TIME_FORMAT = %Y-%m-%d %H:%M:%S.%3N %:z
MAX_TIMESTAMP_LOOKAHEAD = 32
SHOULD_LINEMERGE = False
TRANSFORMS-squashpassword = squashpassword
[web_error]
TIME_FORMAT = %Y-%m-%d %H:%M:%S.%3N %:z
MAX_TIMESTAMP_LOOKAHEAD = 32
TRANSFORMS-squashpassword = squashpassword
local/transforms.conf
[squashpassword]
REGEX = (?mi)^(.*)password[=:][^,&]+$
FORMAT = $1password=########$2
DEST_KEY = _raw
props-app
local/props.conf
[app1]
TIME_FORMAT = %Y-%m-%d %H:%M:%S.%3N
MAX_TIMESTAMP_LOOKAHEAD = 25
BREAK_ONLY_BEFORE = ^\d{4}-\d{1,2}-\d{1,2}\s+\d{1,2}:\d{1,2}
[app2]
TIME_FORMAT = %Y-%m-%d %H:%M:%S.%3N
MAX_TIMESTAMP_LOOKAHEAD = 25
BREAK_ONLY_BEFORE = ^\d{4}-\d{1,2}-\d{1,2}\s+\d{1,2}:\d{1,2}
props-db
local/props.conf
[db_error]
MAX_TIMESTAMP_LOOKAHEAD = 25
props-west
local/props.conf
[db_error]
TZ = PST
[web_error]
Chapter 11
[ 365 ]
TZ = PST
props-east
local/props.conf
[db_error]
TZ = EST
[web_error]
TZ = EST
```

- Finally, an app specifically for our indexers:

```
indexerbase
local/indexes.conf
[volume:two_year_home]
path = /small_fast/two_year_home
maxVolumeDataSizeMB = 300000
[volume:one_year_home]
path = /small_fast/one_year_home
maxVolumeDataSizeMB = 150000
[volume:two_year_cold]
path = /big_slow/two_year_cold
maxVolumeDataSizeMB = 1200000
[volume:one_year_cold]
path = /big_slow/one_year_cold
maxVolumeDataSizeMB = 600000
[volume:large_home]
path = /big_fast/large_home
maxVolumeDataSizeMB = 900000
[volume:large_cold]
path = /big_slow/large_cold
maxVolumeDataSizeMB = 3000000
[web]
homePath = volume:large_home/web
coldPath = volume:large_cold/web
thawedPath = /big_slow/thawed/web
[app]
homePath = volume:large_home/app
coldPath = volume:large_cold/app
thawedPath = /big_slow/thawed/app
[main]
homePath = volume:large_home/main
coldPath = volume:large_cold/main
thawedPath = /big_slow/thawed/main
local/inputs.conf
[splunktcp://9997]
local/server.conf
[license]
master_uri = https://spl-license.foo.com:8089
```

This is a minimal set of apps, but it should provide a decent overview of what is involved in configuring a distributed configuration. Next, we will illustrate where these apps should go.

Configuration distribution

As we have covered in some depth, configurations in Splunk are simply directories of plain text files. Distribution essentially consists of copying these configurations to the appropriate machines and restarting the instances. You can either use your own system for distribution, such as puppet or simply a set of scripts, or use the deployment server included with Splunk.

Using your own deployment system

The advantage of using your own system is that you already know how to use it.

Assuming that you have normalized your apps as described in the section *Using apps to organize configuration*, deploying apps to a forwarder or indexer consists of the following steps:

1. Set aside the existing apps at $SPLUNK_HOME/etc/apps/.
2. Copy the apps into $SPLUNK_HOME/etc/apps/.
3. Restart Splunk forwarder. Note that this needs to be done as the user that is running Splunk, either by calling the service script or calling su. In Windows, restart the splunkd service.

Assuming that you already have a system for managing configurations, that's it.

If you are deploying configurations to indexers, be sure to only deploy the configurations when downtime is acceptable, as you will need to restart the indexers to load the new configurations, ideally in a rolling manner.

Do not deploy configurations until you are ready to restart, as some (but not all) configurations will take effect immediately.

Using the Splunk deployment server

If you do not have a system for managing configurations, you can use the deployment server included with Splunk.

Some advantages of the included deployment server are as follows:

- Everything you need is included in your Splunk installation
- It will restart forwarder instances properly when new app versions are deployed
- It is intelligent enough to not restart when unnecessary

- It will remove apps that should no longer be installed on a machine
- It will ignore apps that are not managed
- The logs for the deployment client and server are accessible in Splunk itself

Some disadvantages of the included deployment server are:

- As of Splunk 4.3, there are issues with scale beyond a few hundred deployment clients, at which point tuning is required
- The configuration is complicated and prone to typos

With these caveats out of the way, let's set up a deployment server for the apps that we laid out before.

Step 1 – deciding where your deployment server will run from

For a small installation with less than a few dozen forwarders, your main Splunk instance can run the deployment server without any issue. For more than a few dozen forwarders, a separate instance of Splunk makes sense.

Ideally, this instance would run on its own machine. The requirements for this machine are not large, perhaps 4 gigabytes of RAM and two processors, or possibly less. A virtual machine would be fine.

Define a DNS entry for your deployment server, if at all possible. This will make moving your deployment server later, much simpler.

If you do not have access to another machine, you could run another copy of Splunk on the same machine that is running some other part of your Splunk deployment. To accomplish this, follow these steps:

1. Install Splunk in another directory, perhaps `/opt/splunk-deploy/splunk/`.
2. Start this instance of Splunk by using `/opt/splunk-deploy/splunk/bin/splunk start`. When prompted, choose different port numbers apart from the default and note what they are. I would suggest one number higher: 8090 and 8001.
3. Unfortunately, if you run `splunk enable boot-start` in this new instance, the existing startup script will be overwritten. To accommodate both instances, you will need to either edit the existing startup script, or rename the existing script so that it is not overwritten.

Step 2 – defining your deploymentclient.conf configuration

Using the address of our new deployment server, ideally a DNS entry, we will build an app named `deploymentclient-yourcompanyname`. This app will have to be installed manually on forwarders but can then be managed by the deployment server.

This app should look somewhat like this:

```
deploymentclient-yourcompanyname
local/deploymentclient.conf
[deployment-client]
[target-broker:deploymentServer]
targetUri=deploymentserver.foo.com:8089
```

Step 3 – defining our machine types and locations

Starting with what we defined under the *Separate configurations by purpose* section, we have, in the locations west and east, the following machine types:

- Splunk indexers
- db servers
- web servers
- app servers

Step 4 – normalizing our configurations into apps appropriately

Let's use the apps that we defined under the section *Separate configurations by purpose* plus the deployment client app that we created in the section *Step 2 – defining your deploymentclient.conf configuration*. These apps will live in `$SPLUNK_HOME/etc/deployment-apps/` on your deployment server.

Step 5 – mapping these apps to deployment clients in serverclass.conf

To get started, I always start with example 2 from `SPLUNK_HOME/etc/system/README/serverclass.conf` example:

```
[global]
[serverClass:AppsForOps]
whitelist.0=*.ops.yourcompany.com
[serverClass:AppsForOps:app:unix]
[serverClass:AppsForOps:app:SplunkLightForwarder]
```

Let's assume that we have the machines mentioned next. It is very rare for an organization of any size to have consistently named hosts, so I threw in a couple of rogue hosts at the bottom, as follows:

```
spl-idx-west01
spl-idx-west02
spl-idx-east01
spl-idx-east02
app-east01
app-east02
app-west01
app-west02
web-east01
web-east02
web-west01
web-west02
db-east01
db-east02
db-west01
db-west02
qa01
homer-simpson
```

The structure of `serverclass.conf` is essentially as follows:

```
[serverClass:<className>]
#options that should be applied to all apps in this class
[serverClass:<className>:app:<appName>]
#options that should be applied only to this app in this serverclass
```

Please note that:

- `<className>` is an arbitrary name of your choosing.
- `<appName>` is the name of a directory in `$SPLUNK_HOME/etc/deploymentapps/`.
- The order of stanzas does not matter. Be sure to update `<className>` if you copy an `:app:` stanza. This is, by far, the easiest mistake to make.

It is important that configuration changes do not trigger a restart of indexers.

Let's apply this to our hosts, as follows:

```
[global]
restartSplunkd = True
#by default trigger a splunk restart on configuration change
####INDEXERS
##handle indexers specially, making sure they do not restart
[serverClass:indexers]
whitelist.0=spl-idx-*
restartSplunkd = False
[serverClass:indexers:app:indexerbase]
[serverClass:indexers:app:deploymentclient-yourcompanyname]
[serverClass:indexers:app:props-web]
[serverClass:indexers:app:props-app]
[serverClass:indexers:app:props-db]
#send props-west only to west indexers
[serverClass:indexers-west]
whitelist.0=spl-idx-west*
restartSplunkd = False
[serverClass:indexers-west:app:props-west]
#send props-east only to east indexers
  [serverClass:indexers-east]
whitelist.0=spl-idx-east*
restartSplunkd = False
[serverClass:indexers-east:app:props-east]
####FORWARDERS
#send event parsing props apps everywhere
#blacklist indexers to prevent unintended restart
[serverClass:props]
whitelist.0=*
blacklist.0=spl-idx-*
[serverClass:props:app:props-web]
[serverClass:props:app:props-app]
[serverClass:props:app:props-db]
```

```
#send props-west only to west datacenter servers
#blacklist indexers to prevent unintended restart
[serverClass:west]
whitelist.0=*-west*
whitelist.1=qa01
blacklist.0=spl-idx-*
[serverClass:west:app:props-west]
[serverClass:west:app:deploymentclient-yourcompanyname]
#send props-east only to east datacenter servers
#blacklist indexers to prevent unintended restart
[serverClass:east]
whitelist.0=*-east*
whitelist.1=homer-simpson
blacklist.0=spl-idx-*
[serverClass:east:app:props-east]
[serverClass:east:app:deploymentclient-yourcompanyname]
#define our appserver inputs
[serverClass:appservers]
whitelist.0=app-*
whitelist.1=qa01
whitelist.2=homer-simpson
[serverClass:appservers:app:inputs-app]
#define our webserver inputs
[serverClass:webservers]
whitelist.0=web-*
whitelist.1=qa01
whitelist.2=homer-simpson
[serverClass:webservers:app:inputs-web]
#define our dbserver inputs
[serverClass:dbservers]
whitelist.0=db-*
whitelist.1=qa01
[serverClass:dbservers:app:inputs-db]
#define our west coast forwarders
[serverClass:fwd-west]
whitelist.0=app-west*
whitelist.1=web-west*
whitelist.2=db-west*
whitelist.3=qa01
[serverClass:fwd-west:app:outputs-west]
#define our east coast forwarders
[serverClass:fwd-east]
whitelist.0=app-east*
whitelist.1=web-east*
```

```
whitelist.2=db-east*
whitelist.3=homer-simpson
[serverClass:fwd-east:app:outputs-east]
```

You should organize the patterns and classes in a way that makes sense to your organization and data centers, but I would encourage you to keep it as simple as possible. I would strongly suggest opting for more lines than more complicated logic.

A few more things to note about the format of `serverclass.conf`:

- The number following `whitelist` and `blacklist` must be sequential, starting with zero. For instance, in the following example, `whitelist.3` will not be processed, since `whitelist.2` is commented:

```
[serverClass:foo]
whitelist.0=a*
whitelist.1=b*
# whitelist.2=c*
whitelist.3=d*
```

- `whitelist.x` and `blacklist.x` are tested against these values in the following order:
  - `clientName` as defined in `deploymentclient.conf`: This is not commonly used, but it is useful when running multiple Splunk instances on the same machine, or when the DNS is completely unreliable.
  - **IP address**: There is no CIDR matching, but you can use string patterns.
  - **Reverse DNS**: This is the value returned by the DNS for an IP address.

  If your reverse DNS is not up to date, this can cause you problems as this value is tested before the value of hostname, as provided by the host itself. If you suspect this, try ping `<ip of machine>` or something similar to see what the DNS is reporting.

  - Hostname as provided by forwarder: This is always tested after reverse DNS, so be sure your reverse DNS is up to date.

- When copying `:app:` lines, be very careful to update the `<className>` appropriately! This really is the most common mistake made in `serverclass.conf`.

Step 6 – restarting the deployment server

If `serverclass.conf` did not exist, a restart of the Splunk instance that is running deployment server is required to activate the deployment server. After the deployment server is loaded, you can use the following command:

```
$SPLUNK_HOME/bin/splunk reload deploy-server
```

This command should be enough to pick up any changes in `serverclass.conf` a in `etc/deployment-apps`.

Step 7 – installing deploymentclient.conf

Now that we have a running deployment server, we need to set up the clients to call home. On each machine that will be running the deployment client, the procedure is essentially as follows:

1. Copy the `deploymentclient-yourcompanyname` app to `$SPLUNK_HOME/etc/apps/`.
2. Restart Splunk.

If everything is configured correctly, you should see the appropriate apps appear in `$SPLUNK_HOME/etc/apps/`, within a few minutes. To see what is happening, look at the log `$SPLUNK_HOME/var/log/splunk/splunkd.log`.

If you have problems, enable debugging on either the client or the server by editing `$SPLUNK_HOME/etc/log.cfg`, followed by a restart. Look for the following lines:

```
category.DeploymentServer=WARN
category.DeploymentClient=WARN
```

Once found, change them to the following lines and restart Splunk:

```
category.DeploymentServer=DEBUG
category.DeploymentClient=DEBUG
```

After restarting Splunk, you will see the complete conversation in `$SPLUNK_HOME/var/log/splunk/splunkd.log`. Be sure to change the setting back once you no longer need the verbose logging!

Using LDAP for authentication

By default, Splunk authenticates using its own authentication system, which simply stores users and roles in flat files. The other two options available are LDAP and scripted authentication.

To enable LDAP authentication, perform the following steps:

1. Navigate to **Manager | Access controls | Authentication method**.
2. Check the LDAP checkbox.
3. Click on **Configure Splunk** to use LDAP and map groups.
4. Click on **New**.

You will then need the appropriate values to set up access to your LDAP server.

Every organization sets up LDAP slightly differently, so I have never managed to configure this properly the first time. Your best bet is to copy the values from another application that is already configured in your organization.

Once LDAP is configured properly, you can map Splunk roles to the LDAP groups through the admin interface. Whether to use an existing group or create Splunk-specific groups is, of course, up to your organization, but most companies I have worked with opted to create a specific group for each Splunk role. The common groups are often along the lines of: `splunkuser`, `splunkpoweruser`,

`splunksecurity`, and `splunkadmin`. Rights are additive, so a user can be a member of as many groups as is appropriate.

New in Splunk 4.3 are the ability to use multiple LDAP servers at once, support for dynamic groups, support for nested groups, and more. The official documentation can be found at the following URL:

```
http://docs.splunk.com/Documentation/Splunk/latest/Security/
SetUpUserAuthenticationWithLDAP
```

Using Single Sign On

Single Sign On (SSO) lets you use some other web server to handle authentication for Splunk. For this to work, several assumptions are made, as follows:

- Your SSO system can act as an HTTP forwarding proxy, sending HTTP requests through to Splunk.
- Your SSO system can place the authenticated user's ID into an HTTP header.

- The IP of your server(s) forwarding requests is static.
- When given a particular username, Splunk will be able to determine what roles this user is a part of. This is usually accomplished using LDAP, but could also be accomplished by defining users directly through the Splunk UI or via a custom-scripted authentication plugin.

Assuming that all of these are true, the usual approach is to follow these steps:

1. Configure LDAP authentication in Splunk.
2. Configure your web server to send proxy requests through to Splunk: When this is configured properly, you should be able to use Splunk as if you were accessing the Splunk web application directly.
3. Configure your web server to authenticate: With this configured, your web server should ask for authentication, and you should still be asked for authentication by Splunk.
4. Look for the HTTP header containing the remote user: Proxying through your web server, change the URL to `http://yourproxyserver/debug/sso`.

   You should see your username under **Remote user HTTP header or Other HTTP headers**.

5. Configure SSO in `$SPLUNK_HOME/etc/system/local/web.conf`: You need to add three attributes to the `[settings]` stanza, as shown in the following code:

```
[settings]
SSOMode = strict
remoteUser = REMOTE-USER
trustedIP = 192.168.1.1,192.168.1.2
```

That should be it. Usually, the hardest part is convincing the web server to both authenticate and proxy. Use the `/debug/sso` page to help diagnose what is happening.

There can also be issues with punctuation in the header fieldname. If possible, removing any punctuation in the header name may eliminate unexpected problems.

Load balancers and Splunk

Some organizations that have invested heavily in load balancers like to use them whenever possible to centralize network management. There are three services Splunk typically exposes, mentioned in the following sections:

web

Usually on port 8000, the Splunk web server can be load balanced when configured with search head pooling. The load balancer should be configured to be sticky, as the web server will still rely on user sessions tied to the web server that the user started on.

See the *Multiple search heads* section for more information.

splunktcp

Usually on port 9997, `splunktcp` is itself stateless. Splunk auto load balancing is very well tested and very efficient but does not support complicated logic. For instance, you could use a load balancer to prefer connections to the indexers in the same data center, only using indexers in another data center as a last resort.

The problem is that when only one address is provided to a Splunk forwarder, the forwarder will open one connection, and keep it open indefinitely. This means that when an indexer is restarted, it will never receive a connection until the forwarders are restarted.

The easy solution is to expose two addresses on your load balancer and list both of these addresses in `outputs.conf`. The two addresses must either be two different ports or two different IP addresses. Two different CNAMEs on the same port will not work, as Splunk resolves the addresses and collapses the list of IP addresses.

The deployment server

Usually on port 8089, the deployment server listens using SSL, by default, with a self-signed certificate. There are a couple of problems with using a load balancer with the deployment server; they are as follows:

- The protocol is essentially REST over HTTP, but not quite. Use a TCP load balancer, not a load balancer that understands HTTP.

- While it is theoretically possible to load balance deployment servers, the issue is that, if the different deployment servers are out of sync, deployment clients may flap, loading one set of apps and then the other.

A better approach is probably running multiple deployment servers and using DNS or load balancers to ensure that certain sets of hosts always talk to a particular server.

Multiple search heads

Using the search head pooling feature, it is possible to run multiple search head instances. The feature requires a share of some sort behind the servers acting as search heads, which effectively means they must be in the same data center. The setup looks essentially like the following figure:

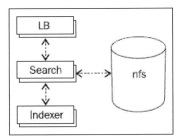

In short, the steps to configure the search are as follows:

1. Mount the NFS volume on each search head.
2. Enable the pooling feature on each instance.
3. Copy the existing configurations to the NFS volume.
4. Test the search heads.
5. Enable the load balancer.

The official documentation is available at `http://docs.splunk.com/Documentation/Splunk/latest/Deploy/Configuresearchheadpooling`.

Summary

We have touched upon a wide variety of subjects in this chapter, each of which possibly deserves a chapter of its own. Maybe that will be the next book.

We talked about the different purposes of Splunk instances, how to collect data from a variety of sources, how to install the Splunk binary, how to size your indexers, how to manage the configuration of many instances, and finally, we touched upon a few advanced deployment topics.

In our final chapter, we will write some code to extend Splunk in a variety of ways.

13
Extending Splunk

While the core of Splunk is closed, there are a number of places where you can use scripts or external code to extend default behaviors. In this chapter, we will write a number of examples, covering most of the places where external code can be added. Most code samples are written in Python, so if you are not familiar with Python a reference may be useful.

We will cover the following topics:

- Writing scripts to create events
- Using Splunk from the command line
- Calling Splunk via REST
- Writing custom search commands
- Writing event type renderers
- Writing custom search action scripts

The examples used in this chapter are included in the `ImplementingSplunkExtendingExamples` app, which can be downloaded from the support page of the Packt Publishing website at `www.packtpub.com/support`.

In addition, **Hunk** will be defined and an overview will be given.

Writing a scripted input to gather data

Scripted inputs allow you to run a piece of code on a scheduled basis and capture the output as if it were simply being written to a file. It does not matter what language the script is written in or where it lives, as long it is executable.

We touched on this topic in the *Using scripts to gather data* section in *Chapter 12, Advanced Deployments*. Let's write a few more examples.

Capturing script output with no date

One common problem with script output is the lack of a predictable date or date format. In this situation, the easiest thing to do is to tell Splunk not to try to parse a date at all and instead use the current date. Let's make a script that lists open network connections:

```
from subprocess import Popen
from subprocess import PIPE
from collections import defaultdict
import re
def add_to_key(fieldname, fields):
  return " " + fieldname + "+" + fields[fieldname]
output = Popen("netstat -n -p tcp", stdout=PIPE,
  shell=True).stdout.read()
counts = defaultdict(int)
for l in output.splitlines():
  if "ESTABLISHED" in l:
    pattern = r"(?P<protocol>\S+)\s+\d+\s+\d+\s+"
    pattern += r"(?P<local_addr>.*?)[^\d](?P<local_port>\d+)\s+"
      pattern += r"(?P<remote_addr>.*)[^\d](?P<remote_port>\d+)"
    m = re.match(pattern, l)
    fields = m.groupdict()
    if "local_port" in fields and "remote_port" in fields:
    if fields["local_addr"] == fields["remote_addr"]:
    continue
    try:
    if int(fields["local_port"]) < 1024:
        key = "type=incoming"
        key += add_to_key("local_addr", fields)
        key += add_to_key("local_port", fields)
        key += add_to_key("remote_addr", fields)
    else:
        key = "type=outgoing"
        key += add_to_key("remote_addr", fields)
        key += add_to_key("remote_port", fields)
        key += add_to_key("local_addr", fields)
    except:
     print "Unexpected error:", sys.exc_info()[0]
    counts[key] += 1
for k, v in sorted(counts.items()):
  print k + " count=" + str(v)
```

Before we wire this up, we can test the command using the Python interpreter included with Splunk, as follows:

```
$SPLUNK_HOME/bin/splunk cmd python connections.py
```

If you are using any Splunk Python modules you must use Python included with Splunk, as other Python installations will not find these modules.

On the test machine, this produces the following output:

```
type=outgoing remote_addr=17.149.36.120 remote_port=5223
local_addr=192.168.0.20 count=1
type=outgoing remote_addr=17.158.10.104 remote_port=443
local_addr=192.168.0.20 count=2
type=outgoing remote_addr=17.158.10.42 remote_port=443
local_addr=192.168.0.20 count=5
type=outgoing remote_addr=17.158.8.23 remote_port=993
local_addr=192.168.0.20 count=4
type=outgoing remote_addr=173.194.64.109 remote_port=993
local_addr=192.168.0.20 count=8
type=outgoing remote_addr=199.47.216.173 remote_port=443
local_addr=192.168.0.20 count=1
type=outgoing remote_addr=199.47.217.178 remote_port=443
local_addr=192.168.0.20 count=1
type=outgoing remote_addr=50.18.31.239 remote_port=443
local_addr=192.168.0.20 count=1
```

Now that we have a working script, we need two pieces of configuration, namely inputs.conf and props.conf. As we covered in *Chapter 12*, *Advanced Deployments*, you will want to place these configurations in different apps if you are going to distribute this input across a distributed environment.

The Splunk configuration file called inputs.conf should contain something similar to the following code:

```
[script://./bin/connections.py]
interval=60
sourcetype=connections
```

If the script ends in .py, Splunk will automatically use the included Python interpreter. Otherwise, the script needs to be executable via the command line. If you want to use a different Python executable, you will need to specify the full path to Python as the script, with the script itself as an argument:

```
props.conf should then contain something as follows:
[connections]
SHOULD_LINEMERGE = false
DATETIME_CONFIG = CURRENT
```

This configuration requires that each line be treated as an event and that, in this event, we don't even try to find something that looks like a date.

Let's build a query using the output of this scripted input. A useful query might be ports opened by domain name. This query uses `dnslookup` and then flattens `remote_host` to either a domain name or a subnet:

```
index=implsplunk sourcetype=connections
 | fillnull value="-" remote_addr remote_port local_addr local_port
 | dedup remote_addr remote_port local_addr local_port
 | lookup dnslookup clientip as remote_addr
 | rex field=clienthost ".*\.(?<domain>[^\.]+\.[^\.]+)"
 | eval remote_host=coalesce(domain,remote_addr)
 | eval remote_host=replace(remote_host,"(.*)\.\d+$","\1.0")
 | stats sum(count) as count values(remote_port) as remote_ports
by remote_host local_addr local_port
 | eval remote_ports=mvjoin(remote_ports, ", ")
```

On the machine I'm using, I get the following results:

remote_host ‡	local_addr ‡	local_port ‡	count ‡	remote_ports ‡
138.108.7.0	172.16.14.25	-	2	80
172.16.14.0	172.16.14.25	-	8	55686, 55692, 55696, 61384, 61787, 61788, 61809, 62078
198.171.79.0	172.16.14.25	-	1	80
1e100.net	172.16.14.25	-	34	443, 80
206.33.35.0	172.16.14.25	-	1	1935
208.85.243.0	172.16.14.25	-	2	443, 80
209.170.117.0	172.16.14.25	-	3	80
akamaitechnologies.com	172.16.14.25	-	5	80
amazonaws.com	172.16.14.25	-	6	443
apple.com	172.16.14.25	-	1	5223

Capturing script output as a single event

When you want to capture the entire output of a script as a single event, the trick is to specify an impossible value for LINE_BREAKER. Let's write a shell script to output the different parts of `uname` with nice field names.

You can find the following script at `ImplementingSplunkExtendingExamples/bin/uname.sh`:

```sh
#!/bin/sh
date "+%Y-%m-%d %H:%M:%S"
echo hardware=\"$(uname -m)\"
echo node=\"$(uname -n)\"
echo proc=\"$(uname -p)\"
echo os_release=\"$(uname -r)\"
echo os_name=\"$(uname -s)\"
echo os_version=\"$(uname -v)\"
This script produces output like the following code:
2012-10-30 19:28:05
hardware="x86_64"
node="mymachine.local"
proc="i386"
os_release="12.2.0"
os_name="Darwin"
os_version="Darwin Kernel Version 12.2.0: Sat Aug 25 00:48:52 PDT
2012; root:xnu-2050.18.24~1/RELEASE_X86_64"
```

You would notice that the last line definitely contains a date. Unless we specifically tell Splunk that the entire output is an event in one way or another, it will turn that last line into an event.

`inputs.conf` file should contain something similar to the following code:

```
[script://./bin/uname.sh]
interval = 0 0 * * *
sourcetype=uname
```

Notice the `cron` syntax for `interval`. This will run the script each day at midnight. An alternative would be to set the value to 86,400, which would run the script each time Splunk starts and then every 24 hours thereafter.

`props.conf` file should then contain something similar to the following code:

```
[uname]
TIME_FORMAT = %Y-%m-%d %H:%M:%S
#treat each "line" as an event:
SHOULD_LINEMERGE = false
#redefine the beginning of a line to an impossible match,
#thus treating all data as one "line":
LINE_BREAKER = ((?!))
#chop the "line" at one megabyte, just in case:
TRUNCATE=1048576
```

Once installed, you can search for these events using `sourcetype=uname`, which produces output similar to the following screenshot:

"Image showing a single event resulting from the search"

Because we used the `fieldname="fieldvalue"` syntax and we quoted values with spaces and strange characters, these field values will be automatically extracted.

We can then use these fields immediately for reporting. A useful query might be as follows:

```
earliest=-24h sourcetype=uname
| eventstats count by os_release os_name
| search count<10
```

This query would find the rare `os_release os_name` combinations.

Making a long-running scripted input

Sometimes, a process needs to be long running, for instance if it is polling an external source such as a database. A simple example might be as follows:

```
import time
import random
import sys
for i in range(1, 1000):
print "%s Hello." % time.strftime('%Y-%m-%dT%H:%M:%S')
#make sure python actually sends the output
sys.stdout.flush()
time.sleep(random.randint(1, 5))
```

This script will run for somewhere between 1,000 and 5,000 seconds and then exit.

Since this is a long-running script, our choices are either to treat each line as an event as we did in the *Capturing script output with no date* section or, if we know that there is a date to use, configure the input like a regular log file. In this case, we can see that there is always a date so we will rely on that. The output is, unsurprisingly, as follows:

```
2012-10-30T20:13:29 Hello.
2012-10-30T20:13:33 Hello.
2012-10-30T20:13:36 Hello.
```

`inputs.conf` file should contain something similar to the following code:

```
[script://./bin/long_running.py]
interval = 1
sourcetype=long_running
```

With `interval = 1`, Splunk will try to launch the script every second but will only run one copy of the script at a time.

`props.conf` file should then contain something similar to the following code:

```
[long_running]
TIME_FORMAT = %Y-%m-%dT%H:%M:%S
MAX_TIMESTAMP_LOOKAHEAD = 21
BREAK_ONLY_BEFORE = ^\d{4}-\d{1,2}-\d{1,2}T\d{1,2}:
```

This will create a long-running process that can do whatever is appropriate.

Even though it is convenient to have Splunk execute scripts for you and capture the output, if the information you are capturing is vital it may be safer to simply schedule the script with `cron`, direct its output to a file, and point Splunk at that file. This allows you to use the file in other ways; you can capture both standard output and errors, and the data will still be captured if Splunk is down. However, it does have the disadvantage of having to clean up those logs yourself.

Using Splunk from the command line

Almost everything that can be done via the web interface can also be accomplished via the command line. For an overview, see the output of `/opt/splunk/bin/splunk help`. For help on a specific command, use `/opt/splunk/bin/splunk help [commandname]`.

The most common action performed on the command line is `search`. For example, have a look at the following code:

```
$ /opt/splunk/bin/splunk search 'foo'
2012-08-25T20:17:54 user=user2 GET /foo?q=7148356 uid=MzA4MTc5OA
2012-08-25T20:17:54 user=user2 GET /foo?q=7148356 uid=MzA4MTc5OA
2012-08-25T20:17:54 user=user2 GET /foo?q=7148356 uid=MzA4MTc5OA
```

The things to note here are:

- By default, searches are performed over **All time**. Protect yourself by including `earliest=-1d` or an appropriate time range in your query.

- By default, Splunk will only output 100 lines of results. If you need more, use the `-maxout` flag.

- Searches require authentication, so the user will be asked to authenticate unless `-auth` is included as an argument.

Most use cases for the command line involve counting events to output to other systems. Let's try a simple `stats` call to count instances of the word "error" over the last hour by the host:

```
$ /opt/splunk/bin/splunk search 'earliest=-1h error | stats count by host'
```

This produces the following output:

```
------------ -----
host2 3114
vlb.local 3063
```

The things to notice in this case are as follows:

- `earliest=-1h` is included to limit the query to the last hour.

- By default, the output is in a tabular format. This is nicer to read but much harder to parse in another scripting language. Use `-output` to control the output format.

- By default, Splunk will render a preview of the results as the results are retrieved. This slows down the overall execution. Disable preview with `-preview as false`. Previews are not calculated when the script is not being called from an interactive terminal, for instance, when run from `cron`.

To retrieve the output as CSV, try the following code:

```
$ /opt/splunk/bin/splunk search 'earliest=-1h error | stats count by host' -output csv -preview false
```

This gives us the following output:

```
count,host
3120,host2
3078,"vlb.local"
```

Note that, if there are no results, the output will be empty.

Querying Splunk via REST

Splunk provides an extensive HTTP REST interface, which allows searching, adding data, adding inputs, managing users, and more. Documentation and SDKs are provided by Splunk at `http://dev.splunk.com/`.

To get an idea of how this REST interaction happens, let's walk through a sample conversation to run a query and retrieve the results. The steps are essentially as follows:

1. Start the query (POST).
2. Poll for status (GET).
3. Retrieve results (GET).

We will use the command-line program cURL to illustrate these steps. The SDKs make this interaction much simpler.

The command to start a query is as follows:

```
curl -u user:pass -k https://yourserver:8089/services/search/jobs -
d"search=search query"
```

This essentially says to use POST on the `search=search` query. If you are familiar with HTTP, you might notice that this is a standard POST from an HTML form.

To run the query `earliest=-1h index="_internal" warn | stats count by host`, we need to URL - encode the query. The command then, is as follows:

```
$ curl -u admin:changeme -k
https://localhost:8089/services/search/jobs -
d"search=search%20earliest%3D-1h%20index%3D%22_internal%22%20
warn%20%7C%20stats%20count%20by%20host"
```

If the query is accepted, we will receive XML code that contains our search ID:

```
<?xml version='1.0' encoding='UTF-8'?>
```

```
<response><sid>1352061658.136</sid></response>
```

The contents of `<sid>` are then used to reference this job. To check the status of our job, we will run the following code:

```
curl -u admin:changeme -k
https://localhost:8089/services/search/jobs/1352061658.136
```

This returns a large document with copious amounts of information about our job as follows:

```
<entry ...>
<title>search earliest=-1h index="_internal" warn | stats count by
host</title>
<id>https://localhost:8089/services/search/jobs/1352061658.136</id>
...
<link href="/services/search/jobs/1352061658.136/events"
rel="events"/>
<link href="/services/search/jobs/1352061658.136/results"
rel="results"/>
...
<content type="text/xml">
<s:dict>
...
<s:key name="doneProgress">1.00000</s:key>
...
<s:key name="eventCount">67</s:key>
...
<s:key name="isDone">1</s:key>
...
<s:key name="resultCount">1</s:key>
```

Interesting fields include doneProgress, eventCount, resultCount, and the field we are most interested in at this point, isDone. If isDone is not 1, we should wait and poll again later. Once isDone=1, we can retrieve our results from the URL specified in <link rel="results">.

To retrieve our results, we make the following call:

```
curl -u admin:changeme -k
https://localhost:8089/services/search/jobs/1352061658.136/results
```

This returns the following XML output:

```
<?xml version='1.0' encoding='UTF-8'?>
<results preview='0'>
<meta>
<fieldOrder>
<field>host</field>
<field>count</field>
</fieldOrder>
</meta>
<result offset='0'>
<field k='host'>
```

```
<value><text>vlb.local</text></value>
</field>
<field k='count'>
<value><text>67</text></value>
</field>
</result>
</results>
```

The list of fields is contained in meta/fieldOrder. Each result will then follow this field order.

Though not necessary (since jobs expire on their own), we can save disk space on our Splunk servers by cleaning up after ourselves. Simply calling the DELETE method on the job URL will delete the results and reclaim the used disk space:

```
curl -u admin:changeme -k -X DELETE
https://localhost:8089/services/search/jobs/1352061658.136
```

Just to show the Python API action, here's a simple script:

```
import splunk.search as search
import splunk.auth as auth
import sys
import time
username = sys.argv[1]
password = sys.argv[2]
q = sys.argv[3]
sk = auth.getSessionKey(username, password)
job = search.dispatch("search " + q, sessionKey=sk)
while not job.isDone:
print "Job is still running."
time.sleep(.5)
for r in job.results:
for f in r.keys():
print "%s=%s" % (f, r[f])
print "----------"
job.cancel()
```

This script uses the Python modules included with Splunk, so we must run it using Splunk's included Python, as follows:

```
$ /opt/splunk/bin/splunk cmd python simplesearch.py admin changeme
'earliest=-7d index="_internal" warn | timechart count by source'
```

This produces the following output:

```
_time=2012-10-31T00:00:00-0500
/opt/splunk/var/log/splunk/btool.log=0
/opt/splunk/var/log/splunk/searches.log=0
/opt/splunk/var/log/splunk/splunkd.log=31
/opt/splunk/var/log/splunk/web_service.log=0
_span=86400
_spandays=1
----------
_time=2012-11-01T00:00:00-0500
/opt/splunk/var/log/splunk/btool.log=56
/opt/splunk/var/log/splunk/searches.log=0
/opt/splunk/var/log/splunk/splunkd.log=87
/opt/splunk/var/log/splunk/web_service.log=2
_span=86400
_spandays=1
----------
...
```

For more examples and extensive documentation, check out `http://dev.splunk.com`.

Writing commands

To augment the built-in commands, Splunk provides the ability to write commands in Python and Perl. You can write commands to modify events, replace events, and even dynamically produce events.

When not to write a command

While external commands can be very useful, if the number of events to be processed is large or if performance is a concern, it should be considered a last resort. You should make every effort to accomplish the task at hand using the search language built into Splunk or other built-in features. For instance, if you want to accomplish any of the following tasks, make sure you know what to do, which is what is discussed here:

- To use regular expressions, learn to use `rex`, `regex`, and extracted fields
- To calculate a new field or modify an existing field, look into `eval` (search for `splunk eval` functions with your favorite search engine)

- To augment your results with external data, learn to use lookups, which can also be a script if need be
- To read external data that changes periodically, consider using `inputcsv`

The performance issues introduced by external commands come from the following two places:

- One source of issues is the work involved with launching a Python process, exporting events as CSV to the Python process, and then importing the results back into the Splunk process.
- The source of issues is the actual code of the command. A command that queries an external data source, for instance, a database, will be affected by the speed of that external source.

In my testing, I could not make a command run faster than 50 percent slower than native commands. To test this, let's try a couple of searches, as shown here:

```
* | head 100000 | eval t=_time+1 | stats dc(t)
```

On my laptop, this query takes roughly four seconds to execute when run on the command line with the preview feature disabled, as shown in the following code:

```
# time /opt/splunk/bin/splunk search '* | head 100000 | eval
t=_time+1 | stats dc(t)' -preview false
```

Now, let's throw in a command included in our sample app:

```
* | head 100000 | echo | eval t=_time+1 | stats dc(t)
```

This increases the search time to slightly over six seconds, an increase of 50 percent. Included in the sample app are three variations of the echo app of varying complexity:

- `echo`: This command simply echoes the standard input to the standard output.
- `echo_csv`: This command uses *csvreader* and *csvwriter*.
- `echo_splunk`: This command uses the Python modules provided with Splunk to gather incoming events and then output the results. We will use these Python modules for our example commands. Using each of these commands, the times are nearly identical, which tells me that most of the time is spent shuttling the events in and out of Splunk.

Adding `required_fields=_time` in `commands.conf` lowered times from 2.5 x to 1.5 x in this case. If you know the fields your command needs, this setting can dramatically improve performance.

When to write a command

Given the warning about performance, there are still times when it makes sense to write a command. I can think of a few reasons:

- You need to perform a specific action that cannot be accomplished using internal commands

- You need to talk to an external system (a lookup may be more efficient though)

- You need to produce events out of thin air, perhaps from an external service or for testing

I'm sure you can think of your own reasons. Let's explore the nuts and bolts of different types of commands.

Configuring commands

Before we start writing commands, there is some setup that must be done for all commands. First, every command will need an entry into the `commands.conf` file of your app. Let's take a look at the following sample stanza:

```
[commandname]
filename = scriptname.py
streaming = false
enableheader = true
run_in_preview = true
local = false
retainsevents = false
```

Go over the following attributes and their descriptions:

- `[commandname]`: The command available to search will be the title of the stanza—in this case `commandname`.

- `filename = scriptname.py`: This is the script to run. It must live in the directory bin inside your app.

- `streaming = false`: By default, only one instance of each command will be run on the complete set of results.

  The assumption is that all events are needed for the script to do its work. If your script works on each event individually, set this value to `true`. This will eliminate the event limit, which by default is 50,000 as specified by `maxresultrows` in `limits.conf`.

- `enableheader = true`: By default, your script will receive a header that the Splunk Python modules know how to use. If this is set to `false`, your command will receive plain comma-separated values.

- `run_in_preview = true`: By default, your command will be executed repeatedly while events are being retrieved so as to update the preview in the GUI. This will have no effect on saved searches, but setting this to `false` can make a big difference in the performance of interactive searches. This is particularly important if your command uses an external resource as it will be called repeatedly.

- `local = false`: If you have a distributed environment, by default, your command will be copied to all indexers and executed there. If your command needs to be run on one machine, setting `local=true` ensures that the command only runs on the search head.

- `retainsevents = false`: By default, Splunk assumes that your command returns the transformed events, much like `stats` or `timechart`. Setting this to true changes the behavior to treat the results as regular events.

To make our commands available to other apps, for instance **Search**, we need to change the metadata in our app. Place the following two lines in the `metadata/default.meta` file:

```
[commands]
export = system
```

Finally, to use a newly configured command, we either need to restart Splunk or load the `http://yourserver/debug/refresh` URL in a browser. This may also be necessary after changing settings in `commands.conf` but is not necessary after making changes to the script itself.

Adding fields

Let's start out with a simple command that does nothing more than add a field to each event. This example is stored in `ImplementingSplunkExtendingExamples/bin/addfield.py`:

```
#import the python module provided with Splunk import splunk.
Intersplunk as si
#read the results into a variable
results, dummyresults, settings = si.getOrganizedResults()
#loop over each result. results is a list of dict. for r in results:
#r is a dict. Access fields using the fieldname.
r['foo'] = 'bar'
#return the results back to Splunk
si.outputResults(results)
```

Our corresponding stanza in `commands.conf` is as follows:

```
[addfield]
filename = addfield.py
streaming = true
retainsevents = true
```

We can use this command as follows:

```
* | head 10 | addfield | top foo
```

This gives us the result shown in the following screenshot:

	foo ⬍	count ⬍	percent ⬍
1	bar	10	100.000000

This could be accomplished much more efficiently by simply using `eval foo="bar"`, but this illustrates the basic structure of a command.

Manipulating data

It is useful at times to modify the value of a field, particularly `_raw`. Just for fun, let's reverse the text of each event. We will also support a parameter that specifies whether to reverse the words or the entire value. You can find this example in `ImplementingSplunkExtendingExamples/bin/reverseraw.py`:

```
import splunk.Intersplunk as si
import re
#since we're not writing a proper class, functions need to be
#defined first
def reverse(s):
return s[::-1]
#start the actual script
results, dummyresults, settings = si.getOrganizedResults()
#retrieve any options included with the command
keywords, options = si.getKeywordsAndOptions()
#get the value of words, defaulting to false
words = options.get('words', False)
#validate the value of words
if words and words.lower().strip() in ['t', 'true', '1', 'yes']:
words = True
else:
words = False
#loop over the results
```

```
for r in results:
#if the words option is true, then reverse each word
if words:
newRaw = []
parts = re.split('([^a-zA-Z\']+)', r['_raw'])
for n in range(0, len(parts) - 2, 2):
newRaw.append(reverse(parts[n]))
newRaw.append(parts[n + 1])
newRaw.append(reverse(parts[-1]))
r['_raw'] = ''.join(newRaw)
#otherwise simply reverse the entire value of _raw
else:
r['_raw'] = reverse(r['_raw'])
si.outputResults(results)
The commands.conf stanza would look as follows:
[reverseraw]
filename = reverseraw.py
retainsevents = true
streaming = true
Let us assume the following event:
2012-10-27T22:10:21.616+0000 DEBUG Don't worry, be happy.
[user=linda, ip=1.2.3., req_time=843, user=extrauser]
```

Using our new command, we get the following line of code:

```
* | head 10 | reverseraw
```

Upon running the previous command on the preceding event, we see the entire event reversed, as shown in the following code:

```
]resuartxe=resu ,348=emit_qer ,.3.2.1=pi ,adnil=resu[ .yppah eb ,yrrow
t'noD GUBED 0000+616.12:01:22T72-01-2102
```

We can then add the words argument:

```
* | head 10 | reverseraw words=true
```

We will maintain the order of words, as shown in the following code:

```
2012-10-27T22:10:21.616+0000 GUBED t'noD yrrow, eb yppah. [resu=adnil,
pi=1.2.3., qer_emit=843, resu=resuartxe]
```

For fun, let's reverse the event again:

```
* | head 10 | reverseraw words=true | reverseraw
```

This gives us the following output:

```
]extrauser=user ,348=time_req ,.3.2.1=ip ,linda=user[ .happy be ,worry
Don't DEBUG 0000+616.12:01:22T72-01-2102
```

happy be, worry Don't—Yoda could not have said it better.

Transforming data

Until now, our commands have returned the original events with modifications to their fields. Commands can also transform data, much like the built-in functions top and stats. Let's write a function to count the words in our events. You can find this example in ImplementingSplunkExtendingExamples/bin/countwords.py:

```python
import splunk.Intersplunk as si
import re
import operator
from collections import defaultdict
#create a class that does the actual work
class WordCounter:
word_counts = defaultdict(int)
unique_word_counts = defaultdict(int)
rowcount = 0
casesensitive = False
mincount = 50
minwordlength = 3
def process_event(self, input):
self.rowcount += 1
words_in_event = re.findall('\W*([a-zA-Z]+)\W*', input)
unique_words_in_event = set()
for word in words_in_event:
if len(word) < self.minwordlength:
continue # skip this word, it's too short
if not self.casesensitive:
word = word.lower()
self.word_counts[word] += 1
unique_words_in_event.add(word)
for word in unique_words_in_event:
self.unique_word_counts[word] += 1
def build_sorted_counts(self):
#create an array of tuples,
#ordered by the count for each word
sorted_counts = sorted(self.word_counts.iteritems(),
```

```
key=operator.itemgetter(1))
#reverse it
sorted_counts.reverse()
return sorted_counts
def build_rows(self):
#build our results, which must be a list of dict
count_rows = []
for word, count in self.build_sorted_counts():
if self.mincount < 1 or count >= self.mincount:
unique = self.unique_word_counts.get(word, 0)
percent = round(100.0 * unique / self.rowcount, 2)
newrow = {'word': word,
'count': str(count),
'Events with word': str(unique),
'Event count': str(self.rowcount),
'Percent of events with word':
str(percent)}
count_rows.append(newrow)
return count_rows
#a helper method that doesn't really belong in the class
#return an integer from an option, or raise useful Exception
def getInt(options, field, default):
try:
return int(options.get(field, default))
except Exception, e:
#raise a user friendly exception
raise Exception("%s must be an integer" % field)
#our main method, which reads the options, creates a WordCounter
#instance, and loops over the results
if __name__ == '__main__':
try:
#get our results
results, dummyresults, settings = si.getOrganizedResults()
keywords, options = si.getKeywordsAndOptions()
word_counter = WordCounter()
word_counter.mincount = getInt(options, 'mincount', 50)
word_counter.minwordlength = getInt(options,
'minwordlength', 3)
#determine whether we should be case sensitive
casesensitive = options.get('casesensitive', False)
if casesensitive:
casesensitive = (casesensitive.lower().strip() in
```

```
['t', 'true', '1', 'y', 'yes'])
word_counter.casesensitive = casesensitive
#loop through the original results
for r in results:
word_counter.process_event(r['_raw'])
output = word_counter.build_rows()
si.outputResults(output)
#catch the exception and show the error to the user
except Exception, e:
import traceback
stack = traceback.format_exc()
si.generateErrorResults("Error '%s'. %s" % (e, stack))
```

This is a larger script, but hopefully what is happening is clear to you. Notice a few new things in this example:

- Most of the logic is in the class definition. This provides a better separation of Splunk-specific logic and business logic.
- Testing for `__main__` is done in the Python way.
- Exception handling is also done.
- This is a nicer exception for failed parsing of integer arguments.
- Here, there are field names with spaces in them.

Our entry in `commands.conf` does not allow streaming and does not retain events:

```
[countwords]
filename = countwords.py
retainsevents = false
streaming = false
```

We can then use our command as follows:

```
* | countwords
```

This will give us a table, as shown in the following screenshot:

	count ⇕	Events with word ⇕	word ⇕	Event count ⇕	Percent of events with word ⇕
1	49680	21822	error	50000	43.64
2	47860	41870	user	50000	83.74
3	40075	40070	time	50000	80.14
4	40065	40065	req	50000	80.13
5	39971	39971	logger	50000	79.94
6	25310	12655	this	50000	25.31
7	25243	25243	barclass	50000	50.49
8	25211	25211	don	50000	50.42
9	16131	16131	network	50000	32.26
10	16056	16056	session	50000	32.11
11	13442	13442	mary	50000	26.88
12	12655	12655	worthless	50000	25.31
13	12655	12655	nothing	50000	25.31
14	12655	12655	happened	50000	25.31
15	12655	12655	log	50000	25.31
16	12584	12584	debug	50000	25.17
17	12556	12556	worry	50000	25.11
18	12556	12556	happy	50000	25.11
19	12523	12523	warn	50000	25.05
20	12426	12426	info	50000	24.85
21	12378	12378	hello	50000	24.76
22	12378	12378	world	50000	24.76
23	8106	8106	red	50000	16.21

With my test data, this produced 132 rows, representing 132 unique words at least three characters long in my not-so-random dataset. **count** represents how many times each word occurred overall, while **Events with word** represents how many events contained the word at all.

Notice the value 50000 in the **Event count** column. Even though my query found more than 300,000 events, only 50,000 events made their way to the command. You can increase this limit by increasing maxresultrows in limits.conf, but be careful!

This limit is for your protection.

Try out our options as follows:

```
* | head 1000 | countwords casesensitive=true mincount=250
minwordlength=0
```

This query produces the following output:

	count ⇕	Events with word ⇕	word ⇕	Event count ⇕	Percent of events with word ⇕
1	1000	1000	T	1000	100.0
2	968	837	user	1000	83.7
3	801	801	logger	1000	80.1
4	799	799	ip	1000	79.9
5	798	798	time	1000	79.8
6	798	798	req	1000	79.8
7	531	459	ERROR	1000	45.9
8	490	490	BarClass	1000	49.0
9	473	473	Don	1000	47.3
10	473	473	t	1000	47.3
11	330	330	network	1000	33.0
12	304	304	session	1000	30.4
13	282	282	mary	1000	28.2
14	271	271	INFO	1000	27.1
15	268	268	error	1000	26.8
16	268	268	Error	1000	26.8
17	259	259	Hello	1000	25.9
18	259	259	world	1000	25.9
19	251	251	WARN	1000	25.1

Notice that we now see one- and two-letter words, with entries for both T and t, and our results stop when **count** drops below our value for `mincount`.

Just for completeness, to accomplish this command using built-in commands, you could write something similar to the following code:

```
* | rex max_match=1000 "\W*(?<word>[a-zA-Z]+)\W*"
| eval id=1 | accum id | fields word id
| eventstats count
| mvexpand word
| eval word=lower(word)
```

```
| stats max(count) as event_count dc(id) as events_with_word count as
word_count by word
| sort -events_with_word
| eval percent_events_containing = round(events_with_word/event_
count*100.0,2)
| rename word_count as count
events_with_word as "Events with word"
event_count as "Event count"
percent_events_containing as "Percent of events with word"
| table count "Events with word" word
"Event count" "Percent of events with word"
```

There is probably a more efficient way to do this work using built-in commands but this is what comes to mind initially.

Generating data

There are times when you want to create events out of thin air. These events could come from a database query, a web service, or simply some code that generates data useful in a query. Just to illustrate the plumbing, we will make a random number generator.

You can find this example in `ImplementingSplunkExtendingExamples/bin/ random_generator.py`:

```
import splunk.Intersplunk as si
from random import randint
keywords, options = si.getKeywordsAndOptions()
def getInt(options, field, default):
try:
return int(options.get(field, default))
except Exception, e:
#raise a user friendly exception
raise Exception("%s must be an integer" % field)
try:
min = getInt(options, 'min', 0)
max = getInt(options, 'max', 1000000)
eventcount = getInt(options, 'eventcount', 100)
results = []
for r in range(0, eventcount):
results.append({'r': randint(min, max)})
si.outputResults(results)
except Exception, e:
import traceback
```

```
stack = traceback.format_exc()
si.generateErrorResults("Error '%s'. %s" % (e, stack))
The entry in commands.conf then is as follows:
[randomgenerator]
filename = random_generator.py
generating = true
```

We can then use the command as follows:

```
|randomgenerator
```

Notice the leading pipe | symbol. This is the indication to run a command instead of running a search. Let's test the randomness of our Python code:

```
|randomgenerator eventcount=100000 min=100 max=899
| bucket r
| chart count by r
```

This produces a graph, as shown in the following screenshot:

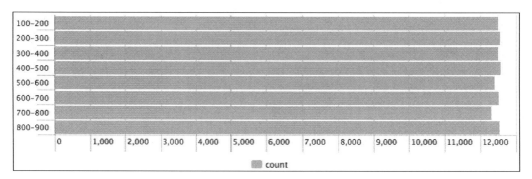

I guess that is not a bad distribution for 100,000 samples. Using Splunk's built-in commands, you could accomplish essentially the same thing using the following code:

```
index=_internal
| head 100000
| eval r=random()/2147483647*100000
| bucket r
| chart count by r
```

That was a very quick overview of commands using fun demonstration commands to illustrate the plumbing required to execute your code. A number of samples ship with Splunk in $SPLUNK_HOME/etc/apps/search/bin.

Writing a scripted lookup to enrich data

We covered CSV lookups fairly extensively in *Chapter 7, Extending Search*, then touched on them again in *Chapter 10, Summary Indexes and CSV Files* and *Chapter 11, Configuring Splunk*. The capabilities built into Splunk are usually sufficient but sometimes it is necessary to use an external data source or dynamic logic to calculate values. Scripted lookups have the following advantages over commands and CSV lookups:

- Scripted lookups are only run once per unique lookup value, as opposed to a command, which would run the command for every event.

- The memory requirement of a CSV lookup increases with the size of the CSV file.

- Rapidly changing values can be left in an external system and queried using the scripted lookup instead of being exported frequently. In the *Using a lookup with wildcards* section in *Chapter 10, Summary Indexes and CSV Files*, we essentially created a case statement through configuration. Let's implement that use case as a script just to show how it would be done in Python. First, in `transforms.conf`, we need the following configuration:

```
[urllookup]
external_cmd = url_lookup.py
fields_list = url section call_count
```

The following are notes about this configuration:

- `fields_list` is the list of fields that will be sent to the script and the list of fields expected in the result

- `fields_list` must contain at least two fields, or the script will fail silently

The script then looks as follows:

```
import sys
import re
from csv import DictReader
from csv import DictWriter
patterns = []
def add_pattern(pattern, section):
patterns.append((re.compile(pattern), section))
add_pattern('^/about/.*', 'about')
add_pattern('^/contact/.*', 'contact')
add_pattern('^/.*/.*', 'unknown_non_root')
add_pattern('^/.*', 'root')
add_pattern('.*', 'nomatch')
# return a section for this url
def lookup(url):
```

```
try:
for (pattern, section) in patterns:
if pattern.match(url):
return section
return ''
except:
return ''
#set up our reader
reader = DictReader(sys.stdin)
fields = reader.fieldnames
#set up our writer
writer = DictWriter(sys.stdout, fields)
writer.writeheader()
#start our output
call_count = 0
for row in reader:
call_count = call_count + 1
if len(row['url']):
row['section'] = lookup(row['url'])
row['call_count'] = call_count
writer.writerow(row)
```

In a nutshell, this script takes the value of url, tries each regular expression in sequence, and then sets the value of the section accordingly. A few points about the preceding script follow:

- The script receives the raw CSV with the fields listed in `transforms.conf`, but only the fields that are needed for lookup will have a value. In our case, that field is url.

- The url field must be present in the data or mapped in the `lookup` command using the as option.

- `call_count` parameter is included to show that this scripted lookup is more efficient than an external command as the lookup will only receive one line of input per unique value of url.

Let's try out the following code:

```
index=implsplunk sourcetype="impl_splunk_web"
| rex "\s[A-Z]+\s(?<url>.*?)\?"
| lookup urllookup url
| stats count values(call_count) by url section
```

This gives us the following results:

url ⭥	section ⭥	count ⭥	values(call_count) ⭥
1 /about/	about	1443	1
2 /bar	root	1383	2
3 /contact/	contact	1389	3
4 /foo	root	1446	4
5 /products/	unknown_non_root	1364	5
6 /products/index.html	unknown_non_root	1389	6
7 /products/x/	unknown_non_root	2899	7
8 /products/y/	unknown_non_root	1430	8

The `values(call_count)` column tells us that our lookup script only received eight rows of input, one for each unique value of `url`. This is far better than the 12,743 rows that an equivalent command would have received.

For more examples of scripted lookups, see the following command:

```
$SPLUNK_HOME/etc/system/bin/external_lookup.py
```

You can also check out the `MAXMIND` app available in Splunkbase.

Writing an event renderer

Event renderers give you the ability to make a specific template for a specific event type. To read more about creating event types, see *Chapter 7, Extending Search*.

Event renderers use mako templates (`http://www.makotemplates.org/`).

An event renderer is comprised of the following:

- A template stored at `$SPLUNK_HOME/etc/apps/[yourapp]/appserver/event_renderers/[template].html`
- A configuration entry in `event_renderers.conf`
- An optional event type definition in `eventtypes.conf`
- Optional CSS classes in `application.css`

Let's create a few small examples. All the files referenced are included in `$SPLUNK_HOME/etc/apps/ImplementingSplunkExtendingExamples`. These examples are not shared outside this app, so to see them in action you will need to search from inside this app. Do this by pointing your browser at `http://[yourserver]/app/ImplementingSplunkExtendingExamples/flashtimeline`.

Using specific fields

If you know the names of the fields you want to display in your output, your template can be fairly simple. Let's look at the `template_example` event type. The template is stored in `appserver/event_renderers/template_example.html`:

```
<%page args="job, event, request, options">
<ul class="template_example">
<li>
<b>time:</b>
${i18n.format_datetime_microseconds(event.get('_time', event.
time))}
</li>
<li>
<b>ip:</b>
${event.get('ip', '')}
</li>
<li>
<b>logger:</b>
${event.get('logger', '')}
</li>
<li>
<b>message:</b>
${event.get('message', '')}
</li>
<li>
<b>req_time:</b>
${event.get('req_time', '')}
</li>
<li>
<b>session_id:</b>
${event.get('session_id', '')}
</li>
<li>
<b>user:</b>
${event.get('user', '')}
</li>
<li>
<b>_raw:</b>
${event.get('_raw', '')}
</li>
</li>
</ul>
</%page>
```

This template outputs a `<ul>` block for each event, with the specific fields we want displayed. To connect this template to a specific event type, we need the following entry in `default/event_renderers.conf`:

```
[template_example]
eventtype = template_example
template = template_example.html
```

Finally, if we want to format our output, we can use the following CSS:

```
appserver/static/application.css:
ul.template_example {
list-style-type: none;
}
ul.template_example > li {
background-color: #dddddd;
padding: 4px;
margin: 1px;
}
```

To test our event type renderer, we need the configuration to be loaded. You can accomplish this by restarting Splunk or by pointing your browser to `http://[yourserver]/debug/refresh`.

At this point, we can run a query and apply the event type manually:

```
index="implsplunk" sourcetype="template_example"
| eval eventtype="template_example"
```

This renders each event in a manner similar to the following screenshot:

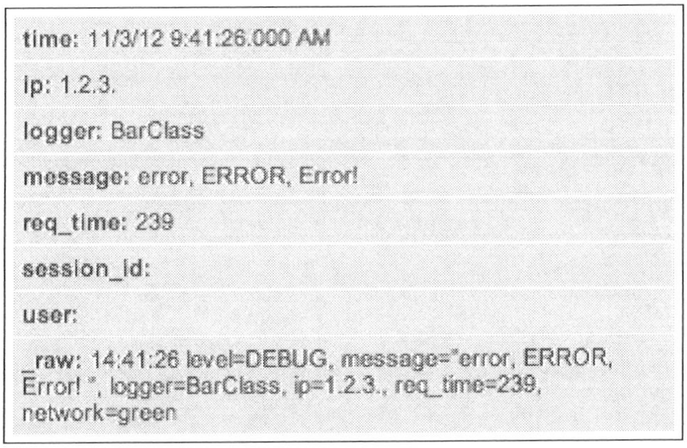

```
time: 11/3/12 9:41:26.000 AM
ip: 1.2.3.
logger: BarClass
message: error, ERROR, Error!
req_time: 239
session_id:
user:
_raw: 14:41:26 level=DEBUG, message="error, ERROR,
Error! ", logger=BarClass, ip=1.2.3., req_time=239,
network=green
```

To make this automatic, we can create an event type definition in `eventtypes.conf`, as follows:

```
[template_example]
search = sourcetype=template_example
```

Now any query that finds events of `sourcetype=template_example` will be rendered using our template.

A table of fields based on field value

Since the template has access to everything in the event, you can use the fields in any way you like. The following example creates a horizontal table of fields but lets the user specify a specific set of fields to display in a special field.

Our template stored in `appserver/event_renderers/tabular.html`, looks as follows:

```
<%inherit file="//results/EventsViewer_default_renderer.html" />\
<%def name="event_raw(job, event, request, options, xslt)">\
<%
import sys
_fields = str(event.fields.get('tabular', 'host,source,sourcetype,line
count')).split(',')
head = ''
row = ''
for f in _fields:
head += "<th>" + f + "</th>"
row += "<td>" + str(event.fields.get(f, '-')) + "</td>"
%>
<table class="tabular_eventtype">
<tr>
${head}
</tr>
<tr>
${row}
</tr>
</table>
</%def>
```

Notice that we have extended the default event type renderer template, which means we will only change the rendering of `field _raw`.

The entry in `event_renderers.conf` is as follows:

```
[tabular]
eventtype = tabular
template = tabular.html
```

Finally, our entries in `application.css` are as follows:

```
th.tabular_eventtype {
background-color: #dddddd;
border: 1px solid white;
padding: 4px;
}
td.tabular_eventtype {
background-color: #eeeeee;
border: 1px solid white;
padding: 4px;
}
```

We are not going to bother giving this event type a definition but we can use it by setting the value of `eventtype` in the query. Let's try it out by running the following query:

```
index="implsplunk" | eval eventtype="tabular"
```

We see the following output based on the default fields specified in the template:

"Image showing two events with the same timestamp. The events list the host, source, soucetype and linecount of the events"

Notice that we still see the event number, the workflow actions menu, the local time as rendered by Splunk, and the selected fields underneath our template output.

We have really only overridden the rendering of `_raw`. If we specify the fields we want in our table in the `tabular` field, the template will honor what we specify in our table:

```
index="implsplunk" sourcetype="template_example"
| eval tabular="level,logger,message,foo,network"
| eval eventtype="tabular"
```

This gives us the output shown in the following screenshot:

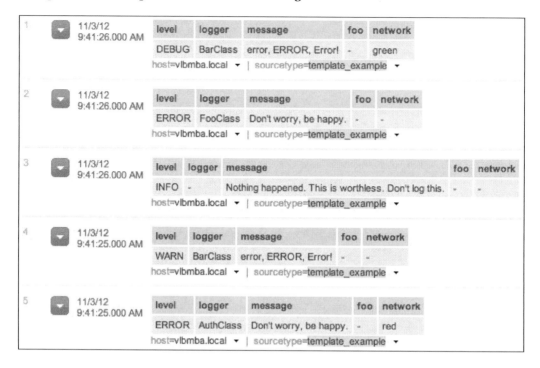

As per the following template code, any field that does not have a value is rendered as:

```
str(event.fields.get(f, '-'))
```

It would be much simpler to use the table command instead of writing an event renderer. This approach is only appropriate when you need a very specific rendering or still need access to workflow actions. For another approach, check out the *Table* and *Multiplexer* modules available in the Sideview Utils app.

Pretty print XML

In this example, we will use Python's *minidom* module to parse and pretty print XML if possible. The template will look for a field called xml or fall back on _raw.

Let's look through the files included in `ImplementingSplunkExtendingExamples`. The template file located in `appserver/event_renderers/xml.html` contains the following lines of code:

```
<%inherit file="//results/EventsViewer_default_renderer.html" />\
<%def name="event_raw(job, event, request, options, xslt)">\
<%
from xml.dom import minidom
import sys
def escape(i):
return i.replace("<", "&lt;").replace(">", "&gt;")
_xml = str( event.fields.get('xml', event.fields['_raw']) )
try:
pretty = minidom.parseString(_xml).toprettyxml(indent=' '*4)
pretty = escape( pretty )
except Exception as inst:
pretty = escape(_xml)
pretty += "\n(couldn't format: " + str( inst ) + ")"
%>
<pre class="xml_eventtype">${pretty}</pre>
</%def>
Our entry in event_renderers.conf is as follows:
[xml]
eventtype = xml
template = xml.html
```

Our entry in `eventtypes.conf` is as follows:

```
[xml]
search = sourcetype="xml_example"
```

We can then simply search for our example source type as follows:

```
index="implsplunk" sourcetype="xml_example"
```

This renders the following output:

```
1    ▼   11/2/12
            8:03:15.000 AM   <bad><time>13:03:15</time><cat>dog</cat><e>egg</e><f /></d>
                             (couldn't format: mismatched tag: line 1, column 57)

                             host=vlbmba.local  ▾  |  sourcetype=xml_example  ▾

2    ▼   11/1/12
            8:03:15.000 AM   <?xml version="1.0" ?>
                             <d>
                                 <time>
                                     13:03:15
                                 </time>
                                 <cat>
                                     dog
                                 </cat>
                                 <e>
                                     egg
                                 </e>
                                 <f/>
                             </d>

                             host=vlbmba.local  ▾  |  sourcetype=xml_example  ▾

3    ▼   11/1/12
            8:03:15.000 AM   <?xml version="1.0" ?>
                             <reg>
                                 <time>
                                     13:03:15
                                 </time>
                                 <b>
                                     5
                                 </b>
                                 <c>
                                     dog
                                 </c>
                                 <e>
                                     egg
                                 </e>
                                 <f>
                                     fly
                                 </f>
                             </reg>

                             host=vlbmba.local  ▾  |  sourcetype=xml_example  ▾
```

The XML in the first event is invalid so an error message is appended to the original value.

Writing a scripted alert action to process results

Another option to interface with an external system is to run a custom alert action using the results of a saved search. Splunk provides a simple example in `$SPLUNK_HOME/bin/scripts/echo.sh`. Let's try it out and see what we get using the following steps:

1. Create a saved search. For this test, lets do something simple and easy such as writing the following code:

   ```
   index=_internal | head 100 | stats count by sourcetype
   ```

2. Schedule the search to run at a point in the future. I set it to run every five minutes just for this test.

3. Enable **Run a script** and type in `echo.sh`:

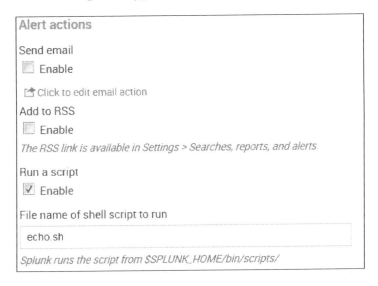

The script places the output into `$SPLUNK_HOME/bin/scripts/echo_output.txt`.

In my case, the output is as follows:

```
'/opt/splunk/bin/scripts/echo.sh' '4' 'index=_internal | head 100
| stats count by sourcetype' 'index=_internal | head 100 | stats
count by sourcetype' 'testingAction' 'Saved Search [testingAction]
always(4)' 'http://vlbmba.local:8000/app/search/@go?sid=scheduler__
admin__search__testingAction_at_1352667600_2efa1666cc496da4' '' '/
opt/splunk/var/run/splunk/dispatch/scheduler__admin__search__
testingAction_at_1352667600_2efa1666cc496da4/results.csv.gz' 'sessionK
ey=7701c0e6449bf5a5f271c0abdbae6f7c'
```

In the bullets that follow, let's look through each argument in the preceding output:

- $0—this is the script path: `'/opt/splunk/bin/scripts/echo.sh'`
- $1—this is the number of events returned: `'4'`
- $2—these are the search terms: `'index=_internal | head 100 | stats count by sourcetype'`
- $3—this is the full search string: `'index=_internal | head 100 | stats count by sourcetype'`
- $4—this is the saved search's name: `'testingAction'`
- $5—this is the reason for the action: `'Saved Search [testingAction] always(4)'`
- $6—this is a link to the search results; the host is controlled in `web.conf`:
  `'http://vlbmba.local:8000/app/search/@go?sid=scheduler__admin__search__testingAction_at_1352667600_2efa1666cc496da4'`
- $7—this is deprecated: `''`
- $8—this is the path to the raw results, which are always gzipped:
  `'/opt/splunk/var/run/splunk/dispatch/scheduler__admin__search__testingAction_at_1352667600_2efa1666cc496da4/results.csv.gz'`
- STDIN—this is the session key when the search ran:
  `'sessionKey=7701c0e6449bf5a5f271c0abdbae6f7c'`

The typical use of scripted alerts is to send an event to a monitoring system. You could also imagine archiving these results for compliance reasons or to import into another system.

Let's make a fun example that copies the results to a file and then issues a cURL statement. That script might look like the following one:

```
#!/bin/sh
DIRPATH='dirname "$8"'
DIRNAME='basename "$DIRPATH"'
DESTFILE="$DIRNAME.csv.gz"
cp "$8" /mnt/archive/alert_action_example_output/$DESTFILE
URL="http://mymonitoringsystem.mygreatcompany/open_ticket.cgi"
URL="$URL?name=$4&count=$1&filename=$DESTFILE"
echo Calling $URL
curl $URL
```

You would then place your script in $SPLUNK_HOME/bin/scripts on the server that will execute the script and refer to the script by name in alert actions. If you have a distributed Splunk environment, the server that executes the scripts will be your search head.

If you need to perform an action for each row of results, then your script will need to open the results. The following is a Python script that loops over the contents of the gzip file and posts the results to a ticketing system, including a JSON representation of the event:

```
#!/usr/bin/env python
import sys
from csv import DictReader
import gzip
import urllib
import urllib2
import json
#our ticket system url
open_ticket_url = "http://ticketsystem.mygreatcompany/ticket"
#open the gzip as a file
f = gzip.open(sys.argv[8], 'rb')
#create our csv reader
reader = DictReader(f)
for event in reader:
fields = {'json': json.dumps(event),
'name': sys.argv[4],
'count': sys.argv[1]}
#build the POST data
data = urllib.urlencode(fields)
#the request will be a post
resp = urllib2.urlopen(open_ticket_url, data)
print resp.read()
f.close()
```

Hopefully, these examples give you a starting point for your use case.

Hunk

To further extend the power of Splunk, Hunk was developed to give a larger number of users the ability to access data stored within the Hadoop and NoSQL stores (and other similar ones) without needing custom development, costly data modeling, or lengthy batch iterations. For example, Hadoop can consume high volumes of data from many sources, refining the data into readable logs, which can then be exposed to Splunk users quickly and efficiently using Hunk.

Some interesting Hunk features include:

- **The ability to create a Splunk virtual index**: This enables the seamless use of the Splunk Search Processing Language (SPL) for interactive exploration, analysis, and visualization of data as if it was stored in a Splunk index.

- **You can point and go**: Like accessing data indexed in Splunk, there is no need to understand the Hadoop data upfront; you can just point Hunk at the Hadoop source and start exploring.

- **Interactivity**: You can use Hunk for analysis across terabytes and even petabytes of data and even enrich Hadoop data with connected data from external relational databases using Splunk DB Connect.

- **Report on and visualize data**: Users can build graphs and charts on the fly as well as use views and reports to create role-specific dashboards that can be viewed and edited on computers, tablets, or mobile devices.

Hunk currently runs on 64-bit Linux, with documentation in the Hunk tutorial found at `http://docs.splunk.com/Documentation/Hunk/latest/Hunktutorial/Tutorialoverview`.

Summary

As we saw in this chapter, there are a number of ways in which Splunk can be extended to input, manipulate, and output events. The search engine at the heart of Splunk is truly just the beginning. With a little creativity, Splunk can be used to extend existing systems, both as a data source and as a way to trigger actions.

Index

Symbol

.conf files
  about 343
  authorize.conf 375, 376
  commands.conf 376
  fields.conf 372, 373
  indexes.conf 373-375
  inputs.conf 351
  outputs.conf 373
  props.conf 344
  savedsearches.conf 376
  times.conf 376
  transforms.conf 361
  web.conf 376

A

acceleration
  about 183
  big data 183
  report acceleration 184, 185
  report acceleration, availability 186
admin interface
  used, for building field 84-86
advanced XML
  reasons, for avoiding 254
  reasons, for using 253, 254
  simple XML, converting to 257-262
  structure 255-257
alerts
  action, options 59
  actions, enabling 58
  creating, from searches 56-58
  search result, saving as 50

sharing 59, 60

AND operator 29
apps
  about 223
  adding, to Splunkbase 247
  appearance, customizing 237
  building 230-234
  customizing, custom CSS used 238
  customizing, custom HTML used 238
  directory structure 246, 247
  Distributed Management Console 224
  gettingstarted 224
  installing 225
  installing, from files 230
  installing, from Splunkbase 226, 227
  Introspection_generator_addon 224
  launcher icon, customizing 237
  purpose 223, 224
  Search & Reporting 225
  splunk_datapreview 225
  SplunkDeploymentMonitor 225
  SplunkForwarder 225
  SplunkLightForwarder 225
  used, for organizing configuration 413
appserver resources 378
apps, Splunkbase
  directories, cleaning up 248, 249
  packaging 250
  preparing 248
  sharing settings, confirming 248
  uploading 251
  URL 247
arguments
  used, for creating macro 208, 209

input attributes 352
native Windows inputs 359
network inputs 357, 358
scripts as inputs 360
input-time attributes 348
intentions
addterm 270, 271
stringreplace 269, 270

L

latency 306-308
launcher icon
customizing 237
layoutPanel attribute 265, 266
Lightweight Directory Access Protocol
     (LDAP)
about 2
using, for authentication 426
load balancers 427, 428
loglevel
extract fields interface, using 79-82
extracting 79
logs
consuming, from database 394, 395
consuming, in batch 389, 390
monitoring, on servers 387, 388
on shared drive, monitoring 388, 389
lookup attributes
about 100-102
child object 103-105
lookup definitions, transforms.conf
about 366
CIDR wildcard lookups 367
temporal lookups 368
wildcard lookups 366
lookups
defining 201-203
troubleshooting 206
used, for enriching data 199
using, with wildcards 316-319
lookup table file
defining 200, 201

M

macro
about 207
creating 207, 208
creating, with arguments 208, 209
mako templates
URL 457
merging order
about 334
outside of search 334
when searching 335
metadata 378-380
metadata fields, transforms.conf
events, routing to different index 365
host, overriding 364
modifying 363
source, overriding 364
sourcetype, overriding 365
minidom module 462
module logic flow 262-265
multiple indexes
working with 403
multiple panels
drilldown, building to 275-279
multiple search heads 429

N

native syslog receiver
using 391-393
navigation
about 377
editing 234-236
object permissions, effects 243, 244
NOT operator 29

O

object permissions
about 243
effects, on navigation 243, 244
effects, on objects 244, 245
issues, correcting 245

object permissions, options
  app 243
  global 243
  private 243
OR operator 29
output
  controlling, for top command 64-66
outputs.conf 373

P

panel
  converting, to report 127-130
  drilldown, building to 274, 275
  options 130
Parentheses (( )) operator 29
parse-time attributes 345-347
Perl Compatible Regular Expressions
        (PCRE)
  URL 76
pipe symbol 61, 62
pivot
  about 105-107
  column value element 110
  example 111-114
  filtering 108, 109
  split column 109, 110
  split row 109, 110
  table, formatting 110
Pivot Editor
  about 107, 108
  pivot elements, managing 108
presets 39
processing stages
  indexing 384
  input 384
  parsing 384
  searching 384
props.conf
  about 344
  attributes 344
  stanza types 348, 349
Proxying
  URL 427

Q

query
  reusing 267, 268
quote marks ("") 29

R

real-time option 40
redundancy, planning
  indexer load balancing 401
  replication factor 398, 399
  typical outages 401, 402
regular expressions 74-76
relative presets 39, 40
report
  search result, saving as 46
report acceleration
  about 184, 185
  availability 186
REPORT, transforms.conf
  dynamic fields, creating 369
  multivalue fields, creating 369
  using 369
REST
  used, for querying Splunk 439-441
results
  categorizing, event types used 194-199
  generating, Google used 221
rex command
  about 78
  used, for prototyping field 83, 84

S

savedsearches.conf 376
scripted alert action
  writing, for result processing 465-467
scripted input
  about 431
  creating 436, 437
  writing, for data gathering 431
scripted lookup
  writing, for data enrichment 455-457

Thank you for buying
Implementing Splunk
Second Edition

About Packt Publishing

Packt, pronounced 'packed', published its first book, *Mastering phpMyAdmin for Effective MySQL Management*, in April 2004, and subsequently continued to specialize in publishing highly focused books on specific technologies and solutions.

Our books and publications share the experiences of your fellow IT professionals in adapting and customizing today's systems, applications, and frameworks. Our solution-based books give you the knowledge and power to customize the software and technologies you're using to get the job done. Packt books are more specific and less general than the IT books you have seen in the past. Our unique business model allows us to bring you more focused information, giving you more of what you need to know, and less of what you don't.

Packt is a modern yet unique publishing company that focuses on producing quality, cutting-edge books for communities of developers, administrators, and newbies alike. For more information, please visit our website at www.packtpub.com.

About Packt Enterprise

In 2010, Packt launched two new brands, Packt Enterprise and Packt Open Source, in order to continue its focus on specialization. This book is part of the Packt Enterprise brand, home to books published on enterprise software – software created by major vendors, including (but not limited to) IBM, Microsoft, and Oracle, often for use in other corporations. Its titles will offer information relevant to a range of users of this software, including administrators, developers, architects, and end users.

Writing for Packt

We welcome all inquiries from people who are interested in authoring. Book proposals should be sent to author@packtpub.com. If your book idea is still at an early stage and you would like to discuss it first before writing a formal book proposal, then please contact us; one of our commissioning editors will get in touch with you.

We're not just looking for published authors; if you have strong technical skills but no writing experience, our experienced editors can help you develop a writing career, or simply get some additional reward for your expertise.

Splunk Essentials

ISBN: 978-1-78439-838-5   Paperback: 156 pages

Leverage the power of Splunk to efficiently analyze machine, log, web, and social media data

1. Make impressive reports and dashboards easily.

2. Search, locate, and manage apps in Splunk.

3. Use the Twitter app to create a dashboard based on Twitter searches of particular topics.

Mastering Splunk

ISBN: 978-1-78217-383-0   Paperback: 344 pages

Optimize your machine-generated data effectively by developing advanced analytics with Splunk

1. Develop simple applications into robust, feature-rich applications to search, monitor, and analyze machine-generated big data with ease.

2. Learn about lookups, indexing, dashboards, navigation, advances transaction with examples.

3. Understand the key features of Splunk by exploring real-world examples and apply the technology in your database.

Please check **www.PacktPub.com** for information on our titles

Splunk Operational Intelligence Cookbook

ISBN: 978-1-84969-784-2   Paperback: 414 pages

Over 70 practical recipes to gain operational data intelligence with Splunk Enterprise

1. Learn how to use Splunk to effectively gather, analyze, and report on the operational data across your environment.

2. Expedite your operational intelligence reporting, be empowered to present data in a meaningful way, and shorten the Splunk learning curve.

3. Easy-to-use recipes to help you create robust searches, reports, and charts using Splunk.

Implementing Splunk: Big Data Reporting and Development for Operational Intelligence

ISBN: 978-1-84969-328-8   Paperback: 448 pages

Learn to transform your machine data into valuable IT and business insights with this comprehensive and practical tutorial

1. Learn to search, dashboard, configure, and deploy Splunk on one machine or thousands.

2. Start working with Splunk fast, with a tested set of practical examples and useful advice.

3. Step-by-step instructions and examples with a comprehensive coverage for Splunk veterans and newbies alike.

Please check **www.PacktPub.com** for information on our titles

49169153R10280